STIGMAS OF THE TAMIL STAGE

an ethnography of special drama artists in south india

SUSAN SEIZER

CALCUTTA 2007

First published by Duke University Press in 2005

This edition printed in arrangement with Duke University Press

For publication and sale in India, Bangladesh, Burma, Bhutan, Sri Lanka, Nepal and Pakistan only

ISBN 81 7046 321 1

Typeset in Quadraat by Tseng Information Systems, Inc.
Book design by CH Westmoreland
Cover design by Sunandini Banerjee using a painting of Valli being bathed.

Published by Naveen Kishore, Seagull Books Pvt Ltd
26 Circus Avenue, Calcutta 700 017

Printed at Lilabati Printers, P54 Ananda Palit Road, Calcutta 700 014

Exclusively distributed in India and South Asia by Cambridge University Press India Pvt Ltd
Cambridge House, 4381/4 Ansari Road, Daryaganj, New Delhi 110 002

Please note: the author's updated url is www.stigmasofthetamilstage.com

Stigmas of the Tamil Stage

To my grandfather David Victor (1910–1989),

whose humane spirit shapes my ideals,

and to four teachers who remain larger than our loss of them,

A. K. Ramanujan, Norman Cutler, K. Paramasivam,

and B. S. Cohn

Contents

PART TWO Comedy

PART THREE Lives

Title page: Actress N. Sansirani (left) and the author.

Video footage of the Buffoon's comedy scene, the Buffoon-Dance Duets, and the Aṭipiṭi scene discussed in the chapters in part two of this book are available on the Web at http://stigmasofthetamilstage.scrippscollege.edu.

Many of the images may also be viewed in larger format on the Web at http://stigmasofthetamilstage.scrippscollege.edu.

List of Illustrations

Plates (between pages 234 and 235)

Acknowledgments

This book owes much to many people, both in India and in the United States. My first debt of gratitude is to the Special Drama artists of the Tamilnadu Drama Actors Sangam, Madurai, whose work makes my own possible. Foremost among the many artists who opened heart and home to me are N. Jansirani, R. Baby Natarajan, and their daughters I. Vijayalaksmi and N. Kavitha. Their love and patience extend beyond anything normally implied by these terms, and I am delighted to call them family.

In India

Several senior artists have passed on since I began this research. I was fortunate to learn from Kalaimamani P. S. Nagaraja Bhagavattar, Kalaimamani A. S. Tangavel Vattiyar, Kalaimamani T. N. Sivathanu, and Kalaimamani M. A. Majeeth about a field significantly shaped by their presence in it. Other renowned artists who generously shared their insights and experiences with me include Kalaimamani N. S. Varatarajan Vattiyar, M. S. Kanagarattinam, M. S. Renukadevi, T. K. Appukutti Bhagavattar, N. M. Sundarambal, N. N. Kannappa, P. L. Ranjani, Dindigal Angurattinam, S. N. Kasimbai Nadana Asiriyar, Kalaimamani S. P. Rettinapattar, Kalaimamani T. M. Pangaja, Vaiyur Gopal, Kalaimamani M. P. Gnanambal, Kalaimamani M. R. Kamalaveni, T. K. Vengadasami, Ayyasami Tesikar, Kalaimamani M. K. Dorairaj, Kalaimamani S. R. Parvati, Kalaimamani Palakavi Vengadachalan Vattiyar, Kalaimamani M. K. Kamalam, A. K. Kaleeswaran, C. R. Sunadararaja, M. K. Kalyana Suntaram, P. R. Pandian, Sundaralakshmi, Chandrika, and Devi Shanmukam, T. R. M. Savitri, Sittradevi, Gangamma, S. P. Mina, S. G. R. Bakkiyalakshmi, S. K. Parvati, R. M. Tamilselvi, R. Jeyalatha, S. Kalashri, T. V. Jeyam, M. P. Viswanathan, A. K. Vanitasan, Karur Ambika, K. R. Indra, Ponamaravathy A. R. Arumukam, A. R. A. Kannan, G. Kasturi, Dindigal K. Patma, Ramalingasivan, Balamurugan, S. A. Rettnamani, M. S. B. Minervadevi, Sennai Sivakami, M. Krishnaveni, Gandhimathi, Manjuladevi, Valarmathi, T. M. Saraswati, "Silk" Kalaiselvi, K. Sardar and family, N. M.

Sridevi, P. K. A. Mustafa, Pudukkottai Ilayaraja, M. K. Sattyaraj, M. S. P. Kalaimani, V. C. Prasat Rajendran, M. S. Sundari, V. S. Mukkaiya, D. P. Kuppusami, and K. Murugan. Each has my deep respect and gratitude.

My academic guides in Tamilnadu, Drs. Mu. Ramasami and the late Shenbagam Ramasami, graciously shared with me their knowledge of the field of Tamil performing arts in all its breadth. Drs. Vijayalakshmi and Navaneetha Krishnan also made me feel welcome in this scholarly field. The ongoing encouragement and support of my scholarship from the Tamil Theatre artist and activist V. Padma (aka Mangai) and Dr. V. Arasu of the Madras University mean much to me; likewise, for a friendship ignited by shared intellectual and activist goals and for their excitement about this project, it was my pleasure to engage with T. Sivakumar and Arouna.

Among the many drama sponsors and drama agents I met, I owe specific thanks to the late "power agent" M. Jeyaraman of Madurai for his candid comments, and to the members of the Karaikudi Music Drama Agents and Actors Sangam, especially their president Mr. P. L. Gandhi, from whose friendship and chivalry I benefited a good deal.

Thanks are equally due to all the audience members with whom I watched dramas, and the many electricians who let me connect video cords into their mixing boards. This is especially true for the 1992–1993 drama seasons in two villages where I stayed for extended periods of time, Valaiyangulam (Madurai district) and Kottamangalam (Chettinadu district), and where I benefited from the hospitality of R. Ponnaiya and family in Valaiyangulam, and Compounder Lakshmanan and family in Kottamangalam. I hope someday to return the pleasure.

Archival Sources

The history of over a century of Special Drama performances that I piece together in the opening chapters of this book owes its strength to multiple archival sources. Given the ephemerality of both live performance itself and the drama notices that index its production in South India, the few existing archival sources of materials on Special Drama played a crucial role in tracing this history. Together these sources provided critical documentary evidence to support the oral narratives of artists that form the ethnographic core of my historical understanding of the genre.

The Roja Muttiah Research Library in Chennai (RMRL) maintains an essential collection of textual material on the Tamil popular arts. I have drawn significantly on its invaluable collection of drama notices from the 1890s through the 1950s. I remain grateful to James Nye, South Asia bibliographer at the University of Chicago library, who worked in a sustained fashion to translate his early visionary appreciation of the importance of this archive into the reality of RMRL, and likewise to Mr. G. Sundar, acting director at RMRL in 2001, who generously facilitated my access to the archives.

Three additional, less-institutionalized archival sources allowed me to create a textual record of Special Drama beyond 1950. First, my private collection of more than two hundred notices from the 1992 and 1993 drama seasons owes its existence to the generosity of the workers at four print shops in Madurai who cheerfully supplied my collecting fetish during these years. Second, many Special Drama artists keep among their personal mementos a few select notices to document their leading performance years, particularly those that honor an especially memorable pairing of performers. I want to specifically recognize senior artists A. K. Kaleeswaran, T. N. Sivathanu, N. S. Varatarajan, M. A. Majeeth, and S. P. Mina for graciously opening their private collections to my inquisitive eye and allowing me to photocopy such important documents. Finally, I know of only one person apart from myself who maintains an archive of video footage of Special Drama in performance. He is Mr. Angumuttu Pillai of Dindigal, tobacco factory proprietor, longtime patron and fan of Special Drama, and fine amateur tabla artist, who has contributed significantly to keeping the art of Special Drama very much alive in the Dindigal district for several decades. While my video archive documents dramas from the 1990s, his preserves the performances of the 1970s, and I am grateful for his foresight and his generosity in sharing these with me.

Research Assistance

I worked with several research assistants over the two-year period from September 1991 to July 1993 in Tamilnadu. These companions variously watched dramas with me all night, accompanied me during interviews, transcribed (and occasionally translated) audio- and videotape recordings, and explained vocabulary, expressions, and concepts. Their help was invaluable. In Madras my assistants were G. Revathy, M. Usha, and V. Sukanya, three remarkable young women who stretched norms to do this work with me; thank you. In Madurai, four comparably remarkable men, K. Ravichandran, Selvaganeshan, P. Velraj, and Krishnaswamy, all gave me insight into gendered aspects of Special Drama performances that I would not have appreciated in the same way without them; thanks for being good anthropologists. Mrs. K. Paramasivam (Shenbagavalli) and family shared a good-natured interest in my work and helped materially in numerous ways; I will never forget the glint in Mrs. K. P.'s eye when she handed me K. P.'s old copies of *The Stage Lover*, saying, "I thought you might find these interesting." Thank you for this recognition and your generosity.

In the United States

This book's first incarnation was as a dissertation submitted to the Department of Anthropology at the University of Chicago in 1997. The members of my dissertation committee—Bernard S. Cohn, Jean Comaroff, Nancy D. Munn, and Norman Cutler—consistently encouraged my best work and supported me as it took its own direction. It is my great good fortune to have learned from them. During the final year of writing, I benefited most significantly from critical readings offered by a writing group of graduate student colleagues—Ira Bashkow, Greg Downey, Anne Lorimer, Teri Silvio, Seung-Hoon Song, and Rupert Stash—who gave me a model for, and a first experience of, the kind of intellectual exchange one dreams of among disciplinary colleagues. The invaluable Anne Ch'ien consistently helped all of us get where we are.

While revising the manuscript in 2001–2002 in Los Angeles, I again benefited from the comradeship of a writing group. Scholarly sustenance joined with its spicier twin as we edited over *idli* and *dosai* at Paru's (thank you, Kannan!). My work improved just by knowing I would submit it to the keen sensibilities of Kajri Jain and Saloni Mathur. There were continuities in our respective approaches to a wealth of Indian material that gave me a welcome sense of being engaged in a broader analytic project than just my own.

Throughout the course of my writing this book, family and friends have provided all kinds of support.

In the initial years of my research in Tamilnadu, I benefited greatly from sharing with Kate Schechter first encounters of all kinds, and likewise from her ability to sustain analytic contact. We did that, Kate.

Teri Silvio did several things I still consider humanly impossible, starting with reading my dissertation from start to finish not one but two times (!)

and then blowing in from Taipei to put the air back in my tires. How can I thank you, Teri? I don't think this book would exist without you.

Then, somewhat later, several genius friends read portions of my writing in various stages, whether as papers or chapters. The necessary moment in a process such as this in a world such as academia is always inconvenient, but these committed comrade-scholars obliged uncomplainingly. For this I am indebted (and in love) with Mary Weismantel, Stephen Eisenman, Dan Segal, Laurie Shrage, Mady Schutzman, Kathryn Hansen, and Elizabeth Chin.

But let me get a good bit more specific here in thanking:

Mary Weismantel, model of verbal and visual elegance, who read the penultimate manuscript of this book during summer 2003 all in a piece, allowing me to see it whole for a critical final revision—you rock, Mary;

Dan Segal, my extraordinary colleague, whose consistently clearheaded apprehension of all that the project of anthropology comprises is a beacon to me;

Stephen Eisenman, for showing me there is no one way to write about art, there are just better ways;

My mother, Fern Seizer, for her unstinting candor in reading my writing and promptly disabusing me of any notion that my prose was already sufficiently free of academic jargon (do you like that sentence, Mom?);

My father, Bob Seizer, for sharing with me his natural flair with a pen and the full-bodied, only slightly self-deprecating laugh on which it rides;

My brother, the first Dr. S. Seizer, for taking that absolutely ludicrous trip to Tamilnadu with me during the hottest May on record in a hundred years and managing to charm everyone he met;

My grandmother, Florence Victor, for loving me, and for waiting impatiently as long as she has to read this book;

The fabulous Jennifer Miller, my best friend and the truest quick-study no-bullshit wise funny gal ever, for being in my life in such a big way for such a long time;

My students at Scripps College, who, more than just avid learners, are real friends: we read each other's work and keep each other honest;

Dean Michael Deane Lamkin of Scripps College, who makes academic life for our faculty more pleasant and fun than anyone else will admit;

The three anonymous readers from Duke University Press who offered such wonderfully detailed readings and genuinely helpful suggestions: your comments were invaluable in giving me a sense of how my words might be read;

Ken Wissoker, Christine Dahlin, and Pam Morrison of the Press, who let me take the time I needed to write the book I wanted;

And finally to my spouse-for-life, Catherine Brennan: I love you on into the next big and littlest things.

Over the years, my work on this project has been made possible by a Fulbright/Hays Doctoral Dissertation Fellowship for research in India, 1991–1992; a Junior Research Fellowship from the American Institute of Indian Studies, 1992–1993; a Charlotte W. Newcombe Foundation Doctoral Dissertation Fellowship, 1994–1995; a University of California–Santa Barbara Women's Studies Program predoctoral teaching fellowship, 1995–1996; dissertation support from the Committee on South Asian Studies at the University of Chicago, 1996–1997; two Scripps College Faculty Research Grants, summer 1999 and fall 2001; and an American Council of Learned Societies ACLS/SSRC/NEH International Area Studies Fellowship, 2001–2002. I am grateful to each of these institutions for their votes of confidence in this work, and for making it possible for me to complete it.

Notes on Transliteration

1. This book employs the international schemes of transcription currently followed for South Asian languages. In these transliteration schemes, long vowels are distinguished from short ones by a dash over the appropriate roman letter substituted for the original language character. The pronunciation of vowels in Tamil is as follows:

Short	Long	Approximately as in the English word:
a	ā	cup; *part*
i	ī	pit; *feed*
u	ū	put; *fool*
e	ē	pet; *ale*
o	ō	book; *hope*

Place names and proper names, as well as those Indian terms that are likely already familiar to English readers in an Anglicized form, have been spelled in the text without any diacritical marks, conforming to the manner in which these names have come to be written in English in India (Swami; Madurai). Otherwise, newly introduced Tamil words appear italicized and with diacritical marks. Frequently used words that make up the basic vocabulary of Special Drama (often themselves hybrid Anglo-Tamil terms) are transliterated only once (e.g., *Stirīpārt*; *Irājapārt*) and are treated thereafter as common English nouns, in a simplified, standard Anglicized spelling (Streepart, Rajapart); they are repeated in this way in the index. Throughout, however, I have retained diacritical marks for one word in particular—*muṟai*—to remind the reader of the fundamental untranslatability of this concept into a single English term. The proper Tamil pronunciation of *muṟai* has a slightly rolling *r* (as in hurrah) and a short diphthong *ai* (as in smile).

2. The italicized word *Valli* is used throughout as an abbreviation of the name of the play most frequently discussed throughout the book, *Valli's Wedding*.

3. Italicized English words embedded in the quoted dialogues of Tamil

speakers signify that the speaker used these words in English in the course of his or her Tamil dialogue. This is a presentational convention used throughout the book; it first appears in the opening conversation of the introduction.

Introduction

> The drama caste has no culture.
> —Special Drama actor P. S. Nagaraja Bhagavattar

Preface: A Conversation on Culture

Time: A late morning in March 1993

Characters in order of appearance: Susan Seizer, an American anthropologist, in her early thirties; P. S. Nagaraja Bhagavattar, a respected Special Drama actor, in his mid-seventies; Vaiyur Gopal, his friend, another wonderful actor, in his early sixties

Scene: The front room of Mr. Bhagavattar's modest bungalow in Ottakadai (beside Elephant Mountain, on the outskirts of Madurai) in Tamilnadu, South India. The participants sit cross-legged on a cement floor. The day is hot, and the doors are left open. Mr. Bhagavattar's wife moves in and out of the room intermittently throughout the conversation, as she is cooking in the adjacent small kitchen. Several neighborhood children have parked themselves near the open front door and stand there staring at the visitor.

Note: This conversation was held in Tamil, though participants insert many English words. The following is a verbatim translation in which *italics* denote words and phrases spoken in English. Numerals (in brackets) indicate pauses in conversation, measured in seconds, while // indicates a line of speech interrupted by the next speaker.

SUSAN SEIZER: You said something earlier that interests me. You said, "Men and women may be equal, but it will be the end of Tamil *culture*." Is that what you said?

NAGARAJA BHAGAVATTAR: Yes.

SS: But somehow, keeping Tamil *culture*, *we must find a way*! There must be a way for women and men to be equal, and yet at the same time for Tamil *culture* to survive.

NB: No, no! This *equality* has already come, *nowadays*.

SS: Has it?

NB: Oh yes, it has come: in the *offices* they *work* together. Everyone together, *male and female* are working together //

VAIYUR GOPAL: That is *foreign*. That is what is meant by *foreign* //

NB: Yes, *foreign* //

VG: This is indeed *foreign culture*.

SS: [*agitated*] Let there be Tamil *culture*, let Tamil *culture* remain! But let us just change this one thing in it. . . .

[1.0]

VG: *Equal* may have already come, but anyway *gents* will never give up their place.

[1.0]

NB: [*with finality*] *To be changed*, anyway, *not approved*. What for *change*? Does one just suddenly change a *husband*?

[1.0]

SS: [*doubtfully*] Unh.

NB: That is forbidden.

[1.0]

VG: [*reflectively*] Now that is just what is happening. That is your *culture*. If that *set* doesn't think things are going right, *Next! Change!*

NB: Immediately, *divorce!*

VG: Here there is a lot of *divorce* happening now.

SS: In the drama world, this has been going on for a long time. . . .

NB: Yes, that's right: in the drama world it has always been like this, right from the very *beginning* it has been this way. It has no *culture*.

SS: [*laughing*] No *culture* at all?

NB: That is, this is a caste with no *culture*. The drama caste.[1]

VG: How's that?

[1.0]

NB: That's how their life has become. Of course, we two never married drama actresses. So then, do we not have *culture*?

VG: [*emphatic*] We do indeed!

I open with this conversation (in which I myself figure as a somewhat embarrassingly naive Western feminist) because it compactly conveys several of the key themes that arose in my research among Special Drama artists. These are now the central themes of this book: (1) that the twin forces of cultural change and exchange have profoundly shaped the history and practice of Special Drama and the lives of stage actors in South India; (2) that Special Drama artists as a community are stigmatized for lacking what they and others often refer to as "Tamil culture," a concept defined in quite particular ways; (3) that the weight of blame for this stigma falls most heavily on female actresses, for an array of reasons both historical and cultural; and (4) that Special Drama artists make a variety of strategic attempts to deflect the effects of this stigma, both onstage and in their offstage lives.

This conversation provides important departure points for each of these themes. Regarding the first, perhaps most immediately striking is how *language* serves as a force of change and exchange. Evident in this conversation to an unusual extent, it nevertheless surfaces in the intertwining of Tamil and English concepts in the vernacular vocabularies of most Special Drama artists. With theatrical terms like "mike" and "light," at its most mundane level this linguistic exchange bespeaks a history of culture contact between British and Indian theater worlds begun in the mid-nineteenth century. In its wider ricochet off of Indian-English catchphrases, however, this conversation reflects the particular experience of senior male artists such as Mr. Bhagavattar (1917–2001), who trained during the colonial period when English was unequivocally the language of political power and social prestige in India. Regardless of subsequent ongoing efforts to decrease its stature and to raise instead the status of the Tamil language in South India (Ramaswamy 1997; Irschick 1969), English remains a language of privilege in Tamilnadu.

On one level, then, Mr. Bhagavattar's use of so much English here asserts a personal linguistic facility of which he was proud. On another level, the particular terms of this exchange reflect profound incommensurabilities within the political lives of these two languages, resulting in the irony of his using hybrid Anglo-Tamil speech to voice a condemnatory, nationalist stance on the negative effects of foreign concepts on "Tamil culture." Our conversation leapfrogs along a dominant narrative, one frequently rehearsed by senior male Tamil drama artists. We land repeatedly—clearly marked by the string of one-second pauses in our conversation—in dense thickets of mostly gendered prerogative: "*gents* will never give up their place . . . [pause]

. . . Does one suddenly change a *husband?* . . . [pause] . . . That is forbidden. . . . [pause] . . . this is a caste with *no* culture . . . [pause] . . ."

In these pregnant pauses reside the beginnings of the second and third themes of this book. The stigma on artists for lacking "Tamil culture" is here deeply enmeshed with the notion that it is actresses who are to blame for this lamentable state of affairs. Male artists can retain their "cultured" identity by avoiding degrading liaisons with actresses. Casting actresses as the culprits in this story of the corrosive effects of modern change is a divisive move that has innumerable repercussions in the lives of both male and female artists.

In South India as throughout South Asia, moral concern over women's movement in public feeds into a dominant ideology of "the home and the world" as separate spheres of propriety for women and men respectively. Women who conduct business in the public sphere are suspect, a suspicion charged with the particular cruelty reserved for accusations of prostitution.[2]

Many of the Tamil terms for actress are also common terms for denoting a whore or prostitute. *Kūtti*, *tāci*, and *tēvaṭiyāḷ* all have the dual meaning of "dancing girl or prostitute" (Fabricius 1972, 505); "dancing-girl devoted to temple service, commonly a prostitute; harlot, whore" (University of Madras 1982, 1825). The two concepts—that of female dancer or performer, whether ostensibly employed in sacred service or not, and prostitute—were so linked in nineteenth-century colonial India that one missionary simply wrote, "A dancing girl is invariably a harlot" (Jensen [1897] 1989, 43). Though such remarks were probably aimed specifically at the women of the Devadasi community, whose artistic service was consecrated to the gods, there is an inevitable slippage, throughout the colonial legal and Anglo-Indian judiciary discourses of the nineteenth century, between the terms "temple dancing girl" and "dancing girl," any and all of whom get lumped together by the colonial courts and criminalized as prostitutes by the early twentieth century (Parker 1998).

The notion of "prostitution" itself under the Raj covered any sexual activity outside marriage (Parker 1998, 566). Simultaneously in England during the 1880s, the Purity Crusade was becoming a mass movement within which prostitution, "hitherto defined as 'sexual intercourse, except for propagation,' was redefined to refer to corruption and moral depravity in life" (Kannabiran 1995, 63). In Tamilnadu all these discourses came together in the social purity movement begun in Madras in the late nineteenth century. Female dancers came to be seen as "characterless ladies" "lost to society" for living outside the bonds of conventional marriage in a world envisioned as organized fundamentally around marriage (Weidman 2003, 198–201).

As *public* women, the accusation that actresses are prostitutes continues to adhere to them, again whether they sell sexual favors or not. Historian Kathryn Hansen's account of Nauṭaṅkī, a comparable genre of popular music theater in North India, confirms my own ethnographic understandings of the stigmatizing situation for Special Drama actresses in the South.

> The selling of sexual favors is not essential to the definition of a stage actress as a prostitute, either in North India or in other societies. Gender roles in this agriculturally based patriarchal society are defined in spatial terms, with women occupying private inside spaces and men public outer ones. Women are valued for their domestic labor and for their reproductivity, which must be controlled for the perpetuation of pure family and caste lines. Enclosure, whether effected by pardā (the curtain or screen of a segregated household), by the canopy of a bullock cart, or by a veil or sari-end drawn over a woman's face, is conceived as necessary to preserve a woman's chastity and, by extension, her menfolk's honor. *Since the social construction of gender places "good women" in seclusion, women who appear in public spaces (such as on stage) are defined as "bad," that is, prostitutes.* Subjected to the gaze of many men, they belong not to one, like the loyal wife, but to all. (Hansen 1992, 21–23; italics mine)

This notion that social purity can be secured through checks on women's mobility and social "mixing" is one that pertains, apparently, throughout South Asia. Such logics are at the base of the stigma on stage artists. Women first mounted the Tamil popular stage in the second decade of the twentieth century. To many, including Mr. Bhagavattar, the actress's entrance inaugurated the descent of the reputation of the dramatic arts in Tamilnadu. The actress is perhaps the most unsettling of theatrical figures precisely in her unsettledness: her seemingly excessive mobility in the public sphere disrupts foundational moral distinctions between the home and the world. These gender dynamics only became clearer as our conversation continued:

NB: If you want to know when the field of *drama* had *culture*, it was when there were only *male actors*. As soon as *female artists* were brought in and *interfered*, that is when *culture* went [*claps his hands for emphasis*]. You see, when males were acting as females, there was no *sexual appeal* to it. But if a man meets a woman, there will be *sexual appeal*; when males were the females there was no such thing as *sexual appeal*. But if a *male* meets a *female*, then definitely, *according to circumstances*, there will be *sexual appeal*.

SS: Are you saying that a male in a female role will not have *sexual appeal*? But indeed, a male in the audience may find a male actor in a female role sexually appealing. . . .

NB: No. *Maybe*. But in any case, that is *mere acting*. But if on that same stage, a male meets a real female, *according to circumstances*—he may touch, talk, sing—and he'll start to think, "Gee, she sings well, she looks good." Like this, the opportunity arises for his heart to change, and for her heart to change also. When a male comes on all dressed up nicely, like a prince, then she may begin to desire this man; seeing him as a hero, seeing him in this role, she may begin to desire him. . . .

SS: *True love* comes. . . .

NB: But this is a very transient thing, it doesn't last. Such *culture* does not exist in this field. Now she wants him; then suddenly if another good-looking man comes. . . . She is not *steady* in her *love*! I have experienced fifty years, a *half century* of experience in this; there is no *culture* here. The very next year, the partners will change [*all laugh*]. What can we do with this? So then, where is our *culture*?

Mr. Bhagavattar here asserts that a particular pattern of gender relations between men and women forms the traditional cornerstone of Tamil cultural identity. Specifically, his assumption is that only lifelong marital bonds *of the proper sort* constitute true "Tamil culture." These are specifically *not* marriages based on the tumultuous grounds of whim and desire, considered transient emotions that will lead quickly from love to divorce. Such transient love is the touchstone of "foreign culture." Tamil culture is built instead on (necessarily heterosexual, he insists) marriages based on the more enduring truths of familial and celestial alignment.[3]

Mr. Bhagavattar's contention is that stage artists "nowadays" lack true (that is, Tamil and not foreign) *culture* because they lack its key distinguishing feature, the constancy of the proper (and properly arranged) Tamil marriage. Instead, your garden-variety drama artists—unlike Mr. Bhagavattar himself or his friend Gopal, to be sure, who did *not* marry drama actresses—regularly engage in the foreign-inflected practice of "love marriage." Stage actresses represent here the pinnacle of such transience: "she is not *steady* in her *love*—the very next year, the partners will change!" This is an all-too-familiar story: the figure of the actress as public woman and prostitute, a loose woman unsteady in her love, makes her someone whom no self-respecting man will marry.

Complicated as it may seem for male artists to base their self-respect on the distance they can establish from those with whom they share the stage, then, imagine the even deeper difficulty of maintaining self-respect as a female stage artist. If men can condemn the actress as the death knell of Tamil culture and themselves stay clean by staying clear of actresses in their private lives, what route of escape is possible for actresses short of leaving the field altogether? As a deferred desire, the latter is what most actresses claim to want for their children: "It is too late for me, but my children should have a different life." For the time being, however, escape takes the shape of performances with an intensity all their own. In these, Special Drama actresses manage to voice condemnatory moralistic attitudes quite similar to those held by their male counterparts, while simultaneously enacting the part of the very women against whom such condemnatory attitudes rail.

Most frequently it is under the guise of comedy that actresses play loose women for laughs. They play themselves—the public woman who threatens Tamil culture with her increased presence in the public sphere—as the butt of their own jokes. In mouthing this dominant moralizing narrative, actresses stand in a complicated relation to their own subjectivity, distancing themselves from the stigmatized social role into which they are repeatedly cast onstage and off. In conversations such as the one I had with Messrs. Bhagavattar and Gopal, the inherent complexity of the stage actress's position as she attempts to deflect this stigma goes unrecognized. It emerges most powerfully, instead, in actresses' own attempts to represent themselves as moral women. Such complex negotiations of self-presentation and representation animate much of my work in this book.

In chapter 8, "The Roadwork of Actresses," for example, I focus on the creative ways actresses use self-erected enclosures to preserve their "goodness" and honor as they travel through the public sphere. In their external behaviors, they reenact a sense of entitlement to privacy and domesticity, a reflection of the internalized moral entitlement that enabled middle-class women in twentieth-century India to remain untainted by their travel outside the home. Likewise I examine the complexities of the role of the wife in the context of a popular comedy sketch on domestic abuse (chapter 6, "The Aṭipiṭi Scene"). The actress performing this role gives a remarkable performance that oscillates between exposing the injustice of domestic gender roles for women and banishing just such exposures to the realm of an unacceptable modernity (the same kind of role-reversing modernity that Nagaraja Bhagavattar deemed "not approved").

The public nature of the acting profession, which frequently displays on public stages what are otherwise meant to be the most private of relations, is problematic for women who attend Special Drama as audience members as well as for actresses. Any woman willing to make herself the object of the gaze of strange men in strange places transgresses the norm of separately gendered spheres. While the transgression is more severe in the case of actresses, who overtly choose to step into the limelight onstage and invite this gaze, it certainly extends to female audience members, who, simply by attending these public events, appear in public outdoor spaces at night. The consequences of audience fears that the reputations of local women will be disparaged simply by their attendance at these events include not only the much lower attendance of women but also important shapings of performances themselves. This is quite overt, for example, in the "Buffoon's Comedy" (chapter 4), wherein an actor masterfully directs his joking address in such a way as to allow women in the audience to salvage their own reputations as good women.

The connections Mr. Bhagavattar made in our rather casual conversation—connections between foreign corrupting influences, cultural instability, the transient nature of women's desires, and the actress as the figure in whom all such terrors condense—represent a nexus of traditionalist, conservative attitudes to which artists of both genders are compared and often conform. They animated the heartbeat between the two questions Mr. Bhagavattar posed back-to-back in our conversation, questions that seemed to me at first to be non sequiturs. When he asked, "What for *change*? Does one just suddenly change a *husband*?" I (not entirely following the leap of his logic) answered doubtfully, "Uh-huh . . . ," and touché! I had managed to give precisely the wrong answer, or rather just the right one to uphold his assumptions about the morals of an American, professional, unmarried female who might well have thought love marriage a socially acceptable practice.

Which brings me, finally, to the overall tenor of this conversation. Because the conversation was held with me, my far-from-silent presence always at least partly shaped what got said. All the understandings I present in this book are similarly doubly filtered through me. First, they took their initial shape in face-to-face fieldwork interactions such as the foregoing conversation, always generated in response both to my presence and to my questions. Second, my own preexisting and developing social interests have shaped my interpretive analyses from those early face-to-face moments through to my viewing and re-viewing of performances and on into these final words I type, as I translate, present, and represent my own ideas alongside those of the artists in every line I write. As I describe what I see, a good part of what you will see is me. The reader is therefore owed the following brief introduction-within-an-introduction to my own entree into this project, and to my enduring commitments within it.

Birth of This Project

This project has changed the ways I use feminist methods in analyzing social relations. I still believe that all women deserve what they consider good lives as defined in their own terms. This commitment has, however, been significantly tested, complicated, and now recalibrated by the exposure of assumptions I didn't realize I held. Somehow I had assumed that improving the quality-of-life standards for women would necessitate the full-scale overhaul of a fundamentally unequal system, direct advocacy for radical social change, and, at the very least, an overt argument. Instead what I encountered in the practices of women I met in the Special Drama community was not much more activist than the desire for their own upward mobility, articulated within the terms of an extant order of hierarchical relations that they seemed content to leave intact. In the first instance, I found this disappointing.

I began, as usual, with all the wrong questions. These invoked generic individuals as well as a generic category, "women": Could individual women acting out of personal interest in their own upward mobility have any broad beneficial effect for Indian women in general? Could such struggles be considered feminist? These questions obscure the particularity of real struggle. The elaborate specificity of actual lives demands subtler measures. Special Drama actresses are indeed each individual women, but they are also a class of women historically stigmatized by their profession. I now see that stigma as the condition of actresses' lives that makes their pursuit of upward mobility remarkable: courageous, complex, and creative.

For given their stigmatized social position, the very act of managing to move up even a notch in an extant social order alters that order, changes it, pushes it open as a path for others to follow. By acting on their desires for social esteem, actresses *expand* the hierarchical order they would join. Their practices foster social change in incremental rather than radical ways. I had to lose my assumption that social change was diametrically opposed to the very existence of hierarchies of value in order to appreciate the strategies of Special Drama actresses. (In a similar move, Louis Dumont criticizes Westerners as so averse to hierarchy that they are now unable to recognize the workings of class in their own society; see Dumont [1966] 1980). Actors do not try to eliminate the systems of hierarchical value within which their lives have meaning. Rather, they seem to accept that hierarchy is what makes social distinction possible, while simultaneously acting in ways that subtly remake those distinctions. These artists are fundamentally engaged, that is, in what I now recognize as the profound and simultaneously ubiquitous social phenomenon of "stigma management" (Goffman 1963).

I never set out to study stigma, let alone the stigma on actors in South India. I came to this project initially through a nonacademic interest in performance. During the early 1980s, I worked as a dancer and choreographer in New York City in what was then a fertile downtown experimental dance scene. I spent a lot of time in dance studios exploring movement possibilities. One afternoon a friend of the family invited me to a performance at Lincoln Center, part of the 1985 Festival of India. The program included Malavika Sarukkai performing Bharata Natyam, a South Indian dance form that the playbill described as "a solo form for women which developed over centuries as part of devotional rituals in south Indian temples and as entertainment in the courts of divine kings." Sitting in those plush velvet seats at that Sunday matinee, I experienced a sort of epiphany. No matter how many hours I spent experimenting in a dance studio, I would never come up with *this*. This surprising combination of feet slapping the floor hard, lyrical hands miming an elephant trunk or a flower (equally graceful), and eyes whose movements were choreographed on a rhythmic beat. In the differences between this dance and my own familiar dance, I suddenly saw the extent to which culture shapes even our most intimate selves, our bodies, and the very ways we move.

I called the Indian consulate the next morning. They gave me the names of several teachers, and I began to study Bharata Natyam, not with the aim of adding it to my own performance repertoire but instead just to experience the differently encultured body it offered. Only after several months did I learn that Tamil was the language to whose sounds we danced. I wanted more. How to engage with the larger questions raised by seeing the extent to which cultures shape bodies? Anthropology. I applied to the four graduate programs at U.S. universities that at the time offered Tamil language study as well as anthropology, and ended up in Chicago.

It wasn't until I went to India for the first time in 1989 to study the Tamil language in situ that I encountered any Tamil performance genres other than those framed as classical Carnatic dance. I began to be able to situate the notion of the "classical" in Tamil arts as a resurrected and relational concept defined against other artistic forms. By happy coincidence, that year I stayed in the very center of town, in the old, crowded heart of the city of Madurai, where just down the street from my flat was a building that proudly proclaimed itself the Tamilnadu Drama Actors Sangam. I had previously been introduced to playwright and Tamil theater scholar Dr. Mu. Ramaswamy of Tanjore University, a man highly knowledgeable about the whole range of folk and classical theater forms, so I sought him out to ask about this organization. To which he promptly responded by dismissing the dramas these actors performed as "boring."

Of course his discouragement immediately intrigued me: Why are they boring? What does "boring" look like in Tamilnadu? To whom (besides him) are they boring? And why did he assume that I too (he knew me only as a member of the category "American scholar") would find them so? In addition to piquing my interest, then, Dr. Ramaswamy's comment was my first intimation of a social reality that would become central to my further study of this very form. From Dr. Ramaswamy I first learned that Special Drama artists and their work are generally dismissed by the Tamil middle class. Only later did I become aware of the specific character of that dismissal. Special Drama is too mixed to be pure, too popular to be art, too modern to be traditional, and too village to be modern.

Ignoring for the time being Dr. Ramaswamy's dismissal, I attended a Special Drama with a friend from the language program. We met several artists in the cast who invited us to their annual Guru Puja Remembrance Day celebration. There we met more artists. One actress in particular, Jansirani, reached out to me. It turned out we lived on the same street; she had noticed me heading off to class in the mornings. She invited me home to lunch. Jansirani was open, forthcoming, and a good cook. I met her husband—she was his "second wife"—and their two young daughters, who stole my heart. I decided to write my term paper for the language program on Special Drama. With Jansi's help in making contacts, I interviewed a few senior artists about their lives in the field of Special Drama. And I went to see more dramas.

Inclined to pursue the suggestive issues that arose even in just these initial encounters, I looked for guidance in previously written research. What I found—or, more precisely, did not find—made me all the more curious to understand why this genre of Tamil theater is so roundly disavowed.

Writing about Special Drama

Very little has been written to date about Special Drama, either in Tamil or in English. Indeed, its existence is recognized only in a few passing mentions, either in survey-style histories of Tamil theater (IAS 1990; Baskaran 1981, 2001; de Bruin 2001a; A. Narayan 1981; Perumal 1981) or in autobiographical reminiscences of stage actors who eventually became famous in Tamil cinema (Shanmugam 1972; Mudaliyar 1998). The larger domain of music drama (icai nāṭakam) of which Special Drama is a subset does, however, play a critical role in Tamil theater historiography. The terms in which music drama is discussed therein continue to profoundly affect the way everyone—historians, artists, and audiences alike—now speak of Special Drama, when and if they do.

The scholarly neglect of Special Drama is a symptom of a larger, elite dismissal of popular theater as "vulgar," what de Bruin calls "an officially advocated aversion" (2001a, 70). The denunciation of popular theater by the Indian middle class, especially vehement around the turn of the twentieth century, has been well documented by scholars of North Indian popular culture (Banerjee 1990; Chatterjee 2001; Hansen 1992; Naregal 2001). These same attitudes contributed to a climate in which the reformulation and reinvention of the "classical" performing arts of South India took place at the expense of more provocative traditions, indeed, often replaced them, as in the case of the *devadasi* tradition, wherein female dancers—whom colonial officials insisted on calling "dancing girls"—dedicated their lives to the arts in service to temple gods (Parker 1998; Kannabiran 1995; Marglin 1985; Bruin 2001a; Singer 1972). Special Drama was just developing during the turn-of-the-century period when the tendency throughout India was for the middle classes to devalue popular traditions and reinvent, through classicization and textualization, high-culture forms such as Bharata Natyam (Erdman 1996; Hansen 1992, 255).

Hybrid theater genres such as Special Drama inhabit the periphery of acceptable Tamil performing arts. Music drama itself has inhabited a gray area in Tamil theater historiography for far too long, somewhere vaguely located between the opposing poles of "village" ritual and "urban" modern theater.[4] (Thankfully this situation seems poised for change; Hanne de Bruin (2001b) has recently offered the fullest consideration of the confluence of styles that resulted, during the colonial period, in what she usefully terms the "hybrid theatres" of India, including the music drama of Tamilnadu.[5])

Dismayed at the dearth of written material on the genre of Special Drama and simultaneously intrigued, I proposed an anthropological study of Special Drama that would situate the genre both historically and among the contemporary performing arts of Tamilnadu. Proposal in hand, I returned to India in 1991. I lived for a good portion of that year and the next with Jansirani and her family and maintained residences in both Madurai and Madras (now Chennai).

During this time, my awareness of the dominant scholarly dismissal of Special Drama was enhanced by my growing sensitivity to the stigma encountered by Special Drama artists in their everyday lives. Everyone, not only scholars, held markedly negative opinions about these artists. Landlords refused to rent to them. People stared at them in the street; rowdy boys sometimes even hurled insults at them as they passed. And middle-class interlocutors quickly lost interest in me, too, when they understood how closely I moved with this class of artists. My study of Special Drama gradually shifted to include a focus on how artists meet—with humor, among other strategies—the stigma that marks their lives.

The position of Special Drama in broader Tamil discourses on the performing arts and the related position of its artists in Tamil social life thus became the subjects of my Ph.D. thesis, for which I conducted primary research during the twenty-two months between September 1991 and July 1993. The present work, now much more focused on the strategies that artists use to redress stigma, draws strongly on this initial period of fieldwork, supplemented by additional materials I gathered during two subsequent, shorter visits to Madurai in 1998 and 2001.

The standard tenor of disavowal that greets Special Drama artists and their work remains my touchstone here, just as it originally piqued my interest in the genre itself. I attempt to redress the lack of scholarship on Special Drama by documenting this genre as it grew outside the charmed circle of scholarly light, as a form fed instead by artists' own creative management of stigma onstage and off. Since this is new scholarly territory, I must introduce the forms and practices of this art before analyzing their relationship to the offstage lives of artists. What makes it possible to do both in one volume is that the rubric linking the offstage and onstage domains of my study also links them in life: the history of the genre and the history of its artists' lives are both shaped by the same dominant, dismissive discourses encountered everywhere one turns.

Methods

I used a range of anthropological research methods to gather the data on which this study is based. These include (1) seventy-five taped, open-ended interviews of varying lengths with drama artists, sponsors, and agents ranging in age from eight to eighty years, from several different regional centers of the Special Drama network; (2) roughly one hundred viewings of live Special Drama performances at a wide range of venues across the state of Tamilnadu; (3) spontaneous, brief, and most often unrecorded conversations with audience members on-site about a performance we just watched; (4) the creation of a video archive of Special Drama performances from which I subsequently worked, with the assistance of native Tamil speakers, through transcription and translation; (5) the collection and consultation of textual and archival materials both from artists' personal collections and from library collections in Chettinadu, Chennai, and Madurai; (6) participant observation at actors sangam scheduled events in Madurai, Pudukkottai, and Dindigal; and (7) extended periods of participant observation, including living for eighteen months with one family in Madurai involved with a range of Tamil popular performing arts, including Special Drama, as well as shorter stays with two families sponsoring Special Dramas in their respective natal villages.

This list warrants further contextualization, beginning with how my own research practices shape the information I gathered for this book. Artists' lives onstage and off are the primary focus of my study. Accordingly, Special Drama artists were the main focus of my interviews as well as of my participant observation practices. In general, to view performances of Special Drama, I traveled to drama venues with artists, either as a group (in a private van) or individually (by public bus), and though I sat in the audience for much of the night, I also frequently spent time backstage with artists. All the time I spent with artists in and around dramas, in preparation for as well as after performance, was rich ethnographic time for me. While at the dramas I also focused my primary interest and attention on artists' activities and discourses.

Only secondarily, then, though increasingly as my fieldwork progressed and I became more familiar with the event structures of Special Drama, did I attend to the activities and discourses of those in the Special Drama audience. I conducted a few demographic surveys of audience members with the help of hired assistants but found that my most valuable learning came from conversations I had with individuals and small groups of audience members spontaneously during and after performances. Such audience responses, coupled with my own observations of their responses as we sat next to each other watching drama, proved invaluable in the analyses of the comic performances I describe in chapters 4 through 6, which form the centerpiece of this book.

Twice, however, I inverted my primary focus on artists, staying for several weeks to a month in each of two villages with local families who regularly sponsor Special Dramas. My research focus during these two inverted periods was on audience relations to the sponsorship of live performance genres, including Special Drama. Each of these villages has a strong, ongoing tradition of Special Drama sponsorship. The first was the village of Valaiyangulam, located twenty kilometers outside of Madurai. There I attended thirty consecutive nights of Special Drama in 1992, and five nights of Special Drama in 1993, and was able to delve quite deeply into the historico-mythic relation many Valaiyangulam villagers see themselves as having with the art form of drama itself (material that unfortunately has no place in the present book). The second site I chose for extended study of audiences and sponsors is the Chettinadu village of Kottamangalam, approximately twenty kilometers from Karaikudi, where I attended a ten-day festival for the goddess Ulakanayaki in 1993. I write of the deep-seated commitment of the sponsorship relations established in these two villages in chapter 2, "Prestige Hierarchies in Two and Three Dimensions: Drama Notices and the Organization of Special Drama," as part of a larger discussion of the wide network of relations that each and every Special Drama event puts into play.

In addition, I would like to offer a word on my interview methods. I tape-recorded all interviews whenever possible. That is, I rarely used the method some anthropologists advocate as "less intrusive" (e.g., Siegel 1987), that of interviewing without a tape recorder and then reconstructing the interview by paraphrasing it in field notes shortly thereafter, a method I used only for spontaneous conversations. Instead, a key to my methodological practice has been the ability to return to audiotaped interviews and videotaped dramas repeatedly in the years subsequent to my initial fieldwork. Such repeated playback allows me to hear and comprehend with increasing detail many things I was unable to hear the first time around.

All dialogues presented in this book, whether from interviews or staged performances, are thus the result of direct translation from recordings. I take ultimate responsibility for these translations, though most often (but not always) they are informed by earlier translations generated with the help of bilingual assistants in Madras and Madurai. These translations in turn owe much to the patient work of several monolingual native Tamil speakers whom I employed to make verbatim transcriptions of dialogues recorded on interview and performance tapes. The many handwritten books of transcriptions resulting from these efforts are an important supplement to the audio- and videotapes that now make up the archive of my 1990s fieldwork in the world of Special Drama.

Geographical Relations and the Historical Ethnographic Present

Special Drama is most actively pursued and performed in the south-central districts of the state of Tamilnadu (see map). The districts of Madurai, Pudukkottai, Pasumpon Muthuramalingam, Tiruchirapali, and Anna—and their respective city centers of Madurai, Pudukkottai, Karaikudi, Karur, and Dindigal—form both the center of the state of Tamilnadu and the center of Special Drama activity. These regions where Special Drama networks are most alive were the primary locations of my fieldwork. By contrast, the state capital of Chennai defines the northeasternmost corner of the state, and the theatrical discourses one finds here are themselves more northern looking and altogether more "modern" and cosmopolitan than those found in the central regions. Historiographic discourses generated in Madras by Madrasi drama historians and critics have nonetheless hugely influenced the way regional theater genres are perceived and discussed by audiences and practitioners alike, a set of relations I trace in chapter 1, "Legacies of Discourse."

At the time of my research, there were approximately 1,500 professional Special Drama artists (actors and musicians) living and working in Tamilnadu. Madurai had the highest concentration of Special Drama artists, a status it has maintained since the earliest days of the genre. Regarding the importance of Madurai to the acting profession at the beginning of the twentieth century, when he and his brothers first entered it, Tamil stage-actor-turned-cine-star T. K. Shanmugam (1972) writes, "The city of Madurai at that time was both mother and home to the acting profession" (Nāṭaka toḷilukke akkālattil tāy vīṭāka viḷaṅkiyatu Maturai mānakaram) (34). This remains the case for the Tamil popular stage today; the nurturing role of Madurai in relation to the other cities and towns where Special Drama actors congregate is captured in the common use of the locution *tāy caṅkam*, or

Map of Tamilnadu, showing the sixteen "actors *sangams*" throughout the state

mother sangam, to refer to the actors' union in Madurai and its relation to the sixteen other drama actors sangams currently operative throughout the state. From 1991 to 1993 there were over 350 artists registered as members of the Madurai Sangam. Another 300 were members of the Pudukkottai Sangam, and nearly 200 of the Dindigal Sangam. After these three largest associations, the remaining thirteen were led in size by the Karaikudi Sangam (located in Chettinadu, historically a district with a strong connection to the dramatic arts) that registered nearly 100 members.[6] The remaining 500 to 600 artists performing in the Special Drama network were spread across twelve other cities and towns throughout the state, each of which had its own actors sangam. These were Karūr, Salem, Sivaganga, Erode, Trichy, Coimbatore, Kōyilpaṭṭi, Maṇappāṟai, Kumbakōnam, Peṅāṭṭam, Perungudi,

Nammakkal, and Manāmaṭurai. In 2001 there were still sixteen sangams total, but three new ones had replaced three earlier ones.[7]

The large actors sangam in Chennai known as the South Indian Actors Sangam (Teṉintiya Ṅaṭikar Caṅkam) is not part of this network of regional actors sangams but rather in its own category. Possessed of a good deal more political clout in the state government than any of the regional sangams, this is primarily a union of film actors serving the prolific Tamil cinema industry. It is the rare artist who belongs to both types of sangam. Notably, the late great M. A. Majeeth, president of the Madurai Sangam during the period of my fieldwork, was just such a crossover artist. His fame was built on devotional song, a skill that is consistently employable in diverse genres of the Tamil performing arts. Able to work both in Chennai and in the regional areas, Mr. Majeeth maintained his primary residence in Madras and commuted to Madurai to preside over the sangam. This trajectory kept him well appraised of dominant state discourses on the arts, and his position as head of the Madurai Sangam made him a well-placed bearer of their moralistic messages. The remedial tenor of these discourses and its effect or lack thereof on regional artists is the subject matter of chapter 3, "Discipline in Practice: The Actors Sangam."

In tracing the discursive influences on Special Drama artists, I too found it useful, as did Mr. Majeeth (though he did not so much trace these discourses as carry them in his very person), to move regularly between the state capital and the regional heartland of Special Drama. My fieldwork tacked back and forth between Chennai and the actors sangams of five south-central cities: Madurai, Pudukkottai, Dindigal, Karaikudi, and Karur. My understanding of the shared dispersal of discourses thus draws on discussions, observations, experiences, and understandings developed through interactions with artists and audiences from well beyond Madurai, though its heart nevertheless most certainly resides there.

I also tack back and forth in time quite a bit throughout the course of the following chapters, supplementing initial fieldwork perceptions with updated reckonings, or with related antecedents. Overall, however, this text takes 1991–1993 "as a historical ethnographic present," to borrow Steven Feld's felicitous phrase (Feld [1982] 1990, 9). The conceit of the historical ethnographic present allows me to treat my conversations with artists in much the same way that literary scholars do their key texts, keeping artistic action alive even when an author or performer has died, by using the active present tense: "Faulkner writes," for example, or "O'Connor demonstrates." And yet by clearly situating my study within the particularities of the historical moment in which I conducted by research—Tamil South India during the last decade of the twentieth century and the beginning years of the twenty-first—I do not write of an indistinct forever (close kin of that ghastly Western specter "timeless India" that still haunts Western journalism and that somehow no amount of scholarship on South Asia can kill). Rather, armed with the conceit of the historical ethnographic present, I can write in 2003 of a conversation I had with an artist in 1993 that "he speaks of actresses as destroying Tamil culture," and by so doing retain something of the vividness of his speech and its present-tense voice.

Why Comedy Is a Good Site for the Study of Culture

While this book is an ethnography of Special Drama artists, it is also the first English-language study of the theatrical genre of Special Drama. However, it is not, nor do I intend it to be, a complete documentation of that genre. A full documentation of the art form of Special Drama would necessarily include a study of its staging of dramatic scenes and focus largely on the centrality of the verbal debates that so characterize them, in all their mythological glory. A study of the genre as a whole would also necessarily devote much more time to the musical aspects of the form. Both the mythological and the musical aspects of Special Drama await further study. The present volume, instead, is an anthropological consideration of the lives of Special Drama artists, onstage and off, within the context of contemporary Tamil society. Within this framework, my analysis of onstage practices focuses almost exclusively on the comedy portions of the performances for several reasons.

First, I gladly admit that I enjoy the direct, colloquial style of the comedic scenes rather more than the stilted style of the dramatic scenes in Special Drama. Clearly, however, this is an overdetermined pleasure inseparable from a larger context of public appreciation as such. The comedy scenes in Special Drama always draw the largest audiences. Indeed, comedy is largely what makes Special Drama "popular" in both senses of the term: appreciated by the masses and oriented to the masses.[8]

Second, in studying artists' lives, I came to appreciate the complexity of the social stigma that stage actors face. In the comedic scenes, artists speak explicitly and colloquially about this stigma, reflecting aloud on issues of gender, class, and Tamil identity. The comedy scenes are their own particular arena—a carved-out space and time with its own communicative style—wherein artists grapple publicly with issues like love marriage, women in the public sphere, attempts to hold on to Tamil culture in the face of the encroachment of the West, and how a poor person finds the strength to carry on. Comedy scenes are thus the improvised, colloquial links between real life and the other life of the mythological dramatic scenes.[9]

The third, and perhaps of all the best, reason to focus specifically on comedy is that comedy itself plays a large role in the history of the stigma on Special Drama artists. In Tamil theater historiography, the vulgarity of stage comedy is presented as a source of the degradation of the art of Tamil drama, rather than being taken seriously as a form of theatrical engagement.[10] As I discuss in chapter 1, only "respectable" drama and its pursuit have warranted a place in the historiography of Tamil theater to date. This historiographic dismissal is then reflected on the ground. As is so often the case with humor, the comedic scenes are greeted by knowing laughter all round, then summarily dismissed as "just comedy."

The terms of that dismissal are the same terms used for condemning unsanctioned sexuality wherever it occurs: *aciṅkam* (dirty), and *ābācam* (vulgar or lewd). During my fieldwork I quickly understood that any attempt to talk about the goings-on in Special Drama comedy scenes would be met, immediately and necessarily, in these moralizing terms. All those with whom I spoke, whatever their class/caste, age, or region, had first (at least when speaking with me) to establish firmly that they were well aware that the comedy scenes were vulgar and dirty and therefore did not warrant serious thought or attention and certainly did not deserve scholarly study.

This dismissal was de rigueur, across the board, and altogether too pat. Or rather, it was altogether ripe for a Foucauldian questioning, first of how such a well-learned disavowal of the public staging of matters sexual (or at all physical) is so very well learned, and second of how this disavowal figures into larger structures of meaning and power in contemporary constructions of Tamil identity. My larger concern in part 1 of this book, then, is to look carefully at the historical and historiographic record to understand the contours of the condemnation of popular theater in contemporary Tamilnadu. Such condemnatory discourses are the context in which Special Drama artists' lives onstage and off necessarily play out, the subjects of parts 2 and 3, respectively.

I do not subscribe to the assumption that analyzing humor deflates it of its critical power, or, for that matter, of its punch. Indeed, I think this defense of leaving humorous events and interactions unanalyzed is simply another way of avoiding, rather than integrating and taking into account, precisely the kinds of sociocultural insights humor often pointedly raises in regard to social situations. I recognize that I am working against the grain of local historiographic practice, as well as of Special Drama artists' own discursive practices, in focusing scholarly attention on the comedic enactments that historians and artists alike assume unworthy of such attention. I hope my work changes this attitude. Indeed, I hope this work convinces all its readers that humor is a good site for the study of culture.

In short, the comedic scenes in Special Drama are the locus for much of the stigma on actors, as well as the arena in which artists most masterfully negotiate the terms and discourses of that stigma itself. Comedy plays off common notions such as that actresses are prostitutes, for example, or that stage artists have neither culture nor morals. Such are the shared stereotypes and stigmatizing accusations that pervade life for Special Drama artists both onstage and off.

What Is Special Drama?

At my first Special Drama, this is what I saw: a sloppy man and a glittery woman played bawdy comedy and danced a scene that ended with what looked like an actual kiss—on the lips!—at which there was a collective gasp from the audience.[11] Then an enormous shift occurred: over half the audience left, and for the next six hours, one after another, heavily costumed actors stood virtually still at stationary mikes in the middle of the stage, facing front, speaking or singing in alternating turns. I understood little of what was said, and it was the performers' affectless and restricted style that struck me most. Like watching a film with the sound off, I was trying to read movement and form but saw only their absence. I was left wondering, why are these actors barely moving? And how did such an oddly still theatrical style develop?

"Special Drama" is a genre of popular Tamil theater that began in the 1890s and continues to the present day. The name refers to the practice of hiring each artist "specially" for every performance, making each performance a "special" event.

These events last all night, from 10 P.M. until dawn. They are now primarily held in villages in conjunction with religious festivals, as dramas are considered entertainment simultaneously pleasing to mortal and immortal audiences; an effigy of a given festival's honorific deity is usually wheeled out on a decorated chariot for the event so that it can watch along with the human crowd.

Dramas are generally performed in a sponsor's hometown (*conta itam*, literally "own place" or "native place") as part of a temple festival to honor a specific deity, usually Hindu, but also Christian.[12] Drama sponsorship is often a devotional act that fulfills, through the sponsorship of public entertainments, a prior vow to honor, recognize, and repay the deity's aid.[13] Such temple festivals, and the performances that enliven them, occur in venues ranging from small villages to large cities spread across the state of Tamilnadu.

The presentational style of Special Drama is a syncretic mix of proscenium staging cribbed from nineteenth-century Parsi and British traveling theater troupes, and the phrasing and broad theatricality familiar from indigenous genres of Tamil epic street theater (Kapur 1991; Karnad 1989; Frasca 1990). The costuming captures well the rather uncanny mix of these two influences: the actors' faces are powdered "realistically" white as any beauty under the Raj, while their bodies are garmented in the saturated colors of mythic Tamil gods and royalty. The content of the plays likewise retells familiar mythological or historical stories, generally branch stories stemming from the two great Hindu Indian epics, the Ramayana and the Mahabharata. By far the most popular Special Dramas, however, enact specifically Tamil stories, to wit, the wedding of Lord Murugan (considered the god of Tamil, youth, and beauty) to his Dravidian wife Valli in the drama *Valli's Wedding*.

The first two hours of a Special Drama are bawdy comedy, enacted by performers in the repertory roles of Buffoon (male) and Dancer (female). These opening comedy scenes are unscripted and improvised, danced and sung and shouted, always in the context of a boisterous meeting of strangers: a girl-woman (who is forever sixteen) and a boy-man (whose age is never an issue).

The remaining six hours of performance make up the dramatic portion of the play. This is the posturally still part of the drama. Here the leading performers enact the relatively more respected repertory roles of Heroes and Heroines, whose behavior is much more staid, befitting higher-class personages: they sing, debate, argue, pontificate, and reign over queendoms as well as kingdoms, for the most part by standing nearly as still as the stationary microphones before them. The cultural logics and sociohistorical discourses that converge to make standing still onstage be valued as "better" acting than if an artist moves around a lot is a subject I take up with relish in chapter 1.

A minimum of ten artists, comprising six actors and four musicians, is required for every Special Drama event. However, there are no troupes or companies in Special Drama: each artist contracts individually for every given performance. For readers familiar with Indian theater, this will likely be a surprising feature of Special Drama's organization, as the majority of South Asian theatrical genres do operate on the troupe or company model (see Appadurai et al. 1991; Richmond et al. 1990).[14] Here, instead, each artist is an independent professional, hired on a freelance basis for every event. In this endeavor, they are aided by men who work as drama agents, booking artists for performances across the state.

Perhaps equally remarkable, this time for readers familiar with Western theatrical traditions, is that there are no rehearsals or directors for Special Drama. Indeed, artists may meet for the first time onstage in performance. All this is made possible by a system of familiar repertory roles —Hero, Heroine, Buffoon, Dancer, et cetera—in a set repertory of plays. Performances use consistent stage conventions that allow individual artists from different cities and towns across the state to perform together, unrehearsed, for eight hours at a time.[15] This unusual organization necessitates an uncommon amount of travel on the part of artists, who might very well appear, during the busy season between March and July, on a different stage in a different village every night.

Special Drama artists represent an unusually broad range of linguistic, ethnic, caste, regional, sexual, and religious identities and community affiliations. Artists are Hindu, Christian, and Muslim; high caste, low caste, scheduled caste, and Dalit; male, female, transgendered, heterosexual, homosexual, married, divorced, widowed, remarried, and unmarried; young, old, retired, semiretired, and ageless. There are artists whose ethnic and linguistic identities are based in states and regions other than Tamilnadu (Saurashtrian, Telugu, Malayali). Some artists come from acting families that have been "putting powder" (*pōṭippoṭu* is the phrase artists use) now for five generations, while others are the first in their families ever to mount a stage.

Such a "maximally inclusive" group identity (Marriott and Inden 1974) is generally negatively regarded as fostering excessive social mixing, seemingly throughout India (Marriott 1998). The positive potential for such a radically inclusive community to be disruptive of otherwise hurtful status quo exclusivities is at least theoretically exciting, as explored in the work of social theorists from diverse scholarly fields concerned with destabilizing prior assumptions regarding the nature of the community concept (Nancy 1991; Laclau 1991; Mouffe 1991; Young 1990; Kaviraj 1993; Halperin 1995;

Sandoval 1991). I find particularly compelling the notion that communities such as this one might raise "the question of a *different* community, a community in and of difference, a community not founded in any autonomous essence" (English 1994, 23). How Special Drama artists themselves see their difference, and how they respond to its recognition by others, are subjects that I view from multiple angles in the following chapters.

The one variable that remains consistent across all others from among all the potential identity markers for artists in the foregoing list is that of class. Professional popular stage acting is a low-class profession in Tamilnadu, and those who enter it do so almost exclusively out of economic need. Special Drama artists are invariably members of the urban poor. Following Sara Dickey's model, I understand the term urban poor to be "a cultural as well as an economic formation" denoting a class whose members share three important features: "poverty, a persistent sense of financial insecurity, and a lack of sociopolitical power" (Dickey 1993, 10). Special Drama artists are actively engaged in attempting to improve their lives on all three of these levels, through a variety of means and with a range of results. Very few artists actually manage to hold onto money into later life, depending largely on other aspects of the fortunes of their domestic lives, including the number and gender of their siblings and their children. But even for the few fortunate enough not to end life this way, poverty is where all began.

Making a Living

Some artists began acting while quite young in life—seven years old, nine years old—especially those who began their careers in "boys companies," as did both Nagaraja Bhagavattar and Vaiyur Gopal. Such children (both boys and girls, the name notwithstanding) were given over by their families to a life with the company that fed, housed, and trained them to act. The money they earned went to the family. Such a decision might be based on the fairness of face or complexion in a child considered appealing to look at and thus likely to do well in an art of appearances. Or perhaps a child's outgoing nature, or a proclivity toward dance or song, was the deciding factor. Equally, though, a dark-skinned girl in a large family (lighter skin being as prized in Tamilnadu as throughout India) might be given to the company because she was one too many mouths to feed and would prove difficult to marry off. Even after the company era, many artists started putting powder before the age of ten; I have heard many versions of childhood-entry-into-the-drama-world stories from artists, all of which turn on the undiminished appeal of child artists onstage as a guarantee to income.

Other artists join the life as adults, looking for work, ready for something different. I met a male artist who worked as a telephone wire installer before deciding to try his hand at drama, and a female artist who had been a nurse in her native Kerala before becoming a quite popular actress in Special Drama. Their stories are fairly uncommon, however. The more frequent entrance into the drama world now comes from some prior familial connection: a maternal aunt acts, and brings her young niece along to dramas as her costume-assistant-cum-chaperone. The girl is all eyes and by age fourteen is dancing herself. Or a father, who himself acted as a child, now books dramas and is training his fairest daughter to sing and dance at home. The teenage son of an actress and an agent begins playing the "all-round drummer" role in a few dramas, and also likes to play dress-up in his mother's costumes, and quickly moves into the role of a Buffoon and becomes known for his cross-dressed roles.

Working as a Special Drama artist pays quite well in relation to other kinds of work available to persons of this class. For example, a woman working as a cook or a maid might earn Rs 75 *per month*, whereas working as an actress she might earn Rs 300 *in one night* (these were average wages in 1993).[16] The drama season, however, lasts only half the year, from February/March to July/August. During this six-month season, artists must earn enough to carry them through the year (it is rare that an artist can find paying work during off-season months). And an artist's earnings depend entirely on his or her popularity that season.

A "leading" artist (to employ the English word that artists use for an artist doing well that season) will perform every night of the month in the high-season months of April and May and earn impressively even by middle-class standards. However, many quite popular artists will be booked only three or four nights a week during this high season, and less frequently still in other months. In addition, an artist's fee must be negotiated for each performance, and as demand lessens, so do fees. The unreliability of an artist's income is thus unnerving. Male actors can generally count on a much longer career as a Special Drama artist; men in their late sixties and early seventies continue to play the Hero/love interest role (that of a fit young bachelor of nevertheless unstipulated age) to a Heroine who is, quite specifically, meant to be a girl of sixteen. That so many of the plots staged in Special Drama turn on the pubescent ripeness of the female heroine doesn't aid actresses in extending the length of their careers. Actresses stop attempting to fill the role of that fictive girl of sixteen usually in their forties, at which point they begin to play the roles of bereaved wives, jilted (if queenly) exes, and mothers or mothers-in-law.

In addition, such high wages for half the year not only must compensate for the loss of social standing attendant on entering this profession (with all the related extra spending that so often accompanies money earned through humiliating circumstances) but must also generally stretch to cover many mouths. Chronic underemployment in Tamilnadu means that a single high earner in a family supports many others who earn insufficiently. One actor in his early thirties working out of Madurai financially supports five younger sisters still living at home in his natal village. Special Drama actresses, in particular, who may be disowned by their families for working in this profession, often live on their own as "second wives" to men who are actors themselves. These women struggle to support children, and perhaps a widowed mother or other relatives in even worse situations, on an unreliable income.

Thus the relatively high wages that artists earn for each performance should not give the impression that Special Drama artists are well-off once they begin on this road. In theory, it should be possible for artists to accumulate a substantial income. In practice, while many do alter their economic situations through this work, they remain enmeshed in relations that substantially drain that benefit. The reasons for this are manifold and deserve a separate study. Briefly, they include (1) the seasonal nature of the work, in a statewide context of underemployment; (2) the horribly exploitative terms of indigenous loan systems that plunge many artists into a debt that eats all their earnings and more than occasionally leads artists to suicide; (3) for actresses, the short span of their viable stage life compared to that of actors; (4) financially "irrational" spending patterns familiar to anyone who has grown up poor under capitalism, involving overcompensatory overspending when money finally arrives, and a lack of trust in savings institutions; (5) the additional costs of prepared food and off-hours transportation inherent in this work, and (6) the practice of a generosity that often helps ease the way for those dependent on the goodwill of strangers.

What Is Special about Special Drama?

"Special Drama" (Speshal Nāṭakam) is a presumptuous name. It assumes that one already knows what—or who—is *special* about this genre of theater.

"Special" functions here as a suggestively floating signifier whose multiple referential possibilities are limited only by one's imagination.

On the most basic level, Special Drama may correctly be understood to identify a drama of *specialties*. As a specific genre within a larger field known as music drama (Icai Nāṭakam), Special Drama's distinction as a genre arises, as previously noted, from the organizational practice of hiring each performer "specially" for each performance, resulting in events that are "special" every night. In this sense the name "Icai Nāṭakam" makes no real break with a standard appellative pattern for Tamil theatrical genres that is (pardon the tautology) quite generic.[17] For example, other contemporary genres of Tamil theater identify their domains as mythological drama, social drama, or modern drama (respectively, Purāna Nāṭakam, for plays based in Hindu mythology; Camuka Nāṭakam, for the bourgeois-realist urban theater of social drama; and Navīna Nāṭakam, for avant-garde, usually amateur, theatrical experiments).

And yet a theater of specialties remains a tantalizingly vague and, potentially, infinitely broad moniker. Indeed, every Special Drama contains mythological *and* social elements, outdoor ritual *and* modern urban attributes. Might "special" then refer to the fact that no single category is privileged above another?

If so, Special Drama would simply be a stage version of the spicy mix —the frequently noted "masala" style—of Tamil films, with their all-of-the-above appeal that banks on providing something for everyone in the audience (action scenes as well as song-and-dance numbers, sexy wet-sari scenes as well as warming family plots). But if its "specialty" had been so thoroughly captured by the medium of film—if film can manage to present all this to the masses so much more cheaply and glamorously, without the material and social encumbrances of actual stage performers—why would the low-tech genre of Special Drama still exist after the advent of film in the 1930s?

Many Indian historians have made the mistake of simply assuming that this theater died an unceremonious death once it had served the purpose of paving the way for the celluloid glory of cinema (Baskaran 1981, 2001; Karnad 1989, 337). This assumption reveals a rather more general ignorance, among the Tamil middle class, of the ongoing life of popular stage drama in Tamilnadu. Such historiographic oversight notwithstanding, Special Drama does still very actively exist in Tamilnadu, and its ongoing survival in the face of a megalomaniacal cinema industry makes the question even more pointed: What is special here?

My full answer to this question fills this book, which may rightly be seen as an extended meditation on what is special about Special Drama. The artists themselves, and their relations with each other as well as the audience's relationship to them, are certainly key. Moreover, much in the phenomenon of its specialness derives from the history and social positioning of the genre, the subject of the following chapter.

Naming Matters

In choosing to use the name "Special Drama" to frame this project, I commit myself to a certain stance in relation to this theatrical form. I have chosen the informal and unofficial over the official nomenclature for the genre. In the state capital of Chennai, theater of the high-cosmopolitan varieties known as social drama or modern drama is performed, while in outlying areas of the city and its broader regional district of North Tamilnadu one may even find troupes or small companies that perform music drama as company drama (de Bruin 2000). Special Drama as such, however, does not exist in Chennai. Only occasionally, for commercial occurrences such as the filming of a performance to be broadcast on a television program dedicated to "village arts," will Special Drama artists from the central regions of the state be contracted to come to the big capital city to perform a Special Drama.

Yet it is in Chennai that the Tamilnadu state government decides on and grants its prestigious artistic service Kalaimāmaṅi (great artiste) awards. Unsurprisingly, at these award ceremonies no artist is ever recognized for participation in Special Drama as such. Rather, when the Kalaimāmani title is awarded to an artist for a lifetime of work in Special Drama, the artist is invariably recognized as a "music drama artiste" (Iyal Icai Nāṭaka Manṛam 1992, 47–49). At such official levels, the particular distinctions of Special Drama as a genre within music drama go unremarked. Nevertheless, "Special Drama" is the term used colloquially among those pragmatically involved in its production: the performers, sponsors, agents, and audiences that make up the network of Special Drama that operates throughout the regions of the state where such dramas are actually performed.

As a cultural anthropologist studying the lives of these artists, my primary allegiance is to the terms and discourses of their lived experience. Such a project necessarily engages me with the full semiotic field in which artists choose their terms, including the relevant domains of comparison between official government rhetoric and discourses, as well as the artists' less-than-official registers and logics.

My decision here may be taken as emblematic of my overall orientation in this work: I am committed to understanding the many implications of the terms in which artists name their own experiences. Note, then, that with my use of "Special Drama," I mean to signal my commitment to documenting the unique organization of the performance phenomenon to which I have been witness, for over a decade now spanning the end of the twentieth and the beginning of the twenty-first centuries, in the same terms that artists themselves use to discuss this drama world. Paradoxically, in this case a commitment to studying artists' lives in their own terms often means working in the assimilated English terms of the colonial era in which their art was forged.

"Speshal Nāṭakam" is a hybrid Anglo-Tamil name. It uses the English word *special* spelled phonetically in Tamil. Such use of an English loan word, rather than a word of Tamil etymological origins that could do descriptively just as well, makes the term *special* meaningful not only as a floating signifier with myriad referential possibilities but also as a *nonreferential* index (Silverstein 1995). That is, the meanings generated by using this assimilated English loan word are not limited to referential meanings—a *special* actor, a *special* drama, a *special* genre, and so forth, wonderfully diverse and floating as these may be—but also index the presence of an indulgent attitude toward the English language itself. Given the devotional attitude to the Tamil language that became so dominant in the politics of twentieth-century Tamilnadu, as we shall see, the continued use of an English word here also conveys something of a nostalgic aspiration to all that English at one time symbolized in India. In the succinct phrasing of novelist Bharati Mukherjee, "To want English was to want more than you had been given at birth, it was to want the world" (Mukherjee 1989, 61).

The English loan word in the name "Speshal Nāṭakam" thus links this form of theater to a certain idea of a foreign cosmopolitanism as desirable, a notion first made available to Indians of a certain class through the advent of the British Raj. Retention of an English word, during the same century that gave birth to the Tamil Self-Respect Movement and an entire related economy of new language-based political identities, is a nod to its past in the Special Drama of the present. It is not that the word asserts that this genre is "special" in any uniquely British kind of way (again a referential possibility) but rather that using the English word indicates a hybrid history—one that draws on multiple theatrical influences, including the Victorian—

that is still deemed salient. Salient enough, that is, to warrant continued use of a hybrid Anglo-Tamil name.

"Hey, Drama People!": Stigma at Work

I was familiar with the locution "drama people" (*nāṭaka makkal*) before the night of the annual festival at the Dindigal Actors Sangam in February 1992. But it was still early in my fieldwork, just six months in, and I wasn't yet attuned to the pejorative connotations this seemingly simple descriptor so often carried. On this night, a particular instance of its use in direct address suddenly brought me up. Of course, as Peter Handke's short story "The Goalie's Anxiety at the Penalty Kick" makes so indelibly clear, any descriptor can be made to function as an identity-insult to which one becomes immediately sensitive: "Hey polka-dot scarf!" or "Red handbag lady!" (Handke [1972] 1977, 65). Such uses make otherwise common terms suddenly marked. In this case, however, I think it was only me who was surprised, who hadn't realized how already marked the term "drama people" is and how frequently it is meant as an insult.

I was sitting in an audience of perhaps three hundred people, all Special Drama artists and their families. This was a performance by Special Drama artists for themselves, for their own entertainment at their own festival and not, for a change, as hired performers at someone else's festival. Dindigal Sangam artists were onstage, in Dindigal, for an audience of artists. Apart from this, the other contextualizing features of the event were standard: it was night, the stage was the usual temporarily erected affair of wood and thatched palm leaf, and the audience sat close together on the dirt ground of the local commons.

Two fluorescent tube lights, ubiquitous both in Tamilnadu generally and on the Special Drama stage, angled over the onstage action. Two stationary microphones, one trained on the musicians and the other on the actors, were cranked up to maximum volume. The drama was proceeding apace until at 1 A.M. a complete power outage occurred and put a stop to the onstage action. Unfazed, everyone stayed put, onstage and off, in the sudden complete darkness. People chatted, seeming confident that power would return.

About half an hour into this hiatus came a loud flatbed truck, its lights suddenly illuminating our blacked-out gathering. The truck swerved wide around us, then slowed ominously. A young man's voice cried out, "Hey drama people! Drama people! The current's off, now you bugger off!" (nāṭaka makkal, nāṭaka makkalē! karant pōccu, nīṅkaḷ ippaṭi pōṅka!). This was followed by the laughter of several other male voices, and then the sound of the truck pulling away.

It was the first time I had heard the phrase "drama people" used in direct address. Coupled with the vaguely threatening manner of the approach, this hurled address brought the whole category "drama people" into the present for me with a jolt. Transformed into an accusatory identity, "Hey drama people!" implicated groups of people in active relations of power and prestige. Perhaps because I too was, under the cover of darkness, inadvertently included in these relations, their force hit me more than before. In any case, I suddenly understood two things: first, that the drama community is named, known, and recognized as such by people outside it, and second, that "drama people" is a stigmatized identity category.

Previously I had heard only actors use the phrase "drama people," among themselves. I had read it, as well, in published autobiographies written by actors about themselves and other actors (e.g., Shanmugam 1972; Mudaliyar [1938] 1998). But this hurled address was how I learned that the acting community exists as such in the public eye, that its name is "drama people," and that this name is a ready insult.

A categorical place for such stage actors clearly exists in the mix of contemporary Tamil society among all the other communities, professions, castes, subcastes, groups, subgroups, and subcultures. Most Tamilians I met were aware of the existence of the popular stage, having come across outdoor dramas one way or another, even if only through the windows of a passing car years ago, as several middle-class friends confessed, or in scenes framed within any number of the frequently aired classics of Tamil film that contain drama-within-a-drama plots. In general, all the people I have met are certainly aware enough of its referent to hold certain beliefs about "drama people." Most common among these is the notion that actors lack *muṟai*, a kind of propriety and sense of social order. Such pervasive, commonly held beliefs about drama people make theirs a community identity of a different order than most, more akin to a rogue state of disorder than to an order at all.[18] To lack *muṟai* is the very definition of stigma in local Tamil social contexts, as we shall see.

In my use of the term "stigma" I rely largely on the sociological work of Erving Goffman. His *Stigma: Notes on the Management of Spoiled Identity* (1963) is a brilliant inventory of the minutiae of possible human responses to the shame of not belonging. As members of a given society, we know how to categorize persons (including ourselves) within its system, and we quickly internalize these social categories. On meeting someone new, we immediately assess him or her: "Society establishes the means of categorizing persons and the complement of attributes felt to be ordinary and natural for members of each of these categories. . . . When a stranger comes into our presence, then, first appearances are likely to enable us to anticipate his category and attributes" (Goffman 1963, 2). Stigma arises when someone we encounter *deviates* from our anticipations of them, and from our normative expectations for them, in some negative way. By failing to meet our normative expectations, the person is discredited. She or he now "possesses a stigma, an undesired differentness from what we had anticipated" (5).

In South India, stage actors are stigmatized and know it. Indeed, "knowing it" is a constituent part of the full-on phenomenon of stigma. In the imagined scenario of social encounter (the imaginary being just as good as the real when it comes to feeling bad), Goffman's "undesired differentness" and its discrediting effects are perceptible not just to those who "do not depart negatively from the particular expectations at issue" (aka "normals" in this context) but to the stigmatized as well. Both parties equally share an awareness of the dominant values of their culture and can play out the fearsome scenarios of stigma both on the ground and in the head. We are all experts at stigma, from whichever side of its cutting edge we encounter it at any given moment: "The stigmatized individual tends to hold the same beliefs about identity that we do; this is a pivotal fact. . . . The standards he has incorporated from the wider society equip him to be intimately alive to what others see as his failing, inevitably causing him, if only for moments, to agree that he does indeed fall short of what he really ought to be. Shame becomes a central possibility" (Goffman 1963, 7). The internalization of shared norms and standards thus both unites and divides those who would be members of a given society or culture. The stigmatized and the "normals" are both aware of what is socially accepted as normal and what is not, as well as that stigma, and shame, lie together on the other side of the swinging door that separates norms from their deviations.[19]

"Actors Have No Muṟai": A Proverbial Lack

Special Drama artists are stigmatized because they transgress Tamil norms of social order. They lack certain social graces; they lack "culture," say some. They lack muṟai, say others, using a Tamil term that covers a wide range of social failings.

Muṟai names a set of densely interconnected concepts regarding the norms of Tamil social organization. It defines a range of cultural expectations for the "normal" course of Tamil life.[20] Used in a simple deictic statement such as "Like this, this is the *proper way* [to do it]" (ippaṭi tān muṟai), muṟai means "proper (manner)" as well as "propriety." It names the accepted way or custom, the "approved course of conduct." To "spoil muṟai" (muṟai kēṭu) is to lapse socially, to act contrary to rule and regulation.[21] In a linked usage, muṟai can also mean regularity in the sense of "repetition" in "time(s)" or "turn(s)," without which proceedings become irregular. To act according to muṟai and custom is to be in the right. Its direct opposite—being *without* muṟai, or *muṟaiyillāmal*—is a state of social disgrace that is seen as not-right, and thus left out.

It is into the state of social disgrace of being without muṟai that stage actors are commonly cast.[22] The sentiment is succinctly captured in a Tamil proverb known by everyone I met, actors and nonactors alike.

> Actors have no muṟai, like a Ganesh-cake has no head.[23]
> [Kūttāṭikku muṟaiyum illai, koḻukkaṭṭaikku talaiyum illai.]

This simple rhyming simile warrants close attention for how tidily it characterizes actors in local social terms. Their *lack* of orderly, proper, normal relations—their lack of muṟai—is here likened to the crudely formed and ultimately topsy-turvy sweet known as a Ganesh-cake (koḻukkaṭṭai). Both are seen as similarly upside-down entities, disoriented and potentially disorienting. The actors' lack of muṟai is like the absence of a head on the koḻukkaṭṭai cake, an analogy of marked absence: actors lack properly ordered relations, as the roly-poly Ganesh-cake lacks a head. In just six words, a world of disorder.[24]

The koḻukkaṭṭai is a sweet made at home to accompany the annual India-wide Hindu celebration of the elephant-headed god Ganesh (aka Vinayakar, among other names), god of auspicious beginnings.[25] Koḻukkaṭṭai are balls of rice flour and coconut dough shaped by hand, often just squeezed in the fist. The resulting shape is irregular, knobby, and dumpling plump with a homemade, childlike quality. The name *koḻukkaṭṭai* reflects something of this cuteness: the verb *koḻu* means "grow fat or be plump," while its noun form *koḻuppu* means "chubbiness, fatness, plumpness."

Kaṭṭai refers to a piece of something solid, often a cut piece of wood, or anything stubby (including the human body or person). Thus an alternate gloss of *koḻukkaṭṭai* might be "chubby-stubby cake." Indeed, iconically, chubby-stubbiness recalls celebrated qualities of the figure of the god Ganesh himself: he is the roly-poly perpetual child of Siva and Parvati. An ongoing subject of an infinite array of often playful visual representations, the figure of the elephant-headed boy-god has been particularly amenable to modern interpretations that emphasize the anomalous trunk and wide ears atop a round stomach and short legs, lending Ganesh an endearing childishness.[26]

So why are actors like a Ganesh-cake?

The koḻukkaṭṭai cake is most unusual in its lack of any visual referent to the elephant head and trunk that usually dominates iconic representations of Ganesh. This cake is like the god only on a more primordial and purely bodily level. Such a headless, all-body state recalls a well-known origin story of the birth of Ganesh. I retell it here for the interesting connections it develops between bodily and divine dirt, connections that seem to play out as well in commonly held Tamil attitudes toward actors.

> It was time for Parvati's daily bath, but she needed someone to keep watch over the privacy of her bathing place and there was no one available. So she scraped off some of the dirt from her own skin, rolled it into a ball, and set it on the bank to guard her bath. Shortly thereafter, Siva came looking for Parvati. The newly formed ball-of-dirt guard did not know that Siva was Parvati's husband, and barred his entry. In anger, Siva pinched off the dirt ball's head and threw it away. When Parvati saw this she was furious, and cried that Siva had killed her child. Siva said, "This blob is your child?" to which Parvati answered, "It was born from my body. What is born from my body is my child, isn't it?" She demanded that Siva replace the child's head. As it was nowhere to be found, Siva went into the forest where an elephant lay newly dead. He cut off the elephant's head and stuck it on the body of the ball, and to this day Ganesh, child of Siva and Parvati, has a boy's body and an elephant's head.[27]

A koḻukkaṭṭai cake is like the ball body of the child Ganesh in its headless, liminal moment, its missing head a marked absence lamented by its mother's cries. It is to this unformed state of being that actors are likened.

The iconicity of the Ganesh-cake to Ganesh thus has nothing at all to do with elephants, though it does have to do with dirt: recall Mary Douglas's famous clarification on the nature of dirt as "matter out of place," something to sweep under the rug like a dirty little secret, or to whisk away entirely—"banished," like actors sent out of Plato's republic.[28] Such is the predicament of those who lack muṟai and are therefore, as it were, "treated like dirt" (Douglas 1966). The iconicity here has everything to do with human, and also perhaps divine, creative processes in all their earthiness: molding, pinching, shaping, scraping, and (re)producing. Parvati's proud defense of her parthenogenic child argues for an inclusive embrace of unusual bodily practices as well as their perhaps unexpected offspring. It is the kind of defense that drama artists could well use, stigmatized as they are by their lack of muṟai.

To lack muṟai is to lack an approved place within a known social order. "Actors have no muṟai, like a Ganesh cake has no head." While the proverb seems on the surface to render the lack of systematicity and order among actors as fairly innocuous, even cute, nevertheless the image it floats of a body without a head is, subtextually at least, menacing. Behind its simple rhyme lies a threat it would dismiss with a chuckle: we laugh at the pithy truth of it (though all such laughter, even when prompted by seemingly innocent wordplay, suggests deeper sources).[29] The social mobility of actors is seen as excessive, even somewhat threateningly so, on a number of levels, from their mimetic practices onstage to their imitative practices offstage. The following chapters turn to the historical origins and the present-day entailments of stigma in the lives of Special Drama artists.

This book is an ethnography of Special Drama artists, intended as an appreciation and a critical examination of the complexity of their lives onstage and off. It is divided into three parts, consisting of three chapters each.

Part 1 documents the history of the genre of Special Drama, focusing on critical discourses that have shaped its theatrical form and influenced the way Special Drama artists themselves speak of their work. Parts 2 and 3 concern the onstage and offstage lives of artists, respectively. The chapters of part 2, "Comedy," document three popular Special Drama comedy scenes in performance. The chapters in part 3, "Lives," focus on three realms of offstage practices in which the stigma on actors affects their community and domestic lives, namely, talk, travel, and family.

Part One: The History and Organization of Special Drama

In these introductory chapters I focus on the discourses that are the context and grounds of the social world in which Special Drama artists live. In chapter 1, I trace the late-nineteenth- and early-twentieth-century origins of the genre, in the process offering a new historical trajectory that recognizes the place of Special Drama in the history of Tamil drama. Writing this history was an interesting and difficult exercise, largely because of the exclusion of Special Drama from the extant body of literature in Tamil theater historiography. The reasons for that exclusion are in themselves telling and form a significant part of the story I tell in this chapter. My intervention into the historiographic record is to supplement it with oral histories given by artists whose lived experiences significantly augment our picture of how the genre of Special Drama, as it is performed today, came to its present form. Chapter 1 thus offers the reader an initial handle on the specialness of Special Drama.

This history is visibly encapsulated in the changing forms of the drama notices I discuss in chapter 2, paper handbills that now bear an iconic resemblance to the stagings they advertise. Special Drama itself, like the notices, is structured by artistic prestige hierarchies. Drama notices communicate information about the full complement of activities and people that together make up the social economy of Special Drama: performers, agents, sponsors, audiences, and honored deities. Notices provide details not just about where and when, but also about why, a drama is being presented, by whom and on whose behalf, all set in a ritual calendar that serves divine as well as human audiences.

In chapter 3, I consider the ideological work of the drama actors sangam, and the attendant disciplinary measures it visits on artists. Sangam ideology recapitulates discourses of vulgarity established in the early twentieth century. Established in 1923, the sangam's rules and regulations continue today to bring such dominant discourses to bear on artists' lives, a reality to which individual artists each respond differently. In this chapter I discuss the strategies of two particular actresses who occupy opposite poles of response to the stigma of their profession. In Michael Warner's useful analytic terms, one is a "stigmaphobe," while the other might be called a "stigmaphile"—or in an even more vivid phrase coined by my undergraduate students at Scripps College, she is a stigma diva.[30] This is Sivakami, who aims for the "big name" of money and fame; in contradistinction, Jansirani seeks the "good name" of moral repute.

Part Two: Comedy

On the Special Drama stage, the careful comedic negotiation of gender norms in the context of humorous indiscretions allows artists the liberty of commenting on contemporary issues of cultural identity. A potent platform for such transgressions, the stage becomes an analogue and a symbolic register on which to represent ideals of social relation, as well as their everyday variants.

As noted, the comedy scenes in Special Drama are the primary locus of its vulgar reputation, and simultaneously its most "popular" scenes. The paradoxical position that artists are placed in by this simultaneous critical devaluation and popular appreciation of their work characterizes their performances on many levels.

In chapter 4, I analyze a sequence of dirty jokes embedded in a Buffoon's monologue. In his performance, I find not vulgarity but rather a reflection of its practiced, anxious use-in-avoidance. I analyze the two separate linguistic footings the performer uses for making moral and immoral comments and the social values that are affirmed by this split. I highlight the narrative connections established in this context between fear of the foreign and fear of the female, consider what such connections index about the remnants of Victorian sexuality in postcolonial Tamilnadu, and discuss the locally reinscriptive effects of such a gendered performance. (Video footage of the 1 April 1992 performance by S. K. Selvam of the Buffoon's comedy scene is available on the Web at http://stigmasofthetamilstage.scrippscollege.edu.)

In chapter 5, I consider multiple performances of a second popular comedy scene, known as the "Buffoon-Dance Duet," to show how the use of stage space in this scene establishes the resonance of its representations to analogous social spaces in everyday life. In a powerful parallelism of the staging of comic and dramatic scenes, the enactment of certain kinds of flirtation, as well as gender role codification, always occurs in specific arenas of the stage. (A video montage of nine separate performances of the Buffoon-Dance Duet—edited to highlight plot progression and to showcase spatial paradigms on the Special Drama stage—is available on the Web at http://stigmasofthetamilstage.scrippscollege.edu.)

The blocking inaugurated in this scene establishes the use of the stage for all scenes to follow. And while ostensibly unrelated, enactments of comedic and dramatic scenes converge in important ways. One such convergence lies in the centrality of the subject of marriage. The bulk of the business that engages the Special Drama stage in both comedic and dramatic modes concerns the pursuit of proper marital relations. The mores and foibles of courtship and marriage are a dominant theme of the dramas (the most popular of which, *Valli's Wedding*, is essentially the dramatization of a prolonged courtship) and similarly are the grounds of the extemporaneous contributions of Buffoons and Dancers.

Chapter 6 is an extended meditation on a much more brutal comic exchange between Buffoon and Dancer, a 3 A.M., nightmarish inversion of the love scene they perform earlier. The Aṭipiṭi scene is a powerful piece of performance in several senses: powerfully performed, powerfully enjoyed in public, and a frightening representation of domestic power relations. Similarly, I had a powerful experience of anthropological "difference" sitting in the audience aghast while ubiquitous laughter rose around me. In subsequently questioning audience members and artists alike about their experiences of and in this scene, I learned that they found it both funny and pleasurable. Trying to understand this response led me to consider the nature of spectatorial relations in Special Drama more broadly. Accordingly, this chapter looks at the Aṭipiṭi scene itself, as well as at the role of the public in it, both onstage and off. (Video documentation of the Aṭipiṭi scene performed by Dancer Sridevi and Buffoon Kalaiarasan on 4 April 1993 is available on the Web at http://stigmasofthetamilstage.scrippscollege.edu.)

Part Three: Lives

The final part of the book offers three offstage chapters that bring the issue of artists' negotiations of stigma down off the stage and into daily life. In this realm fit all the unofficial strategies of artists: a hidden language, ways of passing in public, and kinship practices.

In chapter 7, the "Drama Tongue" is an insiders' argot that nevertheless encodes an outsider sensibility. It is a means of communication that artists primarily use backstage, in that heightened space of permeability between inside and outside that reflects the hybridity of the social identity of stage artists more generally.

Chapter 8 chronicles my growing understanding of the practices I observed actresses engage in on the road, as we traveled to Special Drama performance venues. I refer to these practices as the *roadwork* of actresses, in which, by creating domestic spaces in public places, actresses attempt to pass as "good women."

Chapter 9 concerns the kinship practices of artists and their gendered variations. "Muṟai," as we have seen, is a term that crystallizes notions of how social relations ought to be organized, and as such speaks to normative ideals of kinship. Though artists are accused of lacking muṟai, the kinds of kinship bonds they maintain among themselves reveal that the transgressions of which artists are accused arise rather more from the pluralities of excess than the privations of lack. While actresses use this excess to expand muṟai, male actors attempt to police the boundaries of their domestic lives to prevent its contamination by actresses. I chart the relations of two acting lineages that span five generations to explore this gendered conflict and its present-day entailments.

By way of conclusion I offer an epilogue. A return visit to the Special Drama community in 2001 has allowed me to consider the longer-term efficacy of the strategies documented in preceding chapters. While the passage of time has benefited my perspective, the opposite is true of its effects on the lives of leading actresses. Many of the women whose work and lives I followed in the early 1990s are now in the beginning stages of retirement, facing another wave of hardship. In their vulnerability and perseverance, they are now often alone on paths more ascetic than flamboyant, a shift that requires the kind of facility with mimetic adaptability that make women who act suspect in the first place.

PART ONE

The History and Organization of Special Drama

1 Legacies of Discourse

Special Drama and Its History

Our father was then keeping afloat in the ocean of life by hanging on to that piece of driftwood known as Special Drama.
—T. K. Shanmugam, actor

Special Drama means "as they please: without responsibility." They had no discipline (*kaṭṭuppāṭu*), no regularity or propriety (*oḻukkam*); they talked as they pleased in the dramas, they talked whatever they knew, which amounted to comedy and all that, because they had no *muṟai*.
—A. K. Kaleeswaran, harmonist

The Legacy and Legend of Sankaradas Swamigal

The author of the majority of plays in the dramatic repertory of Special Drama is playwright T. T. Sankaradas Swamigal (1867–1922). Recognized by historians as an important figure in the development of modern Tamil drama, Swamigal is much more than a historical figure to the contemporary Special Drama community. He is revered and honored by Special Drama artists as a guru and as the founder and first teacher of their art form. As such he is actively remembered by artists in speech, song, and worship, as well as in annual collective, commemorative festivals.

For the purposes of this book, Swamigal is an important historical figure primarily because of the disparity between the place he occupies for Tamil drama historians and the position he holds for Special Drama artists. Historians, generally only briefly, mention his work as a bridge between tradition and modernity.[1] Swamigal's oeuvre of over fifty scripted plays includes Hindu mythologicals, Indian histories, Christian devotional stories, and translations of several works of Shakespeare. The scripts alternate sung verse with spoken prose passages and are generally celebrated as popularizations of familiar stories rendered in pleasing prose accessible to the masses. A standard account, from the *Encyclopaedia of Tamil Literature*, reads as follows:

> The significance of Cuvāmikaḷ [Swamigal] as a modern dramatist lies in the fact that he has brought about a creative blend of the old and the new in the Tamil dramatic tradition. He has fused into his plays the elements of the ancient folk dramatic forms, those of the musical plays of the pre-modern days, and the characteristics of the modern Tamil play that came into being under the impact of the West. (IAS 1990, 499)

My sense, having read numerous such accounts, is that the degree of syncretism in Swamigal's oeuvre has rendered both his works and the artists who continue to perform them rather too uncategorizable for historians. Again, both he and they *mix* too much: their art is messy, overly emotionally expressive, and anything but elite. These are not my own terms but rather terms one reads over and again in so many words in the historiographic record. It is a record that either overtly criticizes or else damns by faint praise; as previously noted, extant accounts of the development of Tamil drama make only fleeting reference, if any, to Special Drama, and even then only in the past tense (for a recent example, see Baskaran 2001, 76).[2] Certainly to date, no written account of Swamigal's contributions reflects the kind of following he has inspired among practitioners of his art today.

For example, Swamigal is the frequent subject of actors' own oral elaborations in the form of reverential praise, as well as not-so-reverential anecdotes. These verge on the tall tale, as the ferocity of Swamigal's own acts of devotional worship in turn inspire artists' devotion toward him. In addition to accounts of the frights his own performances visited on female audience members, and of how his heavy disciplinarian hand terrified members of his boys company, the master is said to have angrily hurled songs composed on the spot at the goddess Meenakshi in her temple in Madurai, accusing her of ignoring the plight of the lower classes.

And though it rarely takes written form, appreciation of Swamigal can indeed be found in a plethora of material forms. Colored prints of his portrait circulate throughout the acting community, reprinted and distributed every year on his remembrance day, the anniversary of his death in November 1922 (fig. 1), when Special Drama artists conduct an elaborate celebration and parade through the streets of central Madurai with his image enshrined in a decorated chariot (fig. 2). Similarly, a three-foot-tall plaster statue of Swamigal, seated in the same pose as in the portrait, resides permanently in the Madurai Actors Sangam building. Artists stop in to pay their respects to the guru in devotional gestures and prayers each night before they leave town to perform. On an architectural scale as well, Swamigal has received

1 Portrait of Sankaradas Swamigal, on a poster distributed at Guru Puja, Madurai, 1991.

commemoration in two large auditoriums often used for state-level political functions, one in Chennai and one in Madurai, each bearing his name. Permanent large-scale bronze memorial statues in his likeness have been erected at prominent intersections in Madurai (fig. 3), Dindigal, and Pondicherry (his final city of residence), to which artists annually make pilgrimages.

We must not be misled, then, by the limits of the written record in judging the influence of Swamigal on the contemporary field of Tamil popular drama. For artists, his importance stems from two related aspects of his achievement. The first is his scripting of the majority of the plays in their repertory. The second is his pivotal role in the development of drama companies, the historical precedent to, and condition of possibility for, the current form of Special Drama.

Many of the artists initially trained in drama companies under Swamigal's tutelage went on to teach their art to subsequent generations, establishing a lineage of teachers and students who trace their artistic heritage directly

2 Members of the Tamilnadu Drama Actors Sangam, Madurai, with a processional image of Sankaradas Swamigal, 11 November 1991. *Left*, A. S. Tangavel Vaṭtiyar, drama teacher; *right*, Renuga Devi, Sangam treasurer.

3 Special Drama artists performing *puja* at the permanent statue of Sankaradas Swamigal, Madurai.

to him. This is a lineage in which many of the Special Drama artists whom I interviewed for this book proudly partake. Though recognized by historians—"Those who were trained by him are now famous in the dramatic field" (Varadarajan 1988, 266)—artists who bear this heritage have nevertheless remained an untapped source of ethnographic material for the serious historical study of the roots and subsequent developments of contemporary Tamil popular theater.[3]

What I present here, then, are the beginnings of a history of Special Drama, or rather the beginnings of a revision of the history of Tamil drama that would sufficiently recognize the contributions of the living art of Special Drama. By including artists' voices in this history, I am substantially augmenting the standard historiographic record on Tamil drama. My focus on Special Drama exposes lacunae in a historiographic record that has to date largely omitted this complex theatrical practice from the political and social life of the region. Its inclusion here offers new perspectives on the lived dimensions of the class, language, and regional political struggles that have so defined South India during the past century.

The History of Special Drama

Today, Special Drama is primarily performed in villages. Such rural venues are not, however, where Special Drama began. The genre's roots are much more urban. Special Drama developed in the interstices between the traveling British and Parsi troupes of the nineteenth century and the myriad large Tamil drama companies that came to dominate the Tamil stage in the first decades of the twentieth century (IAS 1990; Kapur 1993; Hansen 1998; Rangacharya 1980). These latter included adult companies as well as companies of child actors, known as boys companies (several of which trained both girls and boys, the name notwithstanding). Companies operated as both disciplinary training ground and home to their year-round charges.

During this period, actors of all ages who left companies after receiving training in their repertory plays circulated on the margins of established troupes and were available for freelance work. Performances that engaged such independent special artists were called Special Drama (Shanmugam 1972; Perumal 1981; Baskaran 1981, 2001; A. Narayan 1981; Navaneethan 1985).

The services of such freelance special actors were often employed to augment company dramas even while a company organizational structure, name, and management remained. That is, even into the 1940s, a drama advertised as being "a special drama" might be put on under a company name; I present and discuss examples of such drama advertisements on handbills in the following chapter. "Since almost all the companies were performing the same plays, it was easier [*sic*] for an actor to desert one and join another to his advantage" (Rangacharya 1980, 110). In certain instances, at least, the company system itself seems to have been fairly dependent on the frequent movement of artists between companies: "A professional company would be having one or two talented singers and actors who would be the main attraction for the audience. After some time the singer and the actor would break away and form his [*sic*] own company" (108), resulting in new "companies" that might consist of no more than a few company players regularly augmented by freelance artists.

By the end of the 1940s, however, the financial burdens of keeping any kind of company structure afloat became increasingly overwhelming, and the vast majority of drama companies had folded. Instead, the appeal of dramas that might be organized entirely through the already existent, albeit informal, network of independent freelance artists grew. It was Special Drama so organized, rather than company drama, that finally proved able to weather the displacement of popular theater occasioned by the advent of the silver screen. Once Tamil talking films began production in Madras in the 1930s, urban drama halls were increasingly converted into cinema halls. By the end of World War II, only a few drama companies remained (the most well-managed ones, to be sure; see Baskaran 2001, 78), and cinema had effectively pushed popular drama off its urban pedestal and out onto the village and "rurban" platforms where it has continued to play ever since.

"Rurban" is a term coined by A. K. Ramanujan (1970) to describe what he perceives as a notion, emergent in both classical and modern Tamil literature, of "a center continuous with the countryside" (242). Madurai, an ancient city frequently described as an overgrown village, is in many ways just such a rurban center. The potential of this hybrid term to capture and characterize something of the quality of life in the regions of Tamilnadu where Special Drama is performed draws me to it; using "rurban" to describe the present-day network of Special Drama helps me conjure a sense of the places it so nimbly links.

Note that this reverse trajectory of progress, this move from the urban-based "company drama" to the rurban "special drama," offers an important corrective to any unidirectional theories of the development of modernity in South Asia. Such theories appear repeatedly in the inescapably teleological accounts of theater in India that have defined its historiography to date.

For example, in his 1989 essay "Theatre in India," Girish Karnad sets the modern Indian theater apart from Indian folk theater on the basis of two key modernizing features: use of the proscenium stage, and the sale of tickets (Karnad 1989, 334–35). Subsequent to these developments, theater, like film, "remained an essentially urban medium" (337). One way to understand the historiographic awkwardness surrounding the subject of Special Drama, so confusingly straddling urban and rural worlds as it does, is to recognize that it muddles the blueprint: this is a theater born of modernity, which in the early twentieth century had both the proscenium stage and the tickets and yet subsequently became part of the ritual economy of the regional countryside, a ritual economy now largely based on the religious and agrarian calendars of village life. Such a reverse trajectory should spell decline, but Special Drama continues to shine (sequins, lamé, and glitter adding powerfully to the effect) from the elevated perch of a proscenium stage that bespeaks a prior life lived very much elsewhere.

The hybrid sensibility captured by this genre thus complicates the straight line of a predetermined rise from rural to urban that has characterized the historiographic narrative of the modernization of Indian theater to date. Indeed, what plays onstage in many out-of-the-way places is a finer articulation of a history that tacks back and forth between "the modern" and "the folk" than such a linear narrative allows.

The history of the development of modern Tamil drama as written by drama historians normally has four stages. They culminate in the development of two styles of drama, the elite amateur style of the *sabhas* and the popular professional style of the commercial theater companies (Baskaran 2001, 78). I now summarize these four canonical stages and then add a fifth that recognizes how the hybrid theater tradition, begun with company drama in the nineteenth century, has continued through the twentieth and into the twenty-first centuries in the form of Special Drama.

Tamil Drama History, Stage One (of Undatable Roots)

An indigenous Tamil theatrical tradition is believed to have existed in Tamilnadu "from time immemorial" (Varadarajan 1988, 255), based on evidence found in stone inscriptions in temples and on allusions in poetic works and their commentaries. Though no ancient texts remain, what evidence there is points to a tradition of staging dramas in temples (IAS 1990, 491–92). A separate tradition of folklore plays in verse and song produced seventeenth- and eighteenth-century texts that do still exist, seen by some as "products . . . of the evolutionary development of the folk dramatic forms" that must have preexisted our written evidence. It is unclear to what extent these seventeenth- and eighteenth-century folk forms influenced the popular form of indigenous Tamil folk theater as it exists today, known interchangeably as *kūttu* (folk drama), *terukkūttu* (street drama), or *kaṭṭaikūttu* (drama with wooden ornaments); on the subject of these names, see Bruin 2000. Indeed, "Little is known about the local forms of theatre that were in existence" before the nineteenth century (Bruin 2001a, 62). One historian writes somewhat despairingly, "the fact remains that whatever Tamil drama or dramatic works might have existed and flourished in the ancient days, not a vestige of it remained or was even remembered" by the end of the nineteenth century (Gopalratnam 1981, 119).

It is nevertheless accepted that folk theater was traditionally performed by villagers for villagers, often as a hereditary occupation. These outdoor ritual performances were enacted in sung verse, the dramatic content of which was puranic, retelling mythic stories from the Hindu epics and puranas. These "night long, ritual like performances" were usually performed during religious festivals (IAS 1990). It is also accepted that before the advent of Western influences on Tamil popular theater, "dramatic performances had been the prerogative of a limited number of (caste) lineages, whose members held locality specific rights-cum-obligations to perform on particular occasions" (Bruin 2001a). This system of local performance rights and obligations defined Tamil theater until the mid-nineteenth century.

While in truth then little is known of its early theatrical form, *terukkuttu* as actively practiced and performed much more recently has come, in the postindependence period, to define Tamil "folk theater" (Frasca 1990; Bruin 2000). Consequently, it is now in relation to *kuttu* that other currently existent forms of Tamil theater, including Special Drama, are understood to be—in the way mutually defining terms such as "traditional" and "modern" so often are—definitionally *other than* indigenous folk theater.

Tamil Drama History, Stage Two

An elite class of Tamil scholars take an interest in drama and begin in the 1860s to translate and adapt Western dramas and literature for a similarly elite audience.[4] "The elitist character of the plays stems from their [authors'] anxiety to raise Tamil drama to the level of the Sanskrit and the western plays" (IAS 1990, 496). This was considered the beginning of *modern* Tamil plays, defined as such precisely because they were based on Western models. At this stage, "Involvement in the theatre came to be considered by the elite to be a fit engagement for persons with a Western education" (Baskaran 2001, 77).

Historians tend to write of this transition in exceedingly colorful terms, a stellar example of which I indulge at some length here:

> The selfless services of erudite scholars have resurrected the Tamil drama from the pits of negligence and withering. In the hands of *street-dancers* drama became worse and worse losing its artistic value. Throughout the night they *shouted and hooted in the name of singing and hopped and leaped instead of acting*. In the morning they went from door to door with stretched arms to get something to fill their belly. Their action on the stage and their behavior in the streets were nothing but a great disgrace to the noble art. Respectable people looked at them with utter contempt. Something substantial had to be done to restore the stage from *the ugly hands of these street dancers*. A few eminent men came forward with great determination. They *modernized* the Tamil stage *with high aims and aspirations*. Since their services were really meritorious and highly valuable they may well be termed the pioneers of modern Tamil drama. (Perumal 1981, 138–39; italics mine)

Note here the marked contrast between the "street-dancers" (a literal translation of *teru-kūttu*) so marked by their physicality—their ugly hands, their empty bellies—and the "high aims and aspirations" of eminent men engaged in the modernizing process. Note also the degradations their performance style visited on the notions of singing and acting, a theme to which I return shortly. The actual theatrical contributions of this "new social class among the natives—the educated middle class men who could neither identify themselves with their fellow men nor find an emotional oneness with the British rulers"—were, however, of only "academic interest" (IAS 1990, 497). It was not until the next stage in this history that your average Tamilian was exposed to new inventions in Tamil drama. The discursive tropes—of elite men rescuing drama from "the pits of negligence and withering"— established in this phase, however, continue to characterize the historiography of Tamil drama.

Tamil Drama History, Stage Three

Parsi drama troupes from Bombay travel to Tamilnadu and perform plays "of puranic and court themes" that incorporate stage conventions "adopted from the English" (IAS 1990, 497).[5] These Parsi companies had their roots in "amateur theatrical activity [that] became fashionable among Parsi college students in Bombay around 1850. Shortly thereafter, Parsi business managers and shareholding actors organised the first professional theatre companies" (Hansen 1998, 2292). The companies charged admission fees from their audiences and are credited with the dubious distinction of beginning commercial theater in India. In the Parsi companies, the "paid employees (including actors) were more disadvantaged with regard to education and family income than company owners" (ibid.), establishing what was to become a class pattern in the organization of commercial theatrical companies across the country.

Stylistically, Parsi theater companies took from British touring companies a new material culture in "styles of advertisements, hand bills, printed tickets and stage machinery," including backdrops of painted cloth scene settings and the architectural innovation of the proscenium arch (Kapur 1993, 86). The framing conventions of the proscenium arch, especially, introduced a visual culture that attempted "to present mythic materials in realistic terms" in the form of gods who, having individual peculiarities and recognizable human faces, might be understood in human terms (Kapur 1993, 97). Further adding to the realism of the stage innovations introduced by Parsi companies was the advent, in the 1890s, of women playing women onstage, a new addition to the extant tradition of male actors expert in female impersonation (Hansen 1998). These two means of representing women onstage vied with each other well into the 1920s in the Parsi theater, allowing the public a choice of images, a legacy that continues in Special Drama today (Hansen 1998, 2292; Bruin 2001a, 69). Commercial Parsi theater companies thus set in motion significant shifts in the spectatorial relations at play in a theater begun in elite, urban cosmopolitan circles but whose impact extended, quite quickly, to working-class audiences and other low-income groups from a range of communities (Hansen 1998, 2292). "The Parsi entrepreneur had to ensure that the fare pleased all tastes and communities and developed a style that was essentially neutral with regard to communal differences and preferences" (Karnad 1989, 336), making it a format easy for subsequent entrepreneurs to adopt.

Tamil Drama History, Stage Four

Tamil drama companies develop along the Parsi model, incorporating both indigenous Tamil material content and the stylistic influences of Western theater made familiar by Parsi troupes. These new Tamil company dramas borrow heavily from the touring Parsi companies that visited the Madras Presidency in the late nineteenth century and the early twentieth.[6] Hanne de Bruin offers a succinct and comprehensive list of the kinds of features Tamil drama companies took from these touring companies:

> Novel features that were incorporated into the emerging *natakam* genre were, for instance, the management of theatre companies as business enterprises, the practice of ticket sales, and the introduction of new visual stage settings and props borrowed from the 19th century Victorian stage, such as the use of an elevated platform or proscenium stage, the "drop curtain," painted back drops and wings, the use of Western musical instruments, such as the harmonium and clarinet, special costumes, and the merging of a melodramatic style of acting with an indigenous performance style . . . and, finally, the casting of women performers in sexually provocative roles. (Bruin 2001a, 56)

Of the new Tamil drama companies that sprang up in the wake of these traveling theatricals, the two most influential were those begun by Pammal Sambanda Mudaliyar, a member of the judicial service, in 1891, and Sankaradas Swamigal in 1910 (IAS 1990, 497). These two companies also inaugurate the split of modern Tamil theater into its two separate streams: the world of elite amateur drama sabhas, and that of professional commercial popular theater companies.

Sambanda Mudaliyar's company, the Suguna Vilasa Sabha, and its repertory represent the beginnings of the elite strain of social drama based on contemporary social themes. It was begun "by a band of bold and enterprising young men of good families with high literary accomplishments to their credit" (Gopalratnam 1981, 123). Such "amateur" actors distinguished themselves by this appellation from those *professional* stage actors who must earn their living from theatrical performance. These amateurs who could afford to engage in this art in their leisure time were notably judges and barristers in the city of Madras. The plays staged in their clubs were mostly Tamil translations of Sanskrit and English works by Kalidasa and Shakespeare (Baskaran 2001, 77).

The values assigned in the West to rankings of theatrical professionals and amateurs are inverted in the world of Tamil theater during this period. The primary determinant of rank is class; the elite amateur need not work but is "free" to act out of a higher sentiment. Tamil drama historians tend not to question the logic of this order, and we find many descriptions like the following:

> Right up to the end of the [nineteenth] century no amateur could be found to interest himself in any manner in Tamil drama. It was entirely in the hands of *professionals drawn from the lowest ranks of society*. The great prejudice in the popular mind against the atmosphere of the drama and all persons engaged in it cannot be said to have been wholly unjustified. (Gopalratnam 1981, 122; italics mine)

In this narrative of a degraded indigenous "professional" drama in need of rescue by great men, Sambanda Mudaliyar figures as the hero who began "the Herculean task of cleaning the Augean stables" of "the internal impurities in the practice of the art itself" with his company of amateur actors of high social standing (Gopalratnam 1981, 122). And yet others note that Mudaliyar's plays were also compromised by his own elite position in society; "his inability to remain faithful to the contemporary social realities might be seen in the context of his social standing, professional status and his having been conferred the 'Rao Bahadur' title by the British government" (IAS 1990, 498). Thus Sambanda Mudaliyar's contribution feeds that stream in Tamil drama of an elite, modern "social" theater by and for middle-class society.

In stark contrast is the other stream of theater influenced by Sankaradas Swamigal. Here theater artists are "in the life" full time. Even before he began his own adult company, from 1891 Swamigal worked with professional artists, holding the position of drama teacher (*vatiyar*) in numerous adult drama companies. Actors recall that "in those days the revered Sankaradas Swamigal was every drama actors' teacher" (Shanmugam 1972, 34). He began a drama company of his own in 1910, the Samarasa Sanmaarka Sabha, about which one historian writes, "its chief claim for fame rests on its having provided an appropriate forum for the shaping of the potential artistes. . . . It was this Company that provided the infrastructure on which were built the [later] dramatic troupes" (IAS 1990, 499).

Swamigal's scripts were performed regularly by drama companies. Shortly after starting his adult company, Swamigal began working with children. In 1918 he founded his own boys company, the Madurai Tattuva Meenalosani Vittuva Bala Sabha. (All the companies used Sanskrit terms in their titles, seemingly in a bid for urbanity; I will return to the subject of changing language politics in twentieth-century Tamilnadu later.)

Swamigal's biographer gives the following explanation for Swamigal's switch from working with adults to children.

> Upon seeing that the adult actors whom he had trained were not speaking and acting as he had taught them, but instead *speaking and acting dialogues however they themselves pleased*, he became heartbroken. He tried to correct them, but they wouldn't be corrected; so he left off working with those who foiled his expectations, and formed a company of the best boy actors and began running that instead. (Ulakanatan 1992, 18)

This notion of willful adult actors who stubbornly pursue their own pleasure onstage against all better counsel recurs repeatedly, and not only in historical accounts of this early formative period of Tamil drama but also in contemporary criticisms of Special Drama. A perceived need to discipline artists out of such habits—their propensity to speak and act however they please—was a hallmark of the company era that is now part of the ideological legacy inherited by Special Drama artists.

The disciplining of the artist's body played a critical role in the smooth functioning of the Tamil drama company. Criticisms of Tamil drama in its postcompany days stress its unfortunate lack of discipline. To understand where Special Drama fits in this narrative, I turn briefly to a more ethnographically informed look at life in the drama companies and outside them before resuming my staged history.

The Disciplined Life of the Drama Company

In his memoir of a celebrated life in the theater, T. K. Shanmugam (1972) stresses the centrality of discipline in the experience of actors in boys companies in the first decades of the twentieth century. One of the first highly respected and well-known Tamil stage-actor-turned-cine-stars, Shanmugam gained his first acting experiences in Sankaradas Swamigal's boys company. There, he writes, discipline focused on the maintenance of good manners (*o̱lakkam*) and the avoidance of the bodily vices of betel chewing, snuff snorting, beedi smoking, and the drinking of alcohol. Any boy caught doing any of the above "was in big trouble. Terrific blows were about to fall, that no one could stop. Afraid of Swamigal's beatings, many actors ran away from the company" (Shanmugam 1972, 41). That is, children who couldn't or wouldn't stay in the disciplined world of the company left it to become part of the far looser world of Special Drama.

I interviewed many Special Drama actors who first learned their art in drama companies and gained from them an understanding of this discourse of company discipline through their experiences in drama companies ranging from the 1920s through the 1960s. One was the renowned harmonist A. K. Kaleeswaran, born in 1917. His career began at a young age, performing child roles in T. K. Shanmugam's company, which was modeled directly on Swamigal's company. Kaleeswaran lasted there just one month, however, before he "got scared and ran away." He joined the company of another of Swamigal's students, where he began training in earnest. He eventually joined the Puliyamana Nagar Boys Co., with whom he traveled widely; his list of the cities he visited while performing with the company includes Singapore, Panang, Kuala Lumpur, Colombo, Kandy, Rangoon. He played both Hero and Heroine roles until age sixteen, when his voice changed and he could no longer do the female parts. He became a harmonist in 1933, and eventually a drama teacher. From 1935 to 1940 he was the proprietor, manager, harmonist, and part owner of a company. After the company folded in 1940, as so many then did due to lack of means, he started working with a cinema music orchestra, and his base shifted to Madras from then on, where he worked with cinema artists and eventually with a classical dance troupe (the Hema Malini Bharata Natyam Dance Troupe) that toured internationally.

Kaleeswaran attributes all that was best about company drama in its heyday, the early decades of the twentieth century, to the intervention of Swamigal and his disciplining of young actors. In Kaleeswaran's words, Swamigal was the one who gave regularity and propriety (oḻukkam) to drama, largely by scripting dialogues and organizing the dramas into scenes.

> The very first boys company, in 1911 [Jeganatha Aiyar's company], was organized by Sankaradas Swami. Before that there were lots of drama companies, Special Drama companies. That is, they put different people in each drama. *They had no discipline [kaṭṭuppāṭu], no regularity or propriety [oḻukkam]: they talked as they pleased in the dramas, they talked whatever they knew, which amounted to comedy and all that, because they had no muṟai.* Only then did Swamigal take some young boys, and put them up front, and he started it all off. Only then did drama become

regularized [oḻuṅkuppaṭutti], and scenes—scenes, and organization—come to be; he was the first to do that.

Kaleeswaran overtly connects lack of discipline and order, and specifically lack of muṟai, with the kind of loose pleasure that characterizes comedy. This dominant attitude toward comedy as inherently lacking in order and discipline crops up repeatedly in discourses of drama criticism in the early twentieth century. Drama was to be distinguished from this disordered world of extempore comedy primarily through its *scripting*. Progress in Tamil drama, for Kaleeswaran as for so many of his era, was born of the improvements wrought by the disciplining hand that wielded that quintessential civilizing tool, the pen. Entextualization—the transformation wrought by encoding bodily practices in written texts—has become a key feature of artists' attempts to classicize their art (and thereby enhance their social status) throughout South Asia.[7]

The presence of words, script, and dialogues makes all the difference here:

> *Terukkuttu* was just a matter of singing one long song. There were no dialogues. Drama, on the other hand, had separate scenes; it was organized by scenes: the Darbar [palace court], the Forest, the Garden. For each scene a *screen* would be put up, and the drama would be conducted. That's the difference between street plays and drama.
>
> When the boys companies began, they brought even further improvements: only that which was taught, whatever it might be, only that was sung onstage. They wouldn't say anything other than that.
>
> Special Drama is not like that. They improvise as they like, each time, apropos to that particular time. In boys companies there is no improvisation. Only that which the teacher has written and given them to speak will they speak.

Discipline, regularity, and regulation of actors' own inherently undisciplined impulses—their impulse to speak as they will, engaging in that lack of discipline and order that defines them as *muṟai illāmal*—appear here as the only hope for attaining a higher art, that is, a truly dramatic art.

Another artist I spoke with was involved in company life during a later era but nevertheless held similar opinions of its virtues. Ramalingasivan was a member of Nawab Rajamanikam's company from the time he joined at the age of twelve, in 1950, until the company finally folded in 1969. This company, officially named the Bala Meena Ranjani Sangeetha Sabha, survived into the postindependence era by virtue of its organizational strengths (Baskaran 2001, 78). When I interviewed Ramalingasivan in 1992, he was in his early fifties and had been playing supporting actor (*Uba Naṭikar*) roles in Special Drama for over twenty years, all roles he had learned during his years in the company. Ramalingasivan is a paradigm of the well-trained actor. Spry and lithe, with a highly animated face, he stood out every time I saw him onstage for the fullness of his embodiment, whether of a servant, a child of the king's court, or a thief disguised as a woman.

Ramalingasivan overtly preferred the company life and its strict work ethic to the freelance life of Special Drama. Unlike most Special Drama artists, who were either kicked out of companies for bad behavior or ran away before they were, Ramalingasivan stayed with this well-managed company until its end. He characterized the experience by saying: "It was more like a university than a drama company. It was an ascetic life; actually it ran more like a Hindu propaganda society, teaching us all the classical dance forms, having us spin our own khadi cloth. We were 250 people working there. All 250 would work together as one machine. Then all 250 would sit together and eat, all in a group, with no differentiation on the basis of caste or creed."

Another artist, V. K. S. Mani, began in acting roles in a boys company as a small child at an only slightly earlier time, in 1947. At puberty his voice broke, and he stopped singing, entering instead into the technical side of the company dramas by operating electrical lights and running scenes with "trick shots" (special effects), skills he took with him to other drama companies after this first one folded in 1953. Mani told me: "Everything I know, I know from the company. The extent to which I can speak now, read now, that's a certain level of knowledge, right? If they hadn't taught it, I'd know nothing. If it hadn't been for them, I'd be a fool now. In those days they taught everything."

In the combined picture I gained from multiple interviews, company life comes across as a kind of world unto itself: there were cooks, tailors, scene painters, dance teachers, dialogue coaches, songwriters, accountants, managers, the big proprietors of the commercial venture, and, of course, the artists, beginning with kids all of four years old. Some boys companies were indeed comprised only of male artists, but others trained both girls and boys. I interviewed several senior actresses then in their sixties and seventies who had begun their careers in boys companies. Once they had trained there, where they could learn all the roles in numerous plays, they could go on to play any role in later life. Many women of this era chose to play Hero as well as Heroine roles in Special Drama (a subject I address in the following chapter).

Companies moved from city to city, camping for months, sometimes even years at a time, in one location before moving on to another. Speaking again of his experiences during the 1950s and 1960s, Ramalingasivan described the traveling company camp (using many English words, which appear in italics in the following excerpt) as

> one big *compound* consisting mostly of thatched sheds, made of coconut frond thatch, big enough to house three thousand members of the *audience*! That's where we would stage the drama. One month before shifting, contractors would go look for a suitable place. We would build one shed to house ill people, another for cooking, then for a prayer room, and a room to sleep in, then a *latrine*. All thatched sheds, all inside a huge *compound*. Have you seen a *circus company*? Just like those tents, only these were thatched sheds: a storeroom, an office room, a ticket counter. This was how the companies functioned.

Moving such an enterprise was a massive organizational endeavor. With all the necessary props, equipment, kitchenware, instruments, and costumes, Ramalingasivan recalls that there were enough

> things to fill 120 lorries. All of us used to help load the goods. These were kept in huge wooden boxes; fifteen persons had to carry one box, it was so heavy. The ankle bells we used while dancing, they would come in huge bundles, in tons! We had props for the different dances, the Ravana dance, the Butterfly dance, an Umbrella dance, a Flower dance (each of which might last all of five minutes when incorporated into the drama). Two tailors were employed all day repairing costumes and stitching on sequins.

In this bulky organizational undertaking that was a drama company, most reminiscent perhaps of eighteenth-century British army caravans, everyone learned all the different kinds of work necessary and participated in the labor of setting up and striking camp (except for the cooks, who only cooked). "When we shift camp to another town, I'd renew the *settings*, and do carpentry. We even used to cut each other's hair; we did such things also." One learned everything in the company life, from the ground up.

And all this functioned on a strict schedule that regulated body and mind. Ramalingasivan again recalls, in a mix of English, Sanskrit, and Tamil that itself reflects a good deal about the ethos of the undertaking and its belief in a kind of civilizing rigor:

> One had to get up at 6 A.M. Then we would get just five big mugs of water to bathe. Who can bathe with just five mugs of water today? The first two mugs were to pour over the head, the third for the body; someone would put soap on our backs and then two mugs of water [*laughs*] whether we are dirty or not!

Then someone will be toweling our hair dry; coconut oil is kept in a big tin, if we want to use it. We have camped even in towns which had no water supply, and the water too will come in lorries. After finishing one's morning *duties* we were given a drink called *wheat coffee* (we didn't know about coffee beans) and then began *sangeetha* [music] *class* for one hour, seven to eight. Eight to nine, *dance class*. We were fifteen people in each *set*. We would undergo training in different things; some would learn the mridangam, some the harmonium, some were painters, though we all learned to draw; during free hours, I used to paint banners, the ones they display outside for publicity. We would concentrate on dramas and acting only during the stipulated times. Then they also used to teach us, through lectures: "Be like this, be like that." Such was the control. No one can maintain order and discipline like this today. They talk about hostels in schools, but this company had much more stringent rules. One had to do everything at the given time.

Life on the Margins of the Companies

In 1918, during the first year of Swamigal's boys company, T. K. Shanmugam and his two elder brothers were pulled from their elementary school studies in the second, fourth, and sixth standards, respectively, to join up. It was the boys' father, himself an actor, who with trepidation made the decision to entrust his boys' future to Swamigal. In recounting his father's weak protests in the face of Swamigal's eager persistence, Shanmugam paints both a larger and a more intimate picture of the drama world than do most of the standard written histories. We learn that his father was "disaffected" with the whole drama business at the time and would have preferred to keep his boys out of it. And we learn, somewhat in passing, of the existence of Special Drama in the following terms: "At that time our father was staying afloat in the ocean of life by hanging on to that piece of driftwood known as 'Special Drama'" (Shanmugam 1972, 35). I myself clung to this stunning characterization of the genre as a piece of driftwood as if it were precious coral, though it wasn't until I spoke with the late great Buffoon T. N. Sivathanu, himself a third cousin of the TKS brothers, that I gained any real understanding of its meaning. We were talking about why actors dropped out of companies or were kicked out, when Sivathanu pointed out quite openly that it was most often because they drank, T. K. Shanmugam's father being a case in point. He was an alcoholic who died of liver disease. The simplicity of this interpretation has profound aspects and implications. It claims that to a certain extent, Special Drama was born of a transgressive overflow from the companies, and that it outlasted them by being better adapted to the vagaries of the alcoholic tide of an actor's life, with its feast-or-famine rhythms of a drama season that lasts only half the year.

Alcohol was a topic that arose frequently in the disparagement of actors' lack of discipline. For example, here was one exchange in my conversation with Kaleeswaran:

SS: Some people say they need drinks to stay awake all night and perform Special Drama.

AKK: That's forbidden [*tappu*]. That's what I'm saying, Special Drama is like that. In the boys companies, all that was *not allowed*. Outside of the boys companies there was no *control*, and those who left could do as they pleased. Not in the boys company; there everything was controlled. Even how much you ate. So no one drank. Only those who left the company drank; in the company, there was *control*.

And yet for all his reputation as a strict enforcer of the teetotaling company, Swamigal himself was no stranger to these waters. According to several artists I interviewed, he may well have meted out his heavy-handed disciplinarian stripes to those who drank from a certain self-knowledge of the lubricated state. The cumulative picture of the man that emerges from artists' reminiscences of Swamigal (those that made it into print, as well as those that thus far have not) is less than exemplary on this front. In addition to his proclivity for doling out beatings, he is said to have channeled the god of death onstage. Before writing plays, Swamigal was briefly an actor, primarily of villain roles. His acting career seems to have been fearfully energetic; he is said to have caused a spontaneous miscarriage when a pregnant audience member reacted with an all-too-real fright to his portrayal of Yemen, the god of death (Ulakanatan 1992, 17). After a second such severe incident occurred, wherein a woman is reported to have fallen dead of fright, Swamigal stopped acting. This was in 1891, when he would have been twenty-four years old; that same year, he began writing dramas.

Based on the oral accounts of my informants, Swamigal was himself almost certainly an alcoholic, and for all his prolific output, much of it written in nightlong creative bursts of imagination, the master remained poor and unmarried until his death. Several artists mentioned to me the bitter irony of these most enduring aspects of the legacy Swamigal left to his successors: to die drunk, unmarried, and poor.

Nevertheless, life in a drama company might initially have had for young boys much the same appeal that running off with the circus held for kids in the West. This was the case for Vaiyur Gopal. When a company came to his town looking for children who sang well, his schoolteacher brought him there. The company offered to pay one hundred rupees per year directly to the boy's parents. Gopal was keen on the idea "because there were so many kids studying and working together, it seemed like fun. If my parents hadn't sent me, I would have gone anyway." And yet the thrill could fade quickly, too. T. K. Appukutti Bhagavattar, the honored mridangam player, first joined a boys company in 1924 at age eight. A mere three years later, he and two friends ran away from the company and took their drums and cymbals with them. He said they ran off "because the company food was lousy." They headed to Madurai and so began a fifty-eight-year career in Special Drama.

An expansive, relatively free-floating world of drama artists working outside the structure of companies has clearly existed since the beginning of the twentieth century. The primary testimonies to this early existence are found in the reminiscences of older Special Drama actors such as I have begun to recount here, supplemented by material evidence contained in drama notices dating to the 1890s that proudly announce "special actors" in "special dramas." Yet the history of Special Drama has never yet been centralized in the historiography of Tamil drama. I am piecing together here marginal mentions, and significantly augmenting them with my own data, in an attempt to construct a historical picture that foregrounds Special Drama.

Tamil Drama History, Stage Five: A New Historical Trajectory

My real intervention thus starts here. By focusing on the legacy of company drama in the practice of Special Drama, from its beginnings to the present, I add a fifth phase to the extant historiography of Tamil drama. I argue that the impressively malleable popular theater genre of music drama (both in its current company drama form in North Tamilnadu as documented by Bruin, and in its Special Drama form in South Tamilnadu as I document here) inaugurates a reverse trajectory to the usual teleological story of the progress of modernity in South Asia. Music drama continues to morph into regionally attuned forms of hybrid theater that become something new—neither purely commercial nor purely ritual theaters, neither purely urban or rural, but rather both.

Such new hybrid forms articulate with localized economic, political, and social formations as part of a process of "vernacularising capitalism" (Jain 2001) that brings commercial and ritual models into articulation in India through a two-way process.

> We might think of this two-way process as one of vernacularising capitalism: not just the incorporation of vernacular constituencies into a regnant capitalism intertwined with bourgeois-modernist ideology, but also the protean adaptations of the axiomatics of capital to varying global circumstances. (Jain 2001)

We need such a concept of new regional economic and social formations to do interpretive justice to the innovations of local practices such as Special Drama. Recent scholarship on "hybrid theaters" in India has begun to map out a terrain where such concepts would be highly applicable (Bruin 2001b).[8] Bruin advocates the term "hybrid theaters" to characterize a historical phenomenon occurring across India during the late nineteenth century and the early twentieth, and her attempt to rescue the reputation of these hybrid theaters from accusations of degeneracy and lack of refinement recognizes that such theaters "provided an interface between rural and urban cultures, and between local traditions and inter-regional and international, cultural and political settings" (Bruin 2001b, 2).

In claiming hybrid theater forms as "the first modern theatres of India," this recent scholarship provides a welcome corrective to previous work that presents modern Indian theater as the exclusive purview of the urban middle class. The opening lines of Farley Richmond's study of modern Indian theater, for example, read: "Modern theatre in India is urban, not rural. It is created by and primarily for people who may be regarded as middle and upper middle class" (Richmond et al. 1990, 387). Under this rubric, he links everything from commercial theater to amateur sabhas to experimental plays.

My contribution to these debates lies in demonstrating that the processes of innovation that resulted in regional hybrid theaters across India did not stop, at least in South India, in the early decades of the twentieth century. Special Drama is not only alive and well but kicking. Its energy remains penned in by dismissive discourses that affect both its production and reception, yet artists consistently find creative ways to make the form responsive and relevant to its changing contexts.

The Legacy of the Company Model in Special Drama

Drama companies have left a considerable imprint on Special Drama today. Their legacy includes the current repertory of dramas as well as the style in which these dramas are learned and performed. The role of the drama teacher in Special Drama is an important piece in this legacy.

Companies employed drama teachers to train actors and teach them the songs for the repertory roles they would play. The role of the company drama teacher describes Sankaradas Swamigal as much as the Special Drama teachers of today, except of course that the safety net of a company payroll no longer exists for Special Drama artists. Drama teachers in the Special Drama network today must rely on their students to pay them according to their means.

> The companies had on their pay-rolls song-writers conversant with classical and folk music who composed songs to suit popular tastes. The main work of the song-writer, known as *vathiar* (teacher), was to write songs and teach them to the actors. As the only person with some formal education in the company, the *vathiar* served as its antenna and the drama reflected his reactions to the political events outside. (Baskaran 1981, 30)

Today the three or four drama teachers in Madurai, and the one or two teachers in each of the other sizable cities in the Special Drama network (Dindigal, Karaikudi, Karur, and Pudukkottai), continue to provide songs to actors in much the same way that company teachers did. They incorporate new ideas into old familiar melodies, and they refit new melodies—including those of current hit cinema songs—to original drama verses.

Swamigal himself employed multiple and varied influences in his scripts. For instance, his directions in the script might indicate that a lyric he wrote be played according to a familiar folk melody or a work song, but equally might refer to a named classical Carnatic raga or again to the tune of a song from another drama popular at the time. His style was intertextual, and his scripts consciously and consistently referenced other entertainment media and performative styles (Navaneethan 1985, 7–38). It is in this way that drama teachers today, I suggest, continue their work in the spirit of Swamigal.

Without any company structure, aspiring actors today still go to drama teachers to learn the songs that fit the repertory roles they would play. The teachers pass on formulaic techniques as well as specific lyrics and lines:

"When the Hero says X, you say Y. If he says Z, you say A," and so on. This technique fuels staged debates consisting of hours of such repartee. In Special Drama performances of *Valli's Wedding*, for example, the trickster sage Naradar piques Murugan's interest in Valli's virtues in a scene that lasts an hour, then Naradar goes and speaks with Valli herself for another hour, and finally Murugan and Valli verbally spar through the several remaining wee hours of the morning, until they wed at dawn. Special Drama is the form that developed debate scenes that fully occupy the stage (Navaneethan 1985, 131). Such long scenes considerably pad the original play scripts of Sankaradas Swami and allow Special Drama performances to last all night.

Given this extended playing time, a great deal of what artists actually perform on the Special Drama stage today was never scripted by Swamigal. This reality sheds an interesting light on the reverential position into which the guru is now cast by Special Drama artists. For while the Special Drama repertory is said to consist primarily of Sankaradas Swamigal's plays, in fact the majority of what takes place on the Special Drama stage has never been scripted at all. A performance that strictly adhered to the dramatic script as written by Swamigal would take barely three hours to perform, even with time liberally allotted to vocal elaboration of his verse songs. During the company days of ticket dramas, performances did indeed last just this long, but once Special Drama moved out into village venues, the ritual slot the dramas filled as entertainment at religious festivals required that these performances conform to a local ritual schedule that assumes events will carry on till dawn.

One reason given for such a schedule is practical: artists must now perform all night because their village audiences need to stay all night. During the heyday of company drama, plays were performed in auditoriums in cities and bigger towns. In these urban venues there was a municipal transportation infrastructure that allowed the audience to take a bus or train home at 11 P.M. or midnight. But in villages there is no transportation at night. People come to the commons in the village by foot, bicycle, ox cart, or horse, and they can't leave in the dark. Thus, as entertainment for village religious festivals, Special Drama performances now run for eight hours, beginning at 10 P.M. and concluding, generally, with an auspicious wedding scene conducted at dawn.[9]

How, then, are the additional five hours of running time for these dramas actually accomplished?

While drama teachers' songs and coached dialogues contribute to the task, the bulk of the additional hours of performance in contemporary Special Drama is the result of actors' improvisation. The formulaic technique that drama teachers impart to their students today consists primarily of an injunction to do the very thing that, recall, supposedly so broke their guru's heart when he ran an adult company: improvise onstage. Their job now is "speaking and acting dialogues however they themselves please" (Ulakanatan 1992, 18). Around a structure of key nodes—certain key Swamigal songs that must be sung, and certain key passages of his prose that must be uttered—actors, guided by drama teachers, add the connecting tissue that fleshes out the nightlong dramas that are Special Drama today. Actors speak, sing, dance, joke, riff, elaborate, and embellish onstage for hours, *karpaṇaiyaka*, "by imagination." For this reason, the formality of even the more formal (that is, literary and literature-based) dramatic scenes in Special Drama is really only a relative formality, as the livelihood of the whole genre now depends on the "special" ability of artists to improvise onstage.

But this ability, this "specialty" of Special Drama, has been roundly criticized. During the heyday of Tamil drama, the period in the first two decades of the twentieth century when Swamigal was so influential in both adult and boys companies, criticism of the improvisational additions made by professional actors to scripted dramas was a common topic of discussion and disdain among the drama elite.[10] This criticism endures in a legacy of shame that the company era has bequeathed to Special Drama. The tropes in which the vulgarity of professional drama was discussed at the turn of the century continue to influence the world of Special Drama. This legacy profoundly shapes the organization of the artists' "official" professional bodies—the drama actors sangams, as discussed in chapter 3—as well as their everyday offstage lives. Here I want to offer a taste of the discourses that confronted professional actors with an image of themselves as vulgar. These discourses are now part of the legacy of the company era for Special Drama artists.

Discourse of Vulgarity, Legacy of Shame

In August 1911 a new magazine began publication in Madras. Entitled *The Stage Lover* in English, and *Nāṭakābimāni* in (a very Sanskritic) Tamil, it was an Anglo-Indian monthly, each issue offering half its essays in English and the other half in Tamil, with titles such as "The Depravity of the Tamil Stage—a Diagnosis" and "Is the Dramatic Profession a Shameful One?" *The Stage Lover*'s annual subscription rate was only three rupees, but a single issue cost

4 Pammal Sambanda Mudaliyar as Hamlet, *The Stage Lover*, 1911.

six: this was clearly a magazine for subscription readers, those able to order ahead and in possession of a settled address at which to receive their subscription—not, that is, for the peripatetic professional actor.

The production values of the magazine were high. Each issue is replete with full-page quality plates. Committed to continuing this style of publication, in the first issue, the editor and proprietor of *The Stage Lover*, Mr. M. V. Ishwar, put out a call to photographers living outside Madras to take pictures of any dramas staged in their area and send them to the magazine, which would pay for the effort. The magazine simultaneously announced that it would award five rupees to the best photograph of a man playing a woman's role, and likewise to the best of a woman playing a man's role (Ishwar, ed., 1911a, 30–31). Through editorial news and notes scattered throughout the magazine, the reader gets a sense of the amount of dramatic activity occurring across the state, and the proliferation of amateur drama sabhas.

The photographic plates are quite striking. The first issue includes a plate of Mr. P. Sambanda Mudaliyar himself in the role of Hamlet (see fig. 4), in full black woolen cape, matching velvet dress, white scarf, and leggings, looking transcendently melancholy. A complementary second plate shows one Mr. C. Ranga Vadivelu, B.A., B.L., in the role of Ophelia, gazing serenely out from a garden in white gown and bonnet. At the back of the magazine are ads. A drama company will offer a good salary to a skilled lady, or a skilled man to play a lady. An engraver offers "process blocks of any size, any grain, mounted on copper, zinc or any metal" at the American Process Studio, Madras, the company responsible for the pictorial images on the pages of *The Stage Lover*. Flute harmoniums made in Calcutta are available, as are painted backgrounds that never fade. And in "a rare opportunity for sabhas," an offer of free packing for "fine bed room pictures with beautiful gold frame, size according to the character."

By the second issue, press clippings are included that sum up the magazine's mission: "Very often the actors on a native stage descend to a low level of morality and by their loose and lascivious expressions on the stage, bring contempt on the dramatic art itself. The regular publication of a journal of this kind is sure to produce healthy results in the progress of the dramatic art" (from the *Desabimani*, Cuddalore, in Ishwar, ed., 1911b, flyleaf). This is clearly the voice of elite amateur drama in its glory. The editor makes his position crystal clear on the front page of the third issue. "Educated people" are right to see popular theater as a real threat, since "theatre has unlimited power of forming the minds and hearts of the people. It is therefore very necessary that, at the earliest possible opportunity educated men should take to stage; else there is a great danger to the morale of the public."

The inherent danger of theater clearly lies in having its power in the wrong hands. The theater that is popular among "the labouring classes" is supremely worrisome. The mutuality of representation and reflection between audience and actors, which is so key to Special Drama as a theater well attuned to its audience, is what the middle-class critic finds most disturbing about such professional theater:

> The Professional theatre managers stage plays . . . [of] gross nonsense. One thing that is much to be regretted is the depravity of the stage, which is due to the undue vulgarity, that has crept in on account of the wrong understanding and desire on the part of the actors to please the groundling by descending very low, overacting their parts and talking vulgarisms at all times. It is a fact which ought not to be ignored that the public taste has in consequence deteriorated and what the public do is, not only that they do not dislike bad plays but like them most—nay adore them. It is a pity that bad plays draw crowded houses. (Ishwar, ed., 1911c, 19)

Note how moral danger is calibrated here in what is clearly a hierarchy of emotions: the lowly actors and their lowly audience mutually *desire* and *adore*, while the middle-class critic responds with *pity*. And pity, it turns out, doesn't leave much room for enjoyment of popular, professional theater.

In such contexts, artists and audiences who might actually enjoy the pleasures of the popular stage learn to do so furtively. Publications such as *The Stage Lover* have the stamp of approval of the educated elite, the powerful barristers and judges of Madras, capital city of the Madras Presidency under the Raj, as well as the backing of commercial businesses boasting the newest foreign technologies. Such early glossy magazines would have been handed around, underlined and dog-eared, and carefully saved in many middle-class homes; indeed, I know the magazine only by being handed just such a stack of the first volume's issues.[11] No popular stage artist I knew had copies of this magazine nor were those with whom I discussed it particularly interested in it. They were already familiar with the attitudes it published: these are elite people who never did, and whose successors still do not, like Special Drama actors or appreciate their art.

How did such dismissive attitudes come to circulate so widely (far more widely than this magazine), and for so long? How exactly is something as *emotional* as the shame of enjoyment in the face of a middle-class dismissal taught and learned; how is it inculcated among artists and audiences of popular theater in Tamilnadu today? The inheritance and inscription of these attitudes is much more complicated than their simple existence in any single media vehicle, including this fortuitously found journal so densely packed with dismissives. Rather, the inheritance and reinscription of these attitudes is a matter of practice. Many of the practices of Special Drama today contribute to this reinscription. One simple example: rather than refute the accusation that this popular theater is vulgar, its artists and audiences instead spar about who is to blame for this state of affairs. Audiences claim that vulgar language (and cine-songs) are all these artists have to offer, while artists claim that these are all audiences today want. Ultimately, of course, to earn a living, professional actors must find ways to please their audience, as complicatedly furtive as both the pleasing and the pleasure taking may have become. As Bruin writes, "Parallel to an 'officially' advocated aversion, the contemporary popular *natakam* [drama] elicits a particular kind of appreciation and hidden pleasure" (2000a, 70). Of which much of the particularity resides, to be sure, in comedy.

In comedy scenes, such attitudes may be conveyed, ridiculed, perpetuated, and avoided, all in the course of one act. Special Drama is itself a complex site for the negotiation of the legacy of shame. In the analyses that follow, I begin by looking at what artists actually do onstage in the face of inherited shame and dominant discourses of vulgarity. Standing before them, artists negotiate their audiences' surreptitious desires. Artists are the magnet to which the stigma of the popular stage adheres. They absorb some of it, and they give some of it back. Artists' ability to do this professionally, for a living, in the context of the contemporary marketplace of Indian entertainment, impresses me and fuels my own desire to watch and understand their art.

Context: The History of Modernity in Tamilnadu

It remains to ground the discourses so far explored within the larger political context of the late nineteenth century and the early twentieth in Tamilnadu. This period when dismissive discourses about popular theater were first unleashed was simultaneously the formative period for Special Drama, the decades when Sankaradas Swamigal wrote the plays that have become its repertory base and a time of intense intellectual foment and radical idealism across the South. The excitement generated during these decades carries over into the reformist ideals that continue to shape artists' political goals today.

The politics of the late nineteenth century and the early twentieth in Tamilnadu have been the subject of a good deal of historiographic attention (Irschick 1969, 1986; Barnett 1976; Washbrook 1989; Ramaswamy 1997). Without rehearsing the finer points and arguments of this work, my aim here is to introduce the active political tenor of the time and give a sense of the kinds of issues that shaped notions of progress during this period.

A central concern of South Indian politics during the late nineteenth century and the early twentieth was the pursuit of an egalitarian society, envisioned simultaneously as a revival of a Tamil golden age and as a leap forward into the modern world. Revivalist ideology—the attempt to return to a former period of happiness and restore a golden age (Irschick 1986)—made modernity palatable by allowing Tamilians to embrace egalitarian social reform without losing a sense of regional pride. That is, revivalism presented modernity in the guise of an authentic Dravidian past. That the pursuit of more egalitarian social relations should have been shaped very much within and through colonial relations is, as the Comaroffs forcefully demonstrate for the South African context, one of the central ironies of colonialism (Comaroff and Comaroff 1995).

In South India, the development of a self-consciously Tamil historical consciousness is rife with such colonial paradoxes. The mobilization of an indigenous Dravidian identity for Tamilians was effected through a distinction between Brahmans (as Aryan invaders) and non-Brahmans (as indigenous natives), a distinction itself made possible by the studious interventions of European missionaries.

> The roots of the concept "non-Brahmin" are intrinsically tied to the idea of the cultural unity and integrity of south India based on a Dravidian past. Paradoxically, this Dravidian-ness was first postulated by Europeans. . . . Many symbols associated with Tamil political identity reach deep into Tamil history and culture. Paradoxically, politicization of these ancient cultural symbols was a concomitant of social change associated with modernization. (Barnett 1976, 15, 17)

Likewise in the history of Tamil theater, Western paradigms of theatrical representation—acts, scenes, dialogues, proscenium arches, and stories with contemporary social relevance—were conceived of as necessary props to the realization of ideals of modernity and social progress for a modernized Tamil theater. Discourses of modernity prevalent around the turn of the century, replete with the ideals of egalitarianism, secularism, and progress, informed programmatic statements seeking to rearrange the Tamil theater (such as we have seen) and simultaneously gave artists a way to think about themselves and their work in the context of larger social goals.

Drama Actors Sangams

The Special Drama acting community continues to pursue political goals first articulated during this period. Within a year of Sankaradas Swamigal's death, in 1923, drama artists founded an official association in Madurai. Known as the Tamilnadu Drama Actors Sangam (Tamiḻnāṭu Nāṭaka Naṭikar Caṅkam), it represents the codification of a collective strategy to better the social and economic status of artists. A primary goal is "to encourage the progress" of members of the drama community, effected through the revival of an ancient concept for modern aims.

The term "sangam" might be translated as "an academy or fraternity," but to substitute any of these English terms would be to lose the resonance of a

Tamil word that references a nodal point in Tamil literary history. I have thus chosen to retain the Tamil term throughout this book. "Sangam" evokes "antediluvian kingdoms extending back many millennia" that "included immortal gods, sages, and kings as member poets" (Ramanujan 1967, 99). Of the large body of poetic works thought to have been composed by three separate sangams of poets over three separate, and very long, periods (the three sangams are said to have lasted 4,440, 3,700, and 1,850 years, respectively), only some two thousand poems now remain, dating from the third and final sangam, part of the "early heroic age" before any Aryan contact (IAS 1990). The sangam era now figures as a period of "prelapsarian bliss [that] came to an end with a series of floods, which destroyed the original Tamil civilization" (Ramaswamy 1997, 45). It is this sense of the heights of Tamil civilization being defined by the creative brilliance of an academy of poet-artists that carries over into the usage of the term by present-day Tamil arts sangams.[12]

Today a network of sixteen drama actors sangams stretches across the central portion of state and facilitates the functioning of Special Drama (see map 1). These sangams are ideological sites of considerable influence on the genre of Special Drama itself as well as on its producers and consumers. (Chapter 3 is devoted to the careful ethnographic consideration of the workings of the Madurai Sangam, and especially to the range of artists' relations to it.)

For our purposes here, a sense of how the progress of the drama community is linked to concepts of modernist reform may be found in a booklet entitled "Rules according to the Sangam's founding laws of 1975 and 1978, detailing organization, the Sangam's goals, and the way it is structured." Under the heading "Goals of this Sangam" are the following:

> III. To take the actions necessary to protect from destruction the Tamil Music Drama art, to reform it, and to encourage the progress of the actors and actresses who undertake it.
>
> IV. To protect old dramas filled with the values of patriotism, cooperation, love, nonviolence, and chastity, and to help conduct the new dramas of the present time [according to such values].

The latter goal suggests that the content of the dramatic repertory itself contains values that can help situate the community in good stead. To understand this claim, we must understand the broader context of these values and the political aspirations to social reform dominant in the period when Swamigal wrote his plays.

In the early decades of the twentieth century, influential Tamil political reform movements such as the Justice Party, founded in 1916, allied with colonial rule against the ascendant forces of the Brahman-dominated Indian National Congress (Ramaswamy 1997, 28). The conflict was pitched as one between "an Aryan-Sanskritic-Brahman Hinduism which inevitably spelled doom for Tamil and its speakers in the emergent nation" and the other 97 percent of Tamilians who were non-Brahmans (Ramaswamy 1997, 29). Language was a main determining factor in these political allegiances: the pro-Tamil movement allied with English as the lesser of two evils, as against Sanskrit and Hindi, both of which were seen as the languages of northern imperialism.

By 1926 the Justice Party became the staging ground for the populist call for radical "rationalist" social reform made by Periyar E. V. Ramasami Naicker and his Self-Respect Movement. This led to the rise of the series of official Dravidian political parties that have defined Tamil politics ever since: the DK, the DMK, and the ADMK, which became the AIADMK.[13] All of these are divisively splintered factions of what began as the Dravidian movement in the early twentieth century, when "Dravidianism's fundamental agenda, of course, was to establish the absolute preeminence of Tamil in all spheres of life and being" (Ramaswamy 1997, 65). The complex political realities of aiming to be a proud, self-respecting Tamil-speaking state within a new postcolonial nation, however, engendered such convoluted strategies as the 1950s rallying cry "English Ever, Hindi Never!" that remains prominent among street graffiti in Tamilnadu today.

David Washbrook offers a fairly cynical take on the source of the alliance for the British:

> The entire historical and sociological theory upon which radical Dravidianism rested, of an Aryan conquest of the Dravidian South and the development of an institutional structure built to accommodate Aryan racial domination, is an invention of Evangelical Christian missionaries eager to stir revolt against the brahman priests whom they felt were their competitors. (Washbrook 1989, 214)

In any case, the British focus on the strength of indigenous Tamil literary achievement served the Tamil non-Brahman, Dravidian revivalist cause well:

> British perceptions of Tamil social history [were] that it was a past where an egalitarian society flourished before the Brahman invaders arrived from the north after the fifth century A.D. . . . "Non-Brahmans"—who claimed to be the indigenous inhabitants of the area—used these revivalist and nativist efforts

to claim that "modern" ideas and social institutions existed in the Tamil area long before the British arrived in India; in this way they did not have to accept "modern" (Western) institutions outright. (Irschick 1986, 4)

Thus was born the unlikely alliance between Tamil revivalism and the evangelical West. What, then, were the "modern" ideals on which both sides agreed? They were essentially the values spread by the Victorian social reform movements of the nineteenth century, in which British missionaries, liberal feminists, and elite educated Indians alike participated. At their base was a set of oppositional discourses aimed at exposing oppressive "communitarian" Hindu practices, such as child marriage, widow immolation (*sati*), and caste itself, counterposing them with more egalitarian ideals. The reform movements deployed modernity in an oppositional endeavor: they overtly opposed "traditions" thought to be barbaric, unjust, and oppressive with the egalitarian, just, and compassionate practices they attempted to mandate through governmental legislation.

Such reform movements opposed all that came to be understood and fixed under colonialism as Hindu religious community tradition. Legislation was initiated to ban sati as early as 1829; to sanction upper-caste widow remarriage in 1856; to prohibit child marriage by passing age-of-consent legislation beginning in 1861; to weed out immorality with the "anti-nautch" movement and its resulting "suppression of immoral traffic" legislation (begun earlier but not actually passed until 1946); to abolish untouchability and instate the Harijan right to enter temples through untouchability offense and temple reentry legislations; and to mandate government reservations of lower castes as part of the larger anti-Brahmin movement. Thus in Tamilnadu, modernity in its guise as the alternative to community and tradition became a cause uniting Dravidians and Englishmen, with Brahminic custom their mutual enemy.

It is in this context, then, that Swamigal's dramas were—and continue to be—celebrated by artists as conveying reformist ideals. According to many artists with whom I spoke, Swamigal's *Kovalan Kannaki* exposes the perils of child marriage; his *Sattiyavan Savitri* reinforces notions about the power of chastity; *Nandanar*, of course, argues for the Harijan right to enter temples; his scripting of *Valli's Wedding* stages forceful arguments by a young woman against polygamy. Many Special Drama artists, particularly actresses who play the lead roles in these dramas, feel that they have a personal stake in promoting the ideals celebrated by these dramas, as in their own lives they still suffer from many of the oppressive traditions such reforms oppose.

Onstage these actresses take pride in acting as mouthpieces for reformist ideals, many of which are broadly considered to have been won more than a century ago. Their performances point up how these issues continue to be relevant to their own social oppression as actors, and especially as actresses (see chapter 9).

Nevertheless there is a deep irony in the actors sangams' aligning themselves with reformist discourses as a means of attempting to raise the social status of stage artists, in that a good deal of the original early-twentieth-century reformers' zeal was focused on "purifying" the polity by purging "degraded" forms of theatrical entertainment. Particularly in debates associated with the anti-nautch legislation (Kannabiran 1995; Parker 1998; Marglin 1985; Gaston 1997; Erdman 1996), reformers were interested in restoring (which essentially meant entirely refashioning) Indian arts to their "pure" forms. Such cleansing of indigenous practices, like the temple dance of the Devadasis, resulted in the utter displacement of the original artists (Bruin 2001b; Weidman 2003), often by Brahmans who transformed the practice through entextualization and classicization into sanitized "classical" dance forms of Bharata Natyam and Odissi (Hansen 1992, 255). Indeed, throughout India, "the reformist discourse that resulted from the colonial experience pushed the theatre to the margins of respectability" (253).

It is no coincidence that the theatrical practices targeted by such cleanup measures were often the purview of female performers, given the power of the symbolic place Indian women held in reformist ideology. Satyajit Ray's two hauntingly feminist films *Devi* (1960) and *The Home and the World* (1992) beautifully capture middle-class Indian women's dilemmas during this period. The lives of middle-class women and working-class women were cleaved apart here, as "the struggle to represent ideal female behavior indeed accompanied the struggle of an emergent middle class" (Chatterjee 1993). The Indian woman whom the new Indian middle-class male desired, modeled on British standards of ideal womanly conduct, was the good housewife whose nemesis was the figure of the public, low-class female performer.

How did progressive Tamil statesmen, steeped in revivalist visions as well as in a critique of the depraved state of the Tamil arts, resolve this ideological conflict? In the reformist context of the early twentieth century, revivalists made the renewal of the art of Tamil drama one of their noble goals by resurrecting and then deploying the concept of *muttamiḻ* (three-Tamil). Muttamiḻ again uses an ancient precedent to link and rethink the arts of *iyal* (prose), *isai* (music), and *nāṭakam* (drama).

Reviving *muttamiḻ* allowed an already declared devotion to the Tamil language to function as a charter and injunction to replenish the three linked arts of classical Tamil culture. The actual historical origins of muttamiḻ are hazy; some historians have claimed ancient roots in the sangam age (second century B.C. to second century A.D.; see Arunachalam 1974), while others date the concept only from the seventeenth century (Varadarajan 1988). Saskia Kersenboom, a Dutch scholar who has recently investigated the concept of muttamiḻ and its implications across the Tamil arts, writes that "as early as the sixth century A.D. the Tamils defined their language as being threefold" (Kersenboom 1995, xvi).

Behind the concept of muttamiḻ lies a powerful notion of the ability of the Tamil language to embody divinity. Indeed, in the late sixth century, a Tamil poet-saint described the god Siva as "the One who has become *Muttamiḻ*" (6). Kersenboom clarifies: "The knowledge of Tamil, the words, the sound and its enactment instantiate the divine. . . . God incarnates into the threefold Tamil. The very utterance of Tamil is vibrant with divine presence and power" (ibid.).

Were drama to take up its rightful place in this triumvirate, it could be a divine expression of classical grace. However, instead of being the chiseled gem of expert artisans (also referred to, therefore, as "sanga-tamil"), popular professional drama was, as we have seen, caught "in the ugly hands of street-dancers" and mired in "the ordinary, everyday Tamil, spoken at home and in the market-place . . . [a] bent, uneven, crooked Tamil" (Kersenboom 1995, 6). That actors use the language of the everyday, of the ordinary people, on stages to entertain these same ordinary people, elicited nothing but chagrin and a righteous resolve to rectify the situation.

In the opening passage of his autobiography, T. K. Shanmugam characterizes how the drama world he entered in 1918 prompted his resolve in just these terms:

> It was a time when people said of drama artists, derogatively, "an actor is a man of no profession." Actors were called names like "street player" and "drunk." People wouldn't even rent an actor a house to live in, such a good reputation actors had. People were afraid he would kidnap their young women, and there was even some truth to the fear.
>
> Parents would not allow their children to watch the drama. It embarrassed the young children who did watch to hear what all was being said in front of everyone. And just opposite the theater hall, there would be a liquor shop.
>
> Yes; this shameful state existed in the very land whose own Tamil language engendered the tripartite concept of *iyal-isai-nātakam*. *It was a separate Tamil for*

drama in our land, such was the wretched state of the drama field at the time I entered the drama world! (Shanmugam 1972, 33; italics mine)

The stigma on actors is palpable here. Stage artists are so characterized by *lack* that even their profession is "no profession." Their performances embarrass those who watch, and this shame adheres to the whole field. The social problems of stage artists and the shameful state of their dramas are inseparably connected, a shame that manifests in a bastard language that will not partake in muttamiḻ but rather is its own debased tongue, "a separate Tamil."

Why Actors Stand Still: Onstage Movement as the Embodiment of Vulgarity

Understanding this discursive history helps us make sense of a question left unanswered. *I wondered at the first drama I saw: Why are these actors barely moving? How does such an oddly still theatrical style develop?* (See p. 21.)

The Special Drama convention of standing still to speak and sing is a literal embodiment of all the dominant discourses we have encountered that devalue and stigmatize what is recognized as a propensity to excess in the lower-class, professional actor. In response to over a century of such dismissive discourse, and in an attempt to embody an ideal of prestigious and ordered social behavior, most dramatic actors playing what are considered the serious and prestigious roles in Special Drama curtail all movement and fluidity in their performances. In scenes where artists play characters of high status who are thought to be above the expressive bodily behaviors enacted in the comedy scenes, excessive movement would read as lack of control; to index higher-status personages, actors barely move.[14]

Indeed, in onstage enactments of Special Drama today, different degrees, as well as different kinds, of physical movement are deemed appropriate for different persons. Simply put, persons of higher class and caste remain relatively still, while persons of lower class and caste move around to serve them. Exerting physical energy is a practice generally coded as lower-class in Tamilnadu, where, as in most societies, menial labor is demeaning. Generally in India this proclivity is carefully hierarchized: those who exert a good deal of physical energy do so appropriately only in the service of others who exert less. Risking a detour into ecological functionalism, I remind readers of the hot climate in Tamilnadu, a place where doing less means sweating less. Sitting at home staying cool and having others come to you is a mark of privilege and prestige. Class distinctions between those who expend much physical energy and those who expend less are quite pronounced and are abetted by caste divisions: the lowest menial jobs, like cleaning other people's toilets and other people's clothes, are still done by the "lowest" people, Paraiyars (whence the English word "pariah") and Dhobis (whence the name of a kitchen scouring sponge available on the U.S. market).

In the onstage roles played by Special Drama actors, such hierarchies of prestige, dependent on the status of different types of work and interactive behaviors, are further somaticized in a standard staging. Actors playing kings and queens (or gods and goddesses) are the heroes and heroines of Special Drama. They stand perfectly still before a central standing microphone to deliver prose speeches and sing poetic songs. Moreover, they do so in the cadences of formal Tamil. Artists playing lowly characters in the story and taking on the repertory roles of buffoons and dancers, on the other hand, cavort, dance, gesticulate loudly, and express all manner of emotions, all in the colloquial idioms of spoken Tamil.

In an article detailing the emergence of upper-caste women as performers of classical music on the South Indian stage in the early twentieth century, Amanda Weidman details similar effects of these same discourses on the musical arts. There they resulted in "the curiously disembodied voice" that continues to characterize acceptable feminine singing styles in Tamilnadu: "the ideal became a kind of performance of nonperformance; nothing visible was supposed to happen on the music stage" (Weidman 2003, 214). Onstage movement bears an inverse relation to prestige and to classicism for these female singers, as "ideals of chaste womanly behavior—not drawing attention to one's body or relying on physical charms—became a metaphor for a new kind of 'art'" that they were encouraged to attain (221).

And this new, softer style of "feminine" singing was defined in opposition to what else but the vulgar "shouting" of low-class actors and dancers. None other than the celebrated Tamil nationalist poet Subramania Bharatiyar recommended in 1909 that good middle-class family women who wanted to sing should "stay away from *nataka mettu* (drama tunes)], cheap songs with *koccai moli* (slang)" if they wanted to reclaim music as a respectable Tamil art (Bharatiyar [1909] 1981, 227–28; cited in Weidman 2003, 209).

In the early 1930s, appearing onstage at all was considered too damaging to a well-bred young woman's reputation, so Brahman female singers first sang only on gramophone recordings. This practice inaugurated a split between the voices of the respectable singer who remains behind the scenes and the disrespectable actress who appears onstage. This split endures in Tamil cinema today, as the songs to which onscreen actresses lip-sync and dance are dubbed by more respectable female background singers.

The introduction of the microphone in the 1930s allowed singers with softer voices to shine and simultaneously enacted a shift that critics of vulgar drama would approve of: "the shift from an earlier, higher-pitched style, accompanied by more gesturing, often referred to today as 'shouting,' to a lower-pitched, more introspective style" (Weidman 2003, 206). The standing microphone, in its very materiality as a fixed feature of the performance stage, "provides a kind of physical ballast for a singer . . . a range within which he or she can physically move" (206). Indeed, on the Special Drama stage Heroes and Heroines tether their own bid for moral standing to the upright standing mikes, never straying beyond their shadow.

Thus for those who must appear onstage there is a way to curtail the attendant disgrace of it by minimizing movement and concentrating instead on the voice. Ideas about language itself, then, contribute powerfully to a split between higher and lower characters onstage.

A hierarchy of onstage movement styles continues to exist within Special Drama. That hierarchy depends on a hierarchy of language use. Tamil is a diglossic language, meaning that its written and spoken forms diverge. Written Tamil in its "pure Tamil" form (*centamiḻ*, also *taṉittamiḻ*) is considered by many in the "land of Tamil" (Tamiḻnāṭu) to be the expression of a divine, originary, and classically beautiful language (Ramaswamy 1997). Tamil is considered pure when it is uncontaminated by the foreign etymological influences of past epochs of supposedly civilizing domination, either by Aryan Brahmans or colonial British, each of whom left a linguistic legacy, Sanskritic or English respectively, of loan words and hybrid derivatives. It is possible to read and speak such Tamil aloud, and those who do so are highly praised, both as virtuosic and as morally exemplary (Bate 2000).

However, in more common, informal speech, generally referred to as spoken Tamil (*pēccutamiḻ*), two common deviations from such exemplary language usage are usually made, primarily out of convenience. First, rather than carefully articulating and pronouncing each individual letter appearing in the written Tamil word, speakers lump sounds and even syllables together, bunching them up, collapsing and shortening them for ease of speech. (For example, instead of pronouncing each syllable in *maṉṉittukkoḷḷuṅkaḷ* [forgive me], spoken Tamil says *maṉṉishukoṅga*.) Such shortening is considered lazy; to speak Tamil well, students are taught that "the tongue must dance!" (and moreover it should be the only body part that does).

Second, and of more direct relevance to us here, spoken-Tamil speakers routinely and shamelessly employ expressions of mixed etymological origin. (In written Tamil, one can incorporate foreign loan words as well, but since the late-nineteenth- and early-twentieth-century politicization of the issue and the symbolic importance subsequently attached to maintaining the purity of the Tamil language, one tries not to, and as a result written Tamil tends to be far more self-conscious about incorporative practices than spoken Tamil.) There are convenient grammatical means for doing so. One is the substitution of a foreign noun for a Tamil one—"culture" instead of *paṉppāṭu*, for instance, as peppered Nagaraja Bhagavattar's speech in the conversation with which I began this book. Another is the addition of a Tamil verb meaning "make; do," through which almost any foreign action word can be converted for use as a Tamil verb: "type-paṇṇu," "wait-paṇṇu," even "shut-up-paṇṇu!" (Paramasivam and Lindholm 1980b, 157). Such etymological hybridization is considered impure, and therefore less worthy of the devotion to a "chaste" Tamil that characterized both the Tamil independence movement of the late nineteenth century and the early twentieth, and much of postindependence state politics (Ramaswamy 1997).

Any public Tamil speech that mixes foreign terms and concepts is regarded as undignified, or worse. The rhetoric of Maraimalai Adigal, the leader of the "pure Tamil" movement, strongly criticized those who could not or would not speak pure Tamil: "Defiling one's speech by mixing up with it extraneous elements simply indicates laxity of discipline, looseness of character, and lack of serious purpose in life" (Maraimalai Adigal [1925] 1980; quoted in Ramaswamy 1997, 146).

The harshness of this condemnation may seem surprising to those unfamiliar with the language politics of Tamilnadu (to which the best antidote is Sumathi Ramaswamy's excellent historical account of the years 1891–1970). During this period, Ramaswamy argues, the Tamil language grew to represent the land, the country, the lifeblood and soul, the mother, the ethnicity, and the identity of Tamilians. To "mix up with it extraneous elements" was tantamount to defilement.

Thus during this same period and thereafter, and always in this same charged context of a need to redefine Tamilness in the face of a foreign-born modernity, Special Drama artists struggle for respectability. Maraimalai Adigal's vituperative condemnation is echoed in the condemnatory discourses that greeted stage artists throughout the early decades of the twentieth century, making any actions that mix the Tamil self with a foreign other seem morally unworthy. People who "mix themselves up" in this way *lack discipline* and are *loose of character*—the same accusatory terms that we find used repeatedly to defame Special Drama artists by drama historians, and in turn by certain artists as well.

So it is that the condemnation of language mixing and a disdain for physical mobility come together in an overall devaluation of the overly expressive, mobile, and mixed aspects of artists' onstage lives. These same terms are used to condemn artists in their offstage lives as well, affecting everything from the ways they move through public space to kinship relations in their domestic lives, and from the codifications of the sangam rules and regulations to the purely orally transmitted system of terms and idioms that make up their secret argot.

Unsurprisingly, the same artists who physically move about most onstage use the most colloquial language: in both cases, these are the comic actors and actresses. One senior male Buffoon with whom I spoke made a telling little joke to express these connections between linguistic mixing, physical moving, and the vulgarity of Special Drama comedy today. We were discussing comedic styles in the heyday of Tamil drama. He held the opinion that these have degenerated since then. In the good old days, he said, a comedian would find a way to bring comedy appropriately into a scene, mixing it into dialogues that served to further the dramatic story. "Not like now," he said, "where it just mixes with the dancer!" This use of the verb "mix" (*kala*) has the sexual connotation of "to copulate," which here seems to anthropomorphize and prosthetically animate comedy itself; the comedian mixes his "comedy" with the dancer's female body. "Now in Special Drama, just for entertainment and so the village people will like it, they use *awkward* words, dirty words, *double-meaning* words, and all that."

The Stage Today

The same issues continue to stigmatize Special Drama artists today. Rather than the resurrection of Tamil natakam envisioned by revivalists at the height of the company era, the popular stage was instead translated into the new medium of film. The first Tamil films were essentially stage performances fixed on celluloid. "All the sixty-one films that were made in the first five years of the Tamil talkie were reproductions of successful plays staged by drama companies; and they were exact duplications of the stage show"

(Baskaran 2001, 78–79). The general attitude toward actors was duplicated in the new medium as well, as the elitist aversion to popular drama carried over to an elitist aversion to popular cinema (87).

Artists did gain some measure of increased respect in the heady days of the independence movement in the teens and nineteen twenties, when popular drama artists lent support to the freedom struggle by singing Tamil songs whose political double meanings escaped Raj censorship.[15] Tamil film historian Theodore Baskaran goes so far as to say:

> By entering the political arena, they [popular drama artists] suddenly gained in status. They found themselves at the centre of politics and came to enjoy a respectability they had not experienced before. They sat on political platforms along with well-known political leaders. Political activism was a route to respectability, something for which they had been yearning all these years. (Baskaran 2001, 82)

But the activism of popular drama artists in the nationalist freedom struggle, however proud it made them, did not end the stigma attached to their profession. And not all these artists left the stage for the studio in the 1930s with their political ideals, as Baskaran suggests.[16] While he recognizes that the actors sangam in Madurai was founded "with the aim of guiding the political involvement of the stage artists" in the freedom struggle, Baskaran does not recognize the continuing work of the sangam beyond that era. Primarily a film scholar, Baskaran's stated aim is to trace "the interaction between the stage, the film, and politics," a goal that necessarily interests him in the historical trajectory of company drama artists who went into film. (A fascinating trajectory indeed, as those stage artists who catapulted from the screen to the heights of political life inaugurated "the phenomenon of the filmstar-politician . . . in the social and political scenario of Tamilnadu in a manner that is unparalleled elsewhere in the world" [83].)

His is a restricted focus, however, that does not consider the lives of stage artists who continued on the stage and the ongoing politics of their lives. What forces shape the lives of artists who did not abandon the stage for the screen but rather continue to make popular theater? And how do these artists fit, not into the power realms of cine-superstardom and state politics in the capital, but into the grounded political life of rurban Tamilnadu? These questions animate the present work.

From Urban to Rurban

Special Drama now means outdoor, all-night performances, largely unscripted, wherein freelance artists, each hired specially for the event, meet onstage to enact repertory roles. In dramatic scenes they sing and debate extemporaneously, using key verses from the scripts of Swamigal's plays. In the comic scenes, they add dance and physical comedy to the mix. The degree to which they play up the one over the other style varies according to the tastes of the particular audience at each venue. Special Dramas have thus become events finely attuned to audience attitudes; such malleability is what gives Special Drama its *special* spicy mix, different from the *masala* that audiences can otherwise readily find elsewhere, fixed on celluloid.

Special Drama artists are people of roughly the same class as their audience. When they come onstage with their mix of everyday Tamil and their attempts at more formal verse—none of it particularly chiseled, or sanitized, but rather mixed up with English, Sanskritic, and Hindi influences, all of which reflect the lived history of this genre—artists present a range of everyday Tamil people and everyday Tamil voices familiar to their audience. The Tamil myths they present offer modern ideals, traditional values, poignantly nostalgic aspirations and, occasionally, tentatively resistant postures all in a performative social context that itself displays realities of rurban life in Tamilnadu.

Historians (and particularly film historians, it seems) often assume that rural venues and mythological subjects preclude the possibility of critical agency altogether. Baskaran, for example, laments the fact that in its early years Tamil cinema treated mythological subjects: "That the thematic content of most of these films was mythological, contributed in no small way to the beginning of an uncritical tradition; after all, can puranic presentations be subjected to criticism?" (Baskaran 1996, 12). Though this question is posed rhetorically, it nevertheless prompts one to ask, Well, why not? Why can't puranic presentations be subjected to criticism? Indeed, Special Drama audiences do it all the time. When they respond either with raucous laughter or shy giggles to a joke, when they call out appreciative responses to a performer during a contest of skills, when they selectively attend only portions of the drama, and even when they fall asleep during certain scenes, Special Drama audiences register their responses in ways that performers can read loud and clear.

Similarly, many critics assume that mythological dramas are ahistorical and timeless. Certainly not, especially when we recognize the efforts of playwrights like Swamigal to modernize them, and add to that the extemporaneous "modernizations" effected on these plays by the performers themselves.

It is nevertheless true that village audiences lack some of the cultural capital of urban audiences. The diminishing social status of their audience is one of the changes lamented by senior artists like A. K. Kaleeswaran and P. S. Nagaraja Bhagavattar, both of whom remember the idealism of the company era. As Nagaraja Bhagavattar put it: "These days all *stage discipline* is gone. So how can we call this drama? Then it is only terukkūttu. That is why they have classified this now under *village arts*. In those days, highly respected people in society—judges, and intellectuals—used to watch our plays."

These elders in the field fear that the urban-to-rurban trajectory taken by Special Drama will mean the art form itself regresses to an inconsequential "street play," in their words "mere *kūttu*." Shaped by the days when elite accusations of its vulgarity made *kūttu* a bad word, they lament the "village" tenor in Special Drama, fearing that history will cycle backward and drama will revert to a rough-hewn village art.

In the reminiscences of such senior male artists, the golden era of drama appears as a time when the art itself was respectable: all-male, company educated and trained, and therefore highly disciplined, essentially on the brink of cosmopolitanism. Indeed, the composite picture conjured by Messrs. Kaleeswaran and Bhagavattar is a timeline that looks something like this: first there was street drama (terukkūttu). Then drama teachers came and formed companies, and all was good. Then the companies split up, and women and villagers increasingly entered the field. Their influence, and the influence of illiterate village audiences, are now causing the art form to degenerate into kūttu again.

Such a reconstructionist history is of course highly revisionist—women began performing in drama during the company era itself, not when it ended, for example—and apocalyptically overstated. But what cannot be easily dismissed in such a revisionist account is what it reflects of its tellers' concerns: such accounts give us a sense of the kinds of social markers about which senior male artists like these two care a good deal. Steeped their whole lives in the field of popular Tamil drama and the discourses that surround it, elders like Mr. Kaleeswaran and Mr. Bhagavattar (both of whom have held important elected positions in the acting community) have continued to pass such attitudes on to subsequent generations of Special Drama artists. In particular, their notions about artists' need for increased discipline have largely come to define the terms in which the actors sangam, as the "official" arm of the community, organizes itself.

In practice, the hybrid, rurban theatrical form of Special Drama today is a mix of aesthetic and cultural influences that resists reduction into any single narrative characterization. The form exceeds the interpretive constraints applied to it, being more successful in its improvisational responsiveness to audiences than anyone foretold. It succeeds, ironically, in good part because of the extent to which artists and audiences alike share dismissive, moralistic attitudes about the genre and its artists. Such attitudes were bred in the sociohistorical narratives of exclusion traced here.

These narratives are also condensed in the two-dimensional visual form of drama notices. The next chapter looks specifically at the changing form of these material icons of the genre. There the development of Special Drama from a commercial theater under company management to the full-blown rurban ritual performance phenomenon it is today emerges clearly and colorfully. Chapter 2 moves us through this history and squarely into the organization of Special Drama today.

2 Prestige Hierarchies in Two and Three Dimensions

Drama Notices and the Organization of Special Drama

Drama notices are ephemeral icons. They are usually printed on the cheapest, flimsiest paper available—the same grade of colored paper used for public bus tickets in India, quite thin but pulpy, and with a slightly gritty grain—whose very materiality evokes the fleeting nature of the onetime event. Designed to announce and advertise, and charged with communicating the specific details of personnel, content, and context, these records of planned performance events crammed with written and visual information testify to the specific range of variables at play in any Special Drama production.

Expectations of fragility notwithstanding, the body of drama notices that have survived intact for well over a century now offer an important historical and material record of the transformations in Special Drama since its beginnings in the late nineteenth century. Having established this historical trajectory, I will use contemporary drama notices as my entree into talking about the structure of Special Drama performances today. The formal resemblance that the layout of drama notices bears to the layout and use of the Special Drama stage is striking and provides an eloquent means to begin discussing the hierarchies of prestige and power that characterize contemporary Special Drama.

The range of social and economic relations of production active in Special Drama includes the labor of artists and agents, the patronage of audiences, and the service of professionals who cater to the specific theatrical needs of the genre. Meanwhile the design of Special Drama notices arranges all these relations in and around five main positions: four corners and the center of the visual and spatial field. These five positions demarcate prominent use areas in both the drama notice and the dramatic event, placement within which identifies salient prestige distinctions among the players.

The history of Tamil drama notices begins in 1891, along with the history of modern Tamil drama itself.[1] The collection of historical drama notices at the Roja Muthiah Research Library (RMRL), Chennai, begins here and ends at 1964.[2] To carry the historical narrative conveyed by drama notices into the present, I draw in this chapter on three sources: (1) the RMRL archive, (2) my own collection of drama notices from 1991 to 2001, and (3) select notices from 1954 to 1988 in the private collections of Special Drama artists.[3] The ensuing discussion is thus able to trace both the historic development of notices and the meanings conveyed by their contemporary form.

Early Drama Notices, 1891–1926

The form of the drama notice (*nōṭṭīs*) has changed significantly since it first appeared in Tamilnadu in the late nineteenth century. At first a vertical layout was the prevailing printing convention, as in the 1891 notice printed at Chidambaram (fig. 5) in which the pertinent details of date (Wednesday, 15 April 1891) and drama (the mythic story of *Rukmāngatu*) are penciled in by hand onto a preprinted form. Such a practice was possible because company dramas, such as the production of the Sarvajanarejna Lakshmi Vilasa Sabha announced here, played for an extended run at one auditorium in one locale. Thus details were suitably consistent to allow for bulk printing of a relatively generic form.

In sharp contrast to later notices, the textual material in this early drama notice primarily concerns audience behavior rather than that of performers. It is also quite concerned with ticket details. The single-line second paragraph informs readers that ladies will have a separate place in the fourth class, for which separate tickets will be available. The next paragraph notes that the smoking of cigars and the use of intoxicating substances in the auditorium are forbidden, and there will be no admittance for Harijans (referred to here as *pañcamarkaḷ*, or "persons of the fifth class"). For those of acceptable caste and gender, the following options are available: first-class "easy chair" (*īsi chēr*) tickets costing one rupee; second-class chair tickets costing eighty paise; third-class "bench" (*peñci*) tickets for sixty paise; and fourth-class floor, only thirty paise.

A quarter century later, circa 1917, drama notices are still being laid out vertically (figs. 6–8)—indeed, are often quite long, 45 by 15 cm, 44 by 15 cm, and 58 by 23 cm, respectively—but much has changed. The text is filled with information about the play, and particularly about the players. The particulars that concern audience attendance are relegated to the very

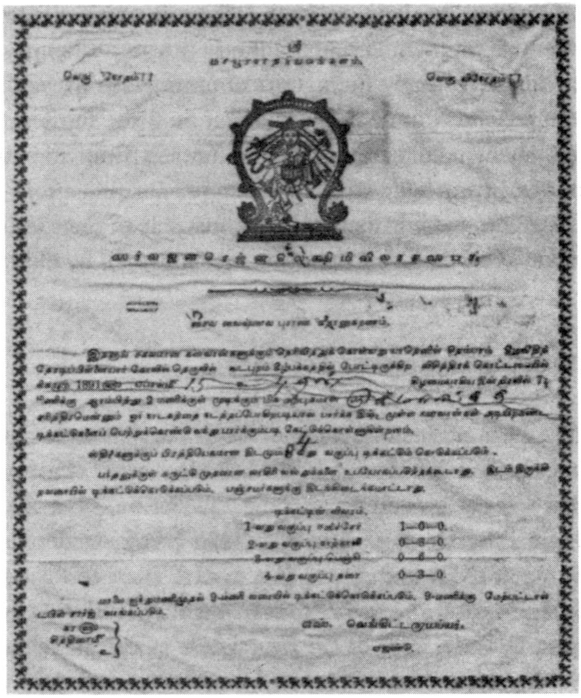

5 Drama notice, 1891. Roja Muthiah Research Library collection, Chennai, India.

bottom of the 1917 notice from Karaikkudi (fig. 6) and include two more classes of ticket: first-class "reserved chair," second-class "chair," third-class "bench," fourth-class floor, fifth-class ladies' floor, and sixth-class mat. No one is explicitly forbidden entrance, and the audience is simply enjoined to remain calm and quiet.

Featured artists become a key advertising draw during this early-twentieth-century period. The large boldface font toward the top of the same notice (fig. 6) reads "Tonight! Tonight! Come! Come see! Two Streeparts! Two Streeparts!" "*Streepart*" ("*Stirīpārṭ*") refers to the role of the dramatic Heroine. The word is a hybrid compound that joins the etymologically Sanskrit word *Stirī*, "lady," with the Tamilized English loan word *pārṭ*, as in a theatrical role or part. The names of the two actresses playing Heroines are given just below this large-font text, P. Vadivāmbāl and T. M. Kamalavēni. The male lead artist doubles as the company manager, as indicated just beneath the two actresses' names. He is M. G. Bhairava Suntaram Pillai, *māṉējmeṇṭ* for the Madurai Nayaki Royal Theatrical Nadaka Company. This title is essentially an amalgamation of all the period buzzwords signaling drama. Faith in the power of repetition in advertising is also apparent in the reiteration of the names of the two female leads in large type running along the right side of the notice, this time with the added descriptor "Parsi Miss P. Vadivāmbāl." The only other large print on the notice names the venue (the city of Karaikkudi) and the play (*Kovilavan Nadakam*).

Using the layout of the typeset notice to represent the centrality of featured artists to the drama has become a hallmark of drama notices. In this early period the strategy was textual. The notice printed in Madurai around 1918 (fig. 7), for example, trumpets "a new Rajapart."[4] "*Rajapart*" ("*Irājapārṭ*"), the Tamil term for the male dramatic hero, is a compound that is etymologically comparable to its feminine paired term. *Irāja* means king in Sanskrit, and is here again joined with the English loan word "part." The exclamatory text at the top of the notice reads: "He's come! He's come! Who? Who?? Who??? New Rajapart Hindustani poet K. M. Dharmalingam Pillai," who, according to the first line of text beneath his name, has come *speshalāy* to sing in this drama. In this production, "Parsi P. Vadivāmbāl" appears as the heroine Valli in the play *Valli's Wedding* (*Vaḷḷi Tirumaṇam*).

Valli's Wedding has long been the most popular play in the Special Drama repertory. Swamigal's script dramatizes the marriage of Lord Murugan (a deity widely revered in Tamilnadu as the god of the Tamil language, as well as of youth and beauty) to his second, Dravidian wife, Valli. In this early notice, the single word "Valli" stands out in enormous font at its center. The centrality of this play to the genre of Special Drama has endured into the present. *Valli's Wedding* is now the signature piece of Special Drama in the Madurai district, to the point where the name of the play is now almost interchangeable with the genre itself. For example, on my most recent visit to Madurai in 2001, an actress who had recently taken part in the filming of a drama staged in Chennai for television broadcast reported that there "they won't know what you mean by the term 'music drama' [Icai Nāṭakam], they might think you mean classical dance-drama or something, and not until you say *Valli* will they know that you mean Special Drama and all that." (A similar transference of the heroine's name from its most popular drama to the name of a theater genre itself occurred in North India with Nautāṅki; see Hansen 1992, 13, 309.)

Many notices from this early-twentieth-century period similarly foreground the word "who" (*yār*), often punctuating it with exclamation points instead of question marks. The emphatic point here is clearly the interest an audience is expected to register in an ever-changing artistic cast. A 1918 notice put out by the Parsi Boys Manamokana Nataka Sabha Company reads:

காரைக்குடியில் ஆட்டம்.

இன்றிரவு! இன்றிரவு!

வாருங்கள்! வந்துபாருங்கள்!

இரண்டு ஸ்திரீபார்ட் இரண்டு ஸ்திரீபார்ட்

P. வடிவாம்பாள் & T. M. கமலவேணி.

M. G. வைரவசுந்தரம் பிள்ளையவர்கள்.

மதுரை தாயிசி ராயல் தியேட்ரிகல்

நாடகக் கம்பெனியாரால்,

காரைக்குடி ... இன்றிரவு 9-30 மணிமுதல் ...

கோவிலவன் நாடகம்.

விசேஷக் குறிப்பு

டிக்கட்டுகளின் விபரம்.

ROJA MUTHIAH
KOTTAIYUR—623 106

ROJA MUTHIAH
KOTTAIYUR—623 106

காரைக்குடியில் ஆட்டம்.

வந்துவிட்டார்! வந்துவிட்டார்!!

யார்? யார்?? யார்???

புதிய இராஜபார்ட் இந்துஸ்தான் கவாய்

K. M. தருமலிங்கம்பிள்ளை

இன்றிரவு! நன்றிரவு!

சமரச தர்த்தன

சௌந்தர ராஜ சபா

நாடகக் கம்பெனியாரும்

இன்றிரவு 9-30 மணி முதல் ...

வள்ளி

புதிய இராஜபார்ட் இந்துஸ்தான் கவாய் K. M. தருமலிங்கம்பிள்ளை

ஸ்திரீபார்ட்

பார்ஸி P. வடிவாம்பாள்...வள்ளிநாயகி

டிக்கட் விபரம்

6 (*left*) Drama notice for *Kovilavan Natakam*, 1917. Roja Muthiah Research Library collection, Chennai, India.
7 (*middle*) Drama notice for *Valli* [1918?]. Roja Muthiah Research Library collection, Chennai, India.
8 (*right*) Drama notice for *Alli Rani*, with English words, 1917. Roja Muthiah Research Library collection, Chennai, India.

"They've come. They've come. Who! Who!! Who!!!" Such notices straddle with obvious expressive gusto a fine line between Special Drama and sabha (company) drama. Featured appearances by new artists and even not-so-new artists (namely, the "Parsi Miss" P. Vadivambal who appeared on two notices for the same venue under two different company banners) do not preclude such productions from claiming to be company drama. Such artifacts add to my overall sense that many of the so-called companies of this era were entities that functioned with considerable reliance on a pool of freelance artists, that is, functioned essentially as Special Drama.

One 1917 notice printed in Karaikkudi (fig. 8) introduces a young actor who went on to achieve considerable fame. S. G. Kittappa (1906–1933) is remembered for his sweet singing voice as "one of the brightest luminaries of the Tamil stage" (Baskaran 1981, 38). Just above the large-font English words "To Night! ALLIRANI" (a play about the matriarchal queen of ancient Madurai, Queen Alli), the notice announces the actor's tender young age as seven. Kittappa would actually have been aged ten or eleven at this time, but the exaggeration of his youthfulness is in keeping with the appeal of child actors in this era of boys companies.[5]

The notice serves as well to introduce the reader to the blend of English and Tamil language text that frequently characterizes notices of this early period. English concepts and aesthetics shot through the hybrid genres of Tamil theater performed on stages across the state during the early twentieth century. Here the injunction to "Miss not this Golden Opportunity" notes "efficient actors, excellent play, wonderful scenes, [and] excellent songs" as the event's attributes. The legacy of such an incorporation of English words and theatrical concepts endures in the language that Special Drama artists still use to discuss the life of the Tamil stage.

The Photograph Enters Notices, 1926–1936

The introduction of photographic plates into the drama notice in 1926 ushered in a period of formal experimentation in notice design. This period eventually resulted in the unusual design form that distinguishes Special Drama notices today, an early version of which first appeared in 1936. The changes begun in this period include a shift to a standard-size paper measuring 23 by 29 cm (or 8.5″ by 11″) (figs. 9–11), the use of a horizontal layout format (figs. 11, 12, 14), and the addition of photographic images of artists (figs. 9–12 and 14).

While researching the historical development of the form in 2001, I asked

9 Drama notice for *Rajendran Natakam*, "with artists trained by T. T. Sankaradas Swamigal," 1926; vertical notice with plates and text. Roja Muthiah Research Library collection, Chennai, India.

a contemporary printer of Special Drama notices about the now-standard layout of drama notices and its history. This second-generation printer, a man of about fifty whose family has been in the business of printing notices since the mid-twentieth century, wasn't sure when the use of photographic plates or the switch to a horizontal format for notices began, as both predated his own experience. He guessed, however, that the horizontal layout began with the use of photographic plates for pragmatic reasons: in his experience, text and photos fit better on the horizontal page, or as he put it, "You can fit more that way."

There is, however, no inherently better quantitative fit between text and photos arranged in horizontal rather than vertical layout (for a good counterexample, see fig. 9). The printer's experience most clearly bespeaks just how naturalized the standard format for drama notices has become among those engaged in its production, perhaps because the aesthetic choices that became standard in drama notices so successfully map a three-dimensional phenomenon onto a two-dimensional form.

Let us look more closely at the experimental stages leading to this now-standard form. The 1926 Pudukkottai notice (again, fig. 9) employs three full-length photographic images of artists, pictured onstage and in costume. The top two photos are single-subject portraits. The Rajapart is pictured in the top left corner, the Streepart in the top right. All the artists are male, and the Streepart is played by one of the TKS brothers, T. K. Muttusami, appropriately cross-dressed in this photo.[6] The central bottom photograph pictures three artists together onstage. Photographs of group action were quickly abandoned in drama notices in favor of single-subject photographs, as individual artists became a primary draw.

A similarly vertically oriented notice using three photographic plates, from roughly the same period but printed in Madras (fig. 10), pictures all artists singly. In *Kovalan*, the drama advertised here, there are two Streepart roles, Mathavi and Kannaki, and the actresses playing these roles are identified beneath their respective photographs. Each artist is again pictured in costume and onstage. Note that the pictured artists are the three leading heroic characters of the drama. The convention of picturing the lead dramatic actors began immediately with the introduction of photography into drama notices and continues to this day. Images of comedic actors were included only later, always as an addition to, and never a substitute for, photographs of the dramatic leads.

There is one highly unusual feature in this Madras notice, however: it advertises a Tamil play entirely in English. Such a full-scale use of English could probably occur only on a notice printed in Madras, where enough people knew enough English to make this an effective advertisement.

The first intimation of what would become the enduring form for the layout of photographs in Special Drama notices appears instead in an all-Tamil notice printed in Madras in 1928 (fig. 11). This is the earliest notice in the RMRL archive to present a photograph of the harmonist, the leader of the orchestra. All music drama performances have live musical accompaniment. (Music drama, recall, is the larger genre of which Special Drama is a colloquially named subset, of which this notice is an excellent example: "Special Actors! Special Dramas!!" is the proud boast of the central box of text in this notice.) The harmonist is here pictured beside his instrument, a foot-pedal bellows harmonium. The addition of his image and its central placement are both significant. Rajapart and Streepart remain in the top two corners of the notice, while the harmonist's placement in relation to

10 Undated Madras drama notice for *Kovalan*; vertical with plates and English text. Roja Muthiah Research Library collection, Chennai, India.

11 Drama notice for *Valli's Wedding*, announcing "Special Actors! Special Dramas!!" 1928; horizontal, harmonist plate center. Roja Muthiah Research Library collection, Chennai, India.

them — centrally between them in a mediating relation — represents well his central position in the drama itself. In addition to providing instrumental accompaniment, harmonists are also "backup singers" (*pinpāṭṭukkararkal*) who effectively shadow each and every artist who sings onstage; because the harmonist has such a centrally mediating role, artists say a drama can only be as good as its harmonist.

The central placement of the harmonist on this early notice may also reflect his actual position on the professional drama stage during this period. Unlike today, when the musicians sit together as a group at stage right in full view of the audience as they interact with performers throughout the night (see chapters 4–6), the musicians' placement onstage in the early decades of the twentieth century seems to have been otherwise:

> Originally the musicians were placed on one side of the stage behind a screen, but as the musicians gained more notoriety it became customary to place the harmonium player on stage in full view of the audience. The most famous of the harmonium players (most of whom were also accomplished vocalists as well) were often placed at center stage as the key figures around which the entire performance revolved. (Hughes, n.d.)

It is unknown whether such a central placement of the harmonist onstage endured for any length of time. However, the convention of placing his representative image centrally on drama notices grew increasingly strong over the course of the century, although during this early period drama notices had not yet settled into a definitive model. Another notice from 1928 (fig. 12), printed in Trichy, pictures its star artist to the exclusion of any other artists. The large boldface text across the top of this horizontally printed notice reads "Mister S. G. Kittappa." Eleven years after a notice in which he was a child draw (fig. 8), Kittappa's full-blown star-of-the-stage status is here reflected in a notice that uses a single, full-length photo of him, cross-dressed, as the lead in *Sri Andal's Wedding*.

And again, in a 1931 notice printed in Karaikkudi (fig. 13), we find a kind of formal throwback in a notice for a performance of *Valli's Wedding*, boldly announced in the top line as a "Special Drama," that uses a vertical layout with no photos at all. Like notices from an earlier period, this notice is printed on nonstandard, narrow paper just 14 cm wide by 23 cm long. The drama also stars "Mister S. G. Kittappa," this time in the Rajapart role; the artist unfortunately died just two years hence, at age twenty-seven.

Many other notices in the RMRL collection from the period between 1926 and 1936 use photographs. These picture Rajaparts, Streeparts, and occasionally harmonists, primarily photographed singly, full-length, in costume

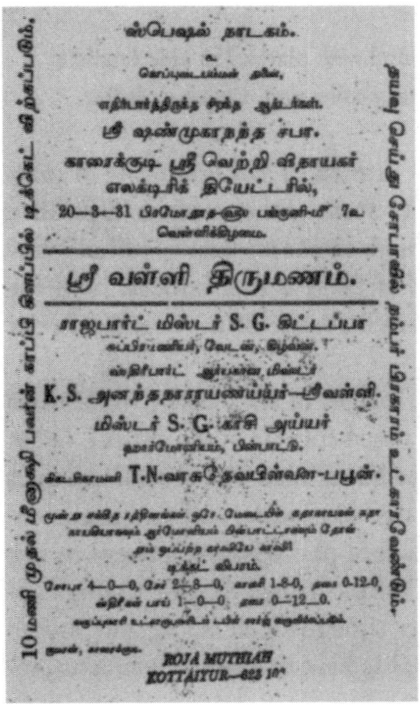

12 Mr. S. G. Kittappa as Sri Andaal in drama notice for *Sri Andaal's Wedding*; horizontal notice, 1928. Roja Muthiah Research Library collection, Chennai, India.

13 Drama notice for *Valli's Wedding* announced as a "Special Drama," 1931; vertical with no plates. Roja Muthiah Research Library collection, Chennai, India.

14 Drama notice for *Pavalakodi*, 1936; horizontal with plates, left side English, right side Tamil. Roja Muthiah Research Library collection, Chennai, India.

and onstage. Two of these notices, both printed in Madurai—one in 1929, the other in 1934—substitute half or bust photos of the actors in the leading roles for the usual full-length shots, though the harmonist is still pictured full-length beside his instrument. None of these earlier notices, however, really prepares one for the full-blown, original style of the oversize notice printed in Madurai in 1936 (fig. 14).

This notice features the photographic images of six artists (two of them twice, their photographs repeated in the upper corners of the notice), rather than only the two dramatic leads and the harmonist. The central group of four photographs portrays the Rajapart, two Streeparts, and the harmonist. The very new addition here is the inclusion of photographic images of two comic actors. Both are male; the list of comic artists for this drama confirms that all the comic artists were male. Though small in size and pushed to the extreme bottom corners, nevertheless here they are: comedians pictured on a drama notice for the first time.

Another striking shift made in this notice is that the artists' images are all uniformly pictured in head-and-shoulder portraits, including the harmonist. They are photographed in full-face, or else slightly three-quarters angled poses. While some appear to be in costume (though suit and tie could equally be daily wear), yet they do not seem to be onstage. The backgrounds of the photographs are empty; these are likely studio portraits. With the name of each artist set squarely beneath his or her image, in a separately boxed frame, individual identification is clearly a primary aim of the layout. The sudden camera shift in to close-ups of the artists' faces seems to bring us closer as well, emphasizing the availability of individual artists to the viewer's scrutiny. As such, it hooks into the advertised appeal of the genre: each artist is appearing specially, "Come see! Tonight only! One and only Special Drama!"

This design captured the spirit of the event in a way that stuck. All subsequent drama notices similarly employ individual artists' photos in head-and-shoulder portrait poses, arrayed across a horizontal landscape in pointed placement, interspersed with written denotational text.

Oversize in a horizontal rather than a vertical layout (29 cm high by 45 cm wide), this 1936 Madurai notice does double duty textually as well as visually. The notice is printed in Tamil on the right side, with (roughly) the same information repeated, through translation and transliteration, in English on the left.[7] This presentation suggests that a hybrid Anglo-Tamil mentality still infused the drama world even at this relatively late date in the independence struggle.

On multiple fronts, then, this 1936 Madurai notice represents a major leap into the formal style that characterizes Special Drama notices today. It marks the end of the period of photographic experimentation in drama notices, and the beginning of a midcentury transition that led directly to the current form. Before discussing midcentury notices, however, I pause here to consider the hold of the English language on the drama world. These linguistic considerations serve simultaneously to introduce the reader to two Special Drama actresses who figure prominently throughout the remainder of this book.

English in the Vocabulary of Special Drama Artists: Jansirani and Sivakami

In the early decades of the twentieth century, the heyday of company drama, India was still under British rule, and there was a good deal of English to be heard in Madras state. English was particularly entrenched in Madras city, the state capital. Even after independence was won in 1947, and even after

Tamil was made the official language of the state in 1956, and the official medium of instruction in the university (1961), English remained the language of everyday life in the city. A commentator on the situation in 1965 wrote:

> In Madras city, English dominates our life to an extraordinary extent. . . . Corporation property tax, electric consumption and water tax bills are only in the English language; all communications of the Collector are in English; in virtually all trade, including the smallest consumer goods, bills, receipts, etc. are made out in the English language. I think it will be no exaggeration to say that a person can live for years in Madras without learning a word of Tamil.[8] (Kumaramangalam, in Ramaswamy 1997, 61)

During the company era, the linguistic registers of the theater world were particularly redolent with terms that reflected the influence of traveling British and Parsi theatrical troupes on Tamil drama. The influence was strongest on the amateur drama sabhas located in Madras city itself, but extended to companies operating throughout the state, as we have seen in drama notices from Karaikkudi and Madurai as well as Madras (figs. 8, 11, and 15). Notices often contained a good deal of English vocabulary, sometimes transliterated into Tamil, but equally often not. One senior artist recalled that during the 1930s, organizers would occasionally have to find someone in the audience who could read English to read out the notice on the auditorium stage, as the artists themselves could not. Regardless of their inability to read it, however, artists were familiar with the English words so often used to characterize their artistic world.

This legacy has been inherited by Special Drama artists today. The dramatic culture contact of the colonial period lives on in a Tamil theatrical vocabulary that is, at least among the Special Drama community, still liberally peppered with English loan words. I first compiled a list of these words a year into my fieldwork. Throughout that year, the Special Drama actress N. Jansirani, the music composer R. Baby Natarajan, and their two teenage daughters Viji and Kavitha had untiringly helped me augment my Tamil vocabulary. One day Jansirani, who is a monolingual Tamil speaker, remarked that she would like someday to speak with me in English. I replied that she had a good start, as she already knew so many English words. She looked skeptical. I compiled the following list of some thirty-odd English words used regularly by Special Drama artists, first, then, to convince Jansirani. This was my list:

> Act, scene, scene setting, notice, photo, light, mike, electricals, trick shot, company, boys company, special, hero, heroine, villain, all-round, buffoon-

comic, dance-comic, dance duet, drama, dialogue, acting, comedy, agent, gents, ladies, amateur, social, advance, ticket, party, costume.

The failure of this list to convince Jansi of anything proved most educational for me rather than her. For even after I read it, Jansi remained unconvinced by my claim that these were, at least originally, English words. Only then did I begin to realize how, in a very real, lived sense for Jansirani and others who, like her, share a background of lifelong engagement in this rurban theater form and only minimal formal education (like many artists I interviewed, Jansi's formal schooling ended at the fourth standard), these are *not* English words and never were. Even for those artists who might be aware of their etymological roots, these words are no longer strictly English; their semiotic context has entirely changed, and they are part of a different grammar and logic now as fully assimilated loan words.[9]

Is there nevertheless still an aura of historical foreignness, an embedded history of culture contact, that clings palpably to these words, such that even when spoken by a monolingual Tamil speaker like Jansirani, they are notably somehow special words, to which some prestige attaches, belonging specially to this theatrical world with its hybrid cultural history? (Or would a similar quality of specialness adhere to the highly specialized words of any professional register, for example, the specifying words a plumber uses to discuss plumbing, or a banker banking, regardless of their etymological origins?)

Drama artists clearly do use these words with that special proprietary relationship that experts in any field have toward the words that name key elements of their working lives. They take pride in expertise over their linguistic register. The historical particularity of this linguistic register, however, additionally partakes of the prestigious historical particularity of English in India, which has everything to do with the fact that English was the language of the elite during British rule. Recall the sublimely succinct phrasing of Bharati Mukherjee's description: "To want English was to want more than you had been given at birth, it was to want the world" (Mukherjee 1989, 61).

When India was under British rule, the command of English—itself the language of command, as Barney Cohn (1988) forcefully reminds us—was prized and also served to land prize jobs for those in the know. Something of this prestige remains a reality in Tamilnadu today, regardless of the prideful Tamil language focus of the Dravidian movement, and regardless of the official end of British rule and the adoption of Hindi as India's national language. "English Ever, Hindi Never!" has remained among the more ubiquitous graffiti on Tamil streets for over half a century, and many Tamilians still take pride in an English made their own. Even for those who, like Jansirani, do not know their etymological roots, these assimilated words, spoken with pride and prestige—indeed, habitually coated with them—get taken up as prestigious words to which a historical aura does still cling.

But of course, quite apart from such commonalties of usage, each artist's relationship to the Englishness of these words (and for that matter to the larger issue of the hybridity of the genre) differs. What is complex and interesting in a community as diverse as that of Special Drama artists is how English language usage and understanding is a particular mix for each artist, a mix that bespeaks the larger political and highly classed world in which he or she lives.

To exemplify the range of linguistic experiences among artists, I want to introduce another Special Drama actress whose relationship to the field of Tamil drama compares tellingly with Jansi's. Her name is Sennai Sivakami. It is her costumed image that graces the cover of this book. In 1990, when Sennai Sivakami, an actress from Madras, took this lovely alliterative stage name to enter the field of Special Drama in Madurai, "Chennai" was not yet the official name of that city. "Sennai," however, was always the city's Tamil name and thus the word one Tamilian might use to another to invoke the city as possessed of a Tamilness that Madras, as we have seen, has not always had. Ironic, really, because by affixing "Sennai" to her stage name, the actress signaled to those in the rurban field of Special Drama that she comes from the big city but speaks of it as they might, an appeal that launched her into popularity as a Streepart on rurban stages.

On the first day I interviewed Sivakami, our conversation was fast and fluid. She spoke about her life in Madras before moving to Madurai, of her current life in Madurai, and of the differences she perceived between these two worlds. We agreed that Madurai and Madras were like different countries; she said, "the Special Drama *type* here in Madurai is one thing, and the Madras drama *type* is another thing entirely. It's very difficult for artists from here to work there, and *vice versa*." Our talk was peppered with English words not belonging to my original list of those canonical to the Special Drama genre. In the course of our talk, Sivakami included words such as *formality*, *prestige*, *type*, *reaction*, *presence of mind*, and *second marriage*.

Though she was only in her early forties, hers was the kind of English usage I had previously encountered only among senior male artists in the field, artists who had themselves lived through the heady hybrid theatrical era of the 1920s, including harmonist A. K. Kaleeswaran and Rajapart P. S. Nagaraja Bhagavattar. But Sivakami was from Madras, not from the rurban spread of the contemporary Special Drama heartland, and that seems to have made all the difference.

Many Madrasis speak fluent English. Or more precisely, fluent Indian-English. Sivakami does not. However, as her own comment indicates, Madras (now Chennai) is a different world from Madurai. Madrasis are still surrounded by far more English speech than Tamilians who live in other towns and cities in Tamilnadu, regardless of government-instigated projects to Tamilize the city. Madrasis generally know when they are using English words and are aware of code switching when they do so. Code switching and hybridity make everyday sense there, and people can play a thing both ways, or move from the big city to a smaller town and back again. For Jansirani, however, Madurai is home, is where she was born and raised, and Special Drama is her whole theatrical world, in which *light* and *mike* are not, and never were, English words.

The differences of experience between these two actresses are clearly affected not only by the language the world uses to describe them but also by the language they use to describe it.

Midcentury Notices and Artists, 1942–1964 (M. K. Kamalam)

The drama notices of the midcentury represent a world of Special Drama that organizes its own representations in a particular way. The notices of this period have fully switched to Tamil language only, occluding the genre's hybrid origins in English and Parsi theatrical models and instead reflecting a new hybridity of borrowings and sharings between the stage and the burgeoning world of Tamil cinema. Such a shift is visible not only in the two-dimensional representations of notices but on the three-dimensional stage itself: "While the popular stage of the 1930s served as the model for the early Tamil films, twenty years later it was the Tamil film, and in particular its songs, acting style, and camera techniques, which were widely imitated by the rural theatre" (Bruin 2001a, 61). During this midcentury period, the drama world both shares in conventions of the cinema world and, increasingly, carves out a different terrain for itself.

A 1942 Madurai notice (fig. 15) from the RMRL collection is a welcome example. As an index of the links between the stage and cinema fields at this time, this notice prioritizes, both visually and in its written text, two stage artists who are simultaneously popular cinema artists: V. A. Chellappa

15 Drama notice for *Sangeetha Kovalan*, 1942. With artists V. A. Chellappa Aiyar, T. S. Durairaj, G. R. Sri Ramulu, S. V. Vasudeva Nayar, and M. K. Kamalam. Roja Muthiah Research Library collection, Chennai, India.

Aiyar, playing the Rajapart role, and T. S. Durai Raj, playing the role of the Second Hero.

Accordingly, the photographic images of Rajapart, Streepart, and Second Hero artists are in the top half of the notice, and as we are already coming to expect, comic artists occupy its lower half. The harmonist's picture, in a deviation from the developing norm, is placed in the lower left corner, probably having been displaced by the plate of the celebrated cine-actor playing the Second Hero role. As if in compensation for this demotion to the visual rank of the comic actors (for the positioning of artists' photos in the lower or upper halves of the notice does convey rank), the harmonist's name is inset in boldface beneath his photo, the only artist on the notice to be so singled out for identification. All the artists appear again in head-and-shoulder poses, studio portrait style. Each artist's image appears in an oval frame surrounded by a linear frame, except in the case of the Rajapart, whose portrait fills the rectangular block.

This particular notice provides a useful illustration not only of the formal organization of drama notices in this period but also of some behind-the-scenes workings of the world of Special Drama. This aspect of the archival function of drama notices relies on privileged and contextualized knowledge. This layer of documentation was pointed out to me by artists in the current Special Drama community whose relatives are featured herein, relatives of the Rajapart, the harmonist, the Buffoon, and the Dancer. Indeed, this 1942 Madurai notice is the earliest I have found that features an artist I myself have met. She is M. K. Kamalam, here playing the Dancer's role of "Iṭaicci" (the shepardess), and this notice is a rather remarkable record of onstage relations that subsequently played out in her offstage life.

Kamalam was an unusually independent and fearless woman. According to one of her granddaughters, "she did everything according to her own desire." I had the pleasure of talking with Kamalam many times during the years before her death in 2000. Her openness with me regarding her life was at least partially a result of my closeness with one of her daughters: Jansirani is Kamalam's fifth child. I write of her history with equal openness here because none of what I write has been particularly kept secret, nor did Kamalam herself discuss these matters with shame. On the contrary, she had an uncommonly proud bearing that she attributes to her foremothers and has likewise passed on to her daughters.

The 1942 Madurai notice features three men, the artists T. S. Durai Raj, G. R. Sri Ramulu, and S. V. Vasuteva Nayar, to each of whom Kamalam bore children. She referred to only one of them, however, as a "husband" (using the English term), the only one likely to reciprocate with the status-conferring term "wife." This was Sri Ramulu, comedian, who had no other wife. The other two artists did: for Durai Raj, Kamalam was a "third wife," and for Vasuteva Nayar a "second wife." Such designations are not legal categories but rather euphemistic figures of speech for commonly lived realities. Common, that is, for drama artists, as many male artists have more than one "wife," and the majority of drama actresses do not have the status of first wives. They are not legally married, just as Kamalam was never legally married to any man.

Kamalam bore eight children, four to Sri Ramulu. She raised these children like a matriarch, the rock at the center of a family grown in the center of Madurai and at the center of the drama world. Kamalam was herself a third-generation stage actress, born in 1925. Her mother, M. D. Kannāmani Ammal, played *gents vesham* (cross-dressed men's roles) in company dramas in the early decades of the twentieth century.

M. K. Kamalam took the initials before her name from her mother: M for Madurai, K for Kannāmani. Generally, Tamil women use the initial of their father's name before their own, until marriage, when they adopt the initial of their husband's name. (For example, N. Viji, daughter of Natarajan, becomes I. Viji, wife of Ilangovan.) Kamalam opted, however, to trace her descent matrilineally. She claimed she did so to honor her mother. She and her sister were also actresses, as was their mother before them. Kamalam's mother and aunt had also taken their mother's initial rather than that of a father or husband. This practice is uncommon and reflects a certain willingness to move outside of cultural norms, and even to flout them;[10] in a granddaughter's words, "she is a different lady, you know?"

In addition, Kamalam's move to trace her descent matrilineally is a rather ingenious means of responding to the stigma that faces a bastard child. Kamalam's mother, and her mother too, were also second wives. Kamalam's decision to take her parental initial from her mother's name honors her mother not as a wife (i.e., by taking her erstwhile husband's initial) but as an actress whose name had its own standing in her professional field. Her decision emphasizes her mother's professional identity rather than looking to define her by marriage. I see Kamalam's bold self-naming as a strategic move, a forcefully proud rebuke to the stigma on actresses. It recognizes the custom of using a parental initial before one's name and boldly expands the parental pool from which initials may be taken to include the female gender, her mother.

The strategy was not invented by Kamalam. Her mother, M. D. Kannāmani Ammal, and her aunt, M. D. Pushparajamani, had equally honored their own mother, Durakannamma, by taking an M for Madurai and a D for Durakannamma, who was a Streepart actress in the late nineteenth century (in Kamalam's words, "before Sankaradas Swamigal"). This prideful tradition of tracing their identity through a lineage of heroic actresses is just one of many creative means for actresses to find self-respect, and to carve out a kind of social standing for themselves in a terrain that would otherwise flatten them. Actresses do not so much fight against or overtly resist the normative practices that would exclude them as they do creatively expand the very bounds of the acceptable itself, here exemplified by altering formulaic naming practices to suit themselves.

Kamalam herself acted all roles, comedic and dramatic, from the 1930s to the 1970s. In due time, three of her own daughters entered the drama world of the 1950s and 1960s, now as fourth-generation actresses. Two of Kamalam's daughters, S. Kalāshri and N. Jansirani, each acted in Special Drama for over thirty years. Jansirani's youngest daughter, the only child in the family to continue in this field as a fifth-generation artist, acted only until adolescence. (Even then, as my youngest and one of my most articulate interview subjects, Kavitha proved a keen observer of the drama world.)

In later life there was one other man whom Kamalam did refer to as her husband, and whose initial she did place before her own in one specific public context. Again, that context was professional rather than legal (from a granddaughter: "She had no need of a certificate!"), reflecting her continued self-determining stance in the drama world. Pichai Ambalam, her last husband, is not an artist himself but rather a village farmer and drama fan who became a drama agent as a side business. When I knew Kamalam, Pichai Ambalam was often at her house in Madurai; he is the father of her last two children. He also has two other wives, both women from his village. Kamalam had retired by the time I knew her, but her name still circulated; when Pichai Ambalam contracted a Special Drama, it was done in Kamalam's name, listed at the bottom of the notice as "Drama Arranged by Kalaimamani M. P. Kamalam, Raja Actress, Madurai." In this context she is no longer M. K. Kamalam but M. P. Kamalam, in an adaptive interpretation of the formulaic usage of a husband's initial to mark instead their professional partnership (see bottom of fig. 20).

I return to the important matter of kinship and marital relations as strategic sites that artists use to counter stigma in chapter 9. Before leaving the 1942 Madurai notice that sparked this discussion, however, there is a second, equally generative story of strategic relations encoded here. Rajapart V. A. Chellappa Aiyar is the elder brother of V. A. Mahadevan, a Special Drama actor who married Streepart actress Renuga Devi. Renuga and I have discussed this notice and the era it evokes. Though now retired, Renuga is an active member of the Special Drama community who continues to serve as treasurer and management committee member of the Madurai Sangam. One of my first interview subjects, Renuga Devi provided me with a strong sense of the history and goals of the artists sangam, and of the strong desire many of its members have to raise the reputation of the art.

Unlike Kamalam, Renuga does not come from an acting family. She was the first and only person in her family to act, and she built her own professional identity in close connection with that of her husband and his family. Her husband was a well-educated Brahman who earned his B.A. in the 1930s. Long after his death, Renuga invokes his memory in public contexts in the drama world. For example, Renuga was personally responsible for providing the printed reproductions of Sankaradas Swamigal's portrait to all who participated in his Guru Puja remembrance day at the Madurai Sangam in 1991. On the bottom of the poster is written, "This is given in the memory of Cinema Prince Soft Singing V. A. Chellappa's brother Raja Actor V. A. Mahadevan" (fig. 1).

In the drama world, artists clearly use the publicness of print media as an arena in which to craft their self-representations and professional identities. Renuga's invocation of her late husband through a sponsorship in print, like Pichai Ambalam's invocation of Kamalam in the text of notices for dramas he contracts, and also like Kamalam's own use of an initial to signal pride in her profession, all partake of this quality of performativity, the accomplishment of things social through words.

The second midcentury notice I will discuss has an entirely different feel from this first document, with all its encoded histories of professional-turned-personal relations. It is a film ad for the mythologically themed movie "Savithiri" printed the same year, 1942 (fig. 16). Its form demonstrates well the increasingly different styles of print representation used by the two concurrent entertainment genres of film and drama.

While both notices are single-sided printed sheets of paper conveying the pertinent details of date, venue, and ticket price of a nightly entertainment to readers, their presentation of featured artists differs greatly. In the film ad, the actors' names are listed, rosterlike, above a single composite image, which is itself a reproduction of the film poster. The poster pictures the two lead artists together in a scene from the film, into which the title of the film, the director's name, and the face of an unidentified actress are inset. The notice is laid out vertically, 23 cm high and only 15 cm wide, essentially a half sheet. The remarkable crossover of artists between these (increasingly divergent) media of screen and stage during this period is pointed, as these two notices share their two leading male artists: both V. A. Chellappa and T. S. Durai Raj feature in the 1942 drama (fig. 15) and the 1942 film (fig. 16).

The crowded close-up visual style of the drama notice that has begun to develop during this period only further intensifies in the next two decades. As drama companies fold, and live theater moves out from the urban auditoriums that increasingly screen films and onto temporarily erected stages in village commons, the genre of Special Drama comes into its own and newly defines its own terrain. The final notice I consider from the RMRL archive

16 Film ad for the mythological *Savithiri*, 1942. Roja Muthiah Research Library collection, Chennai, India.

testifies to the structural changes in the genre in the midcentury period. It is a 1964 notice printed in Madurai (fig. 17), the most recent notice in the RMRL collection.[11]

Visually, this 1964 Madurai notice is quite similar to the 1942 and 1936 Madurai notices that precede it. It features the artists in head-and-shoulder poses, now primarily in rectangular rather than oval format. The harmonist is now squarely placed in the center of the notice. The Rajapart and Streepart are again in the top two corners, the Buffoon and Dancer along the bottom with other supporting artists. But here for the first time there is no delineation of ticket prices. Indeed, no tickets will be sold for this drama at all: instead, it is offered as a "vow drama" (*pirārttaṉai nāṭakam*) by one Sri Ram U. V. Ramasami Chettiyar, free to the public, in honor of his village deity.

The shift from commercial ticket drama to the individual sponsorship of performances for ritual purposes seems to have begun gradually in the 1950s. The Streepart actress Kalaimamani S. R. Parvati shared with me two

17 Drama notice for *Tamil Arasi*, 1964. Roja Muthiah Research Library collection, Chennai, India.

notices from her private collection, dated 1954 and 1955 respectively, in both of which she is a featured Streepart actress. The 1954 notice advertises a ticket drama held in a theater, and ticket prices for both day and nighttime performances are provided on the notice. The 1955 notice has no ticket prices but rather announces two dramas offered on two consecutive days, free to the general public, courtesy of the residents of the village of Perungalur. This 1955 notice, printed at the Muttamil Press in Madurai, is the earliest I have found that advertises a Special Drama offered for ritual rather than commercial purposes.

In accordance with this shift from an overtly commercial to a declaredly ritual function in the framework of Special Drama events themselves, the form of drama notices necessarily took on new functions as well. In addition to announcing the personnel of the drama the notice now also announces those persons for whom the production of the drama is a religiously meaningful event. This new information is added to the formal template established by midcentury of bold photographic images of artists and boldface text advertising the centrality of dramatic personages to the form. Now the notice form allows a whole network of people, connected by each unique Special Drama event, to also have a place in its iconic representation.

The Current Form of Notices: Roles and Ranks

While the local cast of characters engaging in the production of Special Dramas was thus expanding, the notice form itself seems to have undergone the equivalent of a culinary reduction: the drama notice form today has reached a kind of clarified essence. The written text succinctly documents elaborate relations of production, while the visual text now has a set formal layout and a fixed style and placement for artists' photos. There are only five (or at most six) artists pictured in identity-photo-like images, consistently placed according to an established prestige hierarchy of artistic roles.

Nine drama notices, selected fairly randomly from my own collection of drama notices printed during the 1992 drama season in Madurai, here represent the contemporary standard (figs. 18–26).[12]

Note first how each artist figures in a separate single-image photo, set off and framed by a thin line. The hiring processes of Special Drama similarly frame each artist as an individual and an independent professional who is contracted for each performance separately. Yet it is only the assembly of a group of such artists that constitutes a Special Drama, just as only all their images together as a group constitutes a drama notice. In each notice, these images are organized visually as two horizontal pairs, divided into an upper and a lower pair by a line, and a fifth central artist.

The pair of performers pictured above this dividing line are Rajapart and Streepart, who occupy the highest-prestige roles for actors. The pair of performers in the bottom half of the notice are, appropriately, the more lowly Buffoon and Dancer. As paired repertory roles, each duo is engaged in a competitive and sexually charged sparring relationship throughout the night, alternately wooing and insulting, seducing and rejecting. In this, Hero and Heroine primarily match wits, while the Buffoon and Dancer engage each other on a bawdier register.

The central image in the notice will be that of either the harmonist (figs. 18 and 26) or the Second Hero actor (figs. 19, 21–25), and on occasion both (fig. 20). Both these roles require the performer to engage in sustained interaction with all the other players in the drama, here translating into a notice layout that literally pictures them as "central" characters.

18 Drama notice for *Valli's Wedding*, 14 August 1992. Muttamil Press, Madurai, India.
19 Drama notice for *Valli's Wedding*, 26 May 1992. Muttamil Press, Madurai.

20 Drama notice for *Valli's Wedding*, 27 May 1992. Muttamil Press, Madurai.

21 Drama notice for *Valli's Wedding*, 18 June 1992. Muttamil Press, Madurai.

22 Drama notice for *Valli's Wedding*, 18 June 1992. Muttamil Press, Madurai.
23 Drama notice for *Valli's Wedding*, 23 May 1992. Muttamil Press, Madurai.

24 Drama notice for *Valli's Wedding*, 28 May 1992. Muttamil Press, Madurai.

25 Drama notice for *Valli's Wedding*, 2 June 1992. S. R. Printers, Madurai.

26 Drama notice for *Valli's Wedding*, 9 June 1992. Balakrishna Press, Madurai.

In *Valli's Wedding*, for example, the Second Hero actor plays the role of Naradar (*Nāradar*), a trickster sage in Hindu mythology who is "constantly on the move between all the worlds" (R. K. Narayan 1987, 15). In *Valli's Wedding*, he stirs up emotions in other characters as he flits between heaven (*deva lokha*) and this mundane world, inciting Lord Murugan's passions with accounts of Valli's beauty.

This propensity for stirring things up has earned Naradar the name "riot lover" (*kalakapriyā*). T. K. Shanmugam recounts how other children in the boys company teased him with this epithet, calling him "Riot-Lover Naradar" when Sankaradas Swamigal cast him as the trickster sage in four of his dramas. When the teacher heard the taunt, he told the boys: "Naradar does indeed make a commotion; but no one is ever ruined by what he stirs up, and only good grows from it" (Shanmugam 1972, 36). Naradar's ability to instigate a riot, stand at its center, and watch it turn to good is a quality to which many actors aspire. What better model to emulate, particularly if you already belong to a group, such as actors, accused of mixing and moving excessively?

In performance, Naradar is a middleman onstage. He figures in dramatic scenes that take place in the middle of the night. His entrance scene at around 1 A.M. provides forty-five minutes of devotional songs, immediately followed by another forty-five minutes in which he debates with Valli over her plans for marriage. After inflaming the Heroine's ire, he moves to the Hero and in a male-bonding scene that lasts almost an hour, the two plan their conquest of Valli. Interspersed with these dramatic scenes, during his entrances and exits, Naradar engages in comic business with the Dancer and Buffoon. Thus although he moves through the drama on his own rather than in any one pair, Naradar interacts with everyone else onstage. He is central in his constant circulation among others, much as the harmonist is central through his accompaniment of each singer onstage.

The harmonist is similarly on the move musically. While the entire orchestra accompanies the actors throughout the night, the harmonist, in addition to providing instrumental accompaniment, sings backup for each and every performer across every scene in the drama. Performers sing their own repertory of songs, often introducing new lyrics to familiar melodies, into which without prior rehearsal the harmonist must join and lead the other musicians. The harmonist is the necessary center of the successful drama: a drama falls apart in the hands of a weak harmonist, while a good harmonist can cover for a lot of musical errors on the part of off-key singers.

In performance as in notices, then, the presence of such mediating central artists turns the blocky, square configuration of two pairs holding down four corners of a rectangular playing field into a much more mobile arrangement —the hub of a wheel and its spokes—catalyzing a performance in which crosscutting alliances and enmities animate eight hours of onstage activity.

The Photographic Style of Contemporary Notices

Artists are pictured on drama notices both in costume and out of costume, and this depiction is inconsistent across even a single notice: some artists appear in costume, others do not. Presumably both types are equally appealing to viewers, an easy interchangeability that bespeaks a general attitude toward actors as subjects of keen fascination—and stigma—whether onstage or off.

These photographs are provided by the artists themselves. Print shops that regularly print drama notices have stacks of artists' blocks, ready to be set into the frame of any newly ordered notice.

In one particular instance, printers preferentially choose to use an in-costume image. This is to picture a female artist cast in a male role that requires her to cross-dress. In such cases, the in-costume image functions as testimony to the ability of the artist to play the cross-gender role, as well as to the appeal of seeing her do so.[13] In the 26 May 1992 notice for a *Valli* drama in the village of Gandanur (fig. 19), for example, the artist playing the Second Hero is a young woman, Chittiraselvi, pictured in costume as Naradar.[14] Likewise, in the 18 June 1992 notice for a *Valli* drama in the village of Pranmalai (fig. 21), seasoned actress R. S. Jeyalatha is pictured in the Rajapart role of Murugan. In both cases the actresses appear in full-body poses, in all their cross-dressed appeal. In the latter case, using this tall in-costume photo plate required the printer to shift other artists' images around slightly.

In comparison, the 18 June 1992 notice for a *Valli* drama at Muttuvayal (fig. 22) shows a male Rajapart in costume, and a full-length body shot is not necessary to evoke his assumption of the role. He appears here in Murugan's disguise as a hunter (i.e., as a man of Valli's tribe) rather than as deity (fig. 21), signaled by the tiger skin fabric of his dress. Tiger skin prints are the main sartorial symbol of *Valli's Wedding*; the play's action largely takes place in the tribal lands of Valli's family, where everyone evidently wears animal skins. My own photographs of actors in costume for a *Valli* drama in 1992 reveal the marked facial makeup and dress that potentially characterize in-costume images (plates 1 and 2). The distinctive costume for the role of Naradar boasts a topknot hairstyle and a heavily garlanded bare chest; cross-dressed women in the role manage to drape a layer of fabric beneath the garlands. In the 23 May 1992 notice for a *Valli* drama in Chandranpaddi (fig. 23), the actor in costume as Naradar uses a cropped upper-body photo, rather than a full-body photo like that chosen by the cross-dressed actress (fig. 19).

Increasingly, however, artists prefer to be pictured out of costume. In the 28 May 1992 notice for a drama in Koyilpaddi (fig. 24), for example, the printer had to use the only photo the young actress R. Sasikala provided, a picture of her dressed demurely in a sari regardless of the fact that she would play Naradar. To explain this shift, artists tell me they want to appear "modern" (*nakarikamāka*) in their photographs. This is the fashion now; this is how cine-artists are photographed. And of course, without drama makeup and costumes, people will be better able to identify them, further foregrounding the identification of individual artists that has characterized drama notices since the early twentieth century.

There is also a trend toward frontal head-and-shoulders portraits or head shots. Like the early photographs in drama notices, colonial-era photography in India employed a mix of full-face quarter-length portraits, full-length formal portraits, and group shots. British photographers were most interested in visualizing categories of Indian peoples, social groups and castes rather than individuals; in such colonial photography there is no "engagement with the face of the sitter" (Pinney 1997, 31). Such an engagement is, by contrast, exactly what the photos in a drama notice offer: the face, the identity, the character and individuality of each artist. Such images provide a corrective to the collectivizing gaze of types and typification that historically precedes them. As we have seen, individual names, as well as hints at their characters and biographies, are played up in these handbills. (Their style sparks, and supports, my own desire to honor individual artists in this text by using and recognizing their real names, their real histories, and their real faces.)

The frontality of the images in contemporary notices is striking. The direct gaze of artists in these images seems to promise that the forthcoming drama will similarly provide its viewers the opportunity for a direct relationship with the actors on display. According to Anuradha Kapur, the frontality of the performer in early Parsi theatricals was part of the new hybrid realism that the genre introduced into Indian theater. "Parsi theatre companies perform in the proscenium but take as their governing convention an eye and body contact that comes from earlier open stagings" (Kapur 1993, 92). The stagings do away with the imaginary fourth wall of much modern theater in addition to presenting a narrative that in "its fidelity to the continuum of life-time as it were"—that is, by presenting onstage activity as a slice of life that has real precedents and antecedents beyond the frame of the stage—"appears more 'real' than any representational mode prior to it. It is at this intersection of pre-colonial audience relations and a sort of bourgeois realism that [Parsi] mythologicals emerge" (92).

By introducing the phrase "bourgeois realism" into the discussion of the staging of Indian mythologicals, Kapur insightfully connects the introduction of realist characters, in all their human peculiarities and traits, with the introduction of a relationship of desire between viewer and viewed that is quite different from that of a devotee's reverence for an icon of the divine. Kapur refers to an "erotic complicity" (92) newly possible in the Indian theater between real people: "These characters are like people we meet, know, and come to love and hate" (96). The frontality and the direct gaze of Special Drama artists operate in their performance style onstage as well as in the style of their images on drama notices. Artists are indeed personages with whom the audience can both have and imagine having direct contact, in the present, in real time, even right in their own village.

The images on drama notices and the states of desire they might well elicit have more in common with the images of cine-actors one finds in *Film Fare* (or any of the other weekly magazines that circulate to avid readers in India and report on the life and times of the Bollywood rich and famous) than they do with perfected and enduring devotional images of mythic gods and goddesses. The latter circulate in reproductions available at Hindu temples and are recycled each year in Indian calendar art.[15]

Drama notice images thus give new meaning to the "bourgeois" aspect of the stylistic introduction of realism to mythological drama. Artists create images of themselves here that advertise, as much as anything, their ability to enact a certain middle-classness. For rather than divine icons, what the images on contemporary notices now most resemble are identity photos, images that have particular class associations in the Indian context. "The requirements of the state do motivate some image-making, for full-face photographic images are required for use on driving licenses, railway season tickets, college admission forms, bank loan forms and ration cards, in addition to various identity cards required by government agencies, insurance corporations, schools and colleges" (Pinney 1997, 113).

Members of the Indian middle class will have proffered just such images of themselves in official contexts for just such purposes. For the majority of Special Drama artists, however, all the institutional affiliations in this list belong to a realm of respectability beyond their reach. Take Jansirani, who has never had a driving license or a railway season ticket. Nor has she or anyone in her family ever applied for college admission or had a loan from a bank; none of them even has a bank account. Of the various identity cards required by government agencies for conducting official government-sanctioned business, none have ever been required of Jansirani, either for insurance or for educational purposes.

The only official document that many Special Drama artists do possess is a passport. Many older artists who were active in the days of touring company dramas traveled to perform for Tamil-speaking communities throughout the Asian Tamil diaspora, notably in Sri Lanka, Malaysia, Kuala Lumpur, and the country known at that time as Burma. Even now artists are occasionally hired to perform for diasporic Tamil communities, and they must have passports to get there. And in the increasingly globalized world of satellite communications and Internet industrialization, artists, like everyone, are keenly aware of the opportunities for wealth that the United States represents. Most know someone who knows someone who has gone there, and even harbor dreams of someday going there themselves. Having a passport ready is thus regarded as readying oneself for the possibilities opened by

27 The author, seated among Special Drama actresses at the 1992 Guru Puja, Madurai. Photograph courtesy of Buffoon M. K. Sattiyaraj.

foreign travel. Acquiring an Indian passport is not difficult (though visas are another matter), and a passport photo, like identity photos for other officially sanctioned purposes, offers its bearer a middle-class self-image. All the desires for upward mobility that are now condensed in the powerful symbolism of the passport photo come through clearly in the Buffoon's monologue I discuss in chapter 4.

The style of the photographs on contemporary drama notices thus communicates, among other things, artists' own aspirations toward a more bourgeois self-image and middle-class social standing. Special Drama artists are indeed impressively good at playing the part. An artist took a photo of me seated among Special Drama artists and their families at the 1992 Guru Puja in Madurai (fig. 27) that I originally appreciated for how well it captures my own sartorial and postural attempts to fit in with the crowd. Subsequently I have come to appreciate how well this same photo documents artists in the act of mastering the sartorial and postural demeanor of the Indian middle class. Even viewers well versed in the legible distinctions of class usually so evident in the clothing of Indian women would be hard-pressed to identify the women here as popular theater actresses.[16]

These, then, are the communicative features of the current style of notice photos: they offer a frontal presentation of artists as real people, rather than gods, in an identity photo style suggestive of official, middle-class usages. These features are communicated by each photograph singly, on which the grouping and placement of images builds further, relational layers. I turn now to a consideration of some of these additional layers by looking at how the layout of drama notices bespeaks prestige hierarchies of the Special Drama stage.

The Prestige Hierarchies of Artists as Pictured on Drama Notices

The standard artistic roles in Special Drama have two overtly recognized prestige hierarchies, one for actors and one for musicians. These prestige hierarchies are spelled out in a form generated by the artists sangams and used by them to book member artists for performances of Special Drama (fig. 28). The form is a receipt from the sangam management to the drama contractor that binds the listed artists to appear on the given date, at the given place, to perform the given drama.

Of the twelve artistic roles listed, the acting roles are ranked one through seven, and the musicians' roles eight through twelve, as follows:

1. Hero (*Rājapārṭ*)
2. Heroine (*Stiripārṭ*)
3. Second Hero (*Sekoṉpārṭ*)
4. Buffoon (*Papūṉ*)
5. Dancer (*Tāns*)
6. Supporting Actor (*Tuṇai Naḍikar*)
7. [Supporting Actor] (*Tuṇai Naḍikar*)
8. Harmonist (*ārmōṉiyam*)
9. Mridangist (*mirutaṅkam*)
10. All-round (*ālravuṇṭ*),
11. [Clarinet] (*kiḷārneṭ*)
12. Cymbalist (*Tāḷam*).[17]

For the ranking of actors' roles, there are several axes of prestige at play here. There is the privileging of stillness over movement previously discussed: heroic actors stand still to sing and debate, while comic actors prance and dance in parodic physicality. There is also the privileging of

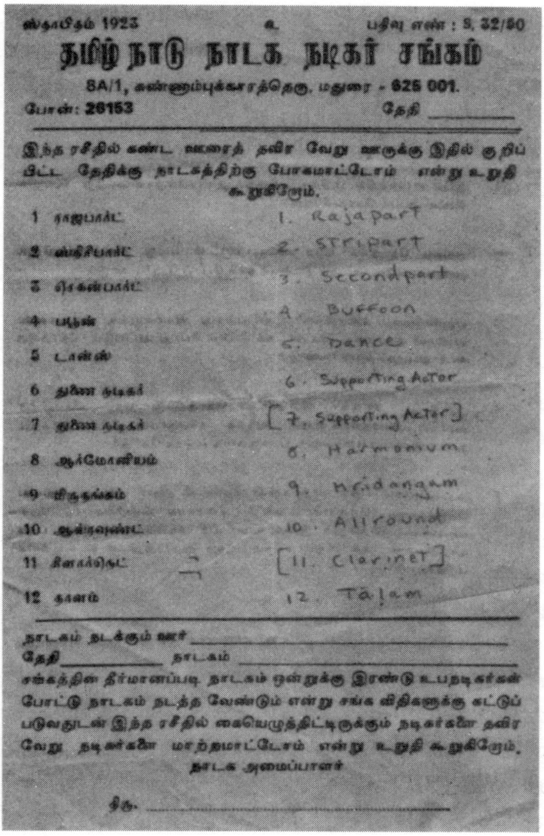

ஸ்தாபிதம் 1923 பதிவு எண் : S. 32/50

தமிழ்நாடு நாடக நடிகர் சங்கம்

8A/1, ..., மதுரை - 625 001.

போன்: 28153 தேதி ________

1	ராஜபார்ட்	1. Rajapart
2	ஸ்திரீபார்ட்	2. Stripart
3	ஸெகண்ட்பார்ட்	3. Secondpart
4	பபூன்	4. Buffoon
5	டான்ஸ்	5. Dance
6	துணை நடிகர்	6. Supporting Actor
7	துணை நடிகர்	[7. Supporting Actor]
8	ஆர்மோனியம்	8. Harmonium
9	மிருதங்கம்	9. Mridangam
10	ஆல்ரவுண்ட்	10. Allround
11	கிளாரினெட்	[11. Clarinet]
12	தாளம்	12. Talam

நாடக அமைப்பாளர்

திரு. ________

28 This is the form—known as a sangam receipt—that sponsors must fill out whenever they hire members of the Tamilnadu Drama Actors Sangam, Madurai. The form numerically ranks those acting and musical roles for which artists are hired to perform in Special Drama.

formal literary, over informal spoken, language: heroic actors engage puranic stories of epic proportions in cadenced verse, while comic actors refer only to the haggles and hustles of everyday life in colloquial banter. There is a privileging of refined social purity over debased mixedness: heroic actors represent kings and queens and gods and goddesses of noble birth who are ever concerned to maintain their lineage through properly arranged marriages, a standard theme of the dramatic plots themselves, while comic actors represent regular folk who are prey to whims of fancy (and lust) and who usually end up eloping.

As noted, these prestige hierarchies are reflected in the positioning of artists in a visual range of high, low, and central positions that correspond to their ranked positions. The accepted prestige hierarchies for actors and musicians remain those in which the Hero heads the actors, and the harmonist the musicians. These status rankings get perpetuated through various practices, from artists' reinforcement of them in their own conversational evaluations of artistic merit, to the unequivocally numbered list on sangam receipts. It is also reinscribed with every printing of a drama notice, as the layout of contemporary notices reflects—in its placement of images as well as in the epithets it uses to describe artists—a higher estimation of musical and literary skill over acting skill.

These epithets exemplify the terms of evaluation on which the prestige hierarchy is based. In the 14 August 1992 notice for a drama in Perumbacheri (fig. 18), the Rajapart is listed first of all the artists, his name appearing beside his picture and just beneath the large-font name of the drama: "Prince of Music supporting his fans through his acting, K. P. Durairaj." In another notice (fig. 20), the same actor is introduced as "Flame of Muttamil Speech, Madurai K. P. Durairaj." Other Rajapart actors are given similar epithets: "Sweet Music Prince Madurai A. K. Vaanidaasan" (fig. 19); "Light-Music Musical Prince P. Lakshmibaalan" (fig. 23), and the same actor again as "Prince of Divine Music Lakshmibaalan" (fig. 25); and "Light of the World of Dramatic Arts P. V. Vijayarajan" (fig. 26).

Similar terms describe Streepart actresses, given with her name just beneath the Rajapart's name: "Musical songbird, Madurai P. S. Vijayatara" (fig. 19); "Poetic songbird, Madurai N. Jansirani" (fig. 20); and my favorite, "Singing songbird of honeyed music from the groves of the human world, Madurai S. A. Rettnaamani" (fig. 22).

Significantly, the one actress whose talents are not praised in terms of music, song, or speech is Sennai Sivakami. She is heralded instead as "Queen of the Art of Acting, Sennai P. Sivakami" (fig. 24). Sivakami is one of the few artists to directly criticize what she sees as a lack of attention to the art of acting in Special Drama performances, as well as in artists' discourses, a style that has earned her more money than friends in the Madurai acting world she now inhabits.

"Secondpart" (or Second Hero) actors are praised in terms similar to those of the leading heroic actors, with a special emphasis on the importance of rhetorical skill for the role of Naradar. The artist is listed first in a text box to the left of the central image on the notice. We have "Great Queen of Speech R. Sasikala" (fig. 24); "He Who Speaks in the Proper Manner T. M. Bala Murugan" (fig. 21); and "Poet Who Is Newly Giving Lessons M. V. Shanmugavel" (fig. 22).

The remaining actors are listed beneath the Secondpart in this same text box. Note how epithets for Buffoons and Dancers, when used, draw on a different palette of descriptors. For the 14 August 1992 Perumbacheri drama (fig. 18), the Buffoon is introduced as "Your *Super Star* M. K. Sattiyaraj" (in a filmic reference to Vijaya Kanth), and the Dancer as "Dance-Warrior, Madurai Sugunarani," not a gentle image. Phrases such as "Star of Comedy" (fig. 20) or "Prince of Comedy" (fig. 23) for Buffoons, and "Queen of Dance" (fig. 24) or "Dance Peacock" (fig. 22) for Dancers are the most common, but equally often a comic artist's name is presented unadorned.

Finally, the name of the supporting actor who will play Valli's father, Nambirajan (a bit part), if given at all, will be placed at the very bottom of the list of actors, beneath the Dancer's name. His is a very brief role, sometimes lasting a total of ten minutes onstage, that is not well compensated financially and is frequently played by nonactors.

On the other side of the central image, in the right-hand text box, is the list of musicians, headed by the harmonist. Epithets for harmonists stress musical ability, as in "Prince of Music, Drama Teacher Madurai N. S. Varatarajan, Harmonium and Backup Song" (fig. 18), or the simpler "*Music* Star V. P. Draviyam, Harmonium and Backup Song" (fig. 24) and "Beautiful Music Artist, Vayalcheri V. S. Mukkaiya, Harmonium and Back-up Song" (fig. 22). The harmonist's name is followed by those of the other musicians, "Mridangam Master Kalvimatai K. K. Sinnasami" (fig. 18) being about the most demonstrative epithet one finds, as most often the remaining musicians are simply listed by name.

In its very simplicity, however, the hierarchy of musicians' roles best illustrates the principles at play in the ranking of all the artistic roles.

The harmonium used in Special Drama is a keyboard instrument, actually a small reed organ with foot-operated blowing pedals, known as a foot (*kāl*) harmonium. The harmonist plays while seated in a chair. The use of any and all keyboard instruments in South India is a marker of European cultural influence, with pianos being the high-culture end of this imported genre (pianos figure in lavish cinema scenes from the 1940s on).[18] The harmonium has become a nativized loan instrument, so much so that it now appears to be a folk instrument (and music drama now figures as the folk genre requiring its use) when compared, for example, with the Korg synthesizers and Yamaha organs currently employed in Tamil "light music" concerts, a performance genre that frequently vies with Special Drama for a performance slot in village temple festivals. Indeed, the history of the harmonium is a microcosm of the history of Special Drama: both seemed terribly modern when they first appeared, but now appear as folkish and quaint in comparison with the more recent higher-tech influences of a postmodern music arts culture spreading globally through the mass media of AsiaSat and MTV.

The mridangam is the elongated, double-headed barrel drum used in classical South Indian Carnatic music. It is a highly articulate drum with voices that range from soft pitter-patters to sharp, high-pitched rings. Often the mridangist also brings one or two tablas, the North Indian single-headed classical drums, to play along with his South Indian drum. The mridangist sits cross-legged on the table that supports his drums.

"All-round" here refers to a second drummer who plays an array of less traditional percussive instruments that generally include a set of bongos and a large cymbal.[19] The all-round drummer is alternately referred to as the "special effects" drummer. Like the mridangist, he sits cross-legged on a table behind his array of instruments.

Tāḷam is a Tamil term that refers to rhythm—to patterns in the beating of time—provided in Special Drama by a musician playing a set of small, hand-held brass cymbals. Specific patterns of damped and ringing (or closed and open) strokes of the cymbals provide a varying number of beats in a repeating cycle articulated by the cymbal strokes. In Carnatic music, the tāḷam is not a particular pattern but a system for articulating a temporal cycle. The tāḷam is played standing. Standing, while others of higher prestige sit, recalls both the servant roles common in contemporary Tamil homes (cooks, for example) and in kingly courts (those who fan the king, for example). The tāḷam player is the lowest-paid artist onstage, earning roughly one-tenth of what the highest-paid male artists earn in one night. A tāḷam player might earn Rs 50, while a higher-ranked artist earns Rs 500.

These are the four basic musicians' roles in Special Drama.[20] Their prestige ranking and pay scales are equally consistent with the order of their listing on the sangam receipt form: harmonium, mridangam, all-round, tāḷam. In addition, this hierarchical prestige ranking does not merely exist in behind-the-scenes pay scales or on paper but rather is visible on the stage itself in the physical postures that musicians adopt while playing their instruments.

Sitting in a chair (that originally European but now staunchly middle-class Indian apparatus) onstage is a marker of higher status than sitting cross-legged "Indian style."[21] The most prestigious and "modern" (read "Western") playing position is that of the harmonist, seated on a wooden chair at his wooden, tablelike instrument. A harmonist's prestige might outrank even that of the lead actors, as seniority comes into play, and harmonists are often the senior members of a drama party. Since the role requires a great deal of musical knowledge as well as familiarity with a broad repertory of songs, harmonists tend to be elders in the drama community.[22]

Seated on either side of the harmonist are the two drummers, who sit cross-legged (Indian style) before their instruments. Again, the lowly tāḷam player, who often hails from a low-caste community, stands.

These same postures index prestige status throughout everyday life in Tamilnadu. In general, sitting on a chair accords more prestige than sitting on the floor, in artistic contexts as well as at home or in the workplace. In a short story about a Tamil singer, R. K. Narayan writes: "Sometimes he would request Selvi to sing, and then dramatically leave the chair and sit down on the floor cross-legged with his eyes shut, in an attitude of total absorption in her melody, to indicate that in the presence of such an inspired artist it would be blasphemous to sit high in a chair" (Narayan 1996, 158). That the modern, Western-style chair should be a prestige marker is merely one highly physicalized sign hinting at the multitude of ways in which a colonial legacy has impacted and continues to shape daily life. A chair here is not just a chair but also a tightly constructed bundle of historical symbolism, while standing conveys servitude.[23]

The ranking of actors is more complicated than that for musicians. With actors, prestige is not the only scale of value: there is also what audiences pay. For actors, pay scales and prestige rankings often diverge. While almost everyone claims (including most comedic actors themselves) to view comedy as low-class work, Buffoons are often more highly paid than Heroes. Comedy, it seems, can earn one fame, popularity, and even money, but not a good moral reputation.

Real struggles of value play out between ideals and practices on the terrain of actors' roles. Without exception, all artists with whom I spoke claimed that roles requiring the greatest musical and literary expertise are the most deserving of high pay and of high status. They thought it fitting that the two highest-paid actors on the Special Drama stage be Rajapart and Streepart, followed closely by the Second Hero. These three actors should be skilled both in literary prose and in Carnatic music; their roles require that they be able to draw on a wide range of literary texts in debate, as well as on a broad array of musical styles in song. The three remaining acting roles, that of Buffoon, Dancer, and Supporting Actor (the latter also frequently a comic role), are said, on the other hand, to be lesser roles deserving of lesser pay.

The determining issue here lies in the *class* or category of work, rather than in either its quantity or quality. In terms of quantity, a Buffoon generally works harder—he spends a longer time onstage and expends a greater amount of improvisational energy there—than a Rajapart. Exerting a lot of energy, however, as previously noted, is itself already a practice coded as lower-class in Tamilnadu, where, as in Western societies, menial labor is demeaning.

Similarly in regard to quality, a Buffoon exhibits remarkable agility in the course of portraying not one but multiple characters during a single night's drama (replete with all the requisite costume changes). He often does so using improvisatory, unscripted monologues and stories of his own creation in performances that generally have the audience in the palm of his hand. Nevertheless, the Buffoon's verbal skills are not necessarily literary skills; his musical abilities do not ensure that he sings classical Carnatic ragas; and his versatility at character acting does not translate into any particularly noble attributes. Instead, the comedian's unscripted speech meets with disdain for straying from the poetry of known masters, and for revealing the seamier side of life in general.[24] Thus while comedy is a crucial element of the genre, Special Drama artists reinscribe in their own discourse a historically dominant dismissive attitude toward it.

Early on in my participation as an audience member at Special Dramas, I was struck by both the impressive amount and quality of work that Buffoons do onstage. I knew that they did not command the same respect as Rajaparts, and assumed this also meant they made less money. In the course of an interview with a Buffoon in Pudukkottai conducted in the main room of that Sangam, he and I were joined by several other comedians eager to add their opinions on the question of how comedy is valued in Special Drama. I was surprised to learn that while the Hero had historically always earned more than the Buffoon, in point of fact, this is no longer the case. Many villagers today are more interested, the comedians informed me, in "entertainment" (they used the English word) than anything else and reward entertainment value by paying comic actors more than they do heroic actors.

Here was certainly an opportunity for comic actors to sing their own praises to me. Instead, rather than celebrating their rising success, they insisted that a Rajapart *should* earn more than a Buffoon, and collectively offered two reasons: first, "he is the hero of the drama," and second, "his knowledge is greater."

Our ensuing discussion of these two points made clear to me the importance of the already established nature of this hierarchy. First, as hero of the drama, the Rajapart's existence makes the existence of all other characters possible, as his story is the central story of the drama. In this a Rajapart fulfills, within the acting community itself, the same role offstage that he plays onstage: he embodies the noble position of the most important man within the community. He is necessary, and his heroism at least partially consists in his assumption of that mantle, that is, in his willingness to appear as the condition of possibility for the drama. The Rajapart's role is thus literally to embody the (kingly, in Dumont's terms) principle of status.

Second, the Rajapart knows Carnatic music and puranic stories, and thus "his knowledge is greater." That is, it is the greater *kind* of knowledge, the knowledge that counts. Again, the underlying issue has to do not so much with quantity or even quality as with a type of knowledge: classical South Indian music (*icai*) and Hindu traditional stories (*iyal*) are the kinds of knowledge that count, while cinema songs, physical comedy, and dirty jokes, popular as they may be, bear no such sanction of tradition and no such similar stamp of "knowledge." Carnatic music is considered an art that "requires prolonged learning and discipline" (Baskaran 1996, 39) and thus is generally the purview of the elite (Baskaran 1981, 121). In contrast, discipline is precisely what Special Drama actors are said to lack, and when they sing onstage, it is only an imitation of "real" singing.[25]

In the stated prestige hierarchies of performers' roles, then, musical and literary skills are overtly valued above comedic skills. However, individual performers earn their reputations as well as their wages according to their desirability to the local audiences who hire them, and audiences pay for what they like. Audiences select both players and play, and what audiences most like, in the heartland of Special Drama, is comedy.

The audience's taste for comedy accounts not only for the discrepancy between pay scales and prestige hierarchies but also for the popularity of *Valli's Wedding* itself. As those involved readily admit, *Valli*, at least as currently performed, is essentially a comedy. An actress who has played both Hero and Heroine in this drama for over thirty years put it as follows:

> *Valli* is full of comedy. Also debate, and the debate is full of comedy too. And fights, they fight too. And in the middle of the Raja-Streepart debate, they sing cine-songs. So the people like it a lot. In the other dramas there is coherence and continuity. Not in this. *Valli* is just small bits strung together. Valli comes and goes, Naradar comes and goes, the Hunter comes and goes. Two people have a debate and there is a lot of comedy in it, that's all, nothing else.

Artists see audience preferences for comedy as responsible for a kind of dumbing-down of drama. To counter this, among themselves they continue to grant the highest respect to roles that demand the greatest musical and literary abilities, perpetuating dominant discourses that devalue comedic, improvisatory work.

It strikes me that the dominant discourse here is prey to an internal contradiction. Does such devaluation of comedic and improvisatory work really support the government-sanctioned goal of a renewed *muttamil̲* tripartite art that equally values "literature-music-drama" (*iyal-icai-nāṭakam*)? Shouldn't muttamil̲ elevate the status of drama as a whole to the greater levels of respect enjoyed by Tamil literature and music? In maintaining the accepted prestige rankings of music and prose above expressive acting, Special Drama artists risk devaluing their own unique art form, a form based on mixing the improvisatory with the scripted. A real restoration of *nāṭaka* to equal par with *iyal* and *icai* would require a willingness on the part of drama artists and historians alike to argue for the appreciation of acting in all its guises: comedic, heroic, improvisatory, and scripted.

Only audiences express such appreciation now. To wit, performances of *Valli's Wedding* comprised 55 percent of all Special Drama performances booked for performance through the Madurai Sangam during the 1992 and 1993 performance seasons.[26] Combined, all the other mythological and historic dramas in the repertory accounted for another 42 percent of performances.[27] And yet the remaining 3 percent of the bookings in 1992 and 1993 are perhaps the most telling figure. These were for an event of "pure comedy" conducted in a vein of social farce known as *Kathambam*. "Kathambam" is a term that can be applied to any *mixture* of diverse elements. It most commonly names strands of mixed flowers, where blossoms of many varieties are strung together in a kind of mess of excessive color (as opposed to the more prized strands of neatly tied white jasmine flowers, daily worn tucked into the tidy plaits of Tamil schoolgirls). Performances so named consist solely of comedic scenes, performed by multiple sets of Buffoons and Dancers, with no roles for heroic actors. "Kathambam" is an apt term to name what is perceived as a messily tantalizing excess of comedy—one that audiences clearly appreciate, even if no one else does (or will admit they do).

The only artists I have heard voice appreciation of the more expressive acting styles are those engaged in pursuit of a "big name" rather than a "good name," artists who openly seek monetary power from their engagement in Special Drama rather than moral prestige (as I discuss in the following chapter). Sennai Sivakami epitomizes this attitude, both in her comments and in her performances. The very voicing of such sentiments, however, ensures that an artist will land outside the approbation of those who frame the prestige hierarchies; indeed, the sangam actually polices those it perceives to be playing too fast and loose with such distinctions, as I document in the next chapter.

Drama notice printers never engage in such debates. They simply set the formulaic template that pictures heroic artists above comic artists, with a mediator in the middle. The same formula exists onstage. After all, the primary job of the notice is to index the dramatic event itself. Notices point the way to the stage, using relations of resemblance to underscore their point. Images and text are laid out like pieces in a board game: here are the players and their basic relations; go see the play for all further developments. The notice is a promissory note for the dramatic stage, where all debates on morality and manners actually belong.

The Iconicity of the Contemporary Notice: Structured Spaces and Places

In linguistic (Peircean) terms, then, a drama notice is a multivalent sign that signifies on all three fundamental levels: as an icon (a sign that resembles the object it signifies), as an index (a sign that points to the object it signifies), and as a symbol (a sign that by convention signifies its object). Its iconic aspects are rather more unusual than the indexical and symbolic signage one expects in advertising. This iconicity inheres in the close likeness, in a two-dimensional and condensed format, that the notice bears to the three-dimensional staged event.

The most obvious visual and framing feature of a contemporary drama notice is its rectangular landscape within which human figures are placed in specific relations to each other. In addition to identifying the spatial use areas of four corners and a center stage, this layout identifies how the drama will unfold in time during a Special Drama performance on a rectangular stage, only in reverse. Reading from left to right and top to bottom, as one does written Tamil text, the most important players are those who appear first on the notice but last onstage. In progressing from night to dawn in a staged performance, one moves from comedy to drama, whereas in reading a notice one moves from drama to comedy.[28]

We have seen that images of artists appear on notices positioned according to a distinct prestige hierarchy of roles. Likewise onstage, particular kinds of artistic activities occupy corners and center in a familiar sequence of scenes, also ranked by prestige. I will use the drama *Valli's Wedding* as a template to explain this progression. The scene sequence essentially moves from least prestigious and auspicious to most prestigious and auspicious, again as if reading a notice from the bottom up. The event begins with two hours of comedy and proceeds through six hours of drama. The dramatic scenes themselves move from those that generously employ comic and supporting characters, to culminating scenes that involve only the heroic actors. Throughout, each of the four corners is regularly put to a different use—one corner is for entering and exiting; another for taking breaks; in a third corner artists enact relational bonds; and in a fourth separations occur—while center stage the central business of debating takes place (see chapter 5).

Over and above this formal iconicity, the drama notice serves as a kind of performative precursor to the event itself. Notices announce the forthcoming event and simultaneously constitute it as an event by articulating its relations of production: this is the drama, these are its producers, here are the players, and this is its purpose. The Buffoon reads the notice aloud in his opening act, an act that thereby allows the notice to deliver on its promises: saying it makes it so. As a product born of the same channels of commerce that produce the drama itself, drama and notice are like mirror-twins; their shared productive context is yet another level on which, and about which, the notice communicates.

Printers and the Circulation of the Drama Notice

Print shops specializing in the printing of drama notices exist in each of the sixteen city centers that boast an actors sangam. In Madurai in the early 1990s there were four such print shops, all located within a three-block radius of the actors sangam. In each, printers typeset notices manually (figs. 29 and 30) and print them on a manual press (fig. 31).

In a standard commission, printers print between 500 and 700 sheets of a notice on a standard-size paper measuring 23 by 29 cm (roughly 8.5" by 11").[29] A commission reaches the printers in the following way. In the month before the event, the sponsor of an upcoming drama will engage one of these press shops to print a notice. The sponsor will travel from his or her village to town to set the notice, thereby inaugurating the route of travel that artists will subsequently follow in fulfilling the sponsor's commission: the sponsor travels from village to town and back, whereas the artists travel from town to village and back. The printed notice travels these same routes, in the hands of those constituting the event, in both directions.

29 Printer typesetting a drama notice by hand. Muttamil Press, Madurai.

At the print shop, the sponsor conveys all the particulars of the upcoming event to the printer: the name of the deity in whose honor this event will be held; the name of the sponsor(s) and his/her/their reason for undertaking this sponsorship; the name of the locale where, and when, the event will take place; the larger ritual context of the event; the name of the drama to be performed; the names of all who will perform in the drama and the roles they will play; the name of the company providing sound, light, and electrical services; the name of the company providing backdrops and scene settings; and finally the name of the agent (aka the contractor) of the event.

Once printed, notices are distributed by bicyclists who cover an area roughly ten kilometers around the locale where the drama will be staged. The cyclist travels the same roads that potential audience members from the region would take to reach the drama. He tacks notices in public places—tea stalls, bus stands, roadside shops, and the like—and hands them out to local residents. Artists will arrive by traveling these same roads. By the night of the drama, when all those responding to its call have come together, one folded-up copy of the notice, pulled from a shirt pocket, is read aloud. The

30 Typeset drama notice plate. Muttamil Press, Madurai.

31 Printer printing a drama notice on a manual printing press. Muttamil Press, Madurai.

Buffoon carefully smooths out the notice as he stands onstage before the microphone, delivering it finally into an oral public address that puts promise into play.

Drama Sponsorship and the Written Text of the Contemporary Drama Notice

Always the first promise announced recognizes the vow made by drama sponsor to deity. Such information is now standard in first lines of drama notices: who is sponsoring the drama and for what purpose. In the top line of text stretching across the page of the 14 August 1992 notice (fig. 18), for example, we learn that "the villagers of Perumpachēri Meṭṭumaṭai will sponsor this drama as part of the oxcart festival for their gracious god Samaiyana Swami; all are invited to come see!" In addition, the first lines of a notice often tell whether this is the first such event, or whether this performance represents a continuing tradition, for example, the third annual (fig. 19) or seventh annual (fig. 23) such religious festival.

People choose to sponsor dramas for a range of reasons, personal and collective. A drama sponsored in fulfillment of a personal vow to a deity is known as *pirārttanai nāṭakam* (vow drama). One such drama I attended, in the village of Valaiyangulam in March 1992, fulfilled a vow made by a sick child's grandfather. The man had promised, in prayers to the village's primary deity Perumal, that should his grandson survive this illness, by the grace of (this) god he would in turn sponsor a drama for the deity. The illness subsided, and with a performance of *Valli's Wedding* on a stage erected in the temple commons, the grandfather honored his vow.

Vow drama sponsorship occurs in exchange for all sorts of divine protections. Residents of the village of Valaiyangulam generally sponsor thirty vow dramas each year, each for different reasons, but all as offerings to Srī Tānāmuḷaitta Taniliṅka Perumāḷ (Perumal of the Unique, Self-Formed Lingam). Valaiyangulam is a village of approximately two thousand homes located just thirty kilometers northwest of Madurai. This annual month of dramas, held in the Tamil month of Māsi at the beginning of the drama season (mid-February to mid-March), makes nearby Valaiyangulam a frequent performance site for Madurai actors. Valaiyangulam is unusual in sponsoring so many Special Dramas each year; in the vast majority of villages, only one or two Special Dramas appear annually.

Valaiyangulam is the first of the two villages in which I chose to study dense drama sponsorships by spending an extended period of time conducting ethnographic research there. Many Valaiyangulam residents have a strong belief in the particular fondness of their deity for dramatic entertainment. One village lineage boasts a family history connecting them with ritual performances for traveling kings held by their kinfolk during precolonial times.[30] The yearly spate of a month of Special Drama in the postcolonial, postindependence era has now, in addition, created experienced drama viewers and an audience that is familiar with the intricacies and variations each performer brings to his or her role. Valaiyangulam audiences have helped me understand the particular pleasures they take in Special Drama at numerous junctures.

One vow drama sponsored in Valaiyangulam in March 1992 was offered to Lord Perumal in return for a rather unusual kind of help. When I met K. Venkatiyamma, the drama's sponsor, she was in her early sixties. She told me that at one time she had been fairly well off. In the course of her life, however, she had lent out the majority of her wealth to friends and relatives. She had kept her wealth in the form of gold jewelry, a common practice among Tamil women. In her old age, Venkatiyamma sought the help of the deity in securing the return of her jewels. Upon the success of that endeavor, she sponsored a Special Drama; I photographed Venkatiyamma adorned in her returned jewels that day (plate 3).

Another performance of *Valli's Wedding* in Valaiyangulam that same month was sponsored by a group of ten young men who called themselves *aṉpu uḷḷaṅkaḷ*, the "love minds." These ten men were all coworkers at a chemical factory located near the village. Some were Valaiyangulam residents, and others traveled from their homes in surrounding villages. They sponsored this drama, one member told me, to ensure the continued prosperity of their collective work. The drama notice for the performance they sponsored on 3 March 1992 lists all their names, introduced simply as "the love minds sponsoring this drama" (innāṭakattai naṭattum aṉpu uḷḷaṅkal). These young workers were an impressive bunch; on the night of the drama, they all dressed alike in shiny gold-brown polyester shirts they had had tailored specially for the occasion.

Such a group endeavor is not an uncommon form of drama sponsorship, particularly in the second village I chose for an extended period of ethnographic study. This is Kottamangalam, a village near Karaikkudi in the region of Chettinadu. The village boasts many homes that are beautiful examples of the architectural style of traditional Chettiyar houses, and is also notably the home of a well-known Tamil playwright and cinema artist from the 1960s. In 1992 I attended the annual ten-day festival held in Kottamangalam in the month of āṉi (mid-June to mid-July) for its village deity Ulakanāyaki (Queen of the World). The entertainments sponsored for the goddess's festival range from cinema screenings to "light music" concerts to classical dance but invariably annually include at least two or three nights of Special Drama.

Several work-related groups regularly sponsor nightly entertainment events during this festival. One such group was known as the "Out-of-Town Workers Association," comprised of men originally from Kottamangalam, all of whom now work in North India. They return each year to their natal village at the time of the Ulakanāyaki festival and unite to sponsor a night's festivities. Another is called the "Local Merchants Group," all of whose members run shops in Kottamangalam. Another sponsor group is known as the "Small Savings Troupe," comprised of local boys under the age of thirteen. Yet another is entitled "The Daughters Union" (makaḷir maṉṟattārkaḷ), a group that brings together approximately one thousand women of the village to sponsor the entertainments they deem worthy of their support for the second day of the festival.

Each of the sponsors or sponsoring groups in Kottamangalam commits to ongoing annual sponsorship. They take responsibility for hiring the entertainment for one particular day of the festival and its nightly entertainment. The first day is sponsored by the village as a whole entity, with monies raised from a common fund requiring the contribution of ten rupees from all married male householders inside the village. The second day is sponsored by the Daughter's Union, the third by one particular man for the continued health of his family. The fourth is sponsored by the Small Savings Group, the fifth by a group of local merchants calling themselves "The Refreshing Association" and consisting of 230 male members. The sixth is sponsored by the Chettiyar community, the largest and most powerful caste group in the village. The seventh day is sponsored by the Local Merchants Group, and the eighth by two separate groups of local workers, one cotton mill workers and the other bank employees. The ninth day belongs to the Out-of-Towners.

The tenth and final day of the festival had for the past five years become the sponsoring responsibility of two friends, both of whom were important men in the village. One, Mr. Lakshmi Narayan, is the village's resident pharmacist (known by the English term "the compounder"). The other is Mr. P. L. Gandhi, an experienced Special Drama agent in the region and founder of the Karaikkudi Agents and Actors Sangam. Mr. Gandhi's residence in the village has ensured that many of the nightly entertainments sponsored by the various village groups in Kottamangalam are performances of Special Drama, and his connections in the drama world help facilitate all the necessary preparations for a drama.

Special Dramas are then frequently only one among a series of nightly entertainments in honor of a deity that together make up a larger festival. The nightly entertainments sponsored by the above groups over the ten days of the Kottamangalam festival in 1992, for example, broke down as follows: one social drama, one dance drama, three nights of double-featured films, two light music orchestras, and two Special Dramas (for a total of nine nights, as the first night had no entertainment, only rituals of worship conducted by locals). In addition to this range of nightly entertainments into which Special Drama is now embedded, generally during the daytime too other forms of ritual practice and celebration are conducted as part of the larger ritual context. Recall the oxcart race in Perumbacheri (fig. 18), a common village form of entertainment involving a contest among men who attempt to tie fabric onto the horns of a running ox. This event was held in the deity's name by day, and a Special Drama later that night. In the 27 May 1992 notice for a *Valli* drama in the village of Gōpālpaṭṭi (fig. 20), the top line announces that for the festival of the Goddess Kāli there will be a party of Karakam-pot dancers. This street folk dance form has a reputation for vulgarity even worse than that of Special Drama, largely due to the fact that the highly physical skill of balance dominates the form and is moreover accompanied by a rustic music of beaten drums and a dance of lewd gestures. In Gōpālpaṭṭi, Karakam dancers from Madurai performed the first night, and a Special Drama was held the next.

In preparation for the fulfillment of the ritual functions of a drama, the honored deity is welcomed to the event through specific and sometimes highly elaborate rituals. These vary widely by village. In most instances the stage will be erected in the direct sight lines of the deity, in accordance with Hindu beliefs about the powers of the divine gaze.[31] If the stage is not located directly in the sight lines of the deity, then an icon of the deity, richly decorated for the occasion, will be led in procession to a spot in the audience that offers full reciprocal visibility for performers and deity. For the ten-day goddess festival in Kottamangalam, beginning on the festival's second day, a daily procession is enacted with a different chariot each day to carry Ulakanayaki's icon to each nightly performance. One chariot was a bullock made entirely of silver; others were a brass lion, a wooden horse, and a jewel-encrusted swan. On the tenth night, a truly spectacular chariot festooned with hundreds of colored electric lights carried the goddess in a procession that circumambulated the entire village. Each morning of the festival, the goddess's processional icon would return from her all-night viewing and be undecorated and lowered from the previous night's vehicle even as the next vehicle was carried out from the temple to be readied for her next appearance.

Finally, in addition to personal vow dramas and dramas sponsored for the collective well-being of a local group, dramas are occasionally sponsored to announce and display the wealth and magnanimity of the sponsor. Such events are a regular occurrence in the town of Dindigal, for example, where the wealthy owner of a local factory, a fine amateur mridangam player in his own right, is also a second-generation fan of Special Drama. Mr. M. V. M. Angu Muttu Pillai, owner of the Angu Vilas Tobacco Company, sponsors several nights of Special Drama every year. He stages the dramas in the center of town and engages more than the usual number of artists for every performance: two Rajaparts, two Streeparts, two Buffoons, two Dancers, two all-round drummers, two mridangists. He sponsors dramas in celebration of human skill and endeavor rather than divine intervention. In addition to their usual fees, at these events artists receive numerous material tokens of appreciation from Angu Muttu Pillai, including lengths of silk and shawls emblazoned with the name of the factory.

Though not often this ostentatious, such tokens are part of a gifting practice that is common at Special Drama events (as it is at many other Tamil performance events), the practice of giving *aṉpaḷippu* or "gifts given as an expression of affection" (Cre-A 1992). Any audience member, not just sponsors, may give aṉpaḷḷipu in appreciation of an artist. During the performance of any given night many scenes are interrupted frequently by gifts ranging from five rupees to one hundred rupees. Each gift is announced over the microphone by a villager, in the name of the giver and to a particular artist. The named artist then greets this honor with a small speech of gratitude, pronounced in formal Tamil, and the play resumes without any sense of a missed beat.

The easy tolerance artists accord such frequent interruptions in a performance marks one important difference between spectatorship norms here and those of contemporary Western theatrical events. The give-and-take between performers and spectators is a central part of Special Drama performances and often reaches a highly interactive pitch in audiences' responsive laughter at comedy scenes (see chapter 6). Here, note that artists are simultaneously present as the characters they play and as actors onstage. They are in no trance, but rather in both roles are well aware of the myriad behind-the-scenes negotiations that enable their appearance on a Special Drama stage.

The Working Network That Makes Special Drama Work

Drama notices list the names of all the key individuals engaged in the production of the event, information that literally frames a notice within its larger network of relations.

The network of flexible service providers whose activities are set in motion with the scheduling of a drama includes those who maintain artists' booking calendars in locations convenient to sponsors; agents, whose job is to connect sponsors with artists they might like to hire; the owners of drama backdrops and scene settings, who rent them for each event; a man hired to run the backdrops and scene settings during the show; the owners and drivers of the vans often hired to take performers to the performance venue; and the owners and operators of mixing boards and electrical lights, who provide sound and light services throughout the night. The names of all these persons are listed across the bottom of a notice.

In the 14 August 1992 notice sponsored by the villagers of Perumbacheri (fig. 18), the information in the bottom text blocks of the notice includes the name of the provider of scenery ("cīn: M. Suntarajan"), of the press printing the notice ("Muttamil Press, Madurai-1"), and of the agent contracting the drama ("drama contracted by drama teacher N. S. Varatarajan, Harmonist, Madurai"). All this is signed off, in large letters, by the villagers of Perumbacheri, informing readers that this drama is sponsored by common funds from the whole village. Such details of sponsorship, production, and organization sandwich the pictorial particulars of the event, appearing at both top and bottom of the notice.

The 23 May 1992 notice for a drama in Chandranpaddi (fig. 23) provides more of such information than usual. In addition to the sound and light provided by Ganapati Sound Service, and the scenery provided by Sri Muttu Mariyamman of Gonaiyur, we learn at the bottom of the notice that a meal will be prepared by P. L. Kalyanasundaram of Chandranpaddi, the stage will be erected by S. Kalyanasundaram of Ilaiyatagudi, the notice is printed by Muttamil Press of Madurai-1, the agent for the drama is N. M. Solamani, and S. Velangudi, proprietor of Ganapati Sound Service, is responsible for its advertising. All such recognition gives credit where credit is due within a local economy of relations of production grounded in their regional, rurban place.

The critical role played by drama agents in Special Drama deserves particular attention. Artists refer to the work of agents as "talking drama" (*nāṭaka pēca*). Talking drama is men's work. It involves moving freely through the public sphere, interacting with many people, introducing oneself and one's opinions to people one barely knows. Many male Special Drama artists act as agents themselves, using their knowledge of the field to extend into its contractual side, as noted for a drama contracted by N. S. Varatarajan in which he was also harmonist (fig. 18). Other men become involved in agent work because they see a business opportunity in their local area. Such agents generally work in specific corridors of villages, in areas they know well, and that include their own natal village (Mr. P. L. Gandhi of Kottamangalam being a good case in point).

Many agents began as drama fans who desired more engagement with the field. Such nonartist agents often marry, or take as "second wives," actresses (as in the previously noted case of M. K. Kamalam and Pichai Ambalam). In Madurai during my research the percentage of actresses whose nonartist husbands worked as drama agents was high—roughly 30 percent among the generation of contemporary leading actresses—making me realize what a mutually beneficial arrangement such a pairing can be. It is a pairing that, above all, makes a highly gendered kind of sense: actresses can maintain the semblance of the reputation of a good woman by not interacting directly with audience sponsors, since her "husband" talks up her talents and arranges for dramas in which she often stars.

Most agents do tend to support particular artists, those whom they know and like. The Karaikkudi Agents and Actors Sangam was quite aboveboard with this fact, its agents almost exclusively booking its artist members in the dramas they contracted. As one might expect, alliances between artists and agents can range from the purely professional to the complexly interpersonal and can further be complicated by interethnic and communal relations. It is a testament to the good-natured majority of artists involved in Special Drama that the business of talking dramas resists being unremittingly ugly. Nevertheless, a strong motivating force in the establishment and maintenance of actors sangams is the desire to regulate relations between artists and agents.

Agents exist because they provide needed services. They are the only link to artists for villagers who want to sponsor a drama but are not themselves familiar with the workings of the drama world. To some extent the stigma on artists keeps agents in business, for if in general people were less wary of artists they might choose to negotiate more directly. As it is, agents negotiate all the variables attendant on a performance on behalf of the sponsor, from identifying suitable artists and ascertaining their availability for booking, to actually hiring artists; from registering the drama with the actors sangam, to arranging for the printing of the drama notice; from arranging for the transportation of artists to the venue, to ensuring that the sponsoring villagers know to prepare the performance venue properly, and to provide the necessities artists require on-site. The provisions that artists require at a drama include a properly constructed stage, a meal before the performance, flowers for the actresses' hair, oil with which actors may remove their makeup, a chair for the harmonist and tables for the drummers, and plenty of hot sweet tea for artists throughout the night.

Apart from these provisions, artists carry with them everything they require for performance. For musicians this means their instruments, while actors carry their own costumes, makeup, and other necessary props for the character(s) they play. All these are the individual property of the artists. Certain of these provisions may be rented, providing yet another offshoot business opportunity. In Madurai, for example, just down the street from the actors sangam is a small shop specializing in the rental of costumes for Rajaparts.

Rajaparts and Streeparts often also bring along a helper, usually an older relative, to whom they pay a token sum. The helper assists by carrying costumes and aiding costume changes. The very act of hiring such a servant adds to an artist's prestige and places him or her a bit higher on the social ladder of who serves whom. A young Dancer or Streepart will generally travel to dramas with a helper-cum-chaperone as a gesture that at the very least exhibits her awareness of the reputation of the profession she enters.

All these people who contribute to the existence of Special Drama—printers, sponsors, and agents, as well as cooks, carpenters, electricians, and helper/chaperones—do so in coordination with a ritual calendar that brings Special Drama to rurban venues at locally meaningful times.

The Ritual Calendar of Drama Sponsorship

Since drama sponsorship is tightly tied to local deities and their annual celebrations, ritual calendars largely determine the current Special Drama season. Villagers select dates for reasons germane to their personal vows as well as in accordance with village-wide ritual calendars. One particular date—the Hindu religious date of Sivanrāttiri (Siva's night), celebrated on the new moon in the Tamil month of Māsi (mid-February to mid-March)—is considered highly auspicious, and many villages interested in sponsoring a drama would simultaneously like to do so on this night. Celebrations of Sivanrāttiri now mark the beginning of the drama season.

Dates appear on drama notices at the top of the central rectangular playing field, within the main area delineated by the placement of the artists' figures. Notices provide the Tamil Hindu year, month, and day as well as the English year, month, and day, as do most commercial Tamil calendars.[32] In the Perumbacheri notice from 14 August 1992 (fig. 18), just to the left of the English date is the name of the Tamil Hindu year (Āṅkīrasa), month (Āṭi) and day (30). Specific details of timing follow, as the next line announces that "after the 2 p.m. oxcart race, at 10 this night the drama *Valli's Wedding* will specially take place in the beautiful arts stage built in Perumbacheri village." This drama, like most, is calibrated to the Tamil Hindu calendar. Fridays in the Tamil month of Āṭi (Āṭi Veḷḷi) are considered auspicious, especially the first and last Fridays of the month; this drama is scheduled for the last Friday of Āṭi.

The ritual calendar accommodates well the seasonal agricultural timetable of village life. Beginning with Sivanrāttiri in mid-Māsi, the five Tamil months that follow—Paṅkuṉi, Cittirai, Vaikāsi, Āṉi, and Āṭi—are the hottest months of the year. Especially in the inland parts of the state, where Special Drama is most popular, daytimes in Paṅkuṉi and Cittirai are virtually too hot for outdoor activity (averaging from 110 to 120 degrees Fahrenheit), so that only in the slightly cooler night temperatures does village-wide outdoor entertainment become a viable possibility. Agricultural work diminishes in villages, and men have more time to attend entertainments. Women, being the household cooks, are not as free to attend, their work being anything but seasonal; staying up all night is much easier when one can sleep the next day. Attendance is thus more physically difficult for women, but the fact that far fewer women than men attend Special Drama performances is only partially due to such pragmatic concerns. Pragmatics here conveniently dovetail with strong ideological notions—about the impropriety of comedy for a female audience, for example—to ensure that fewer women attend dramas (see chapter 4).

The foregrounding of the ritual calendar in drama sponsorship means that artists in the increasingly rurban genre of Special Drama tend themselves to be more attuned at any given time to Tamil Hindu dates than to English dates. Interested parties generally contact artists and engage their services according to the Tamil Hindu calendar, so that artists largely move in a world organized by this calendar. This is itself a marked practice in current-day Tamilnadu, in the sense of markedly "village" and local, as opposed to "modern" and cosmopolitan. Transnational global markets hop and swing on international calendars. The arts festivals of the much more cosmopolitan city of Chennai accord well with the English calendar: classical Carnatic music and classical Bharata Natyam dance concerts, for example, fill Chennai auditoriums in the cooler months of December and January, also conveniently "Christmas break" time for the many tourists who travel to India at this time of year and frequently attend such cosmopolitan events. Opposing values of "village" and "modern" are reinscribed here in the attunement of different Indian performing arts genres to divergent calendars, one of the many less-prestigious differences that now mark the genre of Special Drama and its artists.

The Grounds of a Social Economy

The relations of production between village sponsors and Special Drama artists and service providers link two otherwise dissimilar social entities: a stationary village collectivity and a mobile hired party of independent artists. The movement toward each other is that of unknown people establishing new links, reflecting the essential character of Special Drama. While onstage scenes replay over and again the theme of fortuitous sightings and unexpected meetings between strangers, the same themes have already been set in motion on the ground.

A particularly germinal ground for such movement is the small geographic area that defines the hub of Special Drama activity in the city of Madurai. The area might be described as three square blocks, although Madurai blocks are far from square. In it is located the actors sangam building, as well as a good number of apartment buildings where Special Drama artists live, and all the print shops that produce drama notices. It is located very near the central bus station of the city and is thus officially "Madurai-1," from the last digit of its zip code, 625001. The area is not only close walking distance from the large central city-bus station but equally close to several out-of-town bus stations and to the Madurai railway station.

The centrality of Madurai-1 is convenient to those traveling to the city to book a drama, as well as to artists traveling from the city to far-flung venues across the state. Indeed, all sixteen actors sangams across the state are located in their respective first zip code areas: Dindigal-1, Karaikudi-1, Pudukottai-1, and so forth. Each of these zones denotes the area of town closest to the central bus and train terminals and their connected business, at the heart of the activity of connecting rural and urban lives in India.

The majority of Madurai-based drama artists try to find affordable housing in or near to Madurai-1. For artists, concentrating their living, organizing, and booking activities in this one area eliminates the need to make unnecessary trips to conduct business. It enables a welcome reduction—physically, financially, and socially—in what is known in Tamil as *alaichal*, the kinds of "trouble caused by hectic moving about" and unnecessary walking around (Cre-A 1992, 48). As we have seen, excessive mobility is not well regarded in any case; here, relations between worker bees and the queen bee are an apt model. Excessive mobility particularly compromises women: she who must move about to work is no real queen, however well versed she may be in imitating one (see chapter 9).

The geographic location of the centers of Special Drama business activity within zones of primary rurban connection across Tamilnadu is indicative of the integrated rurban nature of Special Drama today. In this geography, the figures cut by Special Drama artists populate the local rurban landscape. Why then do artists still so frequently figure as outsiders, strangers, and stigmatized others in dominant discourse? An important part of carving out an ideal Tamil identity seems to require imagining actors as a reckless, orderless Other. How the contrast between this reputation and the rurban reality of Special Drama shapes artists' own official organizational strategies is the subject of the next chapter.

3 Discipline in Practice

The Actors Sangam

Sivakami Winks . . .

I am backstage shooting video. Onstage the Buffoon has already begun his opening comedy scene. The public address system is blaring and distorted but I am not listening to the Buffoon's words anyway. I am focusing on Sivakami, whose appearance is mesmerizing. She sits cross-legged behind her open suitcase putting on jewelry and makeup. In my lens she appears framed by several other artists, who also sit behind suitcases and prepare their stage faces. Crouching at Sivakami's shoulder is her eleven-year-old niece, who aspires to enter the drama world. The girl stares unblinking at my lens. I hold the camera still. Sivakami, eyes glinting and sparkling, twists a long strand of hair over the top of her tiara. Looking directly at my camera, she pulls a long black bobby pin from her bag and props it open with her front teeth. Then she squinches up her nose and delivers a long, slow, knowing, and exceedingly flirtatious wink.

Watching this tape again years later, the over-the-topness of Sivakami hits me all over again, and my own laugh echoes back at me on the tape sound track . . .

. . . and Jansirani Disapproves

Later that same night I sit in the audience for the dramatic scenes. My video camera rests on a tripod, capturing Sivakami onstage. An almost exclusively male audience whistles and claps. This performance is taking place at the intersection of two main streets right in the center of Madurai. In this 1993 drama season, Sennai Sivakami is one of the most sought-after Streepart actresses in Special Drama. She has come only recently from Chennai, where for many years she acted in social dramas as a member of a well-known company. Only when the company folded in 1990 did she come to Madurai, to try her luck at Special Drama. She is having considerable success, earning Rs 700 a night.

Beside me sits Jansirani, also now a Streepart actress. Unlike Sivakami, Jansirani has been acting in Special Drama all her life. She was a Dancer for twenty-five years before she moved up into Heroine roles. She grew up in Madurai itself, indeed, just a few blocks from where this drama is taking place. Jansi has accompanied me to watch this drama, and we sit together, VIP style, in folding chairs up front while the rest of the audience spreads out in all directions behind us, sitting on the ground in the middle of the blocked-off street or standing, lining the sides of the road.

In stark contrast to the hoots and hollers of the men all around us, Jansi quietly clucks her disapproval in my ear. She makes that same sound whenever we discuss the present state of the art of Special Drama, how it has changed since the old days when her mother and grandmother acted, when this art (in her opinion) had respect. Her grandmother played Rajapart roles. The times have changed, the audience's expectations have changed, and now the art itself is changing: witness this performance. What Sivakami is doing onstage is "not right," Jansi says. "A Heroine should not dance." At just this moment Sivakami gives a big sideways thrust with her hips—a wink with a different body part—as the all-round drummer crashes his big cymbal and the audience explodes.

Jansirani and Sivakami both began playing the Heroine role in Special Drama in 1990. For Jansi this was the culmination of a lifetime of experience as a Special Drama actress in Dancer roles. She began "putting powder" (*pōṭi poṭukka*)—the expression artists use to capture the essential work of a stage artist—at age eight. She is the fourth generation in a matriarchal line of stage actresses. For Sivakami, by contrast, acting in Special Drama was a switch from a lifetime of experience in the Madras world of social drama, begun at age nine with lessons in classical South Indian dance. The eldest of only two daughters, she is the only one in her family to work as an actress.

There are important similarities in these two women's lives, as well as powerful differences. In 1993 both Jansirani and Sivakami were thirty-nine years old. Both had been Tamil stage actresses for thirty years. Both were now based in Madurai. Both began acting the Heroine role in the 1990 drama season. Here, however, their biographical similarities end, and their very different approaches to, and experiences of, life as Special Drama actresses begin. In many ways these two women's lives represent opposing poles in the range of strategies Special Drama artists use to mitigate stigma. The ability of the community to contain such strategic diversity, and the discourses through which it does so, are the focus of this chapter.

By using the term "strategies," I do not mean to imply that what is at play here necessarily involves the kinds of rational decision making assumed by so much capitalist economic theory on markets and risk management (for a powerful critique of the ethnocentrism of this view, see Sahlins 1996). Rather, in considering strategic choices I am most interested in recognizing both the shared and the individual contingencies of "the material and symbolic factors that impinge on people's choices" (Paxson 2002, 324). I use "strategies" as an umbrella term under which I can consider the range of practices in which artists engage as they negotiate the complex conditions of inequality in their lives.

In studying the sociological negotiations made by those who face stigma, Erving Goffman speaks of "managing" its discrediting effects and offers us "notes on the management of spoiled identity." His is a relational usage with which I concur: to negotiate and manage difficult social situations, people engage in those practices they can—meaning those practices they are both able and willing to employ—to mitigate the situation in a way they see as effective. Such practices range from prayer to procrastination and from apathy to activism and include the full range of forms of everyday resistance (Scott 1985). All to me are *strategies*; I do not intend my use of this term to privilege rationality as the basis on which they are chosen, or to suggest rationality as a fundamental guide to human action. The mix of choices people make is simultaneously historically contingent and more complexly personal than predictive sciences can measure.

The very different strategies pursued by Jansirani and Sivakami, then, in their careers as stage actresses crystallize two opposing stylistic approaches to the management of spoiled identity. Both Jansirani's cluck of disapproval at Sivakami's performance, and Sivakami's persevering pluck in the face of it, are stigma survival strategies. Jansirani pursues a reputation for moral decency, while Sivakami pursues fame.

I will refer to these two different strategies as the pursuit of two different kinds of name: the "good name" or the "big name." Among artists the status of a good name is often opposed by the powerful appeal of a big name, divergent strategies that are evident in both deed and word. In Tamil, the term *periyavarkal*, "big men," names important persons. But as always, there are here different types of importance, as well as different ways of interpreting importance. Analytically it is useful to parse this one blanket term into two more nuanced terms, and to distinguish between those who pursue what I am calling the big name of money and fame, and those who aim instead for the good name (*nalla peyar*) of moral repute. While a big name may command the *power* of wealth and fame, a good name confers the *status* of moral respectability.

The distinction between these two opposed, but mutually defining, means of achieving reputation raises larger issues concerning distinctions between power and status in India more generally. Indeed, it is on their absolute distinction as two opposing forces enacted by kings and priests vying for supremacy at the top of the Indian caste system that Louis Dumont bases his theories of the dynamism of hierarchical systems (Dumont [1966] 1980).[1] The distinction is between a strategy that bases rank on actual rewards given in the material world (kings who pursue power), and a strategy of self-promotion in the terms of extant ideas about status allocation (priests who pursue status). Artists' rankings of themselves and their own actions reflect the tension between these poles in contemporary Tamil life.

The distinction between good name and big name pits morality against fame and maps neatly onto distinctions already drawn between drama and comedy. In historiographic texts, in the visual texts of drama notices, in the casual conversation of artists, as well as in the official rules and regulations of the actors sangam, the prestige of artists is most frequently represented as a hierarchy ranking dramatic over comedic skills. In the following discussion, I move between all these domains of discourse to capture the pervasive nature of the conflict between status and power as it plays out in the competing claims of morality and fame in the lives of Special Drama artists.

Competing Claims: A Matter of Bearing

A person's behavior is her *naṭamuṟai*, the way or manner (*muṟai*) of her walking (*naṭa*). Her naṭamuṟai is how she moves through the world. Naṭamuṟai is a matter of bearing, onstage and off. A conversation with Jansirani's eldest daughter, Viji, gave me a sense of how the two very different naṭamuṟai of Jansirani and Sivakami are appreciated within the community in which they move.

Note that this young woman's ability to make an assessment very much in line with how others talk about these two performers, even though one is her own mother, is at least partly fostered by Special Drama events themselves. Viewers are expected to be able to judge the behaviors of actors, and in particular the morality of their personal behavior and bearing. Such an attitude is precisely what is taught through the avenue of spectatorial relations in Special Drama (see chapter 6). Viji assessed her mother's, as well as Sivakami's, behavioral styles with a trained eye to their professional strengths and weaknesses as Special Drama artists in relation to Special Drama audiences.

Viji characterized her mother as a good worker (*to<u>l</u>ilali*), loyal, responsible, and an all-around *decent type*. (This last phrase she said in English; unlike her mother, Viji is aware of English words as English words and uses them to aid my understanding.) All of these are personal attributes of Jansirani to which I too can attest. Jansi maintains friendly lifelong bonds with many artists and agents throughout the Special Drama network, in Madurai and beyond. She extended these bonds of friendship and loyalty to me, offering me connections of rapport with many artists with whom I would have had no entree otherwise. Her own entree is due equally to her being from an established acting family, to her personal characteristics of trustworthiness and loyalty, and to the fact that Jansirani is a beautiful singer. Both her good reputation and the longevity of her career owe much to the strengths of a singing voice that she herself considers a gift from God (*anṭavan koṭutatu*). It is on the basis of these combined qualities that Jansirani enjoys the respect (*mathippu*) of her colleagues, who regularly praise both her singing and her humility. She has several times been invited, for example, to grace the opening ceremony of an auspicious community event, such as the guru's remembrance day, with a devotional song.

Just as often, however, when Jansirani's name is mentioned, her colleagues wear an expression of sad concern bordering on pity: her humble bearing is matched by her humble material means. Jansirani was never the fair child, and never much favored by her family. She started earning young and has always had to earn her own way. She is an artist's second wife, and both her children are female and have now moved into marital families of their own. Jansirani remains poor and is frequently in debt. Financial debt is one of the cruelest ogres of Special Drama artists' lives. I have known several artists whose suicides are attributed to insurmountable debt. The seasonal nature of the work contributes to inevitable lean periods, and a lack of familiarity with the middle-class institutions of savings banks and insurance plans makes artists vulnerable to loan sharks. In Jansirani, a consistent generosity of spirit fills in these many gaps. Never rich or stately, hers—as her daughter rightly put it—is the naṭamu<u>r</u>ai of the good worker.

To describe the nature of the considerable appeal of Sivakami's persona, by contrast, Viji used a very different expression. Recall the activities of Naradar, the trickster sage of Hindu mythology, who has been accused of enjoying any riot he himself stirs up; this is the same expression used to describe him. "She causes a commotion and excites everyone" (kalakku kalakkiṟanga). The verb *kalakku*, again, means to mix, stir, or disturb; to cause sensation and excite. Doubled up for emphasis as it is in this phrase, it means to mix and really stir things up, to rouse the crowd. The interactive sense of the phrase—its *rasa*, to cast it in terms of Sanskritic aesthetic qualities—is even more sweetly specific in Viji's words. In searching for an English term to characterize Sivakami's naṭamuṟai for me, she struck on "delicious." The dictionary defines *kalakku kalakkiṟanga* as "to stir up the common people, to excite the masses, to cause a sensation, grab their attention and make them notice you" (Cre-A 1992, 267). Viji's additional characterization captures the sense one gets, from watching her perform, that Sivakami enjoys the brew she stirs up, and the attention and applause of crowds finding her delicious. The other English word that Viji used was "jolly." The interactive qualities here are paramount; Sivakami's charismatic stage smile lights up the faces of audience members watching her, too. (One of my early field notes likens Sennai Sivakami to a stylistic combination of Bette Midler and Barbra Streisand.)

Jansirani's critical attitude toward Sivakami's performance on the night we sat together in the Madurai audience is part of a highly specific discourse, propounded by the actors sangam, that reflects an internalization of the criticisms we have seen throughout the historiography of popular Tamil drama. Jansirani's feelings of distaste, and her expression of disapproval that night, embody such internalized values. In aiming to raise the social status of stage artists, sangam discourses overtly value respect above the kinds of power, fame, and glory that are the purview of crowd-pleasing comedy and popular cinema song-and-dance styles. Sangam rules and regulations are attempts to codify the terms on which an artist earns a good name in the genre. For example, the sangam decrees that Heroines "must sing songs appropriate to the drama," rather than cine-songs.

Sivakami, of course, is well aware that she breaks this discursive tradition, as well as sangam rules, by enjoying herself without worrying over the responsibilities inherent in being a Heroine in music drama. Indeed, tensions between herself and the sangam are fairly ongoing. She is regularly fined, for example, for transgressing sangam edicts, though she nevertheless maintains her membership. While others complain that she performs too many popular cinema songs, Sivakami herself told me: "My hands are tied: the audience wants these. They are bored stiff with the old songs, and they won't sit and listen to them. They want *super-star style, Rajini style!*" (referring to cine-star Rajini Kanth). The audience wants glamour and fame, and Sivakami is willing to give it to them. It is a lucrative career move: in 1993 Sivakami earned double Jansirani's fee for every performance.

Jansi claims she overheard men in the audience, the night we watched Sivakami onstage together, saying "*dance over!*"—that is, expressing a criticism about her "dancing too much." I didn't hear these comments; perhaps I was too busy watching Sivakami go for the bold and seeing the audience eat it up. Both things were simultaneously true, of course: too much, and delicious.

The conflict represented between these two actresses' naṭamuṟai—between status and power, respect and fame—plays out repeatedly in the internal proceedings of the acting community. It is a conflict monitored, managed, and overseen by the regulations of the actors sangam. The conflict is so enduring that I have begun to suspect it is a necessary tension, one that now fuels the genre itself: actors live their lives ashamed of their shameful reputation and also dependent on its remaining a constant against which to measure their own actions.

The sangam operates in this breach. Its drive to discipline grows out of a desire to stem accusations about the vulgarity of Special Drama and its artists that long predate the activities of either Jansirani or Sivakami.

Internalized Historiography: Artists' Discourses

The actors sangam is a self-conscious solution to the historical problem of actors' lack of muṟai and discipline. Artists have internalized key aspects of the condemnatory discourses with which historians have generally regarded Special Drama, including a view of comedy as the source domain of vulgarity in popular theater. The kind of looseness on which comedy thrives remains emblematic of all that needs to be disciplined in the genre.

Recall the harmonist A. K. Kaleeswaran's succinct condemnation "Special Drama means, as they please: without responsibility," which casts the genre as marked at birth by a lack of discipline. Beginning with the early company dramas that brought together special artists, the problem with the form was that it had "no discipline [*kaṭṭuppāṭu*], no regularity or propriety [*oḻukkam*]." On its slippery slopes, artists "talked as they pleased in the dramas, they talked whatever they knew, which amounted to comedy and all that, because they had no murai." Without the structure and discipline of teachers, scripts, and company directors, artists' own improvisations would lead headlong into vulgarity.

Enter the actors sangam. Founded in 1923, a year after the death of Sankaradas Swamigal, the actors sangam was created to be that governing and disciplining body without which these artists would remain hopelessly adrift. When I asked Mr. Kaleeswaran directly about the historical role of the sangam, his comments emphasized how without this controlling body, anarchy would reign.

SUSAN SEIZER: Is the sangam necessary?

A. K. KALEESWARAN: Definitely. The sangam is entirely necessary. It helps the actors. Teaches lessons, and principles. Whatever help the actors need, it must do. The sangam exists because our conduct must be disciplined. Without the sangam we could do nothing. The sangam is necessary to foster harmony among the actors. If not, each person would do as he alone pleases.

SS: Then what would happen?

AKK: There would be fighting amongst ourselves. No cooperation. Someone who will give ten rupees comes, and another offers to do the work for only five rupees. If there was a party hired for one thousand rupees, one actor might come and say, "Give me fifty-five rupees advance," and then just take off. In this way many wrongs can occur.

The mandate of the sangam is to rectify—through edicts and punitive measures—these many wrongs. Their very proliferation, as well as their precise nature (as Foucault has so clearly taught), is simultaneously engendered by the authoritative codification of just such an agenda of redress. To wit, certain of the stated goals of the sangam directly address a proliferation of the sorts of interpersonal wrongs Mr. Kaleeswaran mentioned in his example, such as swindling. The following are from the sangam's book of rules and regulations (see appendix 1):

> *Goals of the Sangam, 3d.* To make efforts to settle any disputes which arise between Sangam members and those they interact with.
>
> *Goals of the Sangam, 3e.* To take actions against 1) those who do not give the artists their salary after the performance of a drama, 2) those artists who create unnecessary problems after receiving their money from those who contracted the drama, 3) any others who blackmail or get money from the drama actors and

> actresses in any other improper way, and 4) those who cancel a drama without appropriate reason, after a date has already been fixed and the advance paid.

Other sangam goals, however, target dilemmas peculiar to the cultural and historical subjectivity of drama artists, addressing in particular the stigmatizing perception that they lack discipline. Such injunctions are prefigured by Kaleeswaran's earlier statement: "The sangam exists because our conduct must be disciplined." This internalized discourse translates into punitive actions that, for example, treat Sivakami's penchant for dancing in the role of the Heroine not as a mere charming stylistic idiosyncrasy but rather as a potentially punishable offense falling under the category of "vulgar behavior" within a catalog of wrongs that the disciplining body of the sangam must right.

Controlling Bodies and the Control of the Body

Bodily matters—including drinking, dancing, swindling, and "talking vulgarisms"—are the primary behaviors that the actors sangam attempts to regulate.

Quite shamelessly, the sangam aims to shame its members into submission in the name of a greater good: the reputation of Tamil drama itself. P. S. Nagaraja Bhagavattar succinctly voiced the ideology of the sangam in another of our conversations.

> The Sangam should bring discipline. It's not just that they should ensure that a particular scene is enacted at the end of a particular drama. *Every detail should be looked into.* They should *filter* the drama. They should say, "This is how you should speak. This is how you should act. This is how you should sing." Only if this discipline is there can we ensure that our land's *culture* will not change. For example, if she speaks to him so casually, saying, "pōṭa, vāṭa" [*colloquially*: go there! come here!], what does it mean? When they talk thus, all respect for the institution called *drama* diminishes. All *stage discipline* is gone. So how can we call this drama?

The terms for discipline that recur throughout this conversation are *kaṭṭupaṭu* and *kaṭṭupāṭu*. The former, *kaṭṭupaṭu* (with a short *a*), is an intransitive verb that means "to submit to" or "to be bound (by)," to come under control or be controlled (Cre-A 1992, 232). *Kaṭṭupāṭu* (with a long *ā*) is a noun meaning discipline, restriction, control, and regulation (232). A lack of discipline is tantamount to being loosed, or untied, from cultural webs.

In a society where *tying* is essential to all civilized acts—wearing clothes being an apt example—to be untied is literally to be naked, and thereby uncivilized. South Indian men's and women's primary garments—lungis and dhotis for men, saris for women—are unstitched lengths of fabric, either three meters or six meters respectively, that are tied into place on the body (rather than being cut and sewn to fit like Western clothes). Only "tribals," considered to be outside the civilizing structures of caste society altogether, go naked and unswathed. Nakedness in human adults is considered vulgar, uncivilized, and ugly.[2]

It was a villager from Valaiyangulam who first pointed out to me the similarities between the sangam and a village *panchayat*, the body of disciplinary control in villages throughout India. Like a village, he said, the acting community must tie itself together—must discipline itself, *kaṭṭupaṭu vēṇṭum*—in order to be civilized. Both need a disciplining organization to bind them into civility. If the acting community did not create such ties to bind itself, it would remain vulgarly naked. K. used this metaphor in a conversation we held while standing on the main road to the village, waiting for a bus to Madurai. We talked about the acting community there, with which K. has both consanguineous and affinal bonds. With evident pride in his own decision to continue living a village life in Valaiyangulam, he nevertheless spoke with me as someone who he rightly assumed shared his desire to see drama artists better their position in Tamil society.

> Our village has a panchayat. Just like that, the actors need a sangam. In these times, we need authorities to discipline us. Towns and cities don't have this, and so people there are crazy. For example, we wear shirts to cover our body. In the village, if you don't wear shirts, it's clearly bad conduct. So you'll wear a shirt, because you'll be scared that otherwise people will talk about your bad conduct. But in the town it's not like that: you do anything according to your own wish. In town, whatever one wishes, one can do. Now there will be bad people everywhere; it's not that there are only good people in the village, and only bad people in town. But because of the lack of control, in town 40 percent will be bad, and in the village only 10 percent.

K. provides here a vision of the sangam as a kind of return to traditional Tamil village discipline, offering an increasingly common revivalist overlay on the organizational penchants of modern Indian democracy. (Many contemporary Tamil films present a similarly nostalgic, romanticized image of the traditional village that contrasts, as K. did, the unchecked corruption of modernity in cities to a traditional wisdom and authority of village life. This is now a prevalent and enduring trope of which filmic examples abound; *Patinaru Vayasil*, *Oru Oril Oru Kiramam*, and *Tevar Makan* are just a few examples of very popular films from recent decades whose plots turn on these distinctions.) There are of course both indigenous and colonial models for such disciplinary institutions in India. The actors sangam, founded first under the Societies Registration Act of 1860 (Central Act XXI of 1860) and updated in accordance with the Tamilnadu Societies Registration Act of 1975 (Tamilnadu Act 27 of 1975), clearly draws on both models.

For one, even the updated version of the "Goals, Rules, and Regulations of the Tamilnadu Drama Actors Sangam" share a good deal in overall tone with colonial discourses of progress through modernity. The space carved out for moral guardianship by the Raj seems to have been occupied by the sangam's administrative committee, with the paternalistic Raj replaced by a "mother" (*tāy*) sangam, a term by which artists frequently refer to the Madurai Actors Sangam.

Equally, precolonial models such as the village panchayat are also apt. Before colonial rule, the village panchayat was a caste council wherein the dominant caste of the village decided questions of justice and punishment for the dominated subcastes (Dumont [1966] 1980, 172). Dumont's further description could equally describe the actors sangam's management committee today: "The jurisdiction of the assembly goes beyond the domain of internal justice. It can decree rules and exercise a controlling function" (175). The Sanskritic word *panchayat* comes from the Indo-Aryan *panc* (five). "In reality the word designates a meeting of some notables, 'four or five' as we should say" (172–73). This number neatly matches the obligatory five-member management committee of the actors sangam, the core decision-making group of the organization: president, vice president, secretary, vice-secretary, and treasurer.

More to the point, however, the caste panchayat and the actors sangam share a central concern with reputation: "The jurisdiction of caste panchayats is conceived as extending to any matter in which the men of the caste consider that the interests or reputation of the caste require action to be taken against a member of the caste" (Dumont 1966, 179; quoting H. Hutton 1946, 89). The sangam management committee functions like a "drama caste" panchayat, managing both identity and reputation. The extended analogy would be the district of Madurai-1 as village; drama people as caste; the acting committee as panchayat; and the management committee as its head men. These relations will become clearer later. The goals of the sangam, and the ongoing practices through which it seeks to instantiate these goals, reflect historical efforts by members of the Special Drama community to create an identity for actors that raises both their social standing and the reputation of their art in Tamil society.

Discipline in Practice

A small booklet entitled "Rules according to the Sangam founding laws of 1975 and 1978, detailing organization, the Sangam's goals, and the way it is structured" is available to all members of the Tamilnadu Drama Actors Sangam, Madurai. This booklet is essentially a member's guide to the organization of the sangam, its rules and regulations, and its governing bodies, their composition, and their regular meetings (for a full translation see appendix 1, "Sangam Rules").

The sangam's main governing body is its management committee, a fifteen-member elected group that meets to conduct sangam business on a monthly basis. The minutes of these meetings are printed and distributed to all sangam members after each meeting. Artists informally refer to these published minutes as "sangam notices."[3]

These documents are the internal complement to the publicly circulating drama notices discussed in the previous chapter. During my fieldwork, I collected examples of sangam notices as assiduously as I did drama notices. Their complementarity is total. While drama notices are composed with an eye to visual appeal and printed on brightly colored paper, sangam notices consist only of verbal material set in tight blocks of type, dark ink on a plain white background. Written exclusively in pure Tamil, sangam notices pointedly employ Tamil substitutes even for common Indian-English words; for example, the word "Buffoon" is shunned, replaced instead by *sirippu naṭikar* (comic actor). Both sets of notices are printed by the same four Madurai print shops located in the immediate neighborhood surrounding the actors sangam. While drama notices provide a public record of artists' upcoming performances, sangam notices are rather like a postperformance corrective tonic. Nevertheless their plainer wrapping can hardly disguise their inherently colorful content.

Sangam notices provide a remarkable window on the inner workings of the acting community. They expose the effects of artists' onstage actions in their offstage lives, both in the ideals they assert and as documents of artistic practices that repeatedly fall short of the ideal.

The purview of the sangam's management committee is to oversee and implement the goals of the sangam through disciplinary measures. It is comprised of members in the five named posts of president, secretary, vice president, vice-secretary, and treasurer, and ten members in unnamed posts. As stated in the sangam rules, the ten members constitute an "action committee" empowered to enforce sangam guidelines affecting a wide variety of situations. The nature of these disciplinary measures, and the situations they affect, expose the tensions that define the lives of Special Drama artists.

> *Rule* 5. The Action Committee of the Sangam will decide, examining each situation, the rules to be followed by members amongst themselves, with those taking up the drama art, and with those general people organizing dramas.
> *Rule* 6. The Action Committee will decide whether a member should be suspended from the Sangam or subject to a fine should that member act against the rules of the Sangam, or behave in such a way that might spoil the reputation of the Sangam.

These rules are purposely nebulous to allow the action committee the prerogative of "examining each situation." Attention to the details of actual disciplinary decisions offers a sense of the ideological work of the sangam in practice, as they pursue the stated goal of protecting, reforming, and encouraging "the progress of the actors and actresses who undertake" the art of Tamil Music Drama.

The following are two standard examples of the kind of behavior that is routinely disciplined in this way by the sangam. These decisions were taken by the sangam management on 1 August 1991 and concern related matters:

> 1. Our Sangam member Rajapart Mr. P. V. Vijayarājaṉ has given the committee a complaint regarding our Sangam member Mrs. M. S. Minerva Devi, charging that last 15 July 1991, in Kāppiḷippaṭṭi village near Dindigal, in the drama *Valli's Wedding* organized by Pudukkottai Actors Sangam member Sridaran, Mrs. Minerva Devi used overly cheap language to scold Rajapart Mr. Vijaya Rajan while he was playing the Hunter role, and that she sang songs unrelated to the story, as well as that she prolonged the drama to 7:00 A.M. even after the musicians had wound up, without asking for their consent. The Committee has called upon and inquired among the coactors of that drama so as to ascertain the truth about this matter—namely, Mr. T. N. Palaniyappan, Mrs. T. M. Chitra, Mr. S. L. Raja Rettinam, and Mr. T. M. A. Arun—and has proved the matter to be true. Moreover, that drama was tape-recorded, and the Committee has listened to those recordings, and what has been said about Streepart Minerva Devi has proven to be true. Hence, Minerva Devi was called and during inquiry she regretted her faulty behavior. Hence it was decided Minerva Devi has to give Rs

201 to the Sangam Growth Fund. Hereafter, if this is repeated, the Committee recommends that her membership be revoked.

2. Through listening to the tape recording of the drama *Valli's Wedding* which took place last 15 July 1991 in the village of Kāppiḷippaṭṭi near Dindigal, the Action Committee came to understand during the meeting of 1 August 1991 that our Sangam members Dancer T. M. Chitra, all-round Sardar, and harmonist T. M. A. Arun, all of whom participated in this drama, had transgressed our Sangam rules in the following ways: the Dancer spoke vulgarly with the all-round; the all-round spoke vulgarly with the Dancer; and the Harmonist spoke vulgarly with both the Hunter and Valli. The tape was also played for those named above. Hence, having called them and inquired, and their having promised not to go against the Sangam rules hereafter, it was decided that as contributions to the Sangam Growth Fund, Dancer Chitra should give Rs 101, Sardar Rs 101, and Arun Rs 51.

The presence of an audiocassette recording of the performance in question lends these proceedings an inquisition-like quality. Performances of Special Drama are often taped by the men providing electricals for the event and staffing the sound and light service table. Thus the availability of a taped record against which to check accusations of wrongdoing is not unusual here. Nor are any of the accusations themselves, or the punishments meted out to them.

The minutes of every monthly committee meeting tell similar stories. An actor and actress exchanged words unrelated to the story onstage, and she took off her shoe and slippered him: Rs 401 fine. An actor stood, drunk, in the hallway of the Mariyamman temple across the street from the sangam building and behaved vulgarly: Rs 301 fine. An all-round drank at a drama and stopped playing: Rs 51 fine. A tāḷam player entered the sangam building one afternoon at four o'clock and hit a harmonist, wounding him: Rs 201 fine. Two comedians were inside the sangam building discussing the organization of an upcoming drama when they began arguing, and it came to blows; for this "shameful behavior within the Sangam building itself," each received a Rs 101 fine.

Such decisions refer to and rely on implicit rules, developed over the course of many such action committee meetings, articulating injunctions on artists' behavior both onstage and off. The primary punishable infractions in onstage behavior are cheap language, singing songs unrelated to the story, vulgar behavior (a broad category that includes inappropriate dancing or dance not fitting one's role), performing drunk, and prolonging the drama after dawn has broken. Offstage, similarly, the committee polices any behavior that might be construed as rude or low occurring by artists near the actors sangam building, where such behavior threatens the reputation of the community as a whole. All such behaviors impede the sangam's overarching goal of "protecting and reforming the art of music drama."

In January 1993 a set of rules codifying the actual terms by which artists are expected to abide was published by all the management committees of all the actors sangams in Tamilnadu, collectively. In a joint meeting initiated by the Madurai Sangam, they ratified the following injunctions:

> 1. The artists of all Sangams agree cooperatively to not disgrace music drama, but rather to respect Sankaradas Swamigal's songs, by following all the Sangam rules and regulations so that the dramas proceed properly.
>
> 2. Artists must arrive at the performance venue by 9:00 P.M. Any member who arrives late is responsible for all resultant losses.
>
> 3. Dramas must begin at 10:00 P.M. and conclude at 6:00 A.M.
>
> 4. It is forbidden to go onstage having drunk alcohol.
>
> 5. Artists are forbidden to introduce vulgar actions, dialogues, or songs into a drama.
>
> 6. It is forbidden for a comic actor to behave vulgarly when acting the role of a woman.
>
> 7. In the drama *Valli's Wedding*, Naradar must appear by 12:30 P.M. and Murugan by 2:00 A.M.
>
> 8. In the drama *Valli's Wedding*, the Old Man scene must be enacted, Valli and Murugan must garland each other, and Naradar must reach the garden.
>
> 9. Artists are forbidden to introduce into any drama songs dialogues and actions unsuited to their roles.
>
> 10. Musicians must avoid speaking or singing jokingly with actors and actresses, or leaving their stations to get up and dance with them. Likewise, actors are forbidden to joke and converse with the musicians.

The edict concludes with a list of eight songs written by Swamigal for *Valli's Wedding* that must be sung every time the drama is performed.

Sangam notices chronicle a constant battle on the part of the Sangam's disciplinary body against particular, predictable slips in the behavior of its members. Arriving late, drinking on the job, using foul language, acting vulgarly (particularly when cross-dressed as a woman), engaging in joking banter with musicians, fighting in the sangam building, and singing songs unsuitable to the drama are punishable offenses regularly punished. Their policing has not eradicated such behaviors; instead, these same slips occur during every drama season and are duly investigated in committee meetings. Their ongoing existence poses a conundrum: why do sangam members regularly engage in behaviors that contradict the stated ideals and ratified policies that artists, via their elected representatives, ostensibly erect for their own benefit? Cynicism regarding official representative politics aside, the existence of these prohibitory edicts might itself now partially incite the forbidden behaviors (Foucault 1978). And yet the conflict represented in the sangam edicts long predates the codification of these rules.

The conflict is inherent to working in a stigmatized profession that is famous for one thing but wants to alter its reputation. The conflict for artists is between making a good living in the short term (fame), or working for the good of the community as a whole in the long term (the good name). To be sure, these are questions of idealism and corruption, of personal as well as community politics, and of faith in the possibility of social change. As an observer, I felt the conflict myself: I considered many artists who were active in the sangam management and supportive of its goals to be good friends, while as an audience member I often found the performances of artists who flagrantly violated sangam rules most compelling.

To some extent the conflict is apparent in the sangam rules themselves. One stated aim is "to protect old dramas filled with the values of patriotism, cooperation, love, nonviolence, and chastity, and to help conduct the new dramas of the present time according to such values." Another is to help artists make a good living, and "generally, to take up any and all actions which might aid in securing the well-being and prosperity of the actors, actresses, and musicians." Though these two goals need not necessarily conflict, in reality they do: what sells best in this field, which after all is a recognized commercial endeavor for its participants, are the activities deemed least suitable by the sangam. When they are in their most loosened-up states, these artists offer appreciative audiences suggestive songs and dances, joking banter, and even the genuine fights that occasionally break out between them onstage.

Many artists confront the conflict between rules and realities with a deep sigh of exasperation. I discussed these matters quite directly (and again with some exasperation myself) with Jeyam, a mridangist in his early thirties who already holds a position on the sangam's action committee. I met with him and his elder brother Selvam just after the all-sangam-wide regulations discussed above were circulated in 1993.

SELVAM: If a man acts wrong, he'll do so his whole life. You'd have to change society to change him.

JEYAM: That's how his life will be, generation after generation. A person cannot be disciplined in such a situation. If someone is going to be bad, they are going to be bad. You can't change people.

SUSAN SEIZER: But the sangam keeps putting out these rules; they have just put out the same rules again, which they keep trying to enforce. Year after year, "You must not speak vulgarly. The musicians and the actors must not speak together onstage," et cetera. The same rules. Yet you say artists can't be disciplined. So why does the sangam keep trying?

J: The problem is with the audience's perspective [*kaṇṇōṭṭam*]. How the audience looks at them.

SS: How is that?

J: In those days, because of the way artists conducted dramas and did their work, the audience gave them respect. They all sat quietly and watched, and they appreciated Murugan. If it was Swamigal's drama, the audience demanded that the songs be sung correctly. The audience demanded that in those days. Not anymore.

SS: When was that?

J: Oh, about twenty years ago. I've been working in this field about ten years. This whole time it has been otherwise. The audience only wants cinema songs; that is what they look for. These days they take cinema tunes and put new lyrics in them, and this is what the audience likes. Only for this does the audience like our work. Only for this do they hire us, and only then do we have work. This is their aim. The situation for us is [determined by how] the audience's gaze has really changed.

This conversation moved through stages typical of a logic I encountered repeatedly: artists must be disciplined (even if they can't be, even if such a thing is impossible) because the audience is not; the audience's desires are shaped by cinema now (the cinema referred to shifts in time anywhere between sixty years ago at the birth of the Tamil film industry and sometime in the past decade, dependent primarily on the speaker's own age and circumstance). In the end, whether one blames the audience, or cinema, or the artists themselves, the situation remains the same: the audience pays for artists to perform in precisely those ways the sangam forbids.

The sangam's primary tactic for preventing the encroachment of cinema songs and suggestive dances on "the values of the old dramas" is to maintain a division between comic and dramatic scenes. Sangam rules forbid dramatic Heroes and Heroines from introducing into dramas "unsuitable" songs, dances, or dialogues. Such singing and dancing is, however, expected of comic actors and actresses. The comic portions of the drama have become the place where such crowd-pleasing activities are tolerated and even encouraged in concession to the tastes of contemporary audiences.

There are a few lighter dramatic scenes, however, that blur the strict distinction between comic and dramatic scenes. Sivakami readily notes that the garden scene in *Valli's Wedding* as scripted by Swamigal has the Heroine dancing and singing with lesser characters in supporting roles (who appear in the script simply as her "girlfriends" or "maidservants"). These supporting roles are now generally played by the Dancer and the Buffoon in drag. When Sivakami performs this playful and sometimes parodic scene, she dances and sings cine-songs shamelessly. She defended her choice to me as follows:

> Our men Tangavel Vattiyar and Varatarajan Annan [two respected drama teachers in Madurai] told me to sing only Swami's songs. But the contractor of this drama came and told me directly to sing more cinema songs. Because audiences appreciate only the songs they know. The audience said, "Please sing four cinema songs." What do I say? I said, "I will not sing. Go and ask the Master, he will get angry." Then the audience said, "What, Madam? You are singing the same old songs? How do you expect us to enjoy them?" and they left. Everyone! Only five people were left. The drama was good, but the audience? Artists find that play good, the songs good. But for the audience? One needs a crowd to perform; right, Susan?

A young Dancer raised a similar point in discussing the sangam rule that forbids performers from talking to the musicians onstage. Kasturi, a very popular comic performer, frequently speaks directly to both the musicians and the audience while onstage. Here is her appraisal of the overdetermined ineffectiveness of the sangam rule:

> The audience understands [what we say], and if we talk only to the musicians, they might think something of it. So therefore the sangam made a rule, "You all don't talk, you don't talk: just let the girl look at the audience and speak." But they won't be able to effect that rule. The musicians will be like, "Oh, we can't talk? Let's see!" and they'll urge us to talk a little to them. Anyway, without such talk, it wouldn't be good.

I love this closing admission. It is as though Kasturi is saying, "Anyway, I'm going to do this, because my business after all is to be a good performer!" by which she clearly means good by her own standards and on her own terms. In the sangam's terms, "good" now means proper, even polite. For the audience, good can be flashy and bawdy. But I get the sense here that Kasturi meant "good" as a performer's performance: interesting, playful, and rich.

Overall the rules of the actors sangam reflect a tension between the loosened interactive states that pertain between artists and, to some degree, make their artistic lives possible (that is, the kind of interactive willingness to *mix* and mingle with new people, to meet the demands of different and varied audiences, and to improvise new lines and acts according to the particular situation that allows these artists to pull off an unrehearsed eight-hour drama every night) and the culturally disavowed excesses that such a relaxation of normal interactive relations seems inevitably to breed. Sangam notices reveal this tension in the constancy of their regulatory attempts and their difficulty in ever fully attaining them. The tension is between what the job of acting all-night dramas really involves and the kinds of disciplined behavior deemed ideal to raise the artists' social status.

Indeed, the best and the worst aspects of Special Drama arise from the same feature: Special Drama is special precisely because of the artistic freedoms its organization requires. Every performance is different. The genre requires improvisation (recall that Swamigal's scripts, read line by line, would run for a mere two to three hours in performance; to stretch scripts to eight hours requires embellishment, to say the least). The ability of artists to improvise and add to written scripts—to extend them—is their strength, while the concomitant unloosed, untied, unbounded, and oftentimes unruly state of mind that enables such extension is also their downfall.

Artists must negotiate such conflicting attitudes as tensions that push and pull at an essential excess in their art. The best artists manage, while internalizing many of the disciplinary discourses of which the sangam constantly reminds them, nevertheless to find spontaneity in performance and a way to use the tension between these two poles to enliven, rather than suffocate, their performances.

Take S. P. Mina, an impressive Special Drama actress with years of experience acting in film as well as onstage. Mina prefers stage acting because of just such opportunities. In drama, "we can speak and act however we like, and as well as we like. There's none of that in cinema. There we have to act according to what the director says. We can't go beyond that." What distinguishes Special Drama for her is precisely the opportunity it affords to go beyond someone else's direction. Special Drama offers artists freedom to act and to move beyond external constraints. But this freedom, this "going beyond," can quickly become excessive, and a constant battle against such excess is the purview of the actors sangam. It functions as a collective superego that exists to remind artists, with punitive fines, of the norms by which their actions stand to be judged. The sangam is thus charged with reining in the very freedoms that make Special Drama special.

Nowhere is the relationship between comedy/drama and loose/controlled more visible than in cross-dressing, where the stigmatized (and hence particularly available to comedic representation) status of femininity makes opportunities for men who cross-dress inherently different than those available to women who play men.

Cross-Roles: Marked Men and Funny Women

In the late nineteenth century and very early twentieth, the repertory plays of music drama were performed by all-male troupes. As we have seen, this was a golden age to some (Nagaraja Bhagavattar, for one), when the reputation of the field was not compromised by the bad reputation of "public women." During this period it was standard for men to play women. When female artists entered Special Drama in the 1920s, however, they replaced male artists in the leading female roles.

Today men no longer cross-dress to play leading heroic roles for women in Special Drama. They do, however, continue to play comedic roles in drag. The most frequent cross-dressed performances by male actors are in supporting comedy roles, like the role of second maidservant and girlfriend (*tōḻi*) to the Heroine, whose first maid is played by the female Dancer. Unsurprisingly, it is comedic actors—Buffoons, and occasionally Secondpart actors—who play such low-esteem roles, often parodically.[4] Such cross-dressed comedic performances are hugely enjoyed by audiences, a response that only further stokes the missionary zeal of the actors sangam to curb the vulgarity of comedic performances. Male actors' cross-dressed performances regularly incite heightened disciplinary measures.

Female actresses cross-dress, by contrast, only to perform dramatic roles. As such their performances rarely need to be regulated through disciplinary measures. Indeed, the concerns of actresses playing prestigious male roles closely dovetail with the overall aspirations of the sangam: their own prestige rises in concert with the general prestige of the art form. Women cross-dress only to play the higher-prestige dramatic male roles of Hero and Second Hero (most often Naradar in *Valli's Wedding*), or the child's role of Prince (the latter a staple of the drama *Pavalakkodi*). For women, cross-dressing is an onstage strategy for attaining a good name, an attempt to escape the stigma on women who act by ceasing to be women when they act.

That is, men playing women comedically are (and are expected to be) "bad," while women playing men dramatically are (and are expected to be) "good." For men, playing cross-dressed roles is a fame/bad boy strategy: in playing women they abandon any pretense to playing Heroes. The most popular of these male actors flaunt that abandon to great effect. The pleasure they take in their own comedic moves here can be infectious. In particular, the several gay Special Drama Buffoons I met managed in this role to flaunt their willingness to play bottom in a way that was so overtly sexual that one straight male Tamil friend I brought along to a *Valli's Wedding* performance was so overcome, he was reduced to laughingly repeating, "Too much, Susan, too much!" throughout the entire cross-dressed Tōḻi scene.

Such popular success of course only secures, even for a male actor, the less-valued fame rather than a good name. This seems all that can be hoped for from the lowly comedic role of Dancer in any event, since higher values emanate only from dramatic roles. The ironic pleasure of securing the name of a good girl by successfully imitating a heroic man is reserved for cross-dressing women.

In discussing the North Indian theatrical genre of Nautanki, into which women also entered in the 1920s, Kathryn Hansen suggests that the entrance of women "feminized" the theatrical field, giving all its actors the low status that "results from being identified with the devalued female gender." Such feminization "causes male performers to be viewed (and view themselves) as 'effeminate' and inferior" (Hansen 1992, 256). Such is *not* the case for male Special Drama actors. They do not generally view themselves as effeminate or inferior (much as such tropes are available to gay male Buffoons, should they choose to play them for humor). Gender relations do of course figure importantly into the stigma on Special Drama artists, as we have already seen, as when male artists blame the bad reputation of the art form in general on the entrance of public women onto the stage. Likewise many laypeople assume that actors have confused and disorderly domestic relations, assumptions that affect men and women in the Special Drama community differently and prompt different strategies of redress (see chapter 9).

But the problem for male artists does not stem from a perception that they are effeminate. This mistaken assumption might easily be made, given an unusual feature of their everyday appearance: male Special Drama artists don't wear mustaches. Indeed, they rather proudly announce their profession by being clean shaven. In Tamilnadu, mustaches are virtual seals of masculinity. As far as I know, all Tamil men except those in the acting profession wear mustaches. This is not simply my perception. Mustaches stand in metonymically for men, just as earrings and a *bindi* worn on the forehead do for women. The doors to men's and women's public lavatories in Tamilnadu, for example, give a sense of the ubiquity of these symbols: the distinction is made through bold line drawings of a circle (round head) with a horizontal line where the mouth would be for the male mustache, as opposed to a circle and a dot where the forehead would be for the female bindi.

The different degrees of stigma that confront male and female artists are particularly evident in the different attitudes the two genders take toward the codes of everyday dress they choose to follow. Women try assiduously to blend in, while men actually seem unconcerned that they are easily identifiable as actors. For pragmatic reasons, male actors don't wear mustaches because facial hair interferes with their makeup. They put powder on their clean-shaven faces and then draw on the mustache best suited to the character they will play. Actors want to be able to play any male, even those "effeminate" types who lack virility (like the Husband in the Aṭipiṭi scene discussed in chapter 6), precisely to make hegemonic moral points such as that all Husbands should behave with masculine virility. It is, in a sense, the essence of the acting profession: actors take on multiple roles, they are no one fixed thing, they play fast and loose with muṟai.

Wearing clean-shaven faces without shame in everyday life, male actors seem to encode a certain assertive marking off of their primary affiliation as insiders to this community of outsiders. How else to understand that retired male actors remain clean shaven long after they cease to require the use of makeup? Or that Special Drama musicians, who never put powder in the first place, maintain this simple bodily practice that identifiably marks them as theater artists whenever they set foot in the Tamil public sphere? Shaving seems to cement community bonds among male drama artists. Interestingly, the mechanism through which it renders them immediately recognizable is that of negation, the same that stigmatizes them in the first place: actors lack order, lack regulation, and lack discipline; they also lack a standard feature of Tamil masculinity, a mustache. Yet this lack they wear with pride (see plates 4–6).

Thus though it may seem reasonable that their lack of mustaches could read as a feminization of the whole genre, I do not think this the case. Through this practice male artists are, if anything, able to assert a kind of hypermasculinity: they can play a different mustache every night, if they choose! Rather than an increased femininity marking men, as in the case of Nautanki, here the public life required of artists, with which male actors are quite comfortable, most affects women by compromising their femininity.

The different effect of public visibility on male and female artists is perhaps one of the greatest discrepancies between the offstage lives of women and men in the Special Drama community. As I demonstrate in part 3 of this book, in their offstage lives, actresses regularly employ multiple strategies for fitting into normative Tamil society, and for reducing the discrepancies between themselves and more reputable women. The difference between the public offstage behaviors of men and women in the Special Drama community indexes fundamental gender inequalities in broader Tamil society.

Actresses who struggle to establish for themselves a good name in this field bear a double burden of proof. When male actors parody women through cross-dressed comedic roles, they distance themselves from the most devalued aspects of their profession by laughing, and encouraging the audience to laugh along with them, at a "woman" onstage, as well as at the spectacle of a man trying to be a woman. With their malleable mustaches and mobile masculinities, male actors seem to have ready access to such parodic play. Female actresses, by contrast, can only access such critical commentary by distancing themselves from the female role that conditions their lives onstage as well as off. Indeed, to distance themselves from the stigma of being a woman who acts, some actresses choose to cross-dress and step outside their normal experiences as women.

Drama notices document that women have played male roles in Special Drama since the early decades of the twentieth century. Interviews with senior actresses support my impression that cross-dressing was more common among actresses in these early decades than it is now. Playing the male roles of Hero or Second Hero lent a woman the respect befitting such valiant roles within the drama community. In addition, it removed some of the discomfort many actresses felt at having to play women's roles, for they too felt a desire to distance themselves from what most stigmatizes a woman onstage: having a man touch her in public. One way to avoid such shame and discomfort is to become the Hero oneself, rather than the Heroine.

The specter of being branded "bad" is ever present for actresses, all of whom are affected by any single woman's slip. Public intimacy with any men other than her husband makes a woman vulnerable to accusations of prostitution. Actresses pay fierce attention to when, whether, and how they allow themselves to be touched by a man onstage. One actress answered my questions about the relation of onstage women's roles to the bad reputation of actresses as follows: "Actresses, as part of their profession, have to talk to men, laugh with them, even touch them and be playful with them, and there is therefore no fault in that. It is only when they exceed a certain extent that they are really bad; but you know if one person does something

[bad], ten people get the bad name." Regardless, then, that to convincingly act the part of a wife or daughter an actress might need to be willing to share a bit of staged intimacy, actresses hesitate to do so. For many the threat of increased stigma overshadows the appeal of increased popularity; in such calculations, a fear of infamy trumps any potential pleasures of fame. Actresses' unwillingness to compromise personal reputation for artistic reputation contributes to their participation in that stilted, stiff, motionless style I first found so odd in the dramatic scenes of Special Drama.

It now also becomes plain why some actresses reject altogether the inherent double bind in the role of "actress" and choose instead to play only cross-dressed male roles. N. M. Sunderambal, a lead actress in Special Drama who acted male Hero roles in the thirties, explained to me the logic of her choice as follows: "I didn't want to play Streepart because then the Rajapart would hold my hand, and touch me. So I took up Rajapart roles. I could sing and act, and I also had the courage." Then as now, valor and courage were considered the primary prerequisites for acting the part of a Hero. Of course, to play a woman's role also takes a certain courage, though Sunderambal claims that actresses today are simply "less shy" than she was. Calling them "less shy" rather than courageous is a thinly veiled criticism; Sunderambal sees herself as having a high sense of modesty. The inordinate value placed on female modesty for women in India sharply affects those who play women onstage. Modesty, in addition to being a key component of chastity, is itself perhaps the most frequently praised and strongly asserted virtue of Indian womanhood. Sunderambal's claim that modesty prompted her to take on the valiant role of Hero might well suggest that this particular kind of "courage" be more aptly termed "smarts," as it consisted largely of figuring out how to avoid the stigmatizing public touch of men (see fig. 32).

Female-to-male cross-dressing for Sunderambal grew not out of a concern to displace, or in any way trouble, extant norms of gender ideology, as readers familiar with contemporary Western female-to-male theatrical cross-dressing practices might well assume.[5] Instead it stemmed from her desire to occupy a better position within those extant gender norms: the male position.

Only a few Special Drama actresses today cross-dress to play the most prestigious Rajapart roles such as Murugan in *Valli's Wedding* (see figs. 33–34). When I asked these actresses about their choice to do so, they too invariably replied by invoking the notion of courage. In one artist's words, "I act men's roles because I can. I have the courage as well as the ability to sing and speak." Valor, and the right kind of skill and knowledge—again,

32 An act of modesty: Rajapart T. R. Mahalingam and Stripart S. G. R. Bakkiyalakshmi in a performance of *Alli Arjuna* drama, Kuala Lumpur, 1977. Note the look of shame on the actress's face. Photograph courtesy of S. G. R. Bakkiyalakshmi.

33 Studio portrait of actress Sittra Devi in costume for the Rajapart role of Murugan in *Valli's Wedding*. Photograph courtesy of the artist.

34 Actress Jeyalatha onstage in the Rajapart role of Murugan in *Valli's Wedding*, 1992.

literary and musical knowledge—remain the primary qualities regarded as befitting the male Hero.

But whereas in the earlier twentieth century this move to cross-dress succeeded in gaining many an actress respect, more recently the women who dare to play Rajapart roles encounter difficulties that their predecessors did not. I was told by several women who had recently tried to play male roles that male actors today often resent a woman encroaching on their source of income. In turn, these male artists will not book an actress in a Hero role when they themselves "talk dramas," and will discourage other agents from hiring actresses as well. One male Rajapart, whose reputation was based primarily on his strong singing voice, shared with me his low opinion of one of the most accomplished female Rajaparts in Madurai. His words can only be considered catty: "She has a low voice like a man, and can't hold her notes cleanly on top of it. Since she doesn't sing well she does this *novelty trick* of playing gents' roles." Calling her portrayal of a Hero a "novelty trick," he likens her cross-dressing to a cheap illusion, a false front hiding an empty interior. In so doing, he echoes more widely held attitudes toward stage actors. A female artist might well dread encountering such pettiness from male colleagues who thus set her up as a lightning rod for their own fears, surely contributing to the decline in women willing to take on the role of Hero.

Even more disconcerting and dissuasive is the fact that some Streepart actresses themselves, when playing the female role opposite a cross-dressed Hero, treat a woman in a male role as an impostor and openly criticize her onstage, making the whole conceit all the more difficult to pull off for any who dare. I witnessed one such drama in June 1992, in the village of Pranmalai, during a performance of *Valli's Wedding* where a fight broke out between the two actresses onstage playing Valli and Murugan.

The fight occurred during a drama that had cast one of the few actresses who currently dares to play male Hero roles, R. Jeyalatha of Pudukkottai, as Murugan, and Minerva Devi of Madurai (whose reputation for onstage trouble precedes her) as Valli. In the famous final debate scene of the drama, Hero and Heroine match wits. Murugan, disguised as a Hunter, insists that the deer he pursues has run into the millet fields that Valli guards. Valli insists the deer has not entered. Eventually, as scripted by Swamigal, she asks the Hunter for the distinguishing features (*aṭaiyālam*) of the deer he seeks. He responds by singing "Kāyāta Kaṉ" (In the Evergreen Grove), a song that has itself become the distinguishing feature of Swamigal's drama. The Hunter reveals that this girl herself is the deer he seeks, likening her countenance to that of the spotted deer in a series of suggestively evocative puns.[6]

At the performance in Pranmalai, however, Minerva Devi simply refused to play. Instead she broke character and insisted that this was no Hunter, but rather a woman in disguise, and one who knew nothing about hunting to boot.

Pandemonium reigned, and the debate scene turned into an all-out cat fight, the actresses hurling at one another rather brutal, reciprocal accusations about the seamier sides of their offstage lives. The audience ate it up. By dawn the action had devolved so badly that the drama agent had to intervene, stopping the drama by jumping onstage and declaring the event over. The final garlanding and dawn marriage scene never took place (punishable offenses that were then later duly penalized).

Instead the stage was packed up in a hurry. I shut off my camera, folded up my tripod, and headed back to the van in which we had come the previous night. Midway there, I stopped to ask some audience members what they thought of the drama. I was prepared for the worst, for their accusatory disappointment that a drama in their village had not been properly conducted, and in particular that the garlanding scene, generally regarded as conveying a divine benediction on the venue in which it is enacted, never occurred. I wasn't prepared for what they actually answered. Three older village men assured me, "Oh, this was an excellent drama! This is exactly what we like. A fight between actors makes a drama really good, and today they really fought."

Given such audience preferences, it should be no surprise that Minerva Devi was one of the most popular leading actresses in the field of Special Drama that season. Booked to perform every night for months in a row, she also regularly broke sangam rules and received sangam censure, as the notice cited earlier testifies. Here again the popular actress flourishes, not by adhering to sangam rules but by audaciously flouting them.

While I often appreciate the empowering aspects of such audacity on the part of an actress (as for example in Sivakami's imperturbable preference for dancing in the Streepart role), on that hot June morning in Pranmalai, I felt disheartened as I boarded the van back to Madurai. The spirit of the thing had not been at all playful or beneficent, and its effects carried beyond the stage. Jeyalatha declined to join the others riding in the van. She and her companion-cum-chaperone walked that morning, I later learned, at least ten kilometers from that village to reach the nearest public bus headed back to Pudukkottai.

Multiple Strategies

My point in this chapter has been to show how actors sangam procedures and practices expose the extent to which Special Drama artists have internalized dominant discourses about their lack of discipline. Sangam rules and regulations represent one strategic response to such accusations. The sangam exists as a kind of auxiliary, prosthetic body set up to control the transgressions enacted by artists' own unruly bodies, to which artists respond in diverse ways. Some follow sangam dictums in pursuit of a good name, while others flaunt the same for a big name. I found both of these opposing responses to sangam prescriptions on how they ought to behave in their professional lives active among contemporary special Drama artists.

I also found, however, that artists use many other strategies to mitigate stigma in the course of their everyday lives. These strategies are far less codified than those endorsed and adjudicated by the sangam. They are also less obviously oppositional than the strategies traced here. Rather, artists' strategies for mitigating stigma offstage seem to have one common goal: to lessen public censure and public involvement in their private lives. In part 3, I return to look at three particular offstage domains—talk, travel, and family—in which artists attempt to draw limits on the public exposure of their private business.

First, though, it is time now to look more closely at what artists actually do onstage, and at how stigma and artists' strategies to mitigate it play off each other to create some very funny performances.

PART TWO Comedy

4 The Buffoon's Comedy

Jokes, Gender, and Discursive Distance

Every joke calls for a public of its own.
—Sigmund Freud

The writer of prose does not meld completely with any of [his] words, but rather accents each of them in a particular way—humorously, ironically, parodically, and so forth. That is to say, the words are not his if we understand them as direct words, but they are his as things that are being transmitted ironically, exhibited and so forth, that is, as words that are understood from the distances appropriate to humor, irony, parody, etc.
—M. M. Bakhtin

The Distances Appropriate to Humor

Bakhtin suggests that humor, irony, and parody all involve a certain kind of discursive distancing, a productive separation between author and text, speaker and speech. Special Drama Buffoons deploy jokes in this way, offering them at different distances—either more or less directly—to the men and women in the audience. By skillfully manipulating norms of public discourse, gendered as they are in India, the Buffoon manages to tell dirty jokes to a mixed audience and get away with it. Using "the distances appropriate to humor," the Buffoon's comedy deftly reenacts the very conventions of gendered discourse that the public telling of such jokes would seem to transgress.[1]

This chapter presents a close analysis of a Buffoon's monologue from the opening act of a Special Drama. The monologue is typical in several important ways. First is its subject matter, a fantasy in which modernization would visit upheavals on otherwise docile, static gender categories and securely separate spheres. The theme of modernization and its discontents has, as we have seen, been a staple of debate and conversation throughout twentieth-century India, now offering an array of comic possibilities. A young male protagonist's fears about the withering of privileged male access to the Tamil public sphere drives this particular monologue. Through this narrative conceit, the comedian effectively connects fear of the foreign with fear of the female in a potent illustration of how economical humor can be.

Second, the monologue is typical of its genre. This particular oral text is performed by many Buffoons, none of whom claim it as exclusively their own. Jokes, anecdotes, stories, and tall tales, even turns of phrase and gestural moves, pass freely among Special Drama actors. In performance, artists tailor and alter these to suit their own style, making the texts their own in the telling. There are no written scripts for the comic portions of Special Drama.

Third, the monologue is typical in its staging. It is actually performed as a dialogue between the comedian and the musicians, though still considered the comedian's act. Special Drama artists refer to it simply as the "Buffoon's comedy scene" (*papūṉ kameṭi cīṉ*). While the dialogic quality of this performance is typical of such opening acts, it is pointedly not a duet but rather the lead-up to the Buffoon's duet with the Dancer in the scene that follows this one. Here the Buffoon's repartee with the musicians establishes a relationship of support between male artists, a general tenor of "stage right" and the quality of talk and action that characteristically occurs there throughout the night.

Finally, this performance introduces the provocative use to which the theatrical footing known as a *stage aside* is often put in Special Drama comedy scenes. Goffman uses the term "footing" to refer to the alignment of speaker to hearers. Changes in this alignment are "a persistent feature of natural talk" that allow speakers to make shifts in tone and attitude within the course of a single utterance or string of utterances (Goffman 1979, 5). The defining conceit of a theatrical aside is that certain listeners are excluded from its address. While this basic conceit is maintained in Special Drama, the determination of which listeners will be excluded reverses the conventions of Western dramaturgy. The widely exported Elizabethan paradigm of the soliloquy, for example, has an actor uttering an aside as though the persona represented were alone—either entirely alone, or alone with the audience (think Hamlet)—as a means of communicating something to the audience and apart from the other players. In Special Drama, quite to the contrary, the comedian directs his aside utterances to certain other players, and away from the audience.

Clearly, an aside is an entirely relative phenomenon. When the norm has the actors talking to each other as in contemporary American dramatic theater, the audience of invisible observers is treated as though it were a "fourth wall." A marked break occurs if a performer turns to address a comment directly to the audience. In Special Drama, the norm (or unmarked footing) is that the performer does speak directly to the audience, and there is no imaginary fourth wall. Consequently, the marked footing becomes the address to another artist onstage. In the dramatic scenes in Special Drama, actors generally maintain this formal frontality, facing the audience and speaking directly into the standing microphone before them, using the marked footing of speaking directly to another artist only sparingly, for emphasis. In comedic performances, however, actors often engage in action and comments among themselves, playing and speaking directly to each other (a practice the actors sangam attempts to curtail, as noted in chapter 3). Such moves—shifts in footing—break the formal frontality that otherwise offers actors' words most directly to the audience. Comedy is a frequent locus of such marked breaks in presentational format, another sign of the marked role played by comedy in Special Drama overall: marked by a lack of formality and refinement, comedy is assumed instead to be loose and vulgar.

In this performance, the Buffoon uses the stage aside literally as a sideways communication with a same-sex set of his coplayers. The four male musicians seated stage right become his right-hand men, his intimates and confidants. The stage aside allows the Buffoon the ruse of confiding his more intimate thoughts and feelings to these men's familiar ears alone, rather than to an entire village audience full of unknown persons, women and children included. To this effect, the Buffoon uses a full complement of possible discursive distances, ranging from the casual close speech of intimate familiarity with a same-sex cohort to the far reaches of formal generality in public rhetorical address. Dominant norms of gender propriety in Tamil public behavior and speech assume sex-segregated social spaces and practices: public buses are split down the middle by separate-side seating for men and women; restaurants have separate sections for men only or women and families; movie theaters have not only separate seating for women but a separate queue for ladies to purchase tickets; and not surprisingly, women and men sit separately in the audience at Special Drama.

Sex segregation is a naturalized aspect of the Tamil sex/gender system. On the Special Drama stage, dramatic actors convincingly expound on the importance to Tamil culture of maintaining gender role division. The Buffoon, instead, does so in ways that manage to be simultaneously proper and titillating, exploiting the humorous potential of gender constraints on speech by making a show of abiding by them.

The present analysis focuses on what the Buffoon actually does in performance: how he talks and moves, as well as the actual jokes he tells. The performance event has two tiers, the story and its telling. I refer to these as the "narrated event" and the "narrating event," terms that help distinguish the speaker's different uses of the first person.[2]

In the narrated event, use of the first person singular refers to the fictional protagonist of the story, whose actions take place in the past tense. The narrating event, on the other hand, unfolds in the present, where the Buffoon's "I" refers to himself as narrator and not to a fictional character. The narrated event (the story) is necessarily embedded in the narrating event (its telling). The interplay of these two tiers—what Barbara Kirshenblatt-Gimblett (1975) calls their "text-context fit"—is more powerful than either alone. Indeed, the most intriguing aspect of this performance is how the same cultural assumptions play out in both the narrated and the narrating event, shaping the performance event as a whole.

The Buffoon's Comedy Scene

The actor I saw perform this monologue was a young Buffoon named S. K. Selvam. The venue was the Mariyamman temple grounds in the village of Narayanapuram, on the outskirts of Madurai. This performance on 1 April 1992 was supported by common funds from the villagers, part of a series of performances in honor of the goddess Mariyamman held over three days. The temple grounds abut a main roadside, where buses and lorries passed intermittently throughout the night. Every square inch of ground was otherwise occupied by the bodies of audience members, as roughly one thousand men, women, and children stood, sat, or lay on mats to watch this opening scene.

With a remarkable degree of consistency, audiences for Special Drama segregate themselves by sex and age. The Narayanapuram audience followed suit. Young children and elderly men sat up front, closest to the stage. Other men and boys sat behind them to one side, and women and girls on the other. An aisle, marked out by a thick jute rope, separated the two sex-segregated sides of the audience. Groups of younger men in their late teens through early thirties—bachelors—stood along the perimeter of the audience, on all sides and at the back, a ring of young male spectators forming the audience's outer edge. Figure 35 provides a schematic diagram of the Special Drama stage in its audience context; the encircling ring of young bachelors is represented by stick figures in the diagram. There were perhaps three times as many men as women in attendance. Attending such a perfor-

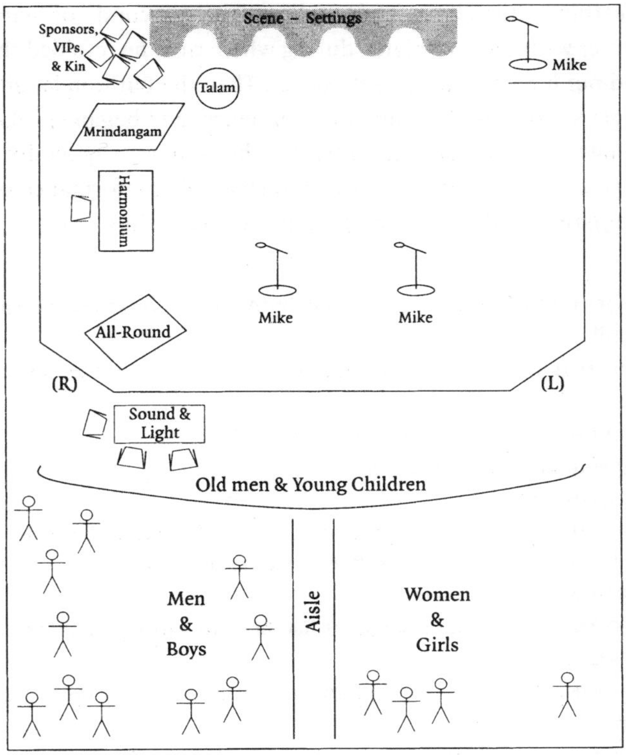

35 Schematic diagram of the Special Drama stage in its audience context.

mance is a much more complicated and problematic psychosocial endeavor for Tamil women than for Tamil men, for reasons that will soon be clear.

For this opening act, the Buffoon wore an entire suit of gold lamé. He entered from the upstage left, crossed over to the musicians' side of the stage, and stood at the mike closest to them. From tailored trousers to wide-lapel jacket, he sparkled under the stage lights. The preliminary scene setting was in place, a canvas backdrop painted with a flamboyant yet reverent religious image of the goddess Parvati riding the back of a tiger. Images of Hindu deities are standard backdrops until the real stage action of the performance begins.

After reading the drama notice aloud and introducing all the players in turn, he introduced himself: "I, Buffoon-Comic S. K. Selvam." Selvam offered the standard, polite gestural welcome to both audience and musicians, palms meeting at his chest. There followed two seconds of semiaudible joking banter with the musicians, during which time he refolded the drama notice and put it back in his jacket pocket. Then the Buffoon laughed, took a beat to get serious, looked out at the audience, and began speaking.

The following is a verbatim transcript of the event (see appendix 2 for the Tamil text), translated into English.[3] (To view this performance on video, go to http://stigmasofthetamilstage.scrippscollege.edu.)

1. BUFFOON: Until the dawn, until the drama ends, please remain calm and peaceful
2. as you are now. I request your support of our artistic service, hereby begun.
3. In your lives you should [*pointing at audience*]
4. struggle to improve yourselves.
5. ALL-ROUND:[4] Unh.
6. BUFFOON: You should not be jealous. Why do I say this? Because in my
7. life I was jealous, and how I suffered because of it!
8. ALL-ROUND: How's that?
9. BUFFOON: My next-door neighbor had been to a foreign country.
10. ALL-ROUND: Unh.
11. BUFFOON: He went to the foreign country, made lots of money, got lots of
12. property, and came back here to Madurai, where he was living comfortably.
13. ALL-ROUND: Unh.
14. BUFFOON: As soon as I saw him I felt jealous.
15. ALL-ROUND: Unh.
16. BUFFOON: Jealous, I went straight to my father.
17. ALL-ROUND: What for?
18. BUFFOON: I went to my dad and asked, "Dad! Dad! I'm going to a foreign country.
19. Give me a little money, please, Dad!" But he said, "You grinning fool!"
20. ALL-ROUND: Unh!
21. BUFFOON: "It's not money you want if you're going to a foreign country.
22. First, you need a passport, and to get that you need a photo. So
23. first go get your photo taken." "Fine," I said, and went straight to
24. the photo studio with my ten rupees.
25. ALL-ROUND, HARMONIST, MRIDANGIST: (inaudible comments), *laughter*.
26. BUFFOON: Unh, yes. I reached the photo studio. Now, does the photo studio give you

27. your photos instantly? They tell you to come back in an hour! Fine;
28. I figure, I have an hour—I can go have a glass of milk. I went straight
29. to the milk stall. I ordered a "special" milk. When I got it, it was boiling hot—
30. ALL-ROUND: Unh.
31. BUFFOON:—so hot I couldn't touch it! Fine, let it go; I figured I'd let it cool some,
32. and placed it on a nearby table and began reading the newspaper. A woman
33. came in all in a rush: it seems her child had no milk! She quickly ordered
34. two milks from the man, hurriedly adjusting the chest-piece of her sari
35. [*throwing it over her shoulder like this*], right? The chest piece of her sari
36. falls over the glass of milk I set down! Now, I want to drink milk.
37. If I want to drink milk, what does that woman have to do?
38. ALL-ROUND: What does she have to do?
39. BUFFOON: What does she have to do?
40. ALL-ROUND: (I don't know!)
41. BUFFOON: You don't know?
42. BUFFOON: If I want to drink milk, that woman has to lift the chest piece
43. of her sari, // man!
44. Musicians and Audience: *laughter*.
45. BUFFOON: Can one go up to a woman and say that? So I figured, forget it.
46. I don't want/need milk. I'll go
47. MRIDANGIST: [*plays a single hit: ding! on his drum*] //
48. BUFFOON: [*slow, exaggerated side-to-side gesture of acquiescence with the head*].
49. directly to the photo studio, pick up my photo, and head straight home.
50. ALL-ROUND: Unh.
51. BUFFOON: I reach the bus stop. Our house is on the route to Fatima College.
52. ALL-ROUND: Unh.
53. BUFFOON: Our house is on that route, so I want/need either the number 7 or the number 73 bus.
54. ALL-ROUND: Unh.
55. BUFFOON: So I'm at the bus stop thinking I'll get on a bus. The crowd at the bus stop
56. is all women! It's morning. Those who go to offices are going to their offices.
57. Those who go to other jobs are going to their other jobs. Each and every one
58. is getting on the bus to go to her respective place of work. Crowd, what
59. a crowd of women! It was like a swarming pack buzzing in my ears.

60. What could I do? I thought, how many buses can I simply let go by
61. while I stand here? Suddenly a bus came. I figured, even though there's this
62. huge crowd of women, it'll be okay; I can adjust. I'll just stand off to one side.
63. So I grab the rail in one hand and my photo in the other,
64. I have one foot on the step of the bus and I'm hanging on.
65. ALL-ROUND: Unh.
66. BUFFOON: But how far can a man go hanging on?
67. ALL-ROUND: Onto what?
68. BUFFOON: The rail, of course! Grabbing the rail—what else can I grab and hang onto? Fine,
69. I tried to forget about it, let it go, thinking I'd hang on all the way.
70. But my hand starts to really hurt. Next to me stands a sixty-year-old woman.
71. ALL-ROUND: Unh.
72. BUFFOON: "Mother, O Mother, excuse me, please, I'm hanging on here for
73. such a long time by one hand! My hand hurts.
74. Please lift your leg and let me climb on!" // that's what I said to her, man!
75. MUSICIANS AND AUDIENCE: *laughter.*
76. ALL-ROUND: What did you say?
77. BUFFOON: You ask what? "Please lift your leg, and I'll climb up onto the vehicle,"
78. that's what I said. But immediately that woman took it differently! She screamed,
79. "What's that you say? How old are you? How old am I?
80. How dare you look at me that way . . . ! Get lost, you!"
81. and gave me a punch that shoved me right in!
82. ALL-ROUND: Unh.
83. BUFFOON: Inside the bulging bus it was totally packed.
84. ALL-ROUND: Unh.
85. BUFFOON: There were women in front, women behind, and women in all
86. the seats. Nothing but women. I'm holding the photo in one
87. hand—my shirt has no breast pocket—I'm holding the photo in
88. one hand, and holding onto the handrail with the other. The bus
89. is going along fine. Suddenly, "sudden-brake" [*hip thrust*].
90. ALL-ROUND: Unh.
91. BUFFOON: Some little goats were crossing the road, right?
92. ALL-ROUND: Unh.
93. BUFFOON: and the driver slams [*hip thrust*] on the brakes. The vehicle
94. rocks. There are women in front of me.

95. ALL-ROUND: Unh.
96. BUFFOON: Directly in front of me is a sixteen-year-old girl. One mustn't bump HER, right?
97. All the women would say that I came onto the bus just to bump them!
98. ALL-ROUND: Unh.
99. BUFFOON: So I tried as hard as I could to keep my balance by reaching out with my other hand
100. [*reaches*], right? And the photo slipped out of my grasp and fell.
101. ALL-ROUND: Unh.
102. BUFFOON: Now couldn't that photo fall anywhere else?!
103. ALL-ROUND: Unh.
104. BUFFOON: No, it fell right beneath that girl's legs!
105. ALL-ROUND: And then?
106. BUFFOON: If I want to get the photo
107. ALL-ROUND: Yes //
108. BUFFOON: I'd have to ask that girl to lift her leg! //
109. AUDIENCE: *laughter* //
110. ALL-ROUND: Unh!
111. BUFFOON: So what could I do? Can one go up to a girl and say,
112. "Lift your leg, I have to take a photo!"?
113. MUSICIANS AND AUDIENCE: *laughter, applause.*
114. BUFFOON: So I figured, I don't want the photo. I don't want the foreign country.
115. Just let it go, let it go, let it go. I figure,
116. "the time's not right; I'll find some other way to earn my living. . . ."

Modernity and Its States of Desire

In this monologue, the Buffoon simultaneously offers and disclaims three utterances that would be considered highly vulgar, in a mixed-gender context, without such disclaimers. Each disclaimed utterance functions as a punch line for the three sequentially related jokes embedded in the story. These jokes are told man-to-man (Buffoon to musician).

The opening lines establish a young male protagonist, jealous of a neighbor who has returned from a foreign country with "lots of money" and "lots of property." The young man determines to get for himself some of the good life, asking Dad for money to go to a foreign country, while Dad, older, wiser, and ever so much more practical, tells his son that first of all he needs a passport, and for that he needs an ID photo. This starts the causal chain of story sequences rolling and establishes the genre of the tale itself: a young man embarking on a kind of identity quest, a coming-of-age tale—he is, after all, pursuing his own identity, the self he would like to see develop, in life as well as on film—and this quest is at least ostensibly sanctioned by the father. Initiated by jealousy and desire for foreign money and the comforts it can buy, it is desire itself that animates the entire adventure to follow. Our protagonist has dared to want more, to want a life he doesn't have, a middle-class life. The father's practicality, his suggestion of sensible steps, actually translates into teaching his son how to channel, and defer, his desire: you want the world, but first you need a passport and your ID photo. With each step, our protagonist sinks deeper into the quotidian realities of his current life, the very local life he dreams of escaping.

The story is enacted in the form of a conversation between the Buffoon and the all-round drummer. This conversational effect between the two men is created and maintained by the musician's verbal and visual responses throughout the course of the story. The all-round consistently utters "Unh" (*uṅ*), a ubiquitous conversational response in Tamilnadu that signals listening. In general such back-channel maintenance responses are less optional in Tamilnadu than in many other places. A visual equivalent is the famous South Indian shake of the head in face-to-face interactions, and though not noted in the transcription, the all-round does a lot of that, too. All throughout the Buffoon's narration, the all-round successfully maintains the listener half of this conversational channel, repeatedly voicing "unh" or otherwise interjecting appropriate verbal and visual encouragements.

In a conversational story, one person will be the intending teller and another person or persons the intended recipient(s) of the telling (Sacks 1974). The telling will be oriented toward its recipient on the level of content as well as of form. Having a male musician as the intended recipient of this story frees the story from the constraints imposed by a mixed audience. As a story told among men, it partakes of common street-corner society conventions that are a familiar component of the popular imagination about the public sphere in Tamilnadu, a domain where men frequent—and frequently loiter at—roadside tea stalls, *iṭli* shops, and rickshaw stands.[5] Such male public spaces are a regular feature of both everyday practice throughout Tamilnadu and contemporary media representations of Tamil life, particularly filmic ones. Common knowledge and common cultural literacy code these all-male settings for all-male conversations as sites where stories can and do have overtly sexual content. The Buffoon's conversational turn to the all-round drummer makes a sexual turn of conversation seem both expected and natural.

Looking at the conversation-like structure of the monologue, it is clear that the all-round drummer in fact supplants the audience role by taking up fairly aggressively the role of intended recipient. The audience for whom the staging of the drama is ostensibly intended—that is, the villagers and the deity for whom they are sponsoring this entertainment—are temporarily circumvented, and a displacement occurs. The village audience remains seated, watching and listening, but the Buffoon now speaks with and to the musicians. An interesting gap is opened, like a trapdoor, stage right.

That door creates the means for moving with relative ease through the barrier that otherwise separates moral from immoral discourses, and mixed-gender from single-sex audiences. On one side of this door, the front, the Buffoon utters moralizing comments directly to the village audience. These begin in lines 3 to 7, when, after his performative opening address to the audience in line 2 (which is actually a performative within a performative: "I request your support of our artistic service, hereby begun"), he offers the audience moral advice: "In your lives you should struggle to improve yourselves. You should not be jealous," and so forth. At the musician's encouraging response "eppaṭi?" (How's that?) (line 8), the Buffoon turns to him to deliver line 9, beginning the tale.

What occurs here is an excellent example of a change of footing. It entails a significant shift in the alignment of speaker to hearers. Shifts in footing frequently involve code switching and changes in tone and pitch, as well as literal changes in stance that include postural repositionings of the speaker's "projected self" (Goffman 1979, 4). The Buffoon employs two distinct footings here. In one he uses a moralizing tone and unequivocally pitches his address to the audience, using a frontal postural stance. From this footing the Buffoon voices his own desires concerning the progress of the narrating event in the eyes of the audience. He establishes a moralizing stance that remains in place throughout his performance, creating a facade behind which (or rather, out the side of which) he slips in order to talk to the musicians.[6] His sideways address to the musicians is the Buffoon's second footing, the extended stage aside. He uses this footing for all the parts of the narrative that might be considered vulgar in a mixed-audience context.

The two footings are stances for moral and immoral comments, respectively, and, while separate from the two tiers of narrated and narrating event, can cross into either of them. An example is the Buffoon's use of the rhetorical question "Can one go up to a woman and say that?" in line 45. The question is part of the narrated event—it advances the plot of the story—but it uses the moral footing established for audience address to do so and allows the Buffoon to monitor the narrating event. Shifting to a frontal footing and looking directly out at the audience when he asks this question, the Buffoon effectively draws the two events, narrated and narrating, together through a moralizing bridge.

The establishment of two separate footings has two face-saving corollaries. First, the aside footing enables the dirty jokes to remain separate from the speaker's frontal, presentational self, and second, it enables the "real" audience to *overhear*, rather than *hear*, these jokes. By alternating use of these two footings, the Buffoon ensures that he has neither lost his audience nor lost face before them. The moralizing facade he erects thus works for their mutual benefit. After each joke, the Buffoon turns to the audience momentarily and, from his frontal footing, secures his moral front with a post-punch-line line that nails his strategy in place: "Can one say that to a woman?" The only proper answer to this rhetorical question, of course, is negative; nevertheless, this is exactly what the Buffoon just did. The Buffoon just managed to utter the socially unutterable and the only social repercussion was laughter.

Let us look at this strategy in practice with the first joke (lines 28–42). The protagonist goes to a milk stand to kill some time while he waits for his photograph. He orders a glass of "special milk" (meaning undiluted whole milk, "original" milk), which is so hot that he has to put it down to let it cool before he can drink. Enter a woman, a mother who has come to secure milk for her child (i.e., a good woman). She orders two milks and adjusts the top of her sari, flinging the end piece up over her shoulder. It falls so that it covers the protagonist's glass of milk. The Buffoon turns to the musicians and demonstrates the gesture of the woman in the story, grabbing an imaginary sari end and throwing it back over his shoulder. Still facing the musicians, he asks, "If I want to drink milk, what does that woman have to do?" (line 37). The all-round responds, repeating the question, which the two men banter back and forth: "What does she have to do?" "What does she have to do?" "I don't know!" "You don't know?" (lines 37–41), as if stalling, building up nerve and postponing the moment of the dread utterance, until the Buffoon gives in and says it: "If I want to drink milk, that woman has to lift the chest piece of her sari, man!" (line s 42–43), at which the audience bursts out laughing.

This sentence is considered vulgar in its double entendre, in its suggestion that lifting the chest piece of her sari would expose the woman's breasts, from which he would then drink "special milk."[7] This is something a decent Tamil man would not say to a decent Tamil woman. Uttering such a phrase at all in public is clearly transgressive. To make absolutely clear that the utterance was meant for the ears of his musician friends, the Buffoon inserted the vocative "man!" at the end of the sentence to clarify the direction of the address. Thus, through the pretense of an aside, the buffoon is able to *mention* "privately" the publicly unutterable phrase while escaping the charge of actually *using* it in public. His aside is a gesture of politeness that attempts to mask the fact of the utterance. The blatant and predictable failure of this masking attempt is its success as a joke.

The distinction effected here between use and mention is analytically important and warrants closer attention. The distinction turns primarily, once again, on the speaker's distance from his speech: *mention* is meta-usage, in which "one expresses an attitude to the content of an utterance" (Sperber and Wilson 1981, 303) rather than simply expressing the attitude conveyed in the content of the utterance itself. Irony is attitude about attitude, a comment on the utterance qua utterance. "USE of an expression involves reference to what the expression refers to; MENTION of an expression involves reference to the expression itself" (ibid.).

Affect as well as attitude is captured in the ironic, quotative meta-usage of "mention." The Buffoon caricatures politeness even as he seemingly enacts it. He never directly addresses any woman, either in the narrated or in the narrating event, with the implied vulgar request "lift your sari so I can drink milk." Instead he mentions only that he has reflected on such an utterance and decided it was too vulgar to use by prefacing the dreaded phrase with "Can one say to a woman . . . ?" The Buffoon has created, in fact, a very special and idiosyncratic context for the potentially vulgar phrase by mentioning it only in a disclaimed usage embedded within a story told as a cautionary tale. Yet there it is. The Buffoon's hesitation, his turn away, his stalling in fear of the utterance, and the care he takes to distance himself from it all point to the vulgarity of the request. The audience laughs, partially in relief at not having had to accept an all-out public use of this phrase, a solecism from which they were saved by the use-mention distinction.

Line 45 marks the change in footing that definitively determines that what the Buffoon puts into play is, in Sperber and Wilson's terms, "an attitude towards the content of an utterance" rather than merely its content (303). The question "Can one go up to a woman and say X?" is a rhetorical tag that reinscribes the code of propriety and public address that the joke has just transgressed. The Buffoon turns directly into his moralizing footing, the facade he erects for the audience, to say this, asking a general, open-ended question, posed to no one in particular and thus ostensibly to everyone present. The question is in marked contrast to the previous statement (lines 42–43) that ended with the directive address "ayya" (man). Here instead he uses an impersonal, tenseless, verbal construction (the infinitive + lām) to ask "Can one say?" (collalāmā?). Again the question turns on social mores of decency, conditioned by and conditional on gendered linguistic usage. It avoids impropriety through a masterful splitting of mention and use, honoring social convention through a strategic, appropriately distanced uttering of the socially unutterable.

The mridangist registers the joke's punch with a congratulatory-sounding ring on his drum (line 47). The Buffoon had begun to move on in his narration (lines 45–46): "Forget it. I don't want/need the milk." On hearing the drum sound, he languishes a moment, drawing out the submissive, acquiescent gesture of agreement—a slow, exaggerated movement of the head from side to side—that marks the protagonist's retreat from his desire. The young man is momentarily cowed; his fear of inadvertently improperly addressing the woman triumphs over his desire for milk: "Fine, I figured, I don't want/need milk."

The word I have translated here as "don't want/need" is *vēṇṭām*, an impersonal negative verbal construction whose semantic range includes both the English "need" and "want." It can thus refer to renunciation of any stripe.[8] Likewise, its positive inverse, *vēṇṭum*, refers to desire of any type, as need and want are seen to be of a piece, and worldly. The notion of renunciation suggests the bliss of desirelessness and the praiseworthiness of ascetic transcendence of all things material. In addition to inspiring epics of popular Hinduism (such as are enacted in some of the stories dramatized in Special Drama, for example in *Sattiyavan Savitri* and *Harischandra*), similar notions about renunciation form part of the daily survival strategies of the millions of people who live below the Indian poverty line, including many in the Special Drama audience. The ability to eliminate or transcend desire is praised, expected, and often necessary. I point this out because it is very unlike life under First World consumer capitalism, where one is constantly exhorted to want more, crave more, and consume more. For those living in poverty in India, desire is still more often a path toward danger than toward good(s). Disappointment is frequent, and traditional Tamil counsel exhorts people not to entertain big—that is, expensive—dreams. The increasing presence of images of the middle class enjoying material success figuratively next door, as the world shrinks, exacerbates the conflict: Ought we dream? Whose dream is this?

But this is precisely the road onto which the young protagonist of our story has just embarked. He harbors big desires: lots of money, a fine house, and the prestige and status of working in a foreign country. Meanwhile he is having a hard time meeting much smaller goals, even that of getting a glass of "special" milk. So he renounces his desire for the milk. He decides instead to head home. At home, perhaps, he and his father could once again strategize his next steps. An image of him and his father, holed up in the safety of their own home, floats here unstated. The world has indeed been turned inside out in this imaginary: there are no women at home; they are all on the streets! Quotidian fears about interaction with the opposite gender loom large, revealing both their humorous and nightmarish potential. In our protagonist's continuing adventures in the public sphere, Woman again enters the picture to foil the fulfillment of even his simplest desires.

The bus stop is teeming with women, and their words are buzzing in his ears (line 59). He feels outnumbered and overpowered, and his worst fears are realized when even a sixty-year-old woman—old enough to be his grandmother—interprets his desires as sexual and literally punches him further into this terrifying world of women and frustrated need. This all-too-literal punch line of the second joke is a variation on the form of the first and third jokes. Here the disclaimed and potentially offensive vulgar statement is actually uttered in the narrated text, not just in the narrating text. The joke is in line 74: "'Please lift your leg and let me climb on,' that's what I said to her, man!" Here our protagonist actually talked to the woman, rather than simply imagining talking to her and thereby safely talking himself out of uttering the offensive line. The problem is again double entendre. In the narrating text, the Buffoon uses the moralizing footing when he tries to extricate himself by making a clarification in line 77, adding, "I'll climb up onto the *vehicle*" to cancel out the offending interpretation that he intended to climb onto the *woman*. The belated correction, however, does not retroactively cancel the joke, which lies precisely in that second meaning, just as the rhetorical question "Can one say that to a woman?" only underscores the forbiddenness of the utterance. The moralizing footing does, however, effectively distance him from the ambiguous utterance through a demonstrative, if belated, disclaimer, before which the double meaning slipped out intact.

Unlike the other two jokes, however, this joke concretizes the threat of discursive transgression. Exemplary retribution—she yells, she punches—occurs within the world of the narrated text itself. Clearly it is a world overrun by serious, self-important women. Their actions instill fear; indeed, their actions live up to all this young man's worst fears. This second joke, by justifying what might otherwise be seen as an unsubstantiated fear of talking to women, accomplishes something very important in thus defining the larger context in which such a story is apt. The entire story turns on such fear, which this joke validates as realistic. In his pain (his hands hurt) our protagonist makes a less-than-prudent decision: he speaks from and of his desire, instead of stifling it. Retribution is swift. He is summarily (mis)judged (line 78, "immediately that woman took it differently!") and sentenced (lines 78–81, "she screamed . . . and gave me a punch") to dwell in a world where women's consensus rules (line 97, "all the women would say that I came onto the bus just to bump them!"). The assumption informing the moralizing rhetorical frame of the first and third jokes—the silent "no" that implicitly answers the rhetorical question "Can one go up to a woman and say X?"—has been upheld beyond a doubt: a man cannot make potentially vulgar utterances around women without courting both bodily injury and profound public humiliation.

In this regard, the third joke revisits the strategy of the first, enlivened by the fear-effects underscored in the second. The third joke and its setup span lines 83 to 112, ending with the sequence "If I want to get the photo, I'd have to ask that girl to lift her leg. So what could I do? Can one go up to a girl and say, 'Lift your leg, I have to take a photo!'?" At this point, claps and laughter erupt from audience and musicians alike. Now the double entendre turns on a semantic overlap within the Tamil verb *eṭukka*, meaning both "to pick up" (as for an object) and "to take" (as for a photograph). If he tries to suggest to the girl that he needs to pick up his fallen photograph—his own fallen image, really, as his identity stares up at her from under the feet of this overwhelming pack of women—he encounters the embarrassing interpretation that what he really desires is to take a photograph between her legs. (Recall that needing versus wanting is indistinct: "I need to pick up a photo" and "I want to take a photo" are both meanings contained in this one sentence, "nān fōṭō eṭukka vēṇṭum," which I have thus translated as "I have to.")

The narrative framing of this final joke uses much the same formula as did the first joke, where an implicit proprietary concern prevents the protagonist from uttering the unutterable. Here, however, the rhetorical question (line 111) precedes the punch line (line 112), and both are spoken to the musicians. The aside footing and the moralizing footing meet in a single utterance and together work to heighten the overall effect of forbiddenness.[9] This young Buffoon seems to feel genuinely shy in the telling of this joke; he speaks quickly, and exclusively now to the musicians. The establishment early on in his performance of two clearly demarcated footings for moral and immoral comments has given way over the course of the narration to a single compound performative address, congealing the likeness of narrated and narrating event. By the end, both the disclaiming hedge ("Can one go up to a girl and say?") and the disclaimed desire itself ("Lift your leg, I have to take a photo") have become more than he can manage to say to any woman, real or imagined.

His final full turn away from women clarifies the gender segregation of discursive worlds that has operated throughout this performance. A men's world of discourse is instantiated onstage in the exchanges between the Buffoon and musicians. A complementary world of women's discourse is implicit in both the narrated and narrating texts. In the latter, the Buffoon assumes that it is necessary to take up a moral tone to address an audience that includes women. In the former, the fictive specter of a world dominated by women's discourse is construed as women "bashing back," yelling, and shaming men. The women's world appears here, to a young man at least, as the inverse of the supportive, same-sex solidarity on which he can rely when telling his right-hand men the woeful tale of his wanderings in the world of women.

A large part of his misery inheres in the fact that women mortify this young man. He'd rather surrender his every desire—his identity, even—than risk the shame of facing women's wrath and censure. The sixteen-year-old before him is just the benevolent, virginal form of the terrifying demoness who punched him. Both are Woman.[10] When his face falls at the sixteen-year-old's feet, it is as though she towers right above his own speechlessness. Staring up at her from beneath her skirt, he faces the ultimate impossibility: speech in the face of everything between her legs. "Can one go up to a girl and say, 'Lift your leg, I have to take a photo!'?" It is unthinkable. Speechless before and beneath her, he finally abandons all desire. The closing renunciative lines of the narrative (lines 114–16) register defeat and rejection as the moral lesson of a cautionary tale. "So I figured, I don't want the photo. I don't want the foreign country. Just let it go, let it go, let it go. I figure, 'the time's not right. I'll find some other way to earn my living. . . .' "

The resignation in these closing lines makes a chilling link between local constraints on desire and their global implications. The protagonist, emboldened by his desire for money, fantasizes about a foreign country. He enlists in an outgoing project wherein his desire for the foreign mingles with his fear of the more immediate and localized other, Woman. His inability to override his fear of the female—exposed by his inability to negotiate communication with the sexualized specter of Woman—leads him to discontinue his pursuit of the foreign. The intimate, inner body parts that his jokes hint at exposing remain forever foreign to him in their femaleness. The narrative thus effectively links the female and the foreign as spheres of (male) activity, equally alien to the local Tamil male subjectivity assumed throughout the narrative.

Indian nationalist discourse has historically cast women as repositories of Indian "tradition" who must assiduously maintain the spirit of "custom" in the domestic sphere, as bearers of both the nation's morality and its very "Indianness" (Chatterjee 1993). In Tamilnadu these visions of woman as the source of indigenous tradition grew even more literal and pointed in the figure of "Tamil-tāy," whose image is revered as the Mother of Tamil (Ramaswamy 1997). In this context, the public sphere evinced in this tale appears unnatural. Its reversals are disorienting and unfamiliar: gone are the expected, conventional separations of domestic and public realms. While the buses are bulging with women, Father sits at home. The message seems to be that the foreign, modernizing influences that send men to work overseas while women take office jobs have finally converted the local public sphere into a foreign territory. As such the tale is a diatribe against the effects of foreign modernity and the states of desire that it breeds. Its telling succeeds because it conforms to existing gender-normative behavior in Tamil discourse. That is, in contradistinction to the reversals of gender roles apparent in the tale itself, its telling reproduces key sociocultural paradigms shaping discourse in contemporary Tamilnadu: first, that Tamil women and men do and should inhabit separate physical and discursive spaces (cf. "Genders are genres. The world of women is not the world of men" [Ramanujan 1991a, 53]); and second, that desire—particularly in its more modern forms, which traverse an ideology of separate spheres—is more trouble than it's worth.

It is important not to confuse the Buffoon's playful circumlocutions and tricky escapes with a politically pointed subversion of dominant gender norms. The parodic recasting of gender norms here, in the inverted-gender world of the narrated text, is more likely to reconsolidate the value of the dominant norms for most in the audience.[11] For while the tale effectively exposes and denaturalizes gender expectations for the Tamil public sphere, it simultaneously reidealizes them by making the vision of their disruption so laughable (silly, unpleasant, frightful). In the way it sutures text and context, the Buffoon's performance indeed seems to exemplify the extent to which successful parody "must be cut from the same cloth as that which it parodies" (Mannheim 1995). Parody is itself often implicated in the same regimes of power it parodies (Butler 1993, 125). This is not to say either, however, that humor does not have fabulous subversive potential; it most certainly does, as many documented cases demonstrate (Jenkins 1994; Newton 1972). However, humor can be put to any use, and there indeed is the rub. One must identify how a particular use of humor facilitates certain social ends, rather than others: "Parody by itself is not subversive, and there must be a way to understand what makes certain kinds of parodic repetitions effectively disruptive, truly troubling, and which repetitions become domesticated and recirculated as instruments of cultural hegemony" (Butler 1990, 139).

As large, public, village-wide ritual events, Special Drama performances offer the kinds of experiences that add to the basic socialization processes of the audience, children as well as adults, and their ongoing learning about the mores of gender behavior in the Tamil public sphere. As briefly suggested earlier, the audience is actually positioned to overhear, rather than hear, the Buffoon's jokes. While potentially present for all members of the audience, the fishbowl effect of watching the interaction of others from the outside is, however, strongest for the women and girls in the audience. This point deserves careful attention, if for no other reason than its Freudian provenance.

Within the Buffoon's moralizing footing, the only footing on which he directly addresses the women in the audience at all, his utterances unequivocally mark the exclusion of women from actual discourse. His use of the generic category "woman" in his key refrain, in the phrase "Can one go up to a woman and say . . . ?" identifies by inference all women as its set of impossible addressees. This rhetorical refrain serves to invoke a fictive, generalized, and indeed faceless Woman (in three standardized life cycle stages: teenage girl, mother, old woman) in place of the real and particular women in the audience, whose predilections are here assumed rather than determined through dialogue.[12] The facelessness of Woman, in her three bodily incarnations, provides an extreme contrast to the young man's pursuit of his own identity specifically through his face, an image of which he struggles to attain although finally it slips from his grasp. The overarching message is that women are not dialogic participants in discourse but rather its objects. In their very embodiedness, they prove to be hindering objects at that.

Based on just such an attitude a hundred years ago, Sigmund Freud attempted to generate a universal theory regarding the gender relations at the basis of dirty jokes. In *Jokes and Their Relation to the Unconscious* (Freud [1905] 1960), his model of triangulated gender relations posits that dirty jokes invariably involve a minimum of three people: one man to tell the joke, a woman to be the object of the joke, and a second man to take pleasure in the joke. In his account the woman is both the object of the joke and the obstacle to male pleasure.[13] It is a blame-the-vixen theory par excellence: women's prudishness frustrates men, forcing them into lewdness. In Freud's words:

> [Jokes] make possible the satisfaction of an instinct (whether lustful or hostile) in the face of an obstacle that stands in its way. They circumvent this obstacle and in that way draw pleasure from a source which the obstacle had made inaccessible. The obstacle standing in the way is in reality nothing other than women's incapacity to tolerate undisguised sexuality. . . .
>
> The power which makes it difficult or impossible for women, and to a lesser degree for men as well, to enjoy undisguised obscenity is termed by us "repression." (120)

Such Victorian notions of the inherent prudishness of women have found expression in nineteenth- and twentieth-century India in nationalist discourses of the home and the world. In its attempts to "take the best from the West and leave the rest," Indian nationalist thought succeeded in linking women with tradition, with spiritual purity and modesty, creating for the developing nation an "inner domain of sovereignty" that could remain untouched and untainted by the outer, interactive world of increasingly materialistic, increasingly Western, "male" concerns (Chatterjee 1993, 117). The good Indian woman of the twentieth century, like the good Victorian woman before her, was assumed to be incapable of "tolerating undisguised sexuality." For Freud, "civilized society" required that smut, seen as the original verbal expression of active (read male) sexuality, be transformed into a joke necessarily told man-to-man.[14] In the case of Special Drama, the twist on the Freudian paradigm lies in the rhetorical device that allows actual Tamil women to hear dirty jokes without falling off their assigned moral pedestal and also without threatening their assumed feminine incapacity to tolerate undisguised sexuality.

In the jokes told here, as in Freud's paradigm, male listeners replace female listeners as addressees. The very idea of talking to a woman stops the narrator from doing so; neither in the story nor in its telling can a dirty joke be told to a woman. In the former, the story's protagonist opts not to say the potentially obscene sentence in instances where a woman might misinterpret it; in the latter, the Buffoon opts not to tell these jokes directly to the mixed audience. Thus the relationship between narrated and narrating events is one in which the thematic content of the story both resonates with and relies on knowledge of the very type of public enactment in which it is itself unfolding: narrated event recapitulates narrating event. In both cases, woman's role as obstacle is satisfied by the mere idea of her: women are conjured, but no female response is solicited. The gender triangle model evacuates female subjectivity altogether, replicating a predetermined ideological role for women while replacing their agency with that of the listening man.

Onto this third party, this male substitute, is displaced not only the role of the addressee but also the burden of appreciating the original libidinal urge for exposure of the woman. Freud writes of this third party as "bribed by the effortless satisfaction of his own libido," seduced by jokes (and indeed often by the joker himself; see Sedgwick 1985) and their "yield of pleasure" into "taking sides without any very close investigation" (Freud [1905] 1960, 103).

This, arguably, is what happens for the women and men attending Special Drama events. The musicians laugh at the jokes, although laughing makes them complicitous. The women and men in the audience are relegated to a noninteractive, deflected audience role, one from which the addressee has been evacuated. Nevertheless they too laugh at the jokes they overhear. Everyone, it seems, is seduced by the jokes, and no one closely investigates the social and discursive paradigms on and into which the jokes play. Of course, women are more suspicious of that seduction than men: it's virtually written into their script that they should be so. Women who laugh at Special Drama comedy thereby risk distancing themselves, by their very act of laughter, from the prudish, morally upright, and irretrievably humorless women represented in stories such as the one analyzed here. Rural India is among the "many cultures [wherein] norms of modesty cause women who laugh freely and openly in public to be viewed as loose, sexually promiscuous, and lacking in self-discipline" (Apte 1985, 75).

The moral reputation of women here concerns everyone in Special Drama audiences, since those women present are none other than the grandmothers, mothers, sisters, daughters, nieces, and cousins of the men present. Indeed, the dilemma for the Tamil comedian is how to get away with telling jokes not simply for his own sake but for the sake of everyone else as well. His successful strategy assumes everyone's familiarity with moralizing discourses of propriety, vulgarity, and the ideology of separate spheres, serious cornerstones of Tamil cultural identity, and not normally laughing matters. Provoking mixed Tamil audiences to laugh together about such things is clearly complicated; many families, constantly concerned with moral standards, prohibit unmarried girls from attending such entertainment. The women who do attend generally do so in accordance with the stipulations Mahadev L. Apte (1985) notes for women's participation in humor so often: "certain social factors such as marriage, advanced age, and the greater freedom enjoyed by women in groups remove some of the constraints ordinarily imposed on them" (69).

The presence of women complicates relations in the public sphere, whether in a fictive world where a shy young man finds them impossible to address, or in their own home village at a temple festival where a shy young actor onstage finds them impossible to address. The women's own laughter seems to confirm the success of the Buffoon's use of a distanced address to tell them jokes. While it may belie discomfort and self-consciousness, the women's laughter is certainly not a protestation of what they have witnessed. The only real protest women make against such tropes is to not attend such performances at all, though, sadly, this refusal is itself all too easily folded back into jokes that naturalize prudishness as a part of women's morality. Thus women's participation in the audience for events that address the very cultural complexities of gendered address in Tamilnadu—indirectly, that is, and precisely so—is inevitably a complicated affair.

Layers of Meaning and the Meaning of Layers

In Tamil, the verb *tūkku* means "to lift." All three of the jokes presented here use the imagined action of lifting as a means of trying to get at that which is hidden but desired: lifting the chest piece of the mother's sari to get milk; lifting the old woman's leg to climb on; lifting the young woman's leg to get a photograph. In the Freudian paradigm, jokes are means of circumventing obstacles to attain desired pleasures by "lifting inhibitions" (Freud [1905] 1960, 169). Here too, lifting is an action desired to get around a (feminine) obstacle to desire. To lift is to expose an underneath, as well as to imply the existence of at least two layers.[15]

The action of lifting, revealing, and exposing at least two layers is encountered not only in the language of the Special Drama Buffoon's jokes but also in many of the concepts I have pulled in to analyze them. I have spoken here of two separate footings, each of which opens onto separate discursive spheres: in one the Buffoon is overtly moralistic, in the other covertly immoral. A similar two-sidedness defines the whole notion of double entendre, where a hidden meaning lies beneath an ostensible one. The notion of renunciation is similarly ambivalent: the desire to be free of desire is itself a desire. "I won't be jealous"; "I don't really want/need any such goods (foreign and/or female)." All these statements, footings, and imagined actions reveal what they conceal, and vice versa. I have thus attempted to analyze this scene as suffused with layers of meaning.

I have also suggested that the agendas of narrated and narrating events are strikingly similar in this performance, and that they support each other as co-texts that reinscribe the same discursive norms. Both employ young male protagonists who must negotiate between their desires to raise their status—which for one involves going to a foreign country to earn a living, and for the other means going onstage and performing witty monologues to earn a living—and their trepidation at transgressing established Tamil codes of mixed-gender discourse and respectability. In sum, the two male protagonists of these two texts not only comment on each other but also serve as tropes of each other. The tone of abnegation and defeat that characterizes the narrated event is precisely what enables the moralizing tone of mastery and success in the narrating event.

Using his pitiable fictional alter ego to do so, the Buffoon is able to act on his desires and achieve his goals. By managing to *mention* without actually *using* transgressive utterances in a public context, the performer maintains the persona of a decent fellow—who turns aside to utter to the company of men remarks that would be unutterable to a company of women—while collecting a tidy sum for his performance. The audience laughs and claps. Another successful opening act has been accomplished. The real punch line of that accomplishment, however, is that nothing has been destabilized: for all the good guffaws elicited by uttering obscene puns in a context seemingly unsanctioned by dominant Tamil mores, the normative organization of gendered spheres of discourse in Tamil social life has not actually been transgressed. So much for romantic theories postulating the innate subversiveness of the joke.[16]

Humor operates here instead most like art as the Russian formalists defined it: a process of defamiliarization, a "making strange." Like the Brechtian use of alienation effects in theater (Brecht [1957] 1964), the defamiliarizing project is liberating only in the sense that it frees one to be, in Fredric Jameson's words, "reborn to the world in its existential freshness and horror" (Jameson 1972, 51). One becomes only free enough, that is, to see the trap in which one is caught. Perhaps the women in the audience laugh in cynicism. The Buffoon himself, by deploying a technique of shifting address and qualified, distanced utterance, manages at least temporarily to slip out of some of the constraints on discursive propriety. He does not, however, alter them. When he leaves the stage, a Cheshire Cat–like image fades much more slowly: a grinning male face staring up the skirt of a sixteen-year-old girl. And while the story's protagonist may have exited with a whimper as the abnegated, innocent child, the Buffoon has achieved a comedic success. The dream he actually pursues is the one in which there is no need for him to hunt far afield for a new way to earn a living: instead he makes his right here at home, exploiting everything he can to do it.

The Ambivalence of Laughter: A Final Consideration

The Buffoon's name, Selvam, retrospectively has the ring of prophecy. The Tamil word *celvam* has three meanings: wealth and riches; the natural resources of a country; and a child. Selvam the Buffoon's wealth certainly lies in the natural resources of home, providing him a discursive state of affairs ripe with possibilities for linguistic play. The foolproof Special Drama Buffoons' strategy for evincing laughter from a platform just the right distance away is his riches. And he and his alter ego together function as inseparable aspects of a male child, one pitiable, the other competent, because of it.

As Keith Basso (1979) points out in his study of Western Apache joking imitations of "the Whiteman," joking situations that require a listener to play along with the joker as the butt of his jokes rely on preexisting relations of goodwill between the involved parties (67–76). Similarly, here the Buffoon relies on the willingness of the women in the audience to suffer his exaggerated fear of them, trusting them to indulge jokes that "affirm conceptions of what is 'right' and proper by dramatizing conceptions of what is 'wrong' and inappropriate" (76). Their patience is tested, as "a relationship in which goodwill is abundantly present is represented as one in which it is conspicuously absent" (76).[17] This concealing ploy makes possible revealing play. In the Special Drama audience, women—mothers, sisters, wives, grandmothers, and cousins of young men—extend considerable goodwill to the much-indulged Tamil figure of the pitiable boy-man. The young Tamil man, who at first appears to be the butt of his own joking story, in fact plays his protagonist's innocence and vulnerability against a standard, generalized female figure of staunchly rigid morality. As beloved boy, he plays on an existing set of culturally coded indulgences.

There is a Tamil expression that succinctly describes the male type that the Buffoon employs here. He is a *pāvam* man. "Pāvam!" is an expression of pity and sympathy, as in "alas, poor thing!" (Cre-A 1992). The pāvam man enlists the audience's compassion and goodwill by seeming vulnerably human in the face of institutional rigidity.[18] In other words, he appeals to the nurturing mother (Ramanujan's "breast mother"; see note 10) in everyone in the audience by exposing his own childlike fear of the avenging mother. His childlike innocence touches his every act. He is a son instructed by his father; he wants "original" milk; he says inappropriately sexual things to women who could be his grandmother. By conjuring up scary women whose goodwill he does not dare assume, he conceals the fact that he already counts on the sympathetic response of those in the audience to extend goodwill to him through their willingness to endure his jokes, and even to laugh at them, much as a parent enables the antics of a child.

Clearly, then, the loving and forgiving mother—absent in the story, but present at its telling—is essential to understanding the machinations of this performance event. Where, then, does the Buffoon's enabling discursive ruse of "use" versus "mention" leave the actual women in the audience for this comedy scene? Does the carefully crafted distinction between appellative hearing and excluded overhearing employed in the Buffoon's performance effectively save their reputations as moral characters in the dominant narrative of their lives as "Tamil women"? Or is sitting in the audience enjoying raunchy comedy a place where women too, perhaps, can partially escape the ubiquitous trope of Woman as Mother as Morality, in all its existential freshness and horror?

The women in the audience laugh. They have been interpellated, through an address at a set, calibrated distance, into both narrating and narrated events, and their presence is an integral part of the spectacle. Here "appropriate distances" provide a means of maintaining status quo positions, positions in which many women sit awkwardly and shyly through such scenes, their own hands held in front of their mouths, laughing in spite of themselves.

5 The Buffoon-Dance Duet

Social Space and Gendered Place

Mise-en-Scène

Scene: a public road.

Backdrop: wide, generic road stretching off vertically to horizon.

Detail: a small gray airplane ascends into sky; clearly a modern scene.

Enter Dancer, stage L.

Action: Sixteen-year-old girl dancing alone in the middle of the road (a fantastic suspension of Tamil norms of conduct for women; no matter).

Enter Buffoon, stage L.

Action: Unknown bachelor unexpectedly bumps into girl dancing on road. Ensuing duet rapidly develops into exploration of illicit love: lewd banter, flirtatious spats, boasts laden with sexual innuendo, coy one-upmanship, cooing love songs. Finally they decide to "do *love*." They *love-marry* and elope.

Exit Buffoon and Dancer together, stage L.

This second scene in a night of Special Drama is known as the "Buffoon-Dance Duet" (*papūn ṭans ṭueṭ*).[1] Following as it does on the heels of the rather stationary Buffoon's comedy scene, the full-bodied performance of the duet opens up the stage by using its full breadth and depth. It also marks the first onstage appearance of a woman. The interaction of the Buffoon and Dancer here literally sets the stage for how relations between men and women play out over the course of a night of Special Drama. This duet establishes the gendered geography of the Special Drama stage.

It is a geography built directly on the platform erected by the Buffoon in the preceding act. He imagines a sixteen-year-old girl out in the public sphere and—"*Oho!*"—suddenly here she is! The actress always enters this scene by singing a chorus of "*Oho! Oho!*" as she whirls, fast and furious, onto the stage.

Broad physical comedy characterizes the Buffoon-Dance Duet. Through exaggerated gestures, mockery, and extreme characterizations, the scene's humor lies in its exposure of its own constructedness. The predictability of this commonplace fantasy of love arising out of an unexpected meeting allows artists to perform and simultaneously to comment on such folly.

While it is thus primarily the representation of a fantasy, this little comedy scene also draws on paradigms active in daily Tamil social life. Indeed, its tropes are so familiar that its existence as a *story* and a *fiction* escapes notice: this is a narrative so naturalized that it disappears. Whenever and whomever I asked about the plot of the Buffoon-Dance Duet—beginning with simple queries such as "Why is she dancing in the middle of the road?" or "What is the story of this duet?"—I was invariably informed, by audience and artist alike, that "there is no story here, this is just *comedy*!" (ingu kataiyē illai, kāmeṭi tāṉ!). It was as though drama and comedy were antithetical terms. "Just comedy" meant that such performances have no touch with the more esteemed realm of the written story, verse, plot, or narrative.

Perhaps because it lives in a realm that no one considers worth serious scrutiny (i.e., that of comedy), the duet captures some of the more uncomfortable ambivalences shaping contemporary Tamil gender relations. It deals with things not often publicly "told." Like the genre of women's folktales usually reserved for private, domestic tellings about which A. K. Ramanujan (1989) writes so eloquently, the duet plays on assumed meanings. It offers messages and images almost too slippery to take the form of a linear, rational narrative. "Tales speak of what cannot usually be spoken. Ordinary decencies are violated. Incest, cannibalism, pitiless revenge are explicit motifs in this fantasy world, which helps us face ourselves, envisage shameless wish fulfillments, and sometimes 'by indirection find direction out'" (258).

Indirectly articulated motifs fill these performances. They inhere in enactments that occur in particular placements onstage, creating a densely symbolic world that communicates through and about social spaces and gendered places. My aim in this chapter is to make visible the contours of the sociospatial world reenacted by and reflected in the Buffoon-Dance Duet, performances of which I have found to be tellingly consistent.

The standardization of the structuring elements in Special Drama—the order of scenes, the use of repertory characters who perform in established musical and rhetorical styles, and the constancy of spatial blocking—makes the unique organization of this genre possible. On any stage, any combination of known or unknown artists can rely, in place of rehearsal or direction, on the continuity of these elements. The sociospatial features of the stage are first established each night in the duet.

My method for articulating the sociospatial paradigms it establishes is to discuss the placement of each key narrative juncture in the duet. I have observed these over many performances, and here I draw on and refer to nine separate duet performances rather than detailing one continuous single performance as I did in the previous chapter.

I originally chose this method of approaching the duet—that of viewing numerous performances as a representative sample of a larger whole, rather than attending to the historical specificity of one particular performance—as a means of proving to myself that the story I perceived in every performance was really there.[2] Seeing the scene performed many times by many different sets of artists, each time I recognized a clear and particular story, though no one else would quite discuss it as such.[3] Those around me took what I write of here as givens, as the unstated grounds of this kind of quotidian comedy.

It is not, I think, that I was determined to find narrative linearity and plot everywhere I looked, but rather that here was a narrative that somehow escaped recognition as such. To satisfy my own desire to understand the narrative stages through which duets progress, then, I spliced together video clips from nine separate performances of the Buffoon-Dance Duet in 1992 (see this edited montage at http://stigmasofthetamilstage.scrippscollege.edu). By lining up key junctures of plot progression one after another, I could see moves recur repeatedly: Buffoon "bumps" Dancer (nine times in a row), she screams (nine times in a row), they start a competitive dance (nine times in a row), and so on. This exercise distilled a structure beneath the comic moves and allowed me to analyze these performances not by analyzing a single text but by looking at a composite of multiple performances.

I now understand the duet as progressing through a contingent series of five relational interactions. The scene moves through these five phases in progressive steps. These relational interactions organize and use the stage space in particular ways that divide it, too, into five areas coded by their specific qualities of gendered interaction.

Each time the Buffoon-Dance Duet is performed, this story that appears to me simultaneously disappears for others into a nonstory as "just comedy" that slides into familiar sociospatial paradigms. Because of its very invisibility as narrative, the comedy duet now strikes me as offering a good place to begin analyzing both the mundane and the fantastic in the representation of Tamil social spaces on the Special Drama stage.

The Five Use-Areas and the Five Story Elements of the Duet

In performance, the narrative progression of the duet develops around five standard bits in a set sequence, five structuring moments in an otherwise improvised scene.[4] They are (1) the Dancer's entrance as a sixteen-year-old girl dancing in the road; (2) the bumpy meeting between Buffoon and Dancer; (3) their discussion of the meaning of a bump between man and woman, *iṭikka* (to bump) having a definite sexual connotation; (4) a contest of skills between Buffoon and Dancer as representatives of the male and female sex, respectively; and (5) mutual admiration and the decision to "do love," that is, elope in a love marriage. Through all this they sing hit cinema songs from the latest popular films, not replicating the choreography of the original cinema numbers so much as quoting filmic conventions of song, dance, and attitude, with all of which they and their audiences alike are already familiar.

There are equally five primary stage areas where such different uses are articulated, familiar to us already from the layout of drama notices: the four corners and center stage. These areas in which the action of the duet takes place each resonate with a certain character and quality of their own, by virtue of the repetition of specific kinds of activities there. The more I watched, the more I saw each of these areas as quality encoded, and the stage itself as a highly articulated social space.

Architecture of the Stage: Inside, Outside, Behind, Above, and Beyond

I have previously noted the general architecture of the Special Drama stage without mentioning its material or symbolic qualities, which are best understood in the context of their use (see again fig. 35). Even before artists mount the stage, however, certain architectural conventions are already in place. The raised rectangular proscenium stage of either dirt, wood, or concrete flooring is surrounded on three sides by thatched walls made of braided palm fronds.[5] These provide back, half sides, and a ceiling to the stage. The thatch extends behind the stage itself to cover the backstage area, which artists use as a greenroom. This backstage area is hidden from frontal view by ceiling-to-floor painted canvases that frame the artists while onstage. These canvases also help mark metaphorical boundaries in onstage action. If a scene calls for a brief and miraculous appearance from a god, for example, the deity's vision, voice, and general otherworldliness emanate from behind this curtain. In the Christian drama *Gnana Saundari*, the Virgin Mary speaks to the Heroine from upstage center and behind this canvas drop (much like the wizard in Oz). This is the "on high" position, directly upstage and behind all the mortal action unfolding onstage. Backdrop scene settings thus simultaneously provide an architectural division that offers intimations of a "beyond" to the antics of the night, and serve as painted representations of realist stage décor that suggest other spaces in other worlds.

In the Buffoon-Dance Duet, all these qualities of the backdrop cloth resonate. Through its exaggerated use of an infinitely receding depth of perspective, the painted road scene that frames the action here suggests a world that extends past the doings onstage, into the beyond. Indeed, this world that exists just beyond the painted canvas road rests on a very real road, where the audience sits and the artists perform. The theatrical demimonde of the drama world (*nāṭaka ulakam*) is a form of the beyond at which audience members often gape with a sort of awe, either when seated in the audience or when sneaking around to peer through holes in the palm frond thatch at the actresses backstage.

Artists demarcate the spaces of backstage and onstage by the terms "inside" (*uḷḷē*) and "outside" (*veḷiyē*), respectively. "Inside" refers to the artists' space backstage, and "outside" to public spaces open to the audience's gaze. These terms reverse otherwise prevalent everyday identities for participants at these events. Performers are usually the quintessential outsiders, while in this context they can temporarily be inside, and insiders to local audiences that remain outside. This rather idealized reversal of the dominant relational dynamics between village locals and itinerant performers temporarily places performers in control of a desirable, semiprivate space of limited access. (The argot that performers use backstage, however, shows that artists are not fooled by this temporary reversal into thinking themselves any less marginal because of it; see my discussion of the Drama Tongue in chapter 7).

Some local men are granted partial insider status by the performers at drama events. Local VIPs, drama sponsors, drama agents, and friends and relatives accompanying performers all enjoy a privileged position that allows them to traffic between the realms of inside and outside during the perfor-

36 The upstage right corner. Sponsors, agents, local VIPS, and relatives and friends of the artists stand beside the musicians during a Special Drama performance, June 1993.

mance. These men often watch the drama from the upstage right corner of the stage, crowding in between the musicians and the far edge of the backdrop (fig. 36). From this vantage point, they are afforded a close experience of the performance. They also thus figure into the performance itself as a staged audience, their every reaction visible to spectators on the ground. As inaugurated by the musicians in the Buffoon's comedy scene, stage right continues here as the locus of an extended representative male audience that, with the addition of these partial insiders, bridges two worlds.

These, then, are the outermost architectural framings of the stage, within which five onstage use-areas take qualitative shape.

Configuring the Stage: The Duet in Performance

While the musicians begin their performance stage right, actors enter from upstage left. From here they move out onto the stage, enacting particular types of activity in its different areas. The general locations of these areas are represented in figures 37 and 38, schematic diagrams indicating the major

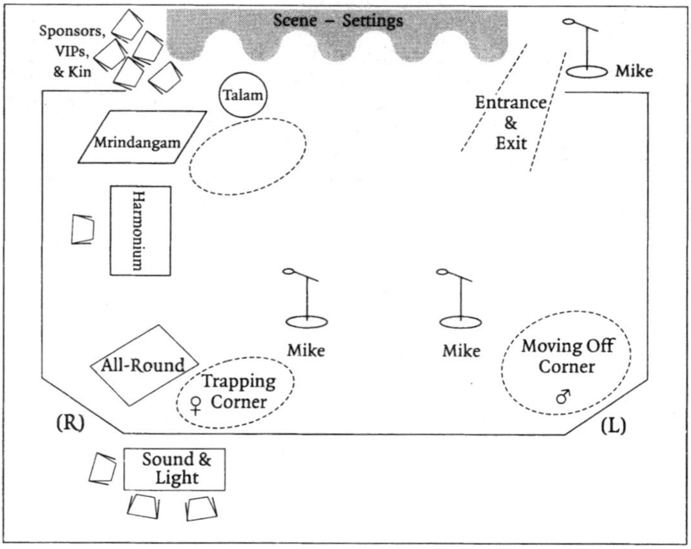

37 The spatial organization of the Special Drama stage.

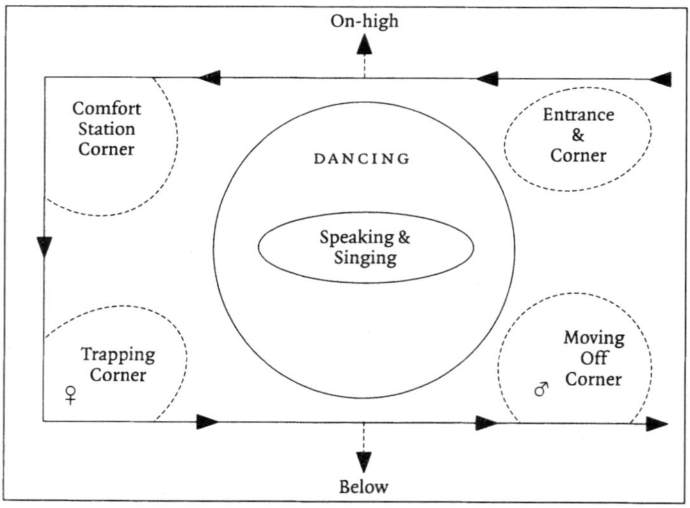

38 Schematic diagram of the use-areas of the Special Drama stage.

39 The upstage left corner. Actress N. Jansirani sings into the microphone located in the stage-left wing in preparation for her stage entrance, April 1992.

use-areas of the stage, whose particular qualities and character emerge as Buffoon and Dancer move through the five story elements of their duet.

The Dancer's Entrance

The upstage left corner is entrance and exit to and from the stage for actors throughout the night. It is the main channel of supply between inside and outside. Strategically opposite the orchestra, here actors can make eye contact with musicians before their stage entrance and coordinate previously unrehearsed entrances to the accompanying music. A microphone located in this corner, behind the wing stage left, facilitates the coordinated timing of the actor's entrance. Actors generally enter the stage singing and begin their songs at this mike in the upstage left corner wing before they are visible onstage (see fig. 39).

The duet begins energetically, the Dancer entering to fast-paced musical accompaniment and circling the central playing area of the stage, moving counterclockwise (fig. 38). Some Dancers' circles are wide and embracing, while others' are so small that they essentially spin in place. Whatever its initial diameter, the flurry of the Dancer's opening circular movement always culminates in a spin and finishes in a flourish. The Dancer thus inaugurates use of the centermost playing space of the stage. Her spin lands her in front of the musicians, stage right. Here the Dancer offers a formal greeting to the musicians, palms together, both a polite quotidian gesture of welcome in Hindu India and a gesture formalized for dancers in the tradition of classical South Indian dance (Bhārata Nāṭyam), where it denotes respect for the players and their instruments, with whom the dancer will share the stage.

Three use-areas of the stage have thus been opened up already in the Dancer's entrance. She moves from the *entrance and exit corner* (upstage left), to the *dancing circle* (center stage), and back upstage into what I call the *comfort station corner* (upstage right).

This upstage right corner is often used as a kind of safe place for actors while they are working onstage. As noted, it is the most populated place on the stage, where actors join others—including family, friends, and men with a certain degree of local prestige—to take brief timeouts. It is where actors both cool off and refuel during the course of a performance. In the midst of a long dramatic scene, for example, while his or her debate partner waxes poetic center stage, an actor may repair to this corner to have a soda or glass of tea, to wipe a forehead or readjust a slipping costume. Unlike the entrance and exit corner, the comfort station corner is not so much an energized channel between outside and inside as it is a piece of the inside—a familiar, community space in which to recharge—situated on the outside.

As such this corner allows actors to drop momentarily out of character and into a net of real-life relations. That is, this onstage safety net provides actors a chance to stand for a moment apart from the character they play, and instead to enact ease and belongingness among a relatively prestigious group. Here prestigious locals as well as drama people, outsiders and insiders, publicly engage in a camaraderie precious in everyday life. In addition to their dramatis personae, then, in this corner actors may embody idealized "real" personae comfortable in public interactions with local VIPs.

The Dancer makes canonical use of the two upstage corners by entering singing from the left and exchanging respectful greetings with the community on the right. She then moves further into center stage and approaches a microphone. She sings one or two popular cine-songs, dancing in a style artists refer to as "Oriental Dance" (the English phrase is used). A wide variety of dance styles have fallen under this changeable rubric in the course of remaking Indian dance in the colonial and postcolonial eras (Erdman 1996). Here "Oriental Dance" is essentially Bharata Natyam lite, a style made familiar by Tamil cinema of the 1950s and 1960s: a few of the simpler hand *mudras* and dance steps, lots of added hip thrusts and shoulder shakes, topped by a megawatt cine-smile.[6] The Dancer does not attempt to replicate the choreography that accompanied the cine-songs in their original filmic context. (Live staged performances that do aim at reproducing cinema choreography as closely as possible belong to a separate genre of contemporary Tamil popular stage performance known as "record dance.") Special Drama Dancers learn the steps they use primarily from watching other Dancers, augmented by the occasional lesson from a local dance master specializing in teaching girls this style. The resulting dance is a loosely interpretive gestural cover of the lyrics of the popular song.

The effect of the Dancer's song and dance at this early moment in a night of Special Drama is to heat things up center stage. Center stage is where the fiery debates, impassioned speeches, and punny monologues that make up the verbal core of Special Drama also take place. The many forms of verbal, postural, and gestural address occurring here enact a tension in performance between arousing the audience and holding them at bay (or, as with the Buffoon's monologue in chapter 4, at an "appropriate distance"). The metaphor that best captures the relation between the Special Drama center stage and its periphery is the centrifuge: activity heats up center stage and then spins off into an edge or corner of a particular qualitative valance.

My video camera captured one such instance of a Dancer heating up the crowd in her entrance act: Patma's exaggerated, slow hip rotation, arms up and body rhythmically circling, received prolonged whistles and hoots from the male audience. At one point a young man stood at the lip of the stage snapping still photographs, his intent posture silhouetted by the brightly lit stage and the glittering figure of the Dancer (this footage may be viewed on the Web at http://stigmasofthetamilstage.scrippscollege.edu).

For the duet scene, actresses wear a glamorized version of a young woman's daily costume. Traditionally, only unmarried young women wear a *tāvaṇi* ("davani," or demi-shawl) and skirt set rather than the full sari worn after marriage.[7] It is meant to be a modest outfit, the shawl providing a second layer of cloth atop the girl's blouse. Dancers' costumes generally consist of a very tight blouse and matching long skirt, decorated with sparkling detail (perhaps even fully sequined; see plate 7), to which three yards of diaphanous fabric may be added, draped across the chest and tucked in at the waist. The contrast between the actress and the role she plays here can be arresting, as many Dancers continue performing this role into their late thirties and early forties, causing a visible transgression of the standard dress code, in which a woman's age-stage is reflected in her clothing. But even for Dancers in their teens and twenties, these costumes are flashy and flirtatiously revealing. The highly visible flaunting of behavioral norms encoded in the Dancer's costume is a good symbol for the kind of fantasy enacted in the duet, in which a full-blown, full-bodied woman behaves, at least initially, as if she doesn't know better.

The Bumpy Meeting

As the Dancer ends her final song, suddenly the Buffoon hurtles out of the upstage left corner and bumps right into her. Their hips collide. The drummers emphasize the collision with an instrumental thud and clang. Most actors play this opening hip bump between Buffoon and Dancer as highly exaggerated physical comedy rather than striving for any impression of realism. No attempt is made to hide the artifice of the meeting or to pretend that either performers, musicians, or audience has not fully expected just this "unexpected" occurrence. Such stagy timing finds its echo in the bump's spatial logic: the bump takes place just at the upstage pinnacle of center stage, simultaneously knocking the Dancer off center and out of center stage while bringing the Buffoon forward. Sometimes he passes right by her after dislodging her from center, continuing on his entrance trajectory across stage, pulling up to greet the musicians just short of hurtling into them. Other times the Buffoon allows the bump to change the direction of his course so that while it pushes the Dancer upstage, the Buffoon winds up center stage at the mike.

The Buffoon's costume communicates a message entirely different from the Dancer's. The clothes he wears may be worn by Tamil males of any age, married or unmarried. His are the everyday comfort clothes men wear around the house: an old sleeveless cotton undershirt or T-shirt and three yards of cotton fabric tied from his waist (a lungi). Over one shoulder he sports a small multipurpose towel, used equally by men to wrap their heads or swat away flies. These items of clothing are supremely ordinary, well-worn, and wrinkled. The Buffoon is dressed as Everyman.

In keeping with this costume style and in contrast to the Dancer's earlier ritualized dance greeting, the Buffoon's greeting to the musicians is casual and colloquial. The Buffoon banters easily with the musicians, as of course they have already met; there is no attempt to hide the fact that this is the same actor, costume change notwithstanding, who performed the previous act. The comfortable repartee among the men here continues in the mode established during the prior scene.

This greeting accomplished, the Buffoon turns his attention to the Dancer. Their first interchange is argumentative: "Why did you bump me?" he asks, to which, offended, she counters, "Me bump you? You bumped me!" and the game begins. At this point the Dancer may offer a defense of her right to mind her own business: "I was simply dancing by myself here on the road, and you came crashing into me!" It is a defense more damning, in context, than not saying anything at all: what would a good Tamil girl ever be doing dancing by herself on a public road? This is the second confirmation that the Dancer is an unusual, and unusually transgressive, Tamil girl/woman.

In Tamilnadu any public dancing is a rather extraordinary affair. For adults, the only nondegrading contexts for dance are either religious and devotional, or sanctioned as a cultural art in the service of national culture. Children, in an example of the latter, learn and perform dance and dance-dramas in school settings and learn to see Indian arts as a matter of service to the nation. Beyond childhood, acceptable artistic contexts include the *Bharata Natyam* genre of classical dance now frequently staged throughout the state and marketed, often through state sponsorship, as part of classical Tamil cultural heritage. As for religious contexts, same-sex folk dancing at religious events is acceptable, as in the circle dance known as *Kummi*. And groups of Hindu devotees on religious pilgrimages, comprised of men as well as (nonmenstruating) women, often dance with great fervor en route to their sacred destinations. The perceived loss of control that accompanies possession by gods is moreover excused by the presence of the divine (Hindu gods regularly do things that would be unacceptable if done by humans). In addition to this catalog of relatively traditional circumstances where public dancing is acceptable, there is now the phenomenon of an urban elite disco-dance scene burgeoning in five-star hotels in cosmopolitan cities throughout India, though these are essentially private clubs due to their admission fees. Apart from these exceptional circumstances then, the norm for public comportment in Tamilnadu is to strictly control extraneous physical movement.

In such a context, the dancing girl's defense of her reputation is no defense at all: she is a dancing girl, after all. When I would ask, "Why is she dancing in the road?" the reply invariably contained the word "summa" (*cummā*), meaning "just because!" or "just like that!"—or rather, for no real reason, and without any purpose. That is, a dancing girl will naturally dance (or again, as the Reverend Jensen noted in his compendium of Tamil proverbs, "A dancing girl is invariably a harlot," [1897] 1989, 43).

This response is in keeping with the general attitude toward the duet from audience and artists alike: it cannot be analyzed; it is "just comedy." The notion of a girl dancing in the road "just because" reinscribes the taken-for-grantedness of this whole mise-en-scène for its participants, as an expected deviation to the normative reality that good girls don't. The deviant possibility that some girls just might, and just might assert that it is their right, hovers like an impossible bubble of autonomy that quickly collapses into a joke.

Right away the intrusive, explosive bump shatters any fantastic autonomous space for this young woman. The bump with the Buffoon is a crash with reality:

BUFFOON UDAIYAPPA (OF PUDUKKOTTAI): "Who are you?"
DANCER PATMA (OF KARAIKKUDI): "Yo! I am a woman, and I am dancing here in this road, and now you've come along and spoiled it!"

The Meaning of a Bump between Men and Women

Such initial argumentative verbal exchanges quickly lead to a more protracted discussion of the meaning of a bump between a man and a woman. The Buffoon and Dancer now stand at the microphones center stage. In their terse exchanges, the repetition of two particular words stands out: *āṇpiḷḷai* (man) and *poṇpiḷḷai* (woman). The bump seems to have sprung open a highly productive space of interactive social anxiety, necessitating fundamental reiterations of the distinctions between the two genders. The bump jolts the Dancer out of what Lacan might term a prelinguistic imaginary, propelling her into the recognition of herself as a signifier in a symbolic, phallic world. Their bump pushes Buffoon and Dancer headlong into the world of logos, carving out a new, specific space onstage in the process.

Morals and mores now tumble out with every utterance emitted from within that oblong hot spot onstage near the microphones. First and foremost, it seems, this pair must establish the difference between them, on which the impropriety of the bump rests:

BUFFOON UDAIYAPPA: Who are you?
DANCER PATMA: I'm a woman.

B: And who am I?

D: You're a man!

B: Right.

D: Right! You're a man! I'm a woman! And for a man to bump a woman is wrong! [*tappu!*]

Suddenly the Dancer's onstage persona is a mouthpiece for just the kind of social censure so often aimed at actresses offstage. This exchange reiterates the most fundamental moral tenets of gendered interaction. The Dancer has just herself introduced a certain discursive reality into what was a purely imagistic fantasy up to this point. And yet this splash of reality only adds to the seductive social appeal of the scene, as now it is clear that she—the female character, and by extension the actress who animates her—knows she does wrong, and does so anyway. Her comments introduce moral discourse embedded in an enactment of its transgression. This cracks the primary fantasy of the imaginary and moves it to a linguistically self-conscious meta-level. In this heightened, charged state, Buffoon and Dancer stand center stage and flirt by flinging at each other prohibitions on just such actions.

The following interchange is from a performance by Dancer Jothi Stri and Buffoon Ravi Kanth, both of Madurai:

B: We bumped into each other, didn't we?

D: Yes!

B: So your hip bumped mine, didn't it?

D: Yes . . .

B: Why did you bump me?

D: Yo! You're saying that I bumped you?! You came and bumped into me, and now you're saying I bumped you?!

B: Unh.

D: [*incomprehensible*]

B: [*looking at his right palm*] There's this hand.

D: [*equally raising her right palm*] There's this hand.

B: [*raising left hand*] And there's this hand.

D: [*raising left hand*] Yes, there are two hands.

B: If you clap the two together, it makes a sound.

D: Indeed, if you clap two hands together, they make a sound!

B: So when two people bump, it makes that too.

D: When two people bump, what does it make?

B: What does it make?

D: Two people bumping also makes a sound.

B: Two people bumping makes lightning [*looking up at sky*] . . .

D: Oh . . . what else does it make?

B: What else? Two people bumping makes a kid!

D: [*forced laugh*]

B: [*parody of her forced laugh*]

What comes of a bump between a man and a woman? Increasingly visible manifestations of their transgression.

Once begun, this loaded exchange quickly becomes contentious, as though arguing might allow them to hammer some way out of the self-consciousness in which they are now trapped.[8] The banter assumes a state of conflict between men and women, evidenced in this impish performance by a Madurai Dancer named Silk:

> I'm a woman. If I want to, I can bear a child. You are a man. So you think I need you; you think that without you I can't do it, isn't that what you think? But I tell you, all that is just your fantasy. That's all the past, man! History! These are modern times. Nowadays, for four thousand rupees I can get an injection and give birth to a kid all on my own. There's no need for you, so *get out!* [*in English*]. [*Turns to look at audience*] At least, that's what I learned from my foreign friend! [*pointing at me and smiling*].

Silk's playful appropriation of modern science here proves that virtually anything (including foreign scholars) can be cunningly harnessed into the timeworn war of the sexes.

The Contest between Men and Women

The contest begins with a challenge. That challenge expands from words, at the microphones standing center stage, into action and the wide-open center of the stage. Its conceit is still fantastic: this woman dancing on the road agrees to engage in a contest of skills with this unknown man, attempting to outstrip him in everything he does. She is the perfect feisty mate, undeterred by the norms we already know she knows.

The following classic exchange is from a performance by Dancer Sugunarani of Madurai and Buffoon Satyaraj of Dindigal during a performance in Valaiyangulam.

DANCER SUGUNA: Man, you really talk!

BUFFOON SATYA: Yo, you really talk! Let's have a contest. Will you dance?

D: I'll dance.

B: Will you sing?

D: I'll sing.

B: Will you run?

D: I'll run.

B: Will you sit?

D: I'll sit.

B: Will you smile?

D: I'll smile.

B: Will you walk?

D: I'll walk.

B: Will you lie down?

D: I'll lie down.

B: Then I'll break your hip!

D: You! You are like mere dust beneath my feet; I blow you off!

B: Well, if I'm dust, you're nothing but hot air! Today we'll see who can break the other's hip. May the best man win!

The best man? Is the Dancer not even recognized as a woman in her overt eagerness for a sexually charged match?

Buffoon Kannan and Dancer Kasturi, both from Pudukkottai, make apparent our sense that the players here are representatives from pitched sides of a gender war through their use of the exclusive first person plural pronoun *nāṅkaḷ*. This exclusive "we" frames two opposing teams of exclusively gendered subjects:

BUFFOON KANNAN: Can you do anything we [nāṅkaḷ] do?[9]

DANCER KASTURI: We'll do it!

B: We'll drive cars.

D: We'll also drive cars!

B: We'll drive buses.

D: We'll also drive buses!

B: We'll drive lorries.

D: We'll also drive lorries!

B: We'll drive you who drive everything!

D: Only if we give it can you drive it; otherwise, there's nothing you can do!

B: No, that's not how it is, woman! All you've got is the "steering" [*gestures with both hands as if holding a steering wheel in front of his chest*], while we have the "gear box!" [*gestures with one arm in a rotary motion in front of his hips*].

Howling laughter greets this barely coded symbolic display of sexual relations. The Dancer looks down at a group of young boys sitting among the small children up front and asks pointedly, "Hey, what is it with you kids? You're laughing too, are you? You think you know anything about all this?!" At this the Buffoon comes to the rescue of the boys, picking one out in particular and saying, "Though he's just a little guy, he is one of our sex [*vark-kam*]. Like a calf, it may be just a small calf, but its horns are big!" The Buffoon's choice of image and word established two definitive sides: "vark-kam" can distinguish class, race, sex, and species, of which his now clearly includes little boys with big horns.

The feistiness of the Dancer's role here seems to have emboldened the actress herself, further blurring the boundaries between performer and role: who exactly is chastising these laughing little boys, a character in a comedy or the actress who plays her? Again, the Dancer is the dancing girl she plays, a slippage about which the young children up front learn as she speaks.[10]

The gauntlet thrown down, Buffoon and Dancer step back from the mikes to begin enacting the physical dimensions of their contest. The musicians strike up a common fast-paced folk tune in a musical genre named for its singsong chorus, *taṇaṇaṇaṉē*. The actors dive into a dance of thrusting hips, big lunges of approach and retreat that expand and contract the circle of center stage. They use wide, strong, voracious steps. The Buffoon has joined the circle the Dancer first traced with her entrance, and together they now spin in a heated whirl.

Their improvisation is a highly attuned mirror. Gradually, in unison, they draw together into a tense, close stance, only their hips moving together rhythmically. The bump that sparked heated words over loudspeakers and a hungry dance over the entire stage has come full circle back into their hips, and for a moment Dancer and Buffoon move together like one pulse. But this tension quickly proves too much for the man: he overtakes her, overzealously thrusting his hips and trying to jump onto her, his overeager excitement ruining the moment; she backs away, trying to escape him. Of course, this is all played for laughs.

At this turn of events, the Dancer always backs up downstage right. Their deceleration out of the charged, whirling circle of big movement left the Dancer positioned between Buffoon and musicians. During that intimate,

40 The downstage right corner. Smiling here for the camera, Dancer Sundari stands trapped in the Duet between the Buffoon (her husband, Prasat Rajendran) and the musicians, June 1993.

sexy quiet moment, there were men both before and behind the Dancer. When she backs up to escape the Buffoon, her only move is to go closer to the musicians. A photograph of Dancer Sundari smiling at the camera in the middle of a performance of the duet finds her positioned in this corner and clearly illustrates its architecture: the bank of musicians behind her stretches all the way to the lip of the stage, just beneath which sit the men in the audience, while in front of her stands the snarling Buffoon (fig. 40).

In Special Drama, the downstage right corner is where women are routinely trapped by men. It is structurally walled off from egress into the audience by the musicians' tables, and the table farthest downstage where the all-round drummer usually sits. His wooden table, his own body, and his all-round array of drums effectively create a wall that separates this downstage corner from the offstage space beyond it. In that offstage space, adjacent to the stage in this same corner, is another table where the electrical sound and light system, and the men who run it, sit (drawn into figures 35 and 37). These two tiers of men seated at their instruments create a vertical wall of enclosure. A woman who is backed into this space cannot pass: this is a corner from which there is no escape. It is here that male actors invariably head when trying to physically overpower an actress. The actor maintains eye contact with the musicians while the actress's back is to them.

When the Buffoon corners the Dancer here in the duet, she literally has to push him away. Most often a Dancer will put her two hands against his chest and shove him off. This is humiliating for her, in that she has had to resort to physically touching a man onstage, and such public contact taints a woman, as the following exchange between Dancer Jothi Stri and Buffoon Ravi Kanth makes clear.

DANCER JOTHI STRI: Hey, don't touch me, man! There are lots of people watching. How am I going to get married, who's going to marry me, if they see me up here getting touched by you?
BUFFOON RAVI KANTH: Oh, are there, are there people watching?
D: Yes, indeed, there are lots of them watching, and they care about that!

This verbal exchange occurred center stage, at the microphones. While talking the Buffoon tapped the Dancer on the shoulder. Her response lays bare an underlying norm that makes the duet such risqué business: a woman's reputation is negatively affected when a man touches her in public; a stigmatized, public woman may never have a proper marriage. The Dancer's frank response is metacommentary on the dangers of disrepute she faces. Not only might she be touched by a man in public, but she might actually have to resort to touching him in public, when she defends herself in the downstage right corner.

The two corners of stage right are thus quite different in valence. The upstage right corner is a possible refuge, security and status provided by its mix of community, while the downstage right corner is a site of humiliation. Whereas upstage right an actress may be seen interacting cordially with important and known men, downstage right she is pushed as far as possible into the gaze of strangers, unknown men in the village audience.

Usually her retreat into this downstage corner, coupled with her retaliating push on his chest, is enough to discourage the Buffoon, and the action folds back into another round of dancing or verbal sparring. I did, however, witness one particular Buffoon-Dance Duet in which a Buffoon's overzealousness at this point in the act definitively crossed that already blurry line between acting and real life and literally stopped the show.

As the wide, hip-thrusting dance circle narrowed into a sexual pulse, instead of merely gesturing at overwhelming the Dancer and driving her into the downstage right corner, Buffoon Udaiyappa went particularly wild, aiming exceedingly high and hostile jumps at Patma. The first time this happened, she adroitly fended him off with her arms and managed to steer them both back into the dance. But when it happened a second time, Patma took the radical step of literally stepping out of the normal playing space of the stage. Her move onto the furthermost downstage proscenium lip of the stage, past the center stage mikes, taught me that the normal playing space of the stage has definite boundaries. She stepped outside them and then turned her back to the audience to directly face and threaten the Buffoon. This was not the frontal show of normal Special Drama staging but its opposite: Patma glared at Udaiyappa. She shook her head no; she put out her hand and shook it no, too. He immediately began chattering nervously, trying to cajole her back into the play. He tried coaxing words, such as "Come, *mā*, come back. What are you going to do out there? Come!" But Patma wasn't playing anymore. She held fast her uncommon ground, making it perfectly clear that unless he stopped his extremely overzealous and sexually aggressive behavior, she would not return.

The moment passed with Udaiyappa seemingly chastised, and they resumed their duet. But each time he veered again toward an overzealous sexual display, she stepped back onto that dangerous front lip, with a look that was a visibly conscious reminder of the precariousness of their agreement, at which he quickly backed down.

There was a heightened edginess and danger in standing between him and the actual audience, instead of between him and the musicians as the fictive "stand-in" audience. Patma is a particularly bold performer, and the unusualness of her move away from the given confines of known men and toward the inherent risks of putting herself nearer to the unknown men in the audience stopped Udaiyappa cold. She had broken out of a prevailing, complicitous dynamic, similar to that of domestic abuse, indignation leading her to forge into open, unknown territory. While moral indignation is an all-too-common stance for women in India—women as the bearers of the nation's morality, and all that this familiar trope implies—in this case it was not simply part of the play but a real frame break. The duality of the Dancer's role struck me again: Patma the actress and the nameless Dancer character she plays merged inseparably in an all-too-real act of moral indignation. Her move punctured the comic frame of the Buffoon-Dance Duet, revealing the ways in which their actions onstage chart similarly real gender relations under a thin guise.

The fifth and final area of the stage opened by the dance contest is the 'ownstage left corner. Like the others, this corner too has recurring stan-

41 The downstage left corner. The contrastive architectural openness of this stage area is quite clear in this second photograph of Sundari and Prasat Rajendran in performance, June 1993.

dard uses throughout the night. Whenever male actors look for an escape from the action onstage, they do so downstage left. In one duet, Dancer Kasturi ducked under Buffoon Kannan's legs to escape his advances, only to find, when she stood up, that he had practically disappeared off stage left. She had to run after him, grab his hand, and pull him back so as not to lose her partner. Similarly, when Dancer Amutha spunkily attempted to force her partner Mani to back up, using a hip-thrusting move like that of Buffoons when guiding Dancers to the downstage right corner, the ploy headed in the opposite direction, and Mani nearly fell off the stage on its open side, stage left. Here again the Dancer had to grab his hand and pull him back on center to continue their play.

This openness of the downstage left corner is dramatically different, and diametrically opposed, to the trapped quality of downstage right (fig. 41). These two downstage corners reflect a strict gender division in use: downstage left is used exclusively by male actors, while right is where women are so often confined. In moving downstage left, the Buffoon straddles a kind of semi-on/semi-off stage position. Here he embodies the ever-present possibility that exists for Tamil men of moving easily out into the public sphere, a possibility that does not exist in the same way for women. The architectural openness of the left side of the stage supports this contrast. Often, late in the night, a Buffoon will dismount the stage to venture out into a sleepy audience with a pail of water to splash, rouse, and startle sleepers. It is always from the downstage left corner that he descends with his pail.

The threats present in both downstage corners feed the contest of skills between Buffoon and Dancer, keeping their play alive. The energy generated from their dancing center stage spikes out, now to one side, now to the other. The spikes take separate directions for separate genders, the women fighting a losing battle not to lose face downstage right, while the men, to escape the prospect of losing place or face, escape downstage left. In the end, both corners present gender separation, while center stage remains the locus of the push-me-pull-you dance that is the centerpiece of the contest phase of the Buffoon-Dance Duet.

Mutual Admiration and "Love Marriage"

The contest segment ends when Buffoon and Dancer each seem to suddenly realize that the other has performed admirably. Back from the scare of either side of the stage, they turn to each other with an admiring gaze and renewed interest. Their tone of voice and comportment completely shift. Sometimes the Dancer begins, in a high-pitched singsong voice, to praise the Buffoon, exclaiming, "Oh! You sing so well! You dance so well! Stay right here, don't go anywhere! I want to bring you home." Equally often, the Buffoon begins by turning to the Dancer and saying, "You sing well. You dance well. What is your name?" followed promptly by the English phrase "I love you."

This saccharine turn of the duet is offset by the parodic flair with which it is performed. For example, my camera captured Dancer Jeeva enacting a send-up of the supposed sincerity of this shift by employing a Freudian pseudoslip: she says, "I'll bite only you!" (uṉai tāṉ nāṉ kaṭikkiṟēn!) instead of "I'll marry only you!" (uṉai tāṉ nāṉ kaṭṭikkiṟēn!). Similarly, when Dancer Sundari flatters insincerely, saying, "Oh! Sir! You are so high up! You have gone, oh, so far somewhere!" her praise simultaneously comments on precisely that evasive prerogative men often exercise, as we have seen. Likewise when Dancer Jothi exclaims, "I want to marry you right away; we are so well suited!" there is a hint of sarcasm in her choice of words, in their suggestion that the reality of that highly sought-after ideal of a suitable marriage could take the form of a courtship such as we just witnessed, filled with fear, anger, and aggression.

But perhaps the hardest-hitting irony of all those couched in this mutual admiration phase of the duet is one displayed by the Buffoon. In the instant after he professes his love for the Dancer, a Buffoon will often turn to some man in the audience and signal him, through hand and head gestures, to meet the Buffoon backstage after the act if he is interested in the woman. He gestures like a classic pimp, "You want her? You'll pay? Meet me in the back as soon as this is over!" At the expense of his female partner's reputation, the Buffoon takes this opportunity to consolidate his same-sex bonds with the men in the audience. He distances himself from her just at the height of the narrative moment in which they ostensibly come together "in love," shredding fantasy with a parodic, cynical realism.

The Buffoon's pimping joke undercuts the moral ground his partner has attempted to stake out for herself as a woman onstage. His actions ensure that stage actresses will never entirely escape their reputation as prostitutes: even a man who has just publicly demonstrated his love for a Dancer and his willingness to view her as a marriageable woman will turn around and pimp her the next instant. With this gesture, the Buffoon reinscribes several extant stereotypes about drama people and the drama world, including the idea that actresses deserve their spoiled reputation. Actresses' own attempts to escape that reputation by enacting the moral stance of a good Tamil woman are foiled by the very men with whom they share the stage.

During such moments, the Dancer does not acknowledge the Buffoon's gesture. The two continue to exchange vows of love and sing a romantic duet during which they clasp each other in an embrace center stage. They smile and coo, holding hands and deciding to elope and perform love marriage. "Love marriage" is the widely used English term that refers to a decision on the part of bride and groom to marry out of love, rather than accept a match arranged by their families. Love marriage is roundly criticized as an import from the West that lacks both traditional moral constraints and common sense, as evidenced by the frequency with which Westerners who "do love marriage" also "do divorce" (see introduction).[11] Love marriage here is a foreign-inflected ending to a scenario traditionally tinged with scandal, that of strangers of the opposite sex meeting, mixing, and matching on a public road.

Their decision to "do love" notwithstanding, there remains a certain tension between the couple center stage. The tautly sprung quality at the center of the duet persists. At this point there are two possible endings for the duet. The first is that the couple complete their song and run offstage together, exiting through the upstage left corner. This is the standard ending to this scene. The second ending is gaining ground, however. In it, the Dancer manages to give the guy the slip: during their love song, she spies her "uncle" coming toward them. She looks out into the distance and calls out, "Uncle!" By politely smiling and bowing to greet this imaginary figure, she extricates herself from the Buffoon's embrace. As the Buffoon turns to follow her gaze out past the audience, she quickly backs away and exits the upstage left corner while his back is turned. The Buffoon is left standing alone to finish the song, and the scene, by himself.

While it would seem to offer the Dancer the last laugh, in this second ending too Buffoons get the last word. They use the opportunity provided by being abandoned onstage to impugn the Dancer verbally, much as the earlier pimping gesture did visually. An elder, well-regarded Buffoon, A. R. Arumugam of Ponamaravathy, spoke as follows after Dancer Patma left him in the lurch with the second ending ruse:

> Blessed woman! She's someone's daughter . . . may you be well! Liking all this is wrong [*tappu*]. It is said, "There is only one woman for one man." And who is that one woman? The one who submits herself to the measure of turmeric cord [i.e., the wife], she's the one. I am not alone in asserting this. The Christian Bible, the Muslim Koran, and the Hindu Kuṟal all say this same thing: "There is only one woman for one man." All these others [*pointing after Patma*] will disappear.

The Buffoon here distances himself definitively from all that he has just enacted in the duet, drawing a sharp line between his real self and the character he played. He asserts that, as a man, he adheres to the authority of traditional and normative morality in the form of the ubiquitous Tamil maxim "only one woman for one man" (orutaṉukku orutti tāṉ), attributing this paean to monogamy not only to the Tiru-k-kuṟal (Tamil sacred sayings) but to the Bible and the Koran too for good measure.

In this moralizing footing of direct address to the audience at the end of the duet, note that Arumugam makes his claim for a distinction between his real self (the actor) and his character (the Buffoon) at the Dancer's expense. His ability to rise above the character he played just seconds ago turns on his dismissal of women *such as her*, an attitude that continues to view actresses and their Dancer characters as collapsed into the single entity "bad women." It is she who is always worthy of disdain.

When a Buffoon uses such a moralizing footing to directly address the audience at the end of the Buffoon-Dance Duet, he creates a tidy closure that not only frames this act but links his two opening scenes. By returning to a footing that he employed in his solo scene, a Buffoon who chooses such a moralizing ending closes the way he began: a Buffoon alone onstage with his male cohort, offering commentary on modern relations between Tamil men and women that portrays antipathy as their natural state.

Analogic Relations Onstage and Off

The Buffoon-Dance Duet is a model for the sociospatial paradigms that organize gender relations in Tamilnadu both onstage and off. Onstage scenes engage these paradigms in both comedic and dramatic modes, while offstage they are part of the ritual event of a rurban Special Drama. Contained in these parallel relations are some disturbing analogies between the gendered spatial uses in this scene and gendered spatial use more broadly.

First, the parallelism between dramatic and comedic scenes: verbal debates, circumstantial encounters, and skill contests between men and women figure repeatedly in both the comedic and the dramatic scenes in Special Drama. As noted, two separate sets of coupled artists play the lead roles in both these scenes, the male Hero and female Heroine in the dramatic scenes, the male Buffoon and the female Dancer in the comedic scenes. For both couples, their interactions always center around marriage, and generally they are cast as unmarried men and women for whom the potential to be drawn, through mutual attraction, into "love marriage" is strong.

In *Valli's Wedding* the play turns on a plot wherein Lord Murugan surprises Valli while she is busy guarding her father's millet fields. Like the earlier dancing girl on the road, the Heroine is outside alone. At Naradar's suggestion, Murugan approaches Valli disguised as a hunter and thus a man of her tribe, searching for a deer. His true divine identity unknown to her, the girl refuses Murugan's advances and instead argues with him, questioning his propriety in addressing her at all (much as the Dancer did when the Buffoon bumped her). Hero and Heroine proceed to debate the morality of arranged marriage versus love marriage (for hours) in a contest of wits, and he finally uses a supernatural trick to frighten her into submission, taking advantage of the girl's fear of elephants in calling on his brother Ganesh to frighten her so much that she runs into his own protective arms. Hero and Heroine eventually tie the knot, and their love marriage ends the drama. Like that of the earlier comic duet, then, the skeletal plot of *Valli's Wedding* is boy meets girl, they argue, then wed.

Despite their ostensible divide, then, the thematic and narrative continuities between comic and dramatic scenes are striking. The duet is essentially a comedic adumbration of the dramatic scenes to follow: in its spatial blocking, it serves as an orienting figuration that diagrams the theatrics to follow. The same paradigms of gendered social relations are found in each event, and just as the narrative texts themselves are organized around interactions between unknown women and men, so is the performance event itself, for audience and performers alike. The potential for an unknown meeting onstage is part of the real and special drama for artists playing these roles, as they potentially meet each other for the first time as unknown persons on a public road.

For the audience, meanwhile, a primary intrigue lies in watching multiple, intertextual layers of meetings unfold between unknown men and women: Buffoon and Dancer; hunter-god Hero and hunted-girl Heroine; actor and actress. The audience is offered the possibility of entering a common fantasy of love in any and all of these domains that conveniently share the same stage. In addition, members of the audience are themselves interacting with people they may never have met before, as well as with others whom they know quite well, all in the heightened space of the village commons.

On multiple levels, then, spatial use on the Special Drama stage reflects and troubles a frequently invoked, commonsense Tamil distinction between "known people" and "unknown people" (discussed in detail in chapter 9). Any interaction with an unknown person is potentially the first step on a path toward increased connectedness with a foreign element, potentially leading to precisely the slippery slope charted in the narrative "boy meets girl, they argue, then elope." New and unknown alliances are generally guarded against, while emphasis is put on strengthening kin connections through endogamous marriage. Women are enjoined to regard known men as their protectors and to see their moral reputation as ensured by limiting outside interaction.

Distinctions between known and unknown persons play out in the use-areas of the stage, as well. The whole of stage right is a continuum of known and semiknown men: the two stage right corners are complementary spaces, upstage being a place to enact the prestige of known relations, downstage a showcase for encountering the fear of the unknown.

What is most revealing, and troubling, here is how well the mapping of social spaces conveys the impossibility of neatly separating the spheres of safe from unsafe, and known from unknown. When the mixing that is modeled in the "known" corner involves men whom the audience knows to be unrelated to the actress seeking comfort there, she is actually anything but safe. Rather, this tenuous performance of the known upstage right shares unsettling features with the tense relations enacted for women downstage right.

The downstage right corner is where men enact sexual aggression, but are these men entirely different from the men who populate the upstage corner? If the upstage corner serves the drama community and its well-wishers as a source of protection, nevertheless downstage we find a confusion of protection and danger within the drama community itself. The mixed message of this contiguous zone stage right resonates in disturbing ways with other Tamil social spaces. The men positioned behind the actress, the musicians, whose wall of musical instruments and furniture keep her in and block her escape, are her community. But what is their role within the comedic performance, in which an unknown man is chasing an unknown woman?

In this the musicians are simply male bystanders: do they offer her any of the protection she might otherwise expect from kin? Instead they often ally themselves with the Buffoon, her adversary, greeting him jocularly, and laughing with him as he makes jokes at her expense. Swept up in the performance, these men become an unknown quantity.

Throughout the first two acts, the Buffoon establishes same-sex bonds of rapport with the musicians that are unavailable to the Dancer. It is, after all, a war of the sexes being enacted in the duet, over and again, one which the musicians do not rise above. As a woman, the Dancer cannot get either the audience or the musicians fully on her side, a situation intensified by the way her real life as an actress and her fictive persona as a Dancer are so often intertwined in the duet, in her own words and actions as well as in the Buffoon's.

All those present at a Special Drama event know that being backed up into this group of men is safer for the actress than being backed up into an audience of complete strangers. But an ambivalence remains: is this downstage right corner home or street? In their role as paradigm audience, modeling for the real audience a kind of engaged but distanced spectatorship, there is an unresolvable tension in the musicians' behavior as they simultaneously egg him on and protect her, raising questions about what any Tamil woman can really expect of the men with whom she lives and works.

In both halves of the performance, comedic and dramatic, the largely unspoken, underlying threats of domestic violence and incest that trouble any easy separation of the home and the world into truly separate domestic and public spheres seem to infuse the area of downstage right, reflecting uncomfortable realities that might play out offstage just about anywhere.

The turning point of *Valli's Wedding* occurs when, after hours of arguing center stage, the hunter traps Valli downstage right. In this corner, he physically grabs her. Valli screams for her brother to come running out to save her. When he arrives, she describes to him all the hunter's disrespectful actions toward her, but instead of helping her get away from this lecherous old man (the guise that Murugan has taken at this point in the play), her brother concludes that such tricksterlike behavior could only be the antics of a god and that this hunter must surely therefore be Lord Murugan in disguise, and that therefore Valli must immediately submit to his will and desires and marry him forthwith. The marriage of Valli to Murugan promptly follows, her brother "giving her away" by supplying the marriage garlands.

Conclusion

The staging of the Buffoon-Dance Duet highlights several levels of analogy between staged spatial paradigms and everyday social landscapes. One level is that of the Buffoon-Dance Duet and the dramatic scenes that follow, and another is that of the sociospatial paradigms embodied onstage and those lived in the daily gendered world offstage. In establishing such analogic continuities, theater creates itself as a space for social commentary. As microcosms of Tamil cultural production, the re-creations of the drama world address some of the largely unstated organizing principles of Tamil social life.

The performers' entrance and exit corner recalls the frequent traffic called for between a known community and an unknown public other. The comfort station corner reflects an accepted pleasure in Tamil life, the existence of a safe space among kin that extends protection out into the larger, public world. Center stage provides the analog for a potentially sparring quality in relations between the sexes in Tamilnadu. And finally, in the two downstage corners, the man-moving-off corner reflects an assumed male freedom leading men to wander and disappear, while the woman-trapping corner downstage right showcases the ambivalent qualities of the domestic sphere for women: Is it desirable and safe? Desirable and unsafe? Or a trap one would rather escape?

The humor of these performances plays off, exposes, occaionally questions, and frequently reinscribes all these existing tensions in everyday life. It maps a series of hinges between the staged world and life offstage. The spatial blocking hammered out in these performances is simultaneously a theatrical stage convention and a map of certain broader conventions of

Tamil sociospatial life. While cast in a comedic mode, here relations between bodies on the ground and bodies onstage play into locally familiar shapings of social space into highly codified, qualified, and gendered place.

Coda

I close this chapter by recognizing an analytic journey similar to the one I have taken here. In an essay on a Kannada women's folktale entitled "The Flowering Tree," A. K. Ramanujan analyzes the series of social spaces through which the tale progresses.[12] It concerns a young woman who is able to become a flowering tree. This special gift is something she wishes to protect, though several of her interactions with others in the course of the story require its display. Ramanujan (1997) writes: "A woman's biological and other kinds of creativity are symbolized by flowering. In this tale, as in a dream, the metaphor is literalized and extended. The heroine literally becomes a tree, produces flowers without number over and again, as the occasion requires. It is her special gift, which she doesn't wish to squander or even display" (221).

In particular, as the tale progresses, there are five different occasions on which the protagonist is called on to display her ability. In recounting these encounters, Ramanujan notes that the story charts "a progressive series of violations" of the woman (222). Each of these violations occurs in a different setting, some indoors and some out, which also speaks to the ambiguity of both public and private spaces in women's lives. Ramanujan's analysis then takes the same turn I found myself pursuing here. He writes: "These five occasions seem pointedly to ask the question: when is a woman safe in such a society? She is safe with her own sister, maybe her mother, but not quite with a newly wedded husband who cares more for a display of her talent than for her safety" (222).

It seems likely that attending to the sociospatial settings and configurations of any South Indian story concerning a display of women's talents will raise disturbing questions about the many unsafe spaces for women that temper their spatial worlds. Though I did not intend it, in analyzing the use of space in the Buffoon-Dance Duet I found myself pondering whether there were any spaces represented here in which a woman was truly safe, or whether perhaps the burden of the act was precisely to present the confusing, precarious position of women who, for whatever reason, engage in public display. A familiar cautionary tale plays out in just such non-stories (those considered "just comedy," or "just entertainment") where one woman on display crystallizes all that is at stake for any woman who opts for the life of the public stage.

6 The Aṭipiṭi Scene

Laughing at Domestic Violence

In case the harvest they reap from representation is reality, we won't allow people to represent a woman as she hurls insults at her husband.
—Plato, *Republic* (395d)

SOCRATES: And do you realize that when we see a comedy, here again the soul experiences a mixture of pain and pleasure.
PROTARCHUS: I don't quite understand you.
SOCRATES: No, Protarchus, for it's somewhat difficult to see this mixture of feelings in our reaction to comedy.
PROTARCHUS: Yes, it does seem difficult.
SOCRATES: Yet the obscurity of this case should make us more eager to examine it, for that will make it easier to detect other cases of mixed pleasures and pain. . . . Our argument shows that when we laugh at what is ridiculous in our friends, our pleasure, in mixing with malice, mixes with pain, for we have agreed that malice is a pain of the soul, and that laughter is pleasant, and on these occasions we both feel malice and laugh.
—Plato, *Philebus* (48b, 50)

I had been in Madurai for twenty months and seen scores of Special Dramas before being disoriented by the performance I write about here. My familiarity with the genre did not prepare me for this experience. A 3 A.M. comedy scene, staged as a break in a performance of *Valli's Wedding* at the Mariyamman temple located on the grounds of the Police Reserve Line, Madurai, was shockingly brutal. Yet the audience all around me laughed riotously, both women and men. I seemed to be the only person not laughing. Instead I was incredulous: "She's bashing him in the teeth! He's kicking her in the groin! Now he's stomping on her while she's sobbing on the floor, and everyone is laughing! What is funny about this pain?"

People often say that humor is the hardest thing to understand cross-culturally, but so far I hadn't found this to be true of the buffoonery in Special Drama. Even the jokes had been pretty transparent (as in the Buffoon's monologue discussed in chapter 4, for example). Here, though, while there was nothing really difficult to understand in the scene itself—its blows and beatings smacked of the all too globally familiar problems of domestic violence—its humor escaped me, and I found the audience laughter as unnerving as the scene itself.

The Aṭipiṭi scene is a powerful piece of performance in several senses: powerfully performed, powerfully enjoyed in public, and a representation of domestic power relations. It seemed worth pursuing the experience of anthropological difference I had confronted in the ubiquitous laughter around me, and so I began questioning audience members and artists alike about their own experiences and learned that they found this scene both funny and pleasurable. In trying to understand the particularity of that response, I began to question spectatorial relations in Special Drama more broadly. Accordingly, this chapter looks at the Aṭipiṭi scene, as well as at the role of the public in it, both onstage and off.

Aṭipiṭi

Aṭipiṭi is a made-up word. Its coinage is built on a fairly common base, as a rhyming twin word comprised of two standard Tamil verb roots playfully joined together. The root *aṭi* means "to hit." *Piṭi* means "to grab or hold." The Aṭipiṭi scene, as the sketch is known, is thus "the hitting-grabbing scene," a blatantly descriptive name for an in-your-face comedy of domestic abuse.

It is performed by Buffoon and Dancer, always in the wee hours of the morning. Its form and content rely heavily on paradigms established in the earlier Buffoon-Dance Duet; it even uses some of the same gags, such as the greeting of an imaginary uncle to escape difficulties with a partner. This later performance, however, is something of a nightmare variation on the earlier fantasy. At this hour, many in the audience are sound asleep and must be roused anew to witness its comic reversals. Either the Buffoon jumps down off the stage (from the downstage left corner, to be sure), bucket of water in hand, or those already awake poke or shake friends and family. Audience members thus begin by rubbing the sleep from their eyes and end by wiping from them streaming tears of laughter.

The artists performing the Aṭipiṭi scene on 4 April 1993, in a drama sponsored by the Madurai Reserve Policemen, were Dancer Sridevi and Buffoon

Kalaiarasan (their performance may be viewed on video at http://stigmasofthetamilstage.scrippscollege.edu). Kalaiarasan and Sridevi are a popular Buffoon-Dance Duet team from Pudukkottai who are frequently hired to perform together (though each may also be hired separately). The Aṭipiṭi scene is a large component of their popularity; they estimate that they are booked together for 80 percent of the performances each does during the drama season, and that for the most part whenever they are booked together they enact the Aṭipiṭi scene.

The basic conceit of the Aṭipiṭi scene has been in standard usage in Special Drama since the 1950s, but Kalaiarasan and Sridevi have taken it to new heights. In Sridevi's words, they claim for themselves the creative vision of the act's physicality:

> Before, it was something like this: the woman used to go and tell her story. Then the man used to tell his, then a small fight between them, but everything was conveyed through dialogues—not acting. They wouldn't hit each other. They'll just have a verbal battle, "How dare you say this?" et cetera, sing a song, and exit. We two are the ones who thought, "Hey, if at this point we did like this, it would be good," and brought this to the stage.

The physicality these two brought others have since imitated, and the Aṭipiṭi sketch now involves blows and beatings whenever it is performed. No actors, however, are quite as impressive in the act as these two: there's a chemistry between them. Nor will either artist act the scene with anyone else. As Sridevi put it, for her, "the scene would be insipid with others" (cīn cuppn̲u poyiṭum; "c[h]up" = tasteless, insipid). In selecting Kalaiarasan and Sridevi's performance to consider more closely, I chose an acknowledged crowd-pleaser; we are looking at a popular hit here, on more than one level.

Anthropologists Viewing Laughter

The experience of incredulous horror at the malicious laughter of others (to borrow Plato's terms) has perhaps been most famously treated in the genre of anthropological fieldwork narratives by Laura Bohannon, writing as Elenore Smith Bowen in *Return to Laughter*. In this novelistic treatment of her experiences in West Africa, Bowen's revulsion at a local joke that poked fun at the helplessness of a blind man provokes a turning point in her otherwise compassionate relations with the Tiv, among whom she lived, and likewise prompts the main philosophical conclusions of her book.

PLATE 1 Hero and Heroine posing in costume as Murugan and Valli in *Valli's Wedding*, backstage at a performance, 1991. (The Heroine is Karūr Indra, whose family lineage is discussed in chapter 9.)

PLATE 2 Buffoon M. K. Sattiyaraj in costume as Valli's brother, onstage in a performance of *Valli's Wedding*, 1992

PLATE 3 Venkatiyamma of Valaiyangulam, wearing all her returned gold jewelry on the day she sponsored her vow drama in the village, March 1992

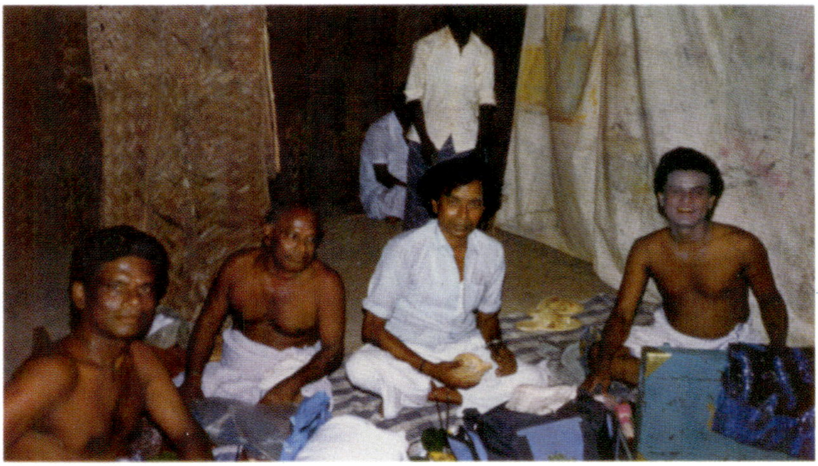

PLATE 4 Four male Special Drama actors backstage, preparing to "put powder"; note their cleanshaven faces.

PLATE 5 The same four male actors fully made up, posing in costume backstage. To represent divinity, the actor playing the god Krishna (blue skin) needs no mustache. Divinity often transcends gender, as in the devotional words of the South Indian medieval saint and *bhakti* poet, Dasimayya:

If they see
breasts and long hair coming
they call it woman,

if beard and whiskers
they call it man:

but, look, the self that hovers
in between
is neither man
nor woman

O Ramanatha
(Ramanujan 1973, 27)

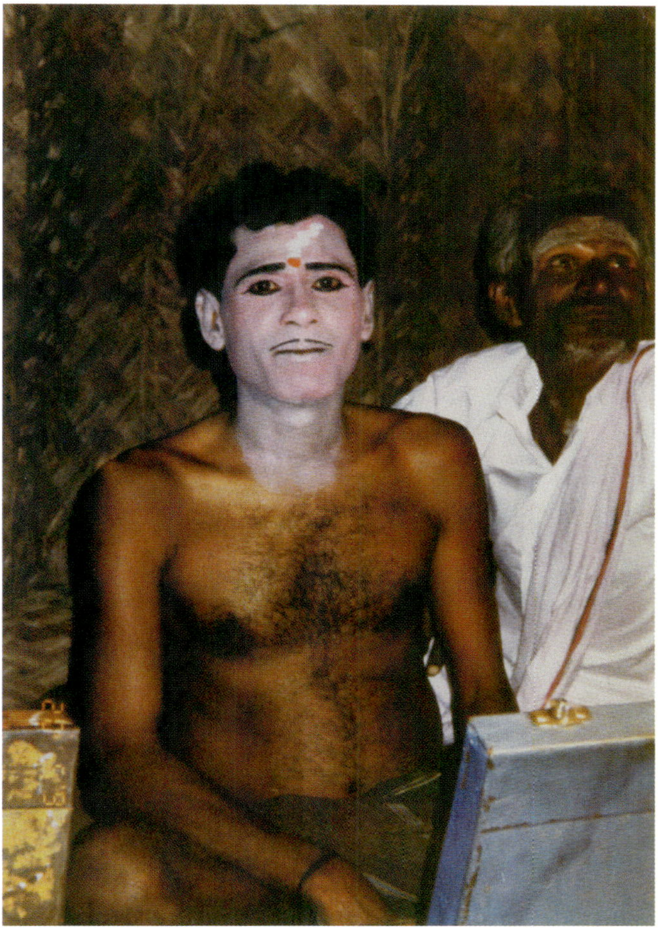

PLATE 6 A Buffoon sitting before his makeup case backstage, halfway through putting powder on his face

PLATE 7 Dancer Patma, during a performance of the Buffoon-Dance Duet, "dancing in the middle of the road." The scene is painted on a canvas backdrop.

PLATE 8 Jeyaraman's booking shop in Madurai, 1993. Artists' calendars line the walls. Mr. Jeyaraman stands at left. Buffoon Ilayaraj stands beside him. A drama agent sits at the booking table.

PLATE 9 Strands of flowers for sale in Madurai

PLATE 10 Three senior actresses just approaching the age of retirement, dressed to go on a Hindu religious pilgrimage in saris of devotional hues (posing with Jansirani and the author in 1992)

Appalled at the laughter of those around her, Bowen found herself exclaiming, "Typical peasant humor, but I am not a peasant, and you are a bunch of savages"; her experience was that "their laughter at suffering was merely one symbol of the gulf between their world and mine" (Bowen 1954, 229, 231). For Bowen, laughter in the face of suffering was decidedly antithetical to her ideas of the entire civilizing process. Indeed, her attempts to fathom this "savage" laughter among those she counted as friends unearthed a whole painful anthropological epistemology: civility for Bowen requires belief in the human ability to change the world, while the only art of savages is to live fatalism gracefully.

Bowen's idea is that Tiv laugh as a means of getting through life. "In an environment in which tragedy is genuine and frequent, laughter is essential to sanity"; "I stood for a while, looking after them. They knew how to live at close quarters with tragedy, how to live with their own failure and yet laugh" (295, 297). Sensible as this may sound, Bowen deems it a nonproductive attitude: such laughter represents to her an acceptance of human failure in a given world, rather than a performative engagement whose effects themselves structure the social world.

The condescension in her attitude infuses the book's final passage:

> These people had developed none of the sciences or arts of civilization. They had not learned to change that which is, to wish for a better life so greatly that they would stake the familiar good that might be lost with the familiar evil. They were not, as we are, greedy for the future. We concern ourselves with the reality of what is, because we wish to direct change wisely, hoping thus to preserve the good on which we are agreed while yet attaining what we believe should be. They did not seek to learn thus purposely. If they knew a grim reality, it was because their fate rubbed it into their very souls. . . .
>
> These people know the reality and laugh at it. Such laughter has little concern with what is funny. It is often bitter and sometimes a little mad, for it is the laugh under the mask of tragedy, and also the laughter that masks tears. They are the same. (296–97)

These conclusions are sad in themselves: why does a concern for the future of civilization, the "wish to direct change wisely," necessarily preclude laughter? The proximity of tragedy and comedy is often not funny, but it may well be civilized. Bowen does not entertain the possibility that laughing at a painful reality might actually be directive, and socially constitutive, of the civilizing process, as the laughter that greets the Aṭipiṭi scene proves to be.

Bowen is unfortunately not alone in failing to think with, and about, all that the laughter of a given social situation entails. Spectators' laughter is all too often treated as foreclosing further speculation about a performance event, rather than prompting it. It shuts down anthropological observation rather than making us "more eager to examine it," as Plato advised. In too many fieldwork accounts, anthropologists allow laughter to cut a kind of firebreak at which they stop an otherwise burning interrogation of cultural difference.

One example is in James Peacock's brilliant study of Ludruk, the Javanese genre of proletarian theater that he analyzed in *Rites of Modernization* ([1968] 1987). Even in this otherwise lucid study, laughter muddies the waters. In discussing the nature of spectatorial relations in Ludruk, Peacock chronicles some six types of spectatorial response, as recorded in audience response reports. He enumerates these responses, presenting them in terms of the frequency with which they occurred in the audience surveys. "The most frequent type of response (51) described or imitated physical motions. . . . The next most frequent response (47) expressed empathy with a character's role or feelings. . . . Thirty-one responses passed moral judgment on a character. . . . Sixteen responses were technical comments, twelve were aggressive shouts, seven were admiring." This informative account then abruptly ends with the statement "and by far the most frequent response was simply laughter" (Peacock [1968] 1087, 69). Simply laughter? That must somehow be differently quantified, and qualified, than any other response? What is simple about that?

A similar blind spot arises in the work of another otherwise supremely careful ethnographer, Esther Newton, who, in writing of her 1960s U.S. fieldwork with gay male drag queens, notes that "one of the most confounding aspects of my interaction with the impersonators was their tendency to laugh at situations that to me were horrifying or tragic" (Newton 1972:109). But rather than push to understand this experience further, Newton is willing to simply see the impersonators as laughing to keep from crying, a position that allays her own confusion by assuming that, at bottom, the drag queens have the same feelings of horror or tragedy that she has, but just cover it up better.

Unwilling to assume any of these attitudes—that this laughter entailed fatalistic acceptance, or that it was somehow an unqualifiable response, or that everyone around me was just as horrified as I but they managed to laugh while crying inside—I decided to further interrogate the laughter I found so disturbing.

It may well be that laughter itself is uniquely resistant to intellectual understanding. Perhaps the appreciation of paradox and incongruity is itself a mental process inherently other than, and opaque to, intellectualization. Or perhaps it is in the nature of symbols to confuse an otherwise sober account of the world by enabling human affects to cathect onto objects; symbols "unite the organic with the sociomoral order" and end up "making the Durkheimian 'obligatory' desirable" (Turner [1969] 1977, 53). There is no dearth of possible, complex reasons why, phenomenologically speaking, laughter might foreclose examination rather than making us more eager to examine it; recall Freud's observation that jokes "bribe us with their yield of pleasure into taking sides without any careful examination." But regardless of how and why the experience of laughter is difficult to scrutinize, this difficulty need not obstruct analysis of the social uses to which it is put.

For the examination of humor in use is necessarily an ethnographic project, precisely because "Humor is an event, not an utterance" (English 1994, 5). Laughter can take many forms, enact widely differing functions, be of any hue.[1] It can be malicious or supportive, socially divisive in some situations and cohesive in others. It can, in Plato's terms, mix pleasure and pain. But the main thing I learned by focusing on it is that the laughter that greets the Aṭipiṭi scene is specific to audience-performer relations in Special Drama.

The Ritual Frame of the Aṭipiṭi Scene

Officially, the Aṭipiṭi scene fills the slot of a short comedy break in the middle of a night of Special Drama, scheduled to occur from 3:00 to 3:15 A.M. In actuality, the scene takes a full forty-five minutes of the 3:00 to 4:00 A.M. hour, providing an extended break in action on several levels. First, it is a hiatus just before the long concluding debate scene of the drama. It is a change of pace for the musicians, who drink tea, rest their hands, take this opportunity to stretch their legs, and generally banter and joke rather than sing throughout the scene.

The scene is considered a freestanding, self-contained act. Framed as an interstice, the figures populating its interstitial world are themselves liminal, "betwixt and between" (Turner [1969] 1977). And as now-classic theoretical considerations of ritual suggest (van Gennep [1909] 1960), liminality is precisely that phase in the progress of a ritual enactment that exposes the cracks in the more stolid states surrounding it. In true ritual character, the Aṭipiṭi scene pokes at the underbelly of all the scenes that precede and follow it. The meeting of Buffoon and Dancer here as beleaguered husband and wife parodies the earlier meeting of Buffoon and Dancer as young bachelor and dancing girl. The parody flips the earlier sweetness of fantasy on its head: where a young man bumps into a carefree girl, here an all-too-worldly wife launches into her careless husband. And where that earlier meeting led to love and elopement, this meeting leads to crashing blows and repentant tears.

Dreams are places where transfigured figments live and die; the 3 A.M. comedy slot is just such a place. Here unrelated and yet similar figures, elements, and themes appear reworked and altered, transformed and transfigured. The sketch itself opens with the wife recounting a dream, albeit one that quickly becomes her nightmare before spectators' eyes.

Aṭipiṭi is a break in another way as well. Its focus on domestic conflicts between a husband and wife disrupts the steady, linear progression of premarital life stages otherwise offered throughout the night, in both dramatic and comedic formats. It leaves behind the pretense of unknown young men and women meeting, messing, and marrying and lurches instead directly into a scene of marital strife. As such this scene reaches beyond the confines of anything else that has happened or is yet to happen onstage. It further breaks dramatic decorum by locating its action not in a mythic palace, an enchanted forest, or even on a generic road, but instead squarely within the working-class home of a squabbling couple.

The Aṭipiṭi scene is thus offering the night's first look, and a cynical one at that, at what may lie ahead in married life, beyond the other action of the drama. It is a sudden and raucous reality check, a kind of splat to earth after several hours of high-minded celestial (and lower, not-so-celestial) romance.

Such a sudden drop is a tactical mainstay of much humor, exploiting both incongruity and relief paradigms, considered by humor theorists to be two of the primary means of arousing laughter (Morreall 1987; Clark 1970). The scene's incongruity in relation to the rest of the night of drama lies in the anomaly of its place in the progression of life stages, while its relief lies in providing an unromantic look at a husband-wife dyad.

But neither incongruity nor relief theories of humor can altogether account for the utter hilarity into which this scene plunges the audience. Its performance also taps into the carnivalesque tradition of bawdy, violent physical comedy, "the great style of popular-festive forms" of medieval Europe, whose parodies were reversals of reigning relations of power (Bakhtin

[1965] 1984, 212). However, while the "grotesque body" in carnivalesque humor signified rude eruptions into relations of state that may actually have recast aspects of those relations, the violent reversals and thrashings enacted in the Aṭipiṭi scene ultimately reverse nothing. In Bakhtin's idealistic rendering of the power of the carnivalesque, "Every blow dealt to the old helps the new to be born" (206). Violence and role reversal also characterize the style of the Aṭipiṭi scene, but they result only in a rebirth of the old order; the publicly applauded spectacle is the act of taming the grotesque female body—in the form of "modern woman" or "worst possible wife"—and bringing her into line with reigning social conventions of domesticity.

That is, here order itself is celebrated, not its toppling. What is repeatedly struck down is the uncivilized, transgressive body, and what is born anew is none other than a renewed commitment to the established order. In this sense, the Aṭipiṭi scene makes a mockery of Bakhtinian idealism, which sees carnivalesque laughter as "a great progressive force, the expression of an ideology that opposes the official and authoritarian languages that dominate our surfaces" (Booth 1982, 61). The only thing overturned here is the insurgent voice; what is repeatedly laughed at and beaten down is the (wife's) dream of a different domestic relationship. Perhaps most frightening of all, the Aṭipiṭi scene ultimately presents domestic violence not as a problem in itself but rather as an appropriate solution to other domestic problems.

The Aṭipiṭi Scene

The scene has three acts. Their order reverses that of the presentation of the earlier comedy scenes. There the Buffoon began with a comedy scene in which he was alone onstage interacting with the musicians. This was followed by the entrance of the Dancer in the Buffoon-Dance Duet, and the Buffoon joined her when she was already onstage. In the Aṭipiṭi scene, this entire sequence is reversed: the Dancer enters first, as wife, and interacts alone with the musicians. She exits. The Buffoon enters next, as her husband, and while he is still onstage, she joins him. Their duet is the third act of the scene.

Act I: The Wife

The Dancer enters from stage left. She is wearing an old sari, tied high as if for housework: the bottom reaches only to just below her knees, exposing her calves, while the usually flowing end piece is wrapped up tightly and tucked in at her waist. Her blouse is faded and stained. She is not a woman dressed to go out; indeed, one wouldn't normally see a woman dressed like this outside at all, unless she had run out of the house momentarily, in a terrible hurry.

Dressed like this, the only bit of the outdoors a woman would regularly enter does not actually count as "outside" at all but rather is the backyard (*kollai*). In the backyard, women regularly wash clothes, hang them to dry, grind spices, sift rice and sort vegetables, burn garbage—and frequently chat with other women doing the same things out behind adjacent houses. In effect, the Dancer's costume immediately locates the scene, and the woman, in the nitty-gritty of female domestic life.

Standing at the microphone nearest the musicians, the Dancer begins her act with a song that clinches this visual effect by adopting the voice of a married woman whose world is defined by the coordinates of home and husband.

> WIFE: [*sings*]
> The man I live with is good like a god, a knowledgeable man
> I've never had to go to the backyard [*kollai*] in frustration and anger
> Nor to the temple to cry over his cruelty.
> He won't gossip, he won't boast
> He won't drink, he won't brawl
> He won't suspect me, or spoil my pleasure
> He won't stop his work and lie lazy on the porch.

In the conversational dialogue with the harmonist that ensues, the wife continues this praise for her good husband.

> That's how he is, my husband! I can go and stand where I like, and he won't suspect me. He'll just think, "This woman goes out and earns good money and brings the cash home to us, she does." If I stand there talking, he will not ask suspiciously, "What are you talking to this guy about?" He's not that kind. There are men who will get all worked up if their wife even stands in the entranceway [*vāsal*] for a moment; they'll start asking, "Who is that you are standing there hoping to see, woman?" and all. My husband won't ask all that. My husband has the kind of character you could inscribe on a golden plate! There's no man like him! He won't stand around all day drinking and fighting; he never hits me, he never beats me. Well, you might ask, "Fine, your husband is not doing all

this. Are you happy?" Up to now he's never left me even to sleep on the porch. If I'm not next to him, he can't sleep. He's never even thought to leave his wife for one instant, going here for ten days, there for ten days.

The two domestic spaces invoked in this description—the doorway (vāsal) and the backyard (kollai)—have distinctly gendered resonances. The vāsal is a more public space than the kollai. It is at the front of the house and is more frequently occupied by men, who interact there with outside visitors. Any interactions at the vāsal are also visible from the street, and the vāsal is an overtly social space of greeting and interaction. The kollai, by contrast, is a domestic space for domestic chores and duties, a space primarily of women's work. The men of the house do enter, as this is often also where bathing occurs, but male visitors do not. The kollai is a space where women gather to work and talk among themselves.

In the line of the song just quoted where kollai is invoked, the knowledge of kollai as women's space is assumed: "I've never had to go to the backyard in frustration and anger" refers to the practice of women sharing their troubles with each other in the kollai. A deprecatory characterization of kollai as a female gossip space is central to the ensuing plot.

The wife's opening song thus paints a picture of her golden man and establishes the domestic peace of her world. And then suddenly she admits that this is all purely dream and desire. "I have so much desire for my husband to be like this, I saw it in a dream: my husband should not cast suspicion on me; he should be happy with me; he shouldn't leave me even for a day. I dream of this!" (Ippaḍi ellam en purusan irukka vēṇḍum eṉṟu enakku rōmba āsai. Kanavil nān pārttēn!). The harmonist interjects, "Oh, this is all just your dream, is it?" She continues: "Yes! If it was this way, how would our family be? Would there be any fights or quarreling? This is how a husband and wife should be, I think!"

The wife's vision here bears much in common with the picture of that upside-down modern world that was so fearsome to the young protagonist of the Buffoon's comedy scene. In the wife's fantasy, the woman works, and the man stays quietly at home. The stage is clearly set, again, for pointed commentary on such a fantasy of reversal, put forward here not by a frightened young man but by an assertive woman herself. The nightmare of modernity seems even closer now, voiced here by the woman herself, and may well require more active intervention than the resigned passivity enacted earlier.

We now see that in truth, this wife is really quite dissatisfied with her husband, who is not at all like her fantasy. He goes out all the time and doesn't tell her where he's been, or when he'll return (all generally quite normal husband behaviors). She stays with him, she insists, only because she's tied to him—because he's the one who tied the *tali* around her neck, after all—but she finds him cruel because he doesn't buy her things, or take her out to movies or festivals, or tell her where he goes when he leaves home. Her complaints are intermingled with curses.

The wife's curses provide the opportunity for a comic bit with the harmonist: every time she reports that she cursed her husband, the harmonist gets defensive, as if she were cursing him. " 'You dastardly sinner, do you deserve a wife?' I said," she cries, and pretending to misrecognize the deictics, the harmonist responds as though there were no quotation marks in her address and as though she were cursing him rather than her husband. Wife: "You diseased leper . . . !" Harmonist: "Hey! Watch it!" With this slippage, the men already seem to form an interchangeable group.

This comic interplay begins a theme that will develop throughout the wife's interactions onstage: the slipperiness of the male character. Both husband and harmonist are in question. She initially praises her husband, then reveals this as a dream. With the harmonist, she initially approaches him based on his reputation as a village leader then later questions his motives.

Though it enters as a comic subtext, the possibility that the harmonist's character is questionable is quickly made explicit. After she complains about her married life, the following dialogue between the wife and the harmonist ensues:

WIFE: He won't come home regularly, he leaves the house at dawn, and where he goes and what he does I can't understand. If I ask, he'll tell me to shut up. So what can I do?

HARMONIST (H♫): You should have come to me! [*male laughter in audience*]

W: That's exactly what I'm doing. Now I've come to you, haven't I? And for what have I come to you? I've come to tell you all the details, and hold a panchayat so that there may be happiness in our family.

H♫: Speak, woman.

W: That's why I've come, sir. You seem to be a decent type. They say you are the one who conducts all the panchayats for this place. They say many families have been spoiled by you . . . /

H♫: / Hey! /

W: / Oops! I mean, they say many families have prospered through you. They say that if I come tell everything to you, everything will work out all right. That's why I now come directly to you . . .

H ♫: Yes! You've come directly to me.

W: [*pointing to mridangist*] They say he's the same way.

MRIDANGIST: Hey! You are a younger sister to me, so don't talk all that!

W: Brother! Brother! I've come to you with the desire to openly tell you everything!

The overall theme of the Aṭipiṭi scene first becomes apparent in this exchange: airing one's domestic troubles publicly is a double-edged sword. Ambiguity is first captured in the wife's exaggerated Freudian slip in an interaction with the harmonist. The harmonist plays a critical role throughout the Aṭipiṭi scene, that of *naṭṭāmai*, or village headman and panchayat leader.[2] The naṭṭāmai is the recognized moral arbiter of local disputes. As such, he is a weather vane of social conscience, though his role here quickly becomes that of a very human character open to parody in his own right. Casting the harmonist as public mediator of disputes deepens the role that musicians already play in being a representative, paradigm audience in Special Drama performances, and the question again arises: Is this a bank of men whom a woman onstage can trust? It arises overtly when, in the very act of introducing the harmonist's role here, the wife slips in a Freudian slip: "Sir, you seem to be a decent type. They say you are the one who conducts all the panchayats for this place. They say many families have been ruined by you . . . / oops! I mean that you have helped many families" (Uṅkaḷāl keṭṭa kuṭumbam nir̲aiya kuṭumbamām! Chee! Uṅkaḷāl vāl̲nta kuṭumbam atikamān̲a kuṭumbamām!).

Such play with slippery ambiguities continues in the common sexual double meaning of "come to me," phrased without a qualifying verb; the bald phrase "I've come to you," and the harmonist's retort "you've come to me," are sexually suggestive (as in, "you've come to sleep with me"). The Dancer does finally insert a qualifying verb in teasing the mridangist, but the damage is done: the suggestiveness of "coming to him" with "the desire to open," and so on, can hardly be mitigated by the late inclusion of the verb "to tell" (Uṅkukkiṭṭa tān nān ellām tir̲antu solla vēn̲ṭum en̲r̲u āsaiyāka vantēn!). In addition, his having to remind her of their mur̲ai, their proper kin relations, by saying, "You are [in the relation of] a younger sister to me, so don't talk like that!" (Nī enakku taṅkacci mur̲ai vēṇḍum, appaṭi ellām pēsātē!), projects onto the actress commonly held stereotypes about actors as lacking proper murai (see chapter 1) and conducting incestuously confused relations.

In this opening bit, then, the wife has brought into the open her dissatisfaction with her marital relations. Both the story she tells and the way she tells it raise the difficult issues that arise for many women in attempting to negotiate gender relations with men. She has gone public here with her desires for her husband's behavior, raising the issue before the entire ūr (village) by asking the village headman to conduct a panchayat. Meanwhile in the narrating frame, all this is simultaneously being presented publicly on the village commons by an actress, notoriously a "public" woman. At both levels, this woman transgresses the norm of treating the husband-wife relation as private and sacrosanct.

The Dancer exits stage left, leaving the arena ready for the husband's entrance. What can the audience expect? Is she right to seek public mediation? How will the husband react to this? Will he defend himself? How will he answer her charges, and her dreamy invocation of a fantastically modern domestic sphere wherein she has power and respect? And finally, how will he react to her rather audacious flirtations with the other men right here onstage?

Act II: The Husband

The Buffoon promptly enters from stage left, singing. He too moves directly to the mike closest to the musicians. He is shirtless and wears a homey, plaid lungi. His shoulder towel is wrapped around his head in the style of a menial laborer. Tamil men often carry a small towel with them, and where and how they wear this towel is as much a sign of their class status as is the tying of the sari for a woman. On entering, the husband unwraps the towel from his head but doesn't wear it over his shoulder as prestigious men do; instead he holds it in his hands, in limbo, as it were, while the status of his character is still in question.

The husband's entrance song is about women, just as the wife's was about men. But if hers was a dream of impossible goodness in a husband, his is a cynical portrayal of the harsh realities of a type of dream woman: he sings about mistresses. Though these are the kind of women of whom men dream, the husband is here to advise them otherwise. Of course, in a further blurring of the boundaries between reality and representation, this is precisely the kind of woman Dancers are thought to be. So instead of his own fantasy, we hear why a married man ought not to want a woman other than his wife, a dismissal of the possibility of pleasure through women such as actresses and clearly, again, a moralizing frame that the Buffoon erects before the audience to shore up his own reputation.

> Don't keep a mistress! [Vaipaḍḍi vaikkātiṅku!] Even if you are a king who follows the righteous path, don't keep a mistress! Even if you [are an ascetic who] transcended earth by eating only to a quarter of your stomach's size, don't be a miserable sinner to your own wife, don't betray her. Don't keep a mistress! She'll ask for a goat, she'll ask for a cow, she'll ask for a nice fluffy mattress. If he says no, she'll tell him, "Scram, Dog!" I tell you in all truth, don't betray the wife you married, don't keep a mistress! Don't keep a mistress! Please—don't keep a mistress!

Here is a husband preaching to other husbands, before an audience of both men and women, recall, not to betray the wife. He seems to sing from experience; has he himself been burned by a mistress, like the mythic, repentant Kōvalan?[3] Or is he perhaps actually the golden husband the wife desired, committed to being faithful? His song readies the audience to hear about the man's relations with women, and he indeed interrupts it frequently with anecdotes about his own hard luck: he lost his money and thus came into the drama field, where he now finds himself "lugging around a suitcase with the rest of these sinners." But wait: the Buffoon is talking about himself here, his real life as an actor, not about the husband character he portrays in this sketch. Like the moralizing frame erected by the Buffoon in the earlier comedy scene, there is a productive ambiguity here: Is this voice the actor's own? The character's? Both?

From subsequent discussion with Kalaiarasan, the actor, I know that the anecdotes he intersperses with his song do indeed refer to his own experiences in his offstage life. Onstage he moves seamlessly from the song to his story in this way:

BUFFOON: Get this! Is there any connection between all this and myself, man? Had I used the 46,000 rupees to set up a grocery store in Pudukkottai, I'd be sitting there now, and would I have any need for this work of lugging around suitcases, man? My father told me right off, "Don't get mixed up with these people . . ."

HARMONIST: Which people, man?

MRIDANGIST: [*defensively*] Hey! Hey!

B: He told me, my dad told me, "Don't get mixed up with these loafers, you'll end up a waste! Keep quiet and stick with our business." Did I listen?

Like most guys these days, I didn't heed my old man's advice. Only now do I realize the results of my actions! I joined with this type instead and lost the 46,000 rupees. Now I go from town to town lifting my suitcase with all you sinners! [*Sings*] "She'll ask for a fluffy mattress. . . ."

The stage conventions are familiar here: the Buffoon tells a first-person tale of a rather pathetic young man who has to go to his father for advice, addressing the account to a male cohort, the musicians. What is new here is that the actor uses a real-life story critical of the drama world, embedded in a song critical of mistresses. The whole thing is utterly believable: this is how people think of the perils of the drama world. The audience is invited to see the Buffoon as a normal guy gone astray, and a married man singing about the treacheries of mistresses and the drama world, all again offered in the comfortable format of a story overheard (that is, ostensibly directed conversationally to the musicians).

On completing this opening song, the Buffoon begins speaking of how he ended up with his wife. His real wife? Or in this skit? How are we to disentangle the two? The actor makes no distinction between the one story as "true" and the other as "fictional." But this story begins in the rhetorical manner that signals the beginning of his longer yarn, and it opens the topic of marriage.

BUFFOON: People marry, don't they, man? You are all married men?
HARMONIST: Why?
B: When I married . . .

And the sketch begins. The husband complains about how little dowry he received from his wife's family. To add insult to injury, he then claims that she turns out to be a shrew:

BUFFOON: When she sees me, she says, "Hey you! Get lost!" [ṭēy! pō 'ṭā!]. That's how she speaks to me, man! "Hey! Get lost! Are you a man or what?" [Nī ellam oru manishan?].
HARMONIST: Hey!
B: To me, that's the way she speaks to me! Who else has made such a sacrifice?
H♫: You're a man, man!
B: I married her with no dowry. I made a sacrifice, right? Hey, look here, today something's gonna happen, I'm telling you—I'm gonna hit her

[*aṭippēn*] and grab her [*piṭippēn*], and anyone who tries to interfere won't make it home whole!

H ♫: Oh, there's something important I forgot to tell you.

B: What?

H ♫: Just now, man, looking for you, your wife came to me! [*audience laughter*]

The plot thickens. Here indeed is the husband of the wife we met. But it turns out that she speaks to him in an insulting way, and he is fed up. He announces his intentions to thrash her something fierce today, to *aṭi* (hit) and to *piṭi* (grab) her, egged on by the harmonist's questioning of his manliness. This is clearly what stings, as the next exchange proves.

BUFFOON: She came to you, did she? Dear Lord! . . . Even directly in front of me, you would say that she came to you? What do you think of me, that I haven't any manly pride [*rōsham*]? What do you think, that I rent out my wife?

The husband's fears are clear: he wants to make sure he is not being cuckolded, accused of lacking manly pride, or of pimping his own wife. The term the Buffoon introduces here to indicate these incursions on his manliness is *rōsham*, and it proves the nerve center that triggers the action that follows.

HARMONIST: Man, she only came here to ask whether her husband had come.

BUFFOON: Then you should have said so right away! All you said was "she came to me." Anyway, she probably came to call for a panchayat. [*Turns to audience.*] Oh, under the guise of the panchayat you can lure all those women to you. . . .

H ♫: Yeah, right, scores of them . . .

B: [*turning to call backstage*] Yo! Woman! Woman inside the house!

DANCER: [*answering from offstage*] Whaddya want, you? [*ēṉ ṭā appu?*]

H ♫: What is this? Is that your own wife addressing you like that?

This testy exchange between the harmonist and the Buffoon about the husband's manliness leads directly into the call to the wife, and to the third and final act of the scene.

To appreciate the insult of the wife's language here, it is necessary to know that Tamil terms of direct address fall into two distinct categories, singular or plural, informal and formal, respectively. The second person singular is conventionally used with persons of lower or commensurate status, or younger age, as well as with intimates. The common examples in use here are *pō* (go) and *vā* (come). The second person plural should properly be employed with persons of higher status or elders, and with those to whom one owes respect, voiced as *pōṅku* and *vaṅku*, respectively.

At issue here are the marital conventions of gendered language use. The husband is normally accorded the linguistic status of a superior vis-à-vis his wife. Conventionally wives address their husbands in the respectful plural, while husbands address wives in the more familiar singular. Children may speak to their mothers in the singular, but not to their fathers. In keeping with the general avoidance of intimate public behavior on the part of husbands and wives, these conventions of status-ranked address are maintained even in the privacy of the home, confirmation for those of us who have always suspected that language is the long arm of the public, and equally that the public is often an extension of that which is (re)produced domestically.

Thus even at home Tamil women add the respectful suffix *-uṅku* to everything they say to their husbands. Most women will not even address their husbands by name, as direct use of a personal name is also reserved for persons of lower or commensurate status. Instead, wives use creative coinages like *hey-uṅku* to get their husbands' attention. Such usage is also a class-inflected practice: middle-class Tamil women, the same who speak English and so on, might speak their husband's name, while women of the urban poor definitely do not. Attributed as often to superstition as to religious doctrine, the majority of Hindu women are careful never to utter their husband's name at all. It is thought to earn them sacred merit (*punniyam*, "favorable effect or blessings accruing through virtuous deeds" [Cre-A 1990]) to pay their husbands this respect.

In discussing these linguistic conventions with the harmonist in the last moments of their exchange before being joined by the wife, the Buffoon takes on a new, less conventionally masculine persona. In this role, he both criticizes the conventional practice and then notes with cynicism that it is not about to change anytime soon. The husband's ability to voice all these conflicting sentiments makes him an almost sympathetic character, caught in a bind that exceeds him. The harmonist, on the other hand, never wavers in his adherence to a strict doctrine of male superiority. Witness the shift in the husband's persona and the rigidity of the harmonist's stance in this final dialogue of the second act of the scene. It is in the eyes of the harmonist, above all, that this husband wants to appear as a man.

HARMONIST: Is it your wife who talks to you like that?

BUFFOON: Like what?

H ♫: If it'd been me in your place, I'd have died on the spot!

B: Die, then, who's asking you not to?

H ♫: But she's saying, "Whaddya want" [*ṭa 'pā*] to you like that . . .

B: So what if she addresses me "*ē̱ṉ ṭā?*" Man, *vā 'ṭā* is exactly how a wife should call her husband!

H ♫: Whoa!

B: That's respect [*maṟiyātai*], man! Don't you know, man? Even Siva himself gave half to Sakti.

H ♫: Half of what?

B: Sir, he gave half of his body! When Siva himself gives half, then between a husband and a wife there should be such closeness [*kajakajappu*]. So she should call him by saying, "Come here, husband! Go there, husband!" [Vā 'ṭā purushā! Pō 'ṭā purushā!]. [*Turns to address audience.*] You all too should speak to your husbands this way, saying, "Come here! Go there!" [Vā 'ṭā! Pō 'ṭā!] [*Turns back to the harmonist and says as an aside:*] So what if they get beaten for it! [*Again turning to audience:*] Who will say anything? When love is great . . . for example, how do we call our daughters? We say, "Come here, dearest! Go there, dearest!" [Vā 'ṭā kaṉṉu! Pō 'ṭā kaṉṉu!]. That's how we address them, right? In the same way, if a wife has great love for her husband she may call him saying, "Whaddya want, king! [ēṉ 'ṭā rājā!]. I'm for equal rights" [nān cama uṟimai koṭukkiṟatu]!

H ♫: Bravo! Bravo! [Palē! Palē!].

B: Only the woman who calls her husband by name will die with merit [*punniyam*], man. And it's the husband who calls his wife by her name who will die in misery. [*Laughing*] I've switched it all around, haven't I?

H ♫: Excellent!

B: [*Turns again to call backstage.*] Yo! What woman is in this house? Yo, woman! [ē! evaḷaṭi avaḷ vīṭṭil? aṭi yē!]

DANCER: [*calling from inside*] Whaddya want? I'm busy! Go away!

B: Today you'll see! With the beating I'm going to give her today, she'll want to flee this town, you'll see! That's how I feel today, yes! [*Turns to face the upstage curtain.*] Yo! What woman is in this house? Yo, woman!

H ♫: What will you do?

The Buffoon has played around glibly in this passage with all kinds of reversals. Not only does he tell women to speak disrespectfully to their husbands, he does so from the footing usually used by Buffoon's to speak directly to the audience about moral truisms (see chapter 4). But it is clear here that he is playing, as he laughingly admits, "I've switched it all around, haven't I?" To jokingly suggest such reversals is one thing; for a woman to really act on them would be, as we soon find out, another thing entirely.

Here the husband calls backstage to his wife in a manner that is much less respectful of her than she might like, but is nevertheless the way husbands usually do address wives. Yet instead of just accepting this as normal Tamil husband behavior, this wife appears as a Fury, scolding him for his disrespect in precisely the language that men usually use to control their wives. The actress's portrayal of this shrewlike wife is a complete reversal of normative gender roles in the Tamil household, foreshadowed in the Buffoon's second act.

In the ensuing action, both husband and wife will flip personae several times. The wife previously introduced two versions of her husband: her dream husband, who would show her respect, and her real husband, who doesn't respect her as she'd like. The Buffoon has also introduced these same two husbands, now cast in the different light of a male perspective: the husband who uncommonly and obsequiously respects his wife (and is seen by the harmonist to be humiliated by this), and the husband who vows to do so no longer. As the scene progresses, these two versions of the husband reappear in interaction with the wife, who herself proves to have two alternate incarnations—one uncontrolled and dangerous, like a fierce amman goddess, the other controlled and benevolent, like the goddess as a paragon of wifeliness.[4] It is through the meeting of these extreme aspects of husband(s) and wife(s) that the scene manages to spark both the carnivalesque laughter of reversal and the malicious laughter of the social corrective.

Act III: Their Meeting

The following is a direct transcription of the remainder of the Aṭipiṭi scene. I have indicated gesture and action throughout. See figure 42 for a storyboard of images marking the progression of this scene, in a series of still frames captured from my videotape of Kalaiarasan and Sridevi in performance.

Wife enters from upstage left, moves behind and bumps husband, slapping him hard on the back with both hands. They spring apart, and she immediately starts ordering him about the stage. The action fills the central use areas of the stage.

WIFE: Come here! Here! Come here! [Vā 'ṭā!] [*She points to the floor, as though gesturing to a dog.*]

HARMONIST (H♫): What is this?

W: The nerve of you to call me like that, saying, [*slapping him on the upper arm*] "What woman is inside?" [*slap*] "What woman?" [*slap*] "What woman?"

H♫: Whoa! Poor fellow!

W: Whom [*slap*] were you calling like that? Whom? [*slap*] Is this the proper way to speak to your wedded wife? [*Slaps him on the cheek.*]

H♫: Ai yai yo!

W: Who put you up to this? Who gave you the nerve? [*Slaps his cheek again.*]

H♫: Ai yai yo!

W: Come here you! [*pointing to floor*] Yo! Come back here! I'm getting mad now! [*slaps his cheek*] Do you know the proper way to address a wife with respect?

H♫: Ai yai yo! He is shaming the entire male race!

W: Come here! Get back here! [*pointing to floor*]

MRIDANGIST: Look here! He's just carrying his towel around! [itō! tuṇṭu eṭuttu koṇṭu varukiṟāṉ.]

W: You don't know how to address the wife you've married with respect. Do you deserve a wife? Come here, I say! Come here! You know what I'm like when I get angry, don't you? [*Slaps him on the mouth.*]

H♫: His mouth is bleeding, ai yo!

W: Do you know or don't you? Do you know or don't you? No respect for the wife. . . . You have always spoken to me respectfully; who taught you to speak to me like this today? Today you said to me, "Get over here, woman!" didn't you?

HUSBAND (H): [*pointing at the musicians and speaking to them*] See, you sinners! That's what I said /

H♫: / What did you say?

W: Don't open your mouth! [*Hits him in the mouth; audience laughs.*]

H♫: Hey!

W: Don't go speak to someone else while I'm talking to you!

H: They said they all call their wives like that, "vā 'ṭi, pō 'ṭi!" [Come here! Go there!].

W: And if that man calls that way, you have to call that way too?

H: Yes!

W: Hey! [*Hits him on the mouth; audience laughs.*] Don't open your mouth. Don't you know what you'll get if you speak while I'm speaking to you? [*Hits*

Wife alone talks with musicians

then Husband alone talks with musicians

saying "What? You're bleeding? Bleed!"

through a trick greeting

. . . and the Harmonist congratulates him

he swats her with his towel

and she sobs

she repents while he sings to her

Wife orders the Husband

she hits him in the mouth

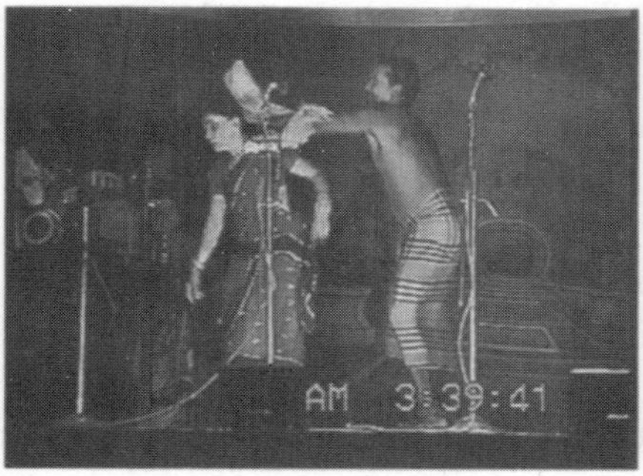

he manages to grab her by the hair

he kicks her while she runs away . . .

she falls to the ground

he stomps on her while she's down

they sing a love song

42 The Aṭipiṭi scene sequence: a storyboard of fifteen digital images taken from a videotape of Sridevi and Kalaiarasan's performance, April 1993, Madurai.

him on the mouth; audience laughs.] Don't be gabbing uselessly, shut up! Are you talking? Be respectful! You must know to always be respectful to your wife. Why are you looking at your hand?

H ♫: His teeth have fallen out!

W: What? You're bleeding? Bleed! [*Slaps his hand away.*] Come here!

[*Points to floor.*] What? Come over here before me! [*Hits him quite hard on the mouth; the audience goes wild with laughter, and some audience members call out.*] Come here! You have no respect for your wife? [*Hits him in the mouth; audience continually laughing.*]

H ♫: He's shaming the whole male race, wretched fellow!

W: Will you speak respectfully? Will you give respect?

H ♫: Yo! Are you a man?

[*Buffoon and Dancer both spin to face the harmonist.*]

H: Forget it, man, you're too much! /

W: You should shut up! /

H: Only if you go look in each and every man's house will you know who's taking the beatings!

[*They turn back to each other.*]

W: Hey! Shut your mouth! How many times have I told you, just stay in the house and do the housework!

H: Yes.

W: I am the one who goes out.

H: You mean I am not allowed to go out even to pee?

W: I go out to work, right? I put it [food] out for you three times a day, don't I? And you can't simply eat and do the housework? And you dare . . . ?

H: She puts it to me three times, while I only put it to her one time, man!

W: You put it? Have you ever even one time put it correctly? Do you put out the food? [*Hits his mouth.*]

H: I put it at night!

W: You put it? [*Hits his mouth.*] You better behave! If I get any angrier, I'll tear you to pieces!

H: Right.

W: You know, right, that if I tear you up, I'll tear you to shreds! Come here! I have told you to stay home and do the housework, don't go anywhere or talk to anyone. [*A man in the audience calls, "Hey, babe!" (ē kutti!)*] From listening to others, if you dare to speak to me that way, I'll beat you senseless! Come here! Thinking he's so great he got married. . . .

H: [*looking out past her, behind her, and bowing with his hands in greeting*] Brother! Welcome, Brother!

[*She spins around to look, and he grabs her by the hair (grabs her bun). Pulling her head back, he kicks her repeatedly in the butt. She runs, but he is right behind her, kicking her. They run like this around the whole stage. She stops, she bends forward in pain, waving her hands, he kicks her a few more times. At each kick, the mridangist hits his drum. The harmonist and the mridangist are smiling broadly.*]

H ♫: Go for it!

H: She's saying "Vā 'ṭā, pō 'ṭā!" to me? What is the meaning of this, sir?

H ♫: Only now are you a man! Shake my hand! [*He stands up behind his harmonium and extends his hand; the Buffoon leans over to him, and they shake. Other musicians extend their hands; the Buffoon shakes them too.*]

H: [*again to Dancer:*] I'll roll you and beat you!

W: Ai yo! He's beating me! [*He kicks her again.*]

H ♫: Beat her, kick her; look how [bold] she is for a scrawny woman!

M: She's the size of a grasshopper.

[*The Buffoon swings his towel up over his neck and proudly pulls it back and forth for a moment, then tugs at the two ends smugly.*]

W: You wretched sinner! Not even one day . . . [*The Buffoon pulls his towel off with his right hand and swats her across the back with it.*] Ai yo! [*He swats her again with the towel, chasing her around and around the central circle of the stage as she runs from him.*] Appa! Do you think I am a washerman's stone, that you should beat me so? That you can beat me like he beats clothes against a stone? Go to hell!

H: [*Slinging his towel up over his right shoulder and wearing it there*] Look you all, still she opens her mouth!

W: Hey! While you are sleeping, I'll come drop a stone on your head and kill you, man! If you keep on beating me, your hands will become leprous!

H: Oh, will they?

W: Go to hell!

H: Sir, she is still saying "Vā 'ṭā" to me! [*Kicks her.*]

W: Ai yo! It hurts!

H ♫: Change the place you hit her, man! What is this? Why do you keep on hitting her in the same place?

W: My parents brought me up so well and all! Oh, you sinner! [*They are now in the downstage right corner. He kicks her yet again, and she cries, looking all around to the musicians for help. Flinging her arms out, she falls to the ground in the downstage right corner and stays there.*]

H ♫: What, man! Kick her both frontside and backside, man!

H: Hey, I'll kill you!

H ♫: Wretched fellow! She's fallen and weak, man!

M: She's as small as a flea.

W: You'll become leprous!

H: Hey! Don't speak! [*He kicks her in the ribs.*] Don't speak! [*He kicks her again in the ribs and then stomps on her foot.*]

W: Don't stomp on my foot! [*she spits.*]

H: She's speaking again! [*Kicks her in the ribs.*] Get up! First get up!

W: Go away! I can't get up! [*He drags her up by her hands, only to swat her again across the arms and back with his towel.*] Ai yai yo! [*She falls back to the floor, now center stage, sobbing.*]

H♫: [*raucous laughter*]

M: Is she laughing or crying?

W: [*to musicians*] *Pō 'ṭā!* Dog!

MUSICIANS: [*laughter*]

H: Will you still talk? [*Again wields his towel in his right hand and swats her with it.*]

W: Pō 'ṭā! No! No! Ai yo! I can't take it! I can't take it! You've never been like this before!

H: Yes, yes.

W: Up to now you've been such a nice quiet man, so I expected the same today. [*He kicks her.*] Ai yo! But today you've started!

H: Right!

W: This is enough for me for a whole year, man!

H: Get up! [*Kicks her.*] First of all, get up! [*Turning to address the harmonist:*] You sinner, man! Aren't you supposed to be a headman? I'm beating her up like this; shouldn't you be coming and putting a stop to it?

H♫: Sure, man. Anyway, now that you've beaten her up like this, what are you going to do at night?

H: What will I do at night? I'll come to your wife. . . .

H♫: I'll slipper you, rascal! [*Audience bursts into laughter.*]

H: [singing in Oppari/lamentation style] On that side of the river, a goya tree in Ayodha. . . .

[*With this song, the husband and wife move swiftly toward reconciliation. He helps her up from the ground. They remain center stage. She sobs in repentance as he sings to her, until finally she clasps him in an embrace and cries into his bare chest. Their dialogue continues with her contrition.*]

H: There there, don't cry, don't cry.

W: My man!

H: Yes . . .

W: I never wanted to oppose you, until all the neighbor women said you had no manly pride [*rōsham*] . . .

B: [*He slaps her on the mouth.*] What, woman? How would the women next door have any idea whether I have manly pride or not?

W: They said, "Your husband is not going out properly to work." They told me that if I give you a good harsh cursing, from the very next day forward you would go properly out to work . . .

H: And in so doing, in cursing me harshly, you have received a beating, haven't you? So don't listen to the talk of the women next door if you don't want to be ruined!

W: Hereafter, I won't listen; this beating is enough for me, man! This is enough for me for two years, man!

H: Hereafter how will you address me?

W: Attāṉ! [kin term for both cross-cousin and husband] [*She touches his chest lightly.*]

They engage in some light banter and end the scene with a romantic love song, "Nighttime."

H and W: [*singing*] Time, nighttime, this is it, nighttime! The colored moon belongs to us! O apple of my eye, your arms are my cradle! Come, come, ours is a bed of flowers! You are like a mother, I like a child; I'll jump to embrace you, and sing joyfully! O apple of my eye, your arms are my cradle! Time, nighttime, O nighttime!

[*Exit together, running off upstage left.*]

Of all the echoing signs of gender trouble that ricochet through this scene, perhaps the most condensed symbol of the stages through which the changing action of the scene progresses is the husband's towel. As noted, a man's towel is a status marker, and how he wears it is significant. The Buffoon entered with his towel wrapped around his head as if he were a menial laborer, then unwrapped it and held it in one hand in a sort of suspended animation while he spoke with the harmonist. When the wife begins beating him, he holds it with both hands and attempts to use it as a shield, clutching it to his chest as she assaults him frontally. He continues clutching it like a baby's blanket for comfort as she orders him around, pointing him to the floor. At one point the mridangist even explicitly comments on the ineffectiveness of this poor excuse of a man by commenting on his relations with his towel: "He's just carrying his towel around!"

Then as soon as he becomes the one delivering the blows, he swings his towel up over his neck, pulling it proudly back and forth, tugging at the two ends now hanging over his puffed-up chest. He is in control now. He takes his towel in his right hand as a weapon, swatting the wife across the back and arms as she runs from him. She comments: "Am I a washerman's stone, to beat like this?" If a washerman is low on the social ladder (and he is, very), the inanimate stone he beats is even lower. The husband has moved up. Now he slings his towel up over his shoulder and wears it there smugly. This is how politicians and prestigious men of town and village wear their towels. The husband wears his like this till the end, when finally he uses his towel to wipe his wife's tears off his chest.

As we have seen, Special Drama comedy scenes often play on and elaborate quotidian fears of gendered interaction. In these acts, the orderly gender world comes unhinged, proper relations mess up, social reprobation looms large, and, as in most nightmares, the worst things imaginable happen. Dreams and nightmares are the manifest content of the Aṭipiṭi scene. The Dancer offers her dream vision, "I have so much desire for my husband to be this way, I saw it in a dream!" which to the harmonist is a nightmare: the "manly pride" of the "entire male race" will be shamed if a wife speaks to her husband without conventional respect markers. The exaggeration is ludicrous, and yet it rings true for some: this is, an audience member told me, "the way it really is with us."

The stage is filled here with characters that epitomize these extremes. The harmonist struggles to instill rigor in the Buffoon, whose terrifying fantasy demoness, the modern working woman so often introduced in Buffoon's monologues, has come to life in the Dancer's embodiment of the worst possible wife, who goes out to work and wants her husband to stay at home.

Hers is the real acting job in this act. It is no mean feat for a woman to do all the things she was told never to do. Of course, stage actresses in Tamilnadu are by definition always already doing precisely that, so for a Special Drama Dancer, this trick is a matter of degree, not of kind. Nevertheless, I am impressed by the actress Sridevi's ability to both give and take abuse so publicly, and by the fullness with which she bodily inhabits the commanding language and cocksure manner of the Tamil husband at home.

Her technique in acting the worst possible wife is simple. She takes gender-role reversal altogether literally and does everything a man does. Her language and her bodily gestures and postures quote verbatim the stereotypical Tamil husband at home. The only twist in the tale lies in its gender inversion; were it not for the fact that they are enacted by the wife, all these domestic behaviors would be standard. When the husband at home is actually a woman, she instantly becomes the worst possible wife.

Were such a simple reversal of roles advocated as a strategy for social change, it would, as feminists have long noted, be a lousy and unsophisticated strategy indeed (e.g., Sandoval 1991). What is its effect when used parodically?

Note first that the object of parody here is not what one might assume. Whereas in contemporary U.S. theatrical culture a parodic gender-reversed portrayal of a husband's aggressive behavior at home would most likely be used to expose problems in the originary gender role (i.e., how ridiculous the husband at home is, as a type, with his smug masculinity, etc.), here the setup is used instead to show the ridiculousness of anything other than the originary gender role. The role reversal is used to show how wrong it is of a wife to attempt to be a husband at home. There is no ostensible critique of the husband at home per se; there is only a critique of the woman who tries to be him. (While the Buffoon may himself be a fool, it nevertheless remains his prerogative, not hers, to cast aspersions on masculinity.) What she does in the male role raises questions only about her, not him. In the Aṭipiṭi scene, it is those who break with convention who are consistently the objects of parody. Only the reestablishment of conventional order brings closure and "peace."

Over the course of this scene, what begins as a reversal of domestic power in a home dominated by a raging and uncontrolled demoness ends in the righting of this obvious imbalance and the taming of the shrew.[5] This fictive enactment provides a platform for (married) men to imagine a backlash against a changing reality of increasingly emboldened wives and the threats to masculinity they pose. Toward this end, the Buffoon is eagerly joined by the musicians, who help him establish a manly (read violent) virility. Putting the wife in her proper place is modeled as the collective responsibility of all the men onstage as the chorus praises the husband for finally acting like a man, shakes his hand, and eggs him on while teasing and laughing at her.

Meanwhile the Dancer enacts the woman-on-top as the mirror of man-on-top. Her worst possible wife uses the same phrases, the same postures, and the same gestures that husbands at home use to their wives. She commands him not to speak but to stay home and do the housework, refusing to allow him to go out or to speak to anyone outside. He is not to stand in the vāsal; he is not to talk back.

The transition to male virility and female subservience is effected through the fake greeting ploy. As used here, the greeting welcomes an imaginary "big brother" to witness the scene, which doesn't simply end with his appearance, as did the earlier Buffoon-Dance Duet. Here instead this imaginary male's appearance sparks a shift that swings all the other men onstage into action: the Buffoon kicks and puffs up his chest; the musicians cheer, hit their drums, and applaud. The audience hoots. The insipid husband has finally found respect for himself as a man—rōsham—and reinstalls himself as the normal husband at home, a role that, miraculously, remains unsullied by the Dancer's parody, leaving the wife alone to suffer for her attempt to usurp him.

Performers and audience alike nevertheless saw wife and husband as equally victorious in this scene, as both attain their proper powers in the end. They argue—to me, as the conversations I present hereafter make clear—that the proper form of women's power is found in the confirmation of men's power. They point out that this end is achieved through a plan hatched by women, after all: talking together in the kollai, women plot to gain proper status, self-respect, and rōsham for the husband. The wife is a vehicle for his coming to power. Both of the women with whom I spoke at greatest length about this scene, one an actress and the other an audience member, tried to convince me that married women (a category in which each includes herself, though in reality neither lives a married life anything like the model she upheld in our talks) desire their subservience to men as the proper state of domestic affairs. Wifely agency, they suggest, inheres in the ability to incite men to the responsibilities of the husband, and the wife's comeuppance raises her husband's, and thus her own, status in the all-important public eye.

This return to an idealized normalcy that ends the Aṭipiṭi scene cannot, however, but be precarious. This act scratches the otherwise glassy surface of the "normal" and reveals lurking terrors. It offers both an initially terrifying reversal and a frighteningly powerful pooling of collective wills (present in both the narrated and the event texts) to rectify that reversal. When the scene ends, comic-break-time ends, and the subsequent, final dramatic scene is the marriage of Hero and Heroine. Can their marriage really seem a bed of flowers after this?

A Discussion with the Artists

In discussing the popularity of this piece with its two main performers, I learned of their overt intention to deliver a moral message. They saw themselves as staging a glimpse of "the wrong way" in order to teach people what not to do. The artists seemed to take particular pleasure in this chance to be the ones to deliver such a moral lesson, as it represents a major reversal of social roles for them. Stigmatized as public performers, Special Drama artists in general rarely get a chance to be heard as purveyors of any kind of morality. In this particular case, Kalaiarasan and Sridevi, as Muslims in a predominately Hindu field, are also minority performers who particularly relished the chance to use their popular repertory hit to prove their ability to assert a sanctioned morality.

At the core of our discussion of the Aṭipiṭi scene was the artists' notion of proper, separate spheres: the family is properly a domestic matter, to be dealt with inside the home, and any move to involve the public in what are meant to be kept as internal disputes will end in tears. This is also the real-life context of their engagement in the art of public performance. Our discussion began with this recognition of the difficult position of Muslim actresses in particular. Sridevi is this actress's stage name, and not her real, Muslim name. She says, "If we use our own Muslim name, advertise it and go to act in some other place, people will speak of us as though we are very cheap, saying, 'Look at that! A Muslim girl has come to act! What a big shame it is for Islam.' They will talk thus amongst themselves, considering it a big shame for the entire village."

Kalaiarasan, the actor, adds, "A humiliation and a shame—they might take action through the *jamaath*" (a Muslim panchayat). This is indeed what happened to Sridevi; the jamaath in her village excommunicated her, cutting her off from all relations with her community. Fortunately, two years later, a more liberal leadership took power in the jamaath. They allowed her to again be part of her community, and allowed her children to study Arabic at the mosque. For men, the prohibitions are not as strict, and Kalaiarasan in fact often introduces himself onstage using both his names: Kalaiarasan, his Hindu stage name, and Mustaffa, his Muslim given name. There are a far greater number of Muslim men acting in Special Drama than women; indeed, Sridevi's family—her mother, her elder sister, Sridevi herself, and now one of her own daughters—were the only Muslim women currently in the field as far as I could gather.

So public opinion is a powerful force shaping these artists' lives, and it varies greatly by gender. As in the Aṭipiṭi scene itself, it is deemed highly important that a man's masculinity be recognized by other men, yet women's talk and the decisions they make among themselves are met with disdain. Sridevi stressed that the unacceptably bold aspect of the wife's character lay in the fact that she dared talk to outsiders (both the neighbor women and the panchayat headman) about problems internal to her marriage. This is why her husband has to hit and discipline her; the main moral of the story, both artists agreed, is "One shouldn't go and tell what happens in the house to others." Both artists adamantly asserted that all problems should be kept quiet in a marriage, and that opening up marital relations to the gossip of outsiders should be avoided at all costs: "peace" in married life means *not* talking about problems in the marriage. In Sridevi's words:

> We should solve all our problems amongst ourselves. Women should generally work within the house and not go around gossiping; otherwise, the family will suffer. When a husband and wife fight, they should forget it immediately. Only then will one's family life be peaceful. Otherwise, if we think, "My husband has bashed me up, and therefore I won't give him any food," the family will be ruined. Man and woman should be united; and when we have kids, we should make sure that we give them a stable family life.

It is a general premise of feminist work against domestic violence worldwide that a couple must first recognize violence against a spouse as a problem before they can begin to address changing it. To do so, one must talk about it and admit that a problem exists. The opposite paradigm is in play here. Domestic violence is, far from being seen primarily as a social problem, treated instead as an acceptable social resolution. Violence is naturalized as an unmarked male action, a given of a husband's behavior. The wife's "complaint" to her neighbors and to the nattāmai leads directly to blows; this eventually "reforms" him, in the sense that it encourages him to establish "normal" husband-wife relations with her by beating her. As Sridevi explained the action of the scene:

> My main aim is to reform him. That's why I hit him; that's why I talked like that: so that he will get rōsham. Once he gets rōsham, then I promise him that I won't talk like that. I say, "We should be like everyone else, like husband and wife." And he also agrees: "Yes. It's my mistake also. Henceforth, I'll go out and earn. Let's live like all other husbands and wives. Let's live peacefully."

What the wife seeks to reform in her husband is his lack of sufficient masculinity, his lack of rōsham. Again, male violence is not the problem here but rather the solution, as well as the desired norm: a man's rōsham is his proper pride and self-respect, which, as we have seen, he attains through his domination of his wife in their home. The original problem in their marriage is the topsy-turvy relation of their household, where the wife was working outside the home. As Sridevi says:

> His wife earns and feels, "Why the hell should I respect this man? I am the one who earns." So she never respects him, but rather calls him "va 'ṭa, pō 'ṭa" [you come, you go].

Thus the wife claims that she engaged in public talk purely as an instrumental move to get her husband to engage publicly with other men and thus find or develop his masculinity. As Sridevi put it, the wife feels that "All these days I behaved in an arrogant manner so that you would get rōsham. At last, you have gotten it." Public exposure here works to ensure that men will continue to hit their wives, and that as long as they do, their wives will stay quiet about it.

What about the publicness of their own performance, I asked? Their performance, the artists felt, works to reinscribe the message that public exposure of marital problems should be avoided. This is clearly understood, they emphasized, as everyone laughs at them. Even children can learn here the values of maintaining an orderly, self-contained Tamil household:

SRIDEVI: In some families, what we show is a fact. The audience will realize [on seeing our act], "Oho! If we talk like this [with outsiders], I suppose this is what will happen." Women should not listen to other women or talk in such a manner to men.

KALAIARASAN: When they see our comedy, families will reform; both some men and some women will reform. After seeing us, they will try to be more united even if they are fighting with their husbands.

The reform urged on families here would not rid them of domestic abuse (seemingly not a salient category of distinction), but rather only of the overly bold speech of a woman, whether to her husband or to outsiders.

The most ironic thing about Sridevi's emphasis on publicness as being wrong for women is that she is using publicness itself to make her point (shades of Anita Bryant). She is in the lowest, most public of professions, for which she is held in disdain by her own Muslim community, yet she stands on ceremony here with normative Tamil ideas about women's non-public persona as the only right role for women. That she herself doesn't find this ironic underscores her very real need to be concerned with what people think. Special Drama actors frequently inhabit such a paradoxical position: their being on public display stigmatizes them, so they attempt to distance themselves publicly from this stigma by enacting a morality critical of public display. The Aṭipiṭi scene is one of the most pointed, and poignant, representations of the painful repercussions of such a strategy.

Given its conveyance of all these moralistic messages, why, I still wondered, is any of this Aṭipiṭi funny? For one thing, of course, the scene comes in the almost irresistible packaging of slapstick physical comedy, some version of which is found across many cultures. Tamil audiences appreciate it in terukkuttu clowns, for example, as well as in celluloid incarnations (the goofy cinema comedy duo Senthil Gowndamani is a case in point).[6] The tried-and-true antics of physical comedy produce an almost knee-jerk laugh response in audiences of all ages. In classic Victorian Punch and Judy puppet shows, Punch trips, and the cymbal clangs! Hands fly up, the body falls down! His arm swings, ding! and connects, causing Judy to reel wider than in real life. The stage performers play the scene for laughs. They attune their gestures through the use of pauses, repetitions, and exaggerations—nevertheless in many respects frightfully realistic, especially the sobbing and doubling over in pain of the wife—to an accompanying whir-slam-bang sound track that provides an overall tenor of cartoon slapstick rather than humanist tragedy.

In Punch and Judy, however, what makes the despicable Punch nevertheless easy for Western audiences to cheer is that he always, if inadvertently, challenges the superego of authority in its many guises, from the cop one should obey (Punch kills him) to the helpless infant one should protect (he abandons it). In his way, Punch is pure subversive id, the kind of character that Western audiences love. I don't know how he would go over in Tamilnadu. He is utterly different from the husband in the Tamil scene: in Aṭipiṭi the husband beats his wife so that all will appreciate his manliness and cheer the reinscription of accepted roles of authority. The anthropological question thus remains: how does the Tamil audience watch Aṭipiṭi, and why do they find it funny?

Four Theories of Spectatorship

It should be unsurprising that the spectatorial relations pertaining between Special Drama and its audiences might be other than those generally held to pertain in Western theater.[7] As we have seen, the Tamil genre of Icai Nāṭakam (music drama) developed at the intersection of multiple theatrical traditions, including the realism of mid- to late-nineteenth-century Parsi and British traveling troupes, as well as indigenous theatrical traditions of Tamil terukkuttu and poetic, devotional song genres. Current stagings of Special Drama continue to blend Western and Indian influences and seem to draw on multiple traditions of spectatorship as well.

The first theory of spectatorship I consider it useful to revisit in trying to understand the spectatorial relations at play in Special Drama is the Platonic model, characterized by its emphasis on *imitation*. Plato distrusted the potentially powerful effects of theater on its spectators, to the extent that theater scholars now characterize his attitude as a "loathing of the theater" (Diamond 1992, 391). In the *Republic*, Plato represents the problem as one of unthinking imitation.

> Instead of being repulsed by the sight of the kind of person we'd regret and deplore being ourselves, we enjoy the spectacle and sanction it. . . . And the same goes for sex, anger, and all the desires and feelings of pleasure and distress which, we're saying, accompany everything we do: poetic representation has the same effect in all these cases too. It irrigates and tends to these things when they should be left to wither, and it makes them our rulers when they should be our subjects, because otherwise we won't live better and happier lives, but quite the opposite. . . . If you admit the entertaining Muse of lyric and epic poetry, then instead of law and the shared acceptance of reason as the best guide, the kings of your community will be pleasure and pain. (*Republic*, 605e–7a)

Given such ideas, in his plan for the ideal republic Plato recommends banishing actors from the city entirely (after anointing their heads with myrrh, to be sure [398b]). In the Platonic/imitative model of spectatorship, the audience members want to be the person they see, and theater leads people into unthinking imitation.

A second classical, Western model of spectatorship is built on Aristotle's brilliant answer to Plato's fears in the *Poetics*. I call this the *inoculation* model. Aristotle effectively rescued theater from Platonic condemnation by proposing "catharsis" as a kind of homeopathic cure: through a small dose of pity or fear, a momentary identification leading to enjoyment or repulsion, the spectator purges himself of the same and thereby attains moral betterment. Here the idea is that the viewer will not copy the bad actions of the actor but rather learn from them what to avoid. By partaking in the bitterness of the tragedy or the foolishness of the comedy staged before them, spectators will be cleansed of any desire to go through the same experiences in their real lives: spectators partake here, so that they need not partake in real life. Theater in this model is an instructive purgatory that offers a useful, inoculating dose of poison, and catharsis strengthens the polity, rather than leading it astray.

A third theory of spectatorship comes not from ancient Greece but from ancient India. This is a theory of spectatorship concerned less with the identifications made by individuals than with a collective appreciation of the theater. The aesthetic theory of *rasa* derives from the classic Sanskrit theatrical tradition, as codified in the early text known as the *Natyasastra*, attributed to the sage Bharatamuni around the third century B.C. In this tradition of theatrical aesthetics, rasa is understood as the taste or mood of the performance, which is generated by the performer's skill and depends on the ability of the audience to taste its flavor. "*Rasa* therefore has essentially a double character: it is 'taste' and it is 'tasted.' It is not possible to separate the two aspects. [. . .] 'Objectively seen *rasa* is the juice, from the subjective point of view it is the relish of the juice. . . . The word *rasa* in fact hangs between the subjective and the objective'" (Heckel 1989, 37). In this model, "the play performed must offer the possibility of tasting," while "a capacity for tasting is likewise required of the audience" (37). The audience relates not to a particular character, or even his or her traits or actions, but rather to the mood of the performance as a whole.

The goal of the audience in this model of spectatorship is to appreciate the artistry of the theatrical representation of human emotion. The idea is that audiences will enjoy the spectacle from a certain distance, exclaiming "So this is how it is!" and appreciating the truths it expresses about the human condition. The *Natyasastra* builds theater from a palette of eight primary *bhavas*, or human emotions: love, humor, anger, compassion, heroism, wonder, disgust, and fear. These eight are then further broken down into four pairs, comprising a source emotion and a derivative emotion. The first paired set of emotions is love (*srngara*) and humor (*hasya*). Of this pair, the text notes that "Humor results when Love is parodied or imitated." The semiotic system that stimulates parodic laughter here relies on exaggeration and disfigurement, distortion and deformity—to read as queer deviations. Simply put, "The comic *rasa* is experienced when something tastes funny" (Siegel 1987, 8).

The rasa of humor is then itself divisible into six varieties, according to whether it is used by high-, middle-, or low-status characters. Each character type is associated with two varieties of laughter. The two used most frequently in the Aṭipiṭi scene are, not surprisingly, those associated with low characters, who employ loud laughter and silly laughter (as opposed to the gentle laughs of the high, or the broad smiles and satirical laughter of the middle types). The silly laughter both used and provoked by low characters is described in the *Natyasastra* as "laughing in the wrong context with tears in the eyes and head and shoulders shaking," while loud laughter is described as "tears flowing from the eyes, voice loud and screeching and sides firmly clasped."

This third model of spectatorship thus recognizes the shared nature of the event that takes place between audience and performer. It suggests not that this experience of give and take leads directly to specific actions in everyday life, but rather that it leads to commentary on such actions. The rasa theory appreciates theater as something the audience judges from a critical distance.

In this sense the Sanskritic theory of rasa provokes performances similar to those that inspired Bertolt Brecht as he developed his theatrical model for activist art. Brecht's early-twentieth-century comparisons of European theater with Asian theater (based on his viewing of traditional Chinese acting as performed by Mei Lan-Fang and company in 1935) led to his celebration of a technique he called "the alienation effect." His comparisons lend themselves well to describing the interactive quality that pertains between spectators and actors in Special Drama:

> Above all, the Chinese artist never acts as if there were a fourth wall besides the three surrounding him. He expresses his awareness of being watched. This immediately removes one of the European stage's characteristic illusions. The audience can no longer have the illusion of being the unseen spectator at an event which is really taking place. . . . He acts in such a way that nearly every sentence could be followed by a verdict of the audience and practically every gesture is submitted for the public's approval. (Brecht [1957] 1964, 91–92, 95)

This notion that audiences *judge* a performance within a shared context of known styles, and standards of common behavior, reappeared in my conversations with artists and audience members alike regarding their appreciation of the Aṭipiṭi scene.

In fact, all three of these theoretical models of spectatorship—the imitative Platonic model, the Aristotelian cathartic model, and the appreciative aesthetic model of Sanskritic rasas and bhavas—reappeared in discussions with those at the scene. Performers spoke of their intention to deliver a moral message, while audience members spoke of how the scene teases their own sense of right and wrong. These conversations strongly suggest yet a fourth model of spectatorial relations, one that engages the audience in an active role of moral patrol.

Why Does the Audience Laugh?

Laughter on its own is a difficult way into the analysis of any spectatorial event. There are too many types of laughter: cynical, tentative, broad, merry, and so on. At the same time, no laughter is any one of these things: a broad laugh may be cynical or a cynical laugh tentative, a merry laugh gentle, or bitter, or even fake. To make sense of any particular instance of laughter, one must consider it in context: which, when, by whom, at what, and with what effect(s)?[8]

The most notable features of the laughter greeting the Aṭipiṭi scene were its conventionality and ubiquity. First, the audience's laughter was quite regularly timed to the stage action. It came in response to punch lines, and thus often in this case to punches. The transcript of the scene presented earlier confirms this tightly interactive, attuned-to-the-action character of the laughter: every time she slaps his mouth, *laugh*; every time he kicks her ribs, *laugh*. The audience laughter here is a regular, reliable feature of the event text.

A primary means of achieving such regularity of response lies in the percussive accompaniment provided by the musicians. The score of percussive beats and bangs, hits, and clangs offered by the two drummers signal punches and punch lines much in the way that vaudeville routines or early animated films used sound. The sound track helps keep the audience on track with the action: pow laugh clang laugh whoosh laugh slam laugh. This nonverbal sound track engages the two sets of observers present at this event, the musicians and the audience, in a mutual, participatory relation that is central to the event.

The other feature marking this laughter as conventional was its ubiquity. Everyone (apart from me) laughed. While it seemed at times uncontrollable and uncontrolled, coming in big breaking guffaws, it was nevertheless contextually normal and regular: laughing out loud was the proper response. From where I sat, as usual among the women in the audience, I was surprised to see that rather than the usual shy giggles, women too laughed openly at the Aṭipiṭi scene. One such laugher was a woman I knew.

An Audience Account

The neighborhood in which this performance took place is in a section of Madurai called Krishnapuram Colony, very near where I lived at the time. The American Institute of Indian Studies school for Tamil language study was located there, and several other American scholars also lived nearby. Neelam is a woman from the neighborhood who provided domestic services to several American residences, including my own.

Neelam fits a common profile of the kind of woman who attends Special Drama performances in urban settings such as this. Working class and lower caste, she is one of the urban poor. She was raising her teenage son alone after her husband left her, for drink, three years earlier. She offered her services as a cook or maid in as many homes as possible to piece together a living.

When Neelam and I spoke on the day after the performance, I didn't quite realize the extent to which her comments answered my questions about audience relations to Special Drama. I was a bit incredulous at the time. Fortunately, I taped our conversation and have been able to listen carefully to it again, so as to present her comments here verbatim.

I asked Neelam why she found the Aṭipiṭi scene so funny. In reply, she recounted the performance to me as she saw it. Her account differs from the transcription I later generated from the videotaped event in revealing ways. Most significantly, Neelam substitutes audience laughter for the critical verbal promptings and interjections of the harmonist.

In Neelam's account, the voice of the nattāmai disappears entirely ("withers," as Plato might have it) and is replaced by a collective, critically interactive public. This substitution suggests that it is a particular subject position, rather than a specific character, with whom Neelam identifies. That is, she does not see herself in either husband or wife but rather finds and defines herself in her experience as an audience member.

As the following excerpts from our conversation reveal, for Neelam, audience enjoyment has more to do with the assertion of a collective moral sensibility in the present, and a collective self defined by moral agreement, than with any Western psychological notions of individual identification.[9] Her recounting of the scene began as follows:

> At the beginning, the husband is like a small child, with a mild-mannered nature. He's sort of crazy. His wife, boldly, makes him do all the housework. "You must wash my saris. You must cook. You must not speak with anyone next door. I'll go out and I'll earn like a man for you. You just eat and listen to me. Whatever I say, you listen. What man, what do you say? What I say goes. Come here! Wash my sari! Put out the food, ṭā!"—this is how she talks to her husband. And like a little child, he fears her and does anything she says: "Okay, 'mā,[10] whatever you say, I'll do it, 'mā.'" So for about ten minutes, he listens to everything she says.

Note immediately how the event text (what occurs in the real time of the performance event) and the narrated text (what occurs in the staged time of the fictional story) merge in Neelam's account. She quotes dialogue from the narrated text but frames it in the real time of the event text, saying, "So for about ten minutes he listens to everything she says" (rather than something like, "So for years he had been doing everything she said," which would have kept her own account in the single plane of the story). In meshing these two time frames, Neelam's account reveals the realness of her experience as an audience member who feels she has a real effect on the onstage action.

Neelam continues by saying that after about ten minutes of listening to everything his wife says—a point on which, by the way, her recollection is uncannily accurate, as testified to by my video time clock—it is finally too much for him, and "he suddenly takes courage." How exactly does this come about, I wondered?

NEELAM: People will laugh, saying, "Ai Yo! See how he does everything his wife tells him to, he irons her saris, he cooks for her, he's so afraid of her!" People will laugh. Then /

SUSAN: / What's funny in that?

N: See, he is submitting to his wife. He is ironing her saris, cooking for her. He has no other go, and because he is living off her income, he is afraid of her and submits to her. If you show this to Tamil people, they'll laugh happily. Then what does he do, immediately he turns around and realizes, "Hey, shit! Everyone is looking at me and laughing!"

It is once the audience's laughter begins that the slippage between the narrated and the event text really comes into its own in Neelam's account, and the event starts to fully "hang between the subjective and the objective" (as a rasa theorist might put it), with no separation between the juice and its tasting: the people laugh, and the performer becomes cognizant that he is laughable.

> He suddenly takes courage: "Whoa! Looking at me, they see that my veshti is tied like a sari, while hers is tied like a veshti! Everyone is looking at me and laughing!" and this gets him going.

Even though the artists never actually cross-dress in this performance, Neelam has here literally clothed the gender reversals of this sketch in the ever-humorous stuff of cross-dressing. Cloth provides her a tidy symbol with which to condense the many issues at stake here into a single image, and Neelam captures the flavor of the gender reversal through this idiomatic exclamation of the shame of psychic cross-dressing: "my veshti is tied like a sari, while hers is tied like a veshti!" is effectively a Tamil parallel to the English idiomatic expression characterizing a topsy-turvy gender situation in a heterosexual home, namely, that the woman wears the pants. Her account continues:

NEELAM: So right away he says to her, "Hey you, you think I'm the kind of guy who will do everything for you? Cook for you and wash your clothes? I will not cook. I will not wash. I will not heed your words"—and with that he raises his veshti [in a fighting gesture] and beats her with blows and kicks. Then she says, "Everyday I talk to you like this, so why have you suddenly taken exception today? Suddenly you are angry? You have been like the wife to me, I've been like the husband to you. Today what, someone taught you that you should beat me like this, kick and beat me like this! You'll come to no good! Your hand will turn leprous!" and she scolds him. And that will be pleasurable for Tamil people. First he was afraid of his wife, but now, finally now, happily, he hits her. . . .

SUSAN: And how did this happiness come about?

N: Right! He realized that everyone was laughing at him. "They must be laughing because they think I'm crazy. So what if I should get the right character, if I should get heroism? Then I show my manliness, and she submits to me." The wife submits. And today the husband moves a step up.

I suspect that by "today" Neelam again refers to a day that simultaneously occupies both story time and telling time, and that the husband moved up a step on both that day and this. Indeed, in her words: "Only now has he become a man. *A man*. And she a wife. And now she surrenders to her husband."

There was an almost wistfully romantic tone to this ending in Neelam's account, a sigh of relief, a contentedness like the happily-ever-after of fairy tales. This is the way it should be. Now he's a man, and she's a surrendering wife; now everything will be okay. When I asked, "But doesn't anyone feel sorry for her?" Neelam answered, "No one will feel for her, because she spoke insolently to him. She didn't treat him with respect. So we'll think, 'Beat her good! Hit her again! Hit her, man! Kick her, man!'"

The effective role claimed for public laughter in this audience account of the event strongly recalls the turn-of-the-century French humor theorist Henri Bergson's treatment of humor as a mechanism of social control and an instrument of moral reform. The use of public laughter as a shaming corrective is central to Bergson's theory, as it seems equally to be of Neelam's.

> Laughter is, above all, a corrective. Being intended to humiliate, it must make a painful impression on the person against whom it is directed. By laughter, society avenges itself for the liberties taken with it. It would fail in its object if it bore the stamp of sympathy or kindness. (Bergson [1900] 1956, 187)

Neelam's retelling of the Aṭipiṭi scene casts the audience's corrective laughter in a key role, erasing any separation between musician as Everyman and audience as everyone. Whereas one might generally talk of a chorus "standing in" for the audience, in Neelam's retrospective portrayal, the two are absolutely undifferentiated subject positions. Audience and chorus are not merely contiguous; they are coterminous. As a result, the harmonist completely disappears from her account, and his contemptuous verbal comments are subsumed into the audience's laughter, which acts to effect the scene's progression.

Neelam's account presents a theory of causality in which shame effects are key. It is the Bergsonian laughter of the audience, "intended to humiliate," that prompts the husband's self-realizations. Likewise it is his shame in the face of the audience that causes him to desire change and thereby to find his manly pride (rōsham). The shared assumption in both Bergson's and Neelam's logic is that shame is highly efficacious in enforcing social norms; as soon as a man realizes that everyone is laughing at him, shame will prompt him to reform and conform.[11] It's as though these ten staged minutes are not a representation of ongoing relations (that could have existed for ten months or ten years) but rather are the very relations themselves. What is happening right here onstage, in the midst of this particular public, is what has to be corrected, and the people right here, as a powerful instantiation of the Tamil public, are the ones doing the correcting.

In this sense, Neelam's account concretizes an abstract public into the current, present public. Working-class women like Neelam and her friends, who attended this performance together, are quite familiar with child rearing and, in Neelam's case, the particular struggles of raising alone boy children into men. When she characterizes the psychological state of the husband as that of a young boy toward his mother—"And like a little child, he fears her, and does anything she says"—she simultaneously notes the sudden shift in authority that marks adulthood. The figure for whom the man must properly perform is the larger public, not simply this one woman, whether wife or mother. The young man's awareness of the broader audience and of himself break into consciousness simultaneously. This sudden self-awareness breaks his orientation to the parental figure, and he abruptly stops orienting his actions to his wife/mother inside the home and starts orienting himself toward the audience, outside in public.

"Going public" is thus both a male life-stage marker and an important step in the proper socialization of male citizens. Going public is right for the man, but wrong for the woman, as going public invites the public in. But for everyone it is clearly the case that only by internalizing the public voice in the first place might you avoid shame and laughter; such are the moral lessons one learns at Special Dramas.

Further, Special Drama seems to draw on every possible model of spectatorship in conveying such socializing messages. The audience partakes of a key aspect of the classic role of the audience in Sanskritic rasa theory, tasting the flavor of the performer's emotional evocation of the human condition. Simultaneously, audience members inoculate themselves, in good Aristotelian fashion, from any need to suffer the same plight as these characters, having learned the consequences of such acts through the performance event itself. And in identifying with the musicians' position, rather than that of the actors, they enjoy this spectacle freed from the Platonic curse of having to be "the kind of person we'd regret and deplore being ourselves."

Through a combination of spectatorial orientations, then, audiences for Special Drama can enjoy scenes like Aṭipiṭi—its upside-downness as well as its uprightness—without disrupting the conventions of morality that order their own lives, for better or worse.

Public voices and public advice, and public commentary on every staged move, are what move the whole event along, through shaming taunts and corrective laughter. The ultimate message seems to be that to avoid actual confrontation with any actual public, one must learn to internalize the public's attitude so thoroughly that one never trips up or needs to go consulting anyone outside. It seems that actors are cast permanently in the role of being people who haven't learned this basic lesson in Tamil life, stuck as they are in this shameful, stigmatizing position of being on the public stage, getting laughed at by an audience who thoroughly enjoy their own ability to claim the moral high ground. Hit (*aṭi*), and hold (*piṭi*): a public celebrates what it knows about public humiliation by reenacting it, in an active role of moral patrol, on actors.

PART THREE Lives

7 The Drama Tongue and the Local Eye

We arrive at dusk. Even before we come to a full stop, a crowd of villagers surrounds us. They are mostly children, though also some old men and women. When we do stop, they press their faces up against the tinted windows of the van, trying hard to see us.

Such an arrival scene played out every time I traveled to a Special Drama with artists. Certain common realities of "first contact" arrival scenes are present here—as for example in Raymond Firth's "We were surrounded by crowds of naked chattering youngsters . . ." ([1936] 1983, 2) or Louis-Antoine de Bougainville's "An immense crowd of men and women received us there, and could not be tired with looking at us" (Bougainville [1772] 1967, 213), both cited in Mary Louise Pratt's illuminating discussion of the "royal-arrival" trope in ethnographic writing (Pratt 1986)—though it also differs in at least one profound way. Here the "we" is not royal at all. This "we" is neither a group of Europeans, as in Bougainville's voyage, nor a single European flanked by native bearers and assistants, as in Firth's landing on Tikopia. Nor do I speak with that plaintive voice of the heroic castaway made indelible by Bronislaw Malinowski in *Argonauts of the Western Pacific*: "Imagine yourself suddenly set down surrounded by all your gear, alone on a tropical beach close to a native village, while the launch or dinghy which has brought you sails away out of sight" (Malinowski 1922, 4). And yet in all these cases, including my own, persons perceived as foreign enter, by means of a relatively modern conveyance and with an impressive array of gear, into the midst of a local population who are rendered understandably curious.

What is distinct about the arrivals I write of here is that the object of the villagers' othering gaze is not me, though I am certainly included in it, as would be almost any woman arriving in a van with these artists. There is a local calculus here that operates regardless of me. Special Drama artists are the ones whom the locals clamor to see. The experience we share by dint of my being with them is, of course, not entirely unfamiliar to me from my travels as a white woman in India, during which I receive regular doses of gawking on my own. But this time it is not the fully foreign but the outsider within who draws the stares. It is she who—within that system of distinctions by which locals judge each other—embodies an otherness whose proportions exceed those of skin and passport color. Here come the Actresses.

The male artists unload suitcases full of costumes and musical instruments and take them backstage. Inside the van, the female artists remain seated, waiting. Because I am female, I wait with them. We wait just that bit longer than the villagers are willing to wait for us (a long time), just until they understand that this is not the moment when they will get to see the actresses.

We leave the van and go backstage. The men have already gone to eat the dinner prepared by the villagers. Someone from the sponsor's house calls us to come eat. On the way, we pass actors who alert us, in code, about the food that awaits us. They say, "Mattimacai mun̲r̲am pūti." No one else would understand it, but what this warns us is: "The local woman's goat meat is bad, don't eat it."

Afterward all the artists gather backstage to prepare their performance faces. Meanwhile the audience gathers outside. They seem excited, restless, eager. Walls of thatched palm fronds separate them from us.

The leaves are big, almost five feet long and three feet wide. Strips are cut into them when they are still green, then braided while still attached along the central stem. When the braided leaf dries, it is stiff and sturdy. The dried leaves lashed together make a porous wall of thatch. Its natural irregularities include spaces where the braiding is not entirely tight.

There are spaces in the thatch that are holes, really, about the size of a human eye. During the night they do indeed fill with village eyes, again pressed up, again trying to see in, to see us. Throughout the night, and particularly at junctures where the onstage action lags, villagers stand and peer through these holes. They are there even at dawn, when the artists can finally remove their makeup.

Thatch walls are a thin membrane for accomplishing any real separation between backstage and offstage, thinner than the tinted glass windows of the darkened van. Through it villagers can stare right into the performers' "inside" space. Indeed, even in what they call their inside space, drama artists are surrounded by local eyes.

It is in this context, where walls literally have eyes and ears, that drama people say to each other, "Mattikkāḷi kāṇkoḷḷutu, nāvāṭātē!" (The centermen are holding eyes, don't wag your tongue!), using words the villagers will not understand.

My central question in the ensuing discussion is this: If even their privacy must be so publicly performed, does the Special Drama community have any interiority that is not already articulated in relation to the gaze of their public?

A Secret Language

Special Drama artists use coded communications in othering situations like these, whether to discuss bad meat or to remark on the presence of villagers. Their code is an argot, a secret language shot through with the relations of stigma that call for its use in the first place. Stigma infuses all its mundane entailments: judgments on food, negotiations over money, and the awareness of staring locals. Its code words themselves are the distilled effects of the stigma that defines actors, as evident in its lexical items.

Of particular interest to me is how this argot encodes the attitudes artists hold about themselves, as well as those they hold about the social relations that define their work. Specifically, Special Drama artists continue to cast themselves as social outsiders even within their own insider language, using it to speak of locals as insiders and "centermen" around whom the artists themselves must hold their tongue.

The self-referential outsider identity that artists maintain suggests that not all marginalized people respond to stigma by attempting to centralize themselves, *even within their own narratives*. Rather, in some cases, self-knowledge and identity are so based in experiences of outsiderness that marginality itself becomes defining.

The expression "The locals are watching, shut up!" best illuminates this sense of the artists' community identity. The sentence is a frequently uttered inaugural phrase in this argot. That is, artists will often use this phrase to signal the need to switch into code: because the locals are watching. This is a fairly straightforward performative function to which the actual lexical composition of the code phrase adds nuance.

The nuance lies in the use of standard Tamil lexical components to create code words. Understanding these lexical elements—and I explain my methods of gaining such understanding in detail hereafter—renders a more Tamil-language-resonant translation of the injunction as "the centermen are holding eyes, don't wag your tongue!" Using an expression that regulates certain persons' tongues (their own) to accord with the actions of certain other persons' eyes (the centermen) is thus how artists induce their own tongues to speak the *nāṭaka bāshai*, the Drama Tongue.

Such a coding reveals the centrality of a highly relational sense of self among Special Drama artists. By "relational sense of self" I mean that artists are keenly aware of how they are perceived in broader Tamil society. Indeed, artists continue to define themselves, even in markedly private speech acts, largely in relation to the norms of a society that treats them as outsiders. Special Drama artists have a savvy and realistic reading of who they are within the larger cultural and historical picture of Tamil social relations. They maintain this relational sense of self in just about everything they do, from the official (exemplified by the sangam rules according to which they self-police) to the unofficial, as in this creative use of a purely orally transmitted argot.

Asserting that artists have an enduring, relational sense of self may strike the reader as too obvious, a platitude of common sense. Yet the case for the perduring effects of social relations, and particularly relations of social stigma, on self-conception and community identity clearly still needs to be made, given influential theories about the "hidden transcripts" of subordinate peoples that argue quite the opposite. Specifically, in his book-length treatment of the subject, James Scott (1990) forcefully argues that subordinate peoples have a certain righteous rage that will be uppermost in their minds, and on their tongues, whenever they are free to communicate privately among themselves. While this may well be true in many situations and societies, and is certainly worth recognizing and even celebrating when it is, such sentiments are not part of the hidden transcript that Special Drama artists encode into their private tongue.

Scott's notion is that private languages (and perhaps even privacy itself?) are inherently liberatory phenomena; I return to Scott's theory in detail later in this chapter. Similar notions are quite common among scholars in the literature on argot. The author of a recent book on Gayle, a gay argot used by Afrikaans speakers in South Africa, for example, claims that "all marginalized groups have an anti-language because they are anti-society" (Cage 2003), as though all argot can be assumed to be both structurally and ideologically oppositional. The link between liberatory and oppositional consciousness here turns on a further assumption that hostile attitudes about others will somehow provoke positive attitudes about the self. The Indian linguist R. R. Mehrotra (1977) suggests precisely this in his consideration of the "general principles and patterns of argot in relation to the deviant behavior of certain criminal and fringe groups" (v): "The hostile and disparaging attitude of the underworld towards the dominant culture is clearly revealed in the argot terms which are used to denote members of the dominant culture. . . . [Such] pejorative expressions provide a sharp contrast to euphemistic terms which members of criminal subcultures use to describe their own group and its activities" (8). Overly generalized as these formulations may be, such ideas clearly have a certain political appeal, as they make the other not only deviant but also defiant, and their "substitute society" into an "anti-society" (8), surely an engrossing fantasy for those bored with their own.[1] The case of the Drama Tongue, however, refutes any such easy universal assumptions about the responses of the stigmatized, whether in relation to a dominant other or to themselves. Not in any sense purely oppositional, the Drama Tongue bespeaks a more complex relationship between language, the social experience of outsiderness, and the formation of identity in the speaking subject.

I am interested here in the specific nature of the linguistic shield that artists as a group wield in the face of a harsh public gaze. I suggest that the actual quality of the "inside" space for artists—the backstage space they call *ullē*, or inside, which is marked off from the stage by drop cloths of painted scene settings and walled around by thatch to separate it from the rest of the commons that stretch beyond the stage—is intimately tied to their own familiarity with their social position as outsiders, and that this dialectic contributes to the tenor of the language itself. The permeable wall of thatch is a good metaphor for the Drama Tongue: it divides inside from out, but it recognizes that this division is social fiction as much as social fact.

The argot itself is a permeable membrane. It is constructed of semitransparent code words that are nonetheless an effective divider between the drama subculture and its larger environs.

Language Matters

The Drama Tongue stems from standard Tamil, the official language of the state of Tamilnadu (the name itself means "Land of Tamil"). Standard Tamil is also the public language in which performances of Special Drama occur. As we have seen, standard Tamil is diglossic, meaning it has two forms, spoken and written, both of which are used (differentially according to the prestige of the role) by artists on the Special Drama stage. And while not all Special Drama artists share Tamil as their mother tongue, all performances are conducted in Tamil, and command of the language is one of the most highly praised skills of a performer.

The nation of India has only two official languages, Hindi and English. The Indian constitution, however, recognizes eighteen different official state languages, one of which is Tamil. It also recognizes 112 mother tongues (this number includes only languages spoken by at least ten thousand persons), as well as 544 dialects (statistics per Encarta online encyclopedia [Microsoft 2000]). Most Indian citizens who travel within the country in their line of work have linguistic capabilities that minimally involve comprehension, if not fluency, in more than one language. Even for a monolingual Tamil speaker, as are most Special Drama artists, life in India sensitizes one to the importance of being able to code switch between languages. Special Drama performers code switch into their Drama Tongue per required need. Simultaneously, the eclecticism of their community membership and their experiences performing for different audiences lead them to appreciate the value of a common language. Standard Tamil is that language, on which the Drama Tongue builds.

Situating the Drama Tongue as an Argot

The Drama Tongue is not a language per se but rather an argot. The term "argot" is generally used to refer to special vocabularies and idioms employed by any social group or class understood to have something to hide, from gay teenagers to gang members, from drug subcultures to secret religious cults (Farrell 1972; Murray 1993; Franklin 1975), and canonically including musicians, prostitutes, convicts, con men, counterfeiters, and carnies whose slang and lingo have by now been documented by scholars too numerous to name. The term "argot" originally referred to secret languages used by bands of criminals who roamed France from the thirteenth through the nineteenth centuries (Bullock 1996, 180). Such historical associations linking argot to disenfranchised subcultural groups are now part of its dictionary definition, as in the following entry from *Webster's*: "a special vocabulary and idiom used by a particular *underworld* group especially as a means of private communication" (italics mine). The notion that underworld groups are the primary users of such coded communiqués infuses the whole associative domain of argot, and the working assumption is that outsider groups have uncommon experiences that insider languages allow them to name.

> A group of researchers on drug subcultures hypothesizes that argots involve an innovative and different use of a distinct language. The meaning of common words is changed in order to provide a vehicle to identify the uncommon experience that characterizes this marginalized group. . . . Vulnerability is the

basic condition which gives rise both to secret societies and the argot. (Kaplan et al. 1990, 142–44)

That is, one way to stave off and combat excessive social vulnerability is to take the power of language, and particularly the power of naming, into one's own hands. Naming one's own experience is a way of claiming it and makes further action possible:

> By distinguishing and naming we prepare ourselves for action. . . . The activities of group members are no longer an undifferentiated stream of events; rather, they have been analyzed, classified, given labels; and these labels supply an evaluation and interpretation of experience. (Sykes 1958, 85–86; quoted in Farrell 1972, 98)

This feature of language making—its ability to evaluate and interpret experience by means of appellation—is particularly revealing when it is most reflexive. "The terms used by members of a community *to designate themselves* frequently reveal the community's salient values and concerns" (Case 1984, 282; italics mine).

But while many scholars of argot recognize that secret languages enable distinctions between the speakers' group and others, few have focused on the specific qualities of personhood—and "the uncommon experience" of being such persons—that characterize marginalized groups (Carole Case [1984] is something of an exception). For example, even in Bryan Reynolds's rich study (1999) of the highly developed cant argot of criminal culture in early modern England, discussion focuses on the official culture's fetishization and commodification of this subcultural world rather than on the experiential world of the subculture itself. In my consideration of Special Drama artists' argot, I attempt to address both the overall sense of outsiderness that propels the Drama Tongue's use and the specific experiences of outsiderness that are now coded into it.

In formal terms, linguists generally recognize two types of argot. The first is the lexical form. Here meaning is masked through the use of substitute words, either new coinages or words whose original meaning has been replaced. The second form, more often referred to by the term "javanais," masks meaning through play with syllables and sounds of words, for example, through affixation or displacements (such as in pig Latin; see Bullock 1996, 190). The Drama Tongue is a lexical form of the first type. It operates by substituting other words for standard Tamil words, while maintaining the syntactical and morphological structure of the dominant language.

These code words effectively hide from those who are unfamiliar with them the meaning of selected utterances. It uses this system of cryptography to create a lexicon of approximately one hundred encoded terms and expressions. Though often new coinages, these coded terms are still clearly Tamil and are employed in a grammar that is fully Tamil and maintains a distinctly Tamil phonology both of individual letter sounds and of sound combining. Many of the Drama Tongue's "new" words are made by creatively combining old, archaic Tamil and Sanskrit lexemes, or by employing lexemes currently in use in standard Tamil but not in precisely the same way or with the same meanings.

Such subcultural linguistic inventions are generally referred to in Tamil by the terms *maṟai moḻi* (hidden language) and *kuḻuukkuṟi* (secret language). The Special Drama community simply refers to their coded speech as *nāṭaka bāshai* (Drama Tongue), as do I.[2]

During the course of my research into the Drama Tongue, people often informed me that many professional groups in Tamilnadu other than drama artists employ similar types of secret languages. The groups most frequently mentioned were the banking and priest communities (and of the latter, Vaishnava in particular). Such professional service communities share with the drama community a need to carry out much of their business under the gaze of noncommunity members, as all these professions involve working with, in, and among the public, and members of these groups might well experience similar desires to communicate specific things among themselves that they would prefer the public not understand. However, I never encountered anyone who was actually familiar with any of these argots, or with any studies of them; the firmest reference I have found is a mention by A. K. Ramanujan of the historical use of hidden languages among religious sects: "In the heterodox and esoteric cults, systems of cryptography were intended to conceal the secret doctrine from the uninitiated and the outsider" (Ramanujan 1973, 49).[3]

Like the Special Drama community, circus and sideshow performers in the United States have their own "circus lingo," perhaps because both sets of artists are, to borrow a phrase, "spectacular subcultures" (Hebdige 1979). In neither case can members escape being viewed as "an attraction" by locals, whether or not they are onstage. Likewise in both subcultures, argot allows speakers to conduct a modicum of private business in public while simultaneously commenting on that public. In discussions of the U.S. "amusement world lexicon" (Bogden 1988, 80–83) or "carnival cant" (Maurer 1931), it is clear that like the Drama Tongue, one of the key uses of circus lingo is to provide its speakers with a hidden means of discussing spectators and spectatorial relations.

There is, however, a striking difference in the tenor of the terms by which speakers do so in each argot. As one documenter of the U.S. case put it, circus and sideshow lingo "is continually fed by the profound contempt which all show-people feel for the 'rubes'" (Maurer 1931, 328). In carnival cant, insiders use their hidden language to name the public as marked outsiders. The spectator is an incompetent: "towners" are "yokels," frequently referred to as "suckers," "marks," and "rubes" (ibid.). Such labeling of the spectator as incompetent outsider is diametrically opposed to the assumptions that spark the Drama Tongue. In the Drama Tongue, artists remain outside the domain of local power, which resides in the hands of "centermen," the insiders of the villages where the artists perform.

The Drama Tongue and circus lingo are thus argots that bespeak two very different strategies for dealing with the complexities of being simultaneously stigmatized and cast center stage. Circus lingo aims at centralizing those previously marginalized; the Drama Tongue, by contrast, keeps the relations of margin and center intact and uses private codes only to comment on their enduring reality. Such commentary fosters a shared perspective among a community as diverse as that of Special Drama artists, giving voice to the group qua group. It stops short, however, of making any moves toward repositioning the community itself in relation to the powers that be. Instead, it recognizes the power of social position to shape social experience.

Researching the Drama Tongue

A brief account of my methods in researching the Drama Tongue will clarify my ensuing presentation of its terms. My methodology was twofold. First, outside of any organic use-context, I initially asked questions of Special Drama artists about their argot. Through this means, I gained a certain familiarity with its terms, and only then was I able to recognize and record instances of its use in situ at drama events. These two research avenues fed into and reflected back on each other in interesting ways.

In the first instance, speaking with artists outside the language's use-context, I was aided by a list of words I encountered in the work of the local Tamil theater scholar M. S. Kodiswari. Her study of music drama artists of the Tanjore district of Tamilnadu during the mid-1980s, including their "hidden language," alerted me to the possibility of an argot in the Special Drama community (Kodiswari 1987, 115–19).

The two drama communities that Kodiswari and I studied differ significantly in their organizational practices. The Tanjore artists work in troupes that regularly perform together, whereas Special Drama artists are each hired as independent professionals. The dramatic repertories of the two communities overlap but there are more plays in the Special Drama repertory. In addition, the relatively insular Tanjore community attunes its performances to the tastes of this one particular regional audience, while Special Drama artists perform throughout the state to a wide variety of audiences. Finding Kodiswari's list thus raised two questions simultaneously: Do Special Drama artists similarly use an argot, and if so, is there overlap in the argots of the two communities? Special Drama artists quickly confirmed the former—seeming universally tickled that scholars should be interested in such things at all—and together we set about checking the latter.

With a photocopy of Kodiswari's list of terms from the Tanjore music drama community in hand, I sat down with Special Drama artists in Madurai to compare two Drama Tongues. Some words overlapped, but many differed. Our sessions quickly generated a new list of words and terms employed exclusively in the Madurai district. I brought these findings to Kodiswari and her research partner Mr. Selvanataraj, meeting with them several times in Madras. Afterward Kodiswari generously typed up a second, comparative Tamil list of Drama Tongue words that now included both her Tanjore music drama terms and the Madurai Special Drama terms I had collected. With this new, comparative list in hand, I continued work in Madurai.

This was work that felt more often like play. None of the artists had ever attempted to write their argot, nor had they ever seen it written, let alone typed. Determining the spelling of the words was a romp in and of itself, and this giddy quality carried over into the participant-observation phase of my research.[4] That phase began as soon as my interest in the Drama Tongue became known. Suddenly at dramas, artists would turn to me with confirming, conspiratorial smiles, making sure I had noted a particular instance of the language in use.

During my research in the Chettinadu village of Kottamangalam, drama agent P. L. Gandhi and his good friend the compounder (the village pharmacist) cosponsored a drama for the annual Ulakanayaki festival (see chapter 2). On the day of the performance, the three of us sat talking together on the compounder's porch, where I asked these two men, both longtime insiders to both the drama community and village life, about the Drama

Tongue. Talking about it delighted them. Both men had been around drama artists since boyhood. Now as well-heeled rurban men in their late forties, they took a boyishly prankish thrill in imagining how funny it would be if I were to say something coded later that night, like "kummāyam pūti" (the food is bad) when we went to a particular villager's house to eat, or if during the drama I were suddenly to stand up and, in hearing range of the actors onstage, say, "neḷivu pūti, kaṭṭumuṭṭā!" (the drama stinks, finish it off!).

I think that particularly in this aspect of my research, my own distance from the norms of Tamil behavior—marked by my American accent, my American gestures, the general boldness of my being female and an anthropologist, and so on—set off well the artists' own distance from behavioral norms as public performers and "disorderly" types. It shifted and recast in nonthreatening ways the notions of insider and outsider that are so central to actors' lives and self-perception, and it put us in cahoots.

Given this mix of research methodologies and experience, my familiarity with the Drama Tongue is oddly idiosyncratic. I began with wobbly text-artifacts of an otherwise purely oral argot and only later gained a more secure sense of its use in context. And most important, my understanding of the Drama Tongue is thoroughly informed by artists' glosses of the terms for my benefit. During our sit-down sessions with typed and handwritten lists of code words, artists would offer me standard Tamil equivalents for each Drama Tongue term. These standard Tamil glosses made the argot comprehensible to me, and I wrote them down alongside the newly inscribed argot terms, thus benefitting from two sets of terms generated by artists themselves in pursuing the analysis that follows.

Terms of the Drama Tongue

In the table that follows, I present eighty-seven Drama Tongue terms and phrases in use among the Madurai district Special Drama community in the early 1990s.[5] Drama Tongue terms appear in the first column, and the second column represents the standard Tamil glosses of these terms given to me by artists. The third column translates the standard Tamil of the second column into English. (For terms that I discuss in detail later, I will at that time also provide an additional fourth column that translates the lexical components of Drama Tongue terms into English, which provides a fuller and more associative sense of the kinds of creative combining that occurs in the Drama Tongue.)

Terms of the Drama Tongue, Madurai District

I. PEOPLE

Drama Tongue	*Artists' Gloss*	*English*
kāḷi	āṇ	man
macai	peṇ	woman
talaiyaṅkāḷi	amaippāḷar	agent
namarikkāḷi	ampaṭṭaṉ	barber
ūlaṅkāḷi	lochārmōniyakkārar	harmonist
kīttaṅkāḷi	piṉpāṭṭukkārar	background singer
muḷakkaṅkāḷi	mirutaṅkakkārar	mridangist
iṇaiya muḷakkam	lochālrauṇṭkārar	all-round drummer
kiṇukkamkāḷi	tāḷam pōṭupavar	talam player
koṇṭikāḷi	irājapārṭṭu	rajapart (hero)
koṇṭimacai	stripārṭṭu	stripart (heroine)
vīttiyakkāḷi	uba naṭikar	supporting actor
nāmakāḷi	kōmāḷi	buffoon
neḷivu macai	naṭaṉamātu	dancer
mūñcāṇ kāḷi	kāvalar	guard, cop
kaṭṭuvāṉkāḷi	purushaṉ	husband
kaṭṭuvāṉmacai	maṉaivi	wife
mattimacai	uḷḷūrpeṇ	local woman
mattikāḷi	uḷḷūrkārar	local man
pūtimacai	keṭṭappeṇ	bad woman
pūtikāḷi	keṭṭa āṇ	bad man
kīñcā macai	kuṟatti	gypsy woman
kīñcāṅkāḷi	kuṟavaṉ	gypsy man
pokka macai	paṟaitti	harijan woman
pokka karavāṉ	paṟaiyāṉ	harijan man
pūṉi macai	pārppaṉatti	brahmin woman
pūṉi karavāṉ	pārppaṉaṉ	brahmin man
kaluvamacai	kiḷavi	old woman
kaluvaṅkāḷi	kiḷavaṉ	old man
cittikāḷi	kuṭikkāraṉ	drunk
cuḷḷāṉ	kuḷantai	child
cullattāṉ	āṇ piḷḷai	boy
cullamacai	peṇ piḷḷai	girl
kuñcu kāḷi	makaṉ	son
kuñcu macai	makaḷ	daughter

II. OBJECTS AND ACTIONS

Drama Tongue	*Artists' Gloss*	*English*
neḷivu	nāṭakam	drama
kentā	uṭai (tuṇi)	clothes, costumes
naṭaiyan̲	seruppu	shoes
coṇappam	nakai	jewels
namari	muṭi	hair
kokkarai	kural	voice
kītam	pāṭṭu	song
potivān̲	pēccu	speech
vākaṭam	vacan̲am	dialogue
kiṇukkam	tāḷam	rhythm
nelippu	naṭippu	acting
kummāyam	cāppāṭu	meal
mun̲r̲am	āṭṭukkar̲i	mutton
pañcana	ṭī	tea
māli	kaḷḷu	toddy (liquor)
citti	cārāyam	arrack (liquor)
kaṇṇappan̲	maḷai	rain
kīttam	muḷakkam	thunder
cakaṭai	vēn̲	van
matti	vīṭu	house
kaṇkoḷ	pār	to see/look
nāvāṭu	pēcu	to speak

III. QUALITATIVE EVALUATION

Drama Tongue	*Artists' Gloss*	*English*
ettu	uyarvu	high, exalted
pūti	tāḻvu; keṭṭa	low, base; bad
vīkkiram	nalla	good

IV. FINANCES

Drama Tongue	*Artists' Gloss*	*English*
nātam	paṇam	money
oruvāṭi nātam	oru rūpāy	1 rupee
patiyam	pattu rūpāy	10 rupees
koṇṭippili nātam	nūṟu rūpāy	100 rupees
periya koṇṭippili nātam	āyiram rūpāy	1,000 rupees
iṇaiya nātam	iraṇṭu rūpāy	2 rupees
iṇaiya patiyam	irupatu rūpāy	20 rupees
iṇaiya koṇṭippili nātam	irunūṟu rūpāy	200 rupees
cūlanātam	mūṉṟu rūpāy	3 rupees
cūlappatiyam	mūpatu rūpāy	30 rupees
cūla koṇṭippili nātam	mūnūṟu rūpāy	300 rupees
cavukka nātam	nāṉku rūpāy	4 rupees
nilak nātam	aintu rūpāy	5 rupees
aṟuvāṭ nātam	aṟu rūpāy	6 rupees
kaṉṉi nātam	ēḷu rūpāy	7 rupees
cittu nātam	eṭṭu rūpāy	8 rupees
nava nātam	oṉpatu rūpāy	9 rupees
patiaivāṭi	patiaintu rūpāy	15 rupees

V. PHRASES

Drama Tongue	*Artists' Gloss*	*English*
mattikāḷi kaṇkoḷḷatu	uḷḷūrkārarkaḷ pārkkiṟarkaḷ	the locals are watching
nāvāṭātē	pēcāmal iru	don't speak/ shut up
mattikāḷi ellām ceṅkiṭṭatu	pārvaiyāḷar kuḷumiṭṭaṉar	the audience is gathered
nātam ceṅkiṭṭu vā	paṇam vāṅkiṭṭu vā	get the money and come
neḷivu pūti	nāṭakam nalla illai	the drama is not good

V. PHRASES (*cont.*)

Drama Tongue	*Artists' Gloss*	*English*
kiṇukkam ettā pōṭu	tāḷam cariyā pōṭu	play the rhythm well
kaṇ koṉṟār	tūṅkukiṟār	he's sleeping
oḷukkal ākka pōkiṟēṉ	ciṟu nīr kaḷikka pōkiṟēṉ	I have to piss
saḷḷi vatiya pōkiṟēṉ	malam kaḷikka pōkiṟēṉ	I have to shit
kaṇṇappaṉ tōṭikkumā?	maḷai varumā?	will it rain?
mattikku cāṉṟēṉ	vīṭṭukku(p) pōkiṟēṉ	I'm going home
kaṭṭumūṭṭai	mūṭṭaikaṭṭu	quit/stop/discontinue

The four topical sections of (1) people, (2) objects and actions, (3) qualitative evaluation, and (4) finances each represent a classic domain of exchange transaction wherein the ability to communicate in a way unintelligible to outsiders would clearly be useful. If, for instance, a question arises concerning finances—such as whether a drama sponsor has paid each artist as promised—the Drama Tongue allows artists to discuss this question as a group before communicating any complaint to the locals.

The fifth section, listing idiomatic phrases within the Drama Tongue, gives us a sense of those phrases artists use often. For example, because artists may travel to a performance venue independently (when they have means of doing so), there is a risk that not everyone will arrive on time. So artists have a coded means for communicating that "the drummer [or anyone else in the cast] has not arrived": "iṇaiya muḷakkam varillai." In such a situation, the other artists might discuss their options for how to proceed by using the Drama Tongue to keep their ideas to themselves for the time being, without the sponsor yet realizing the problem.

All the encoded terms in the Drama Tongue may similarly be understood as words frequently required by the work context of Special Drama artists. As an explanatory example of the formal construction of the Drama Tongue and of the layered and resonant meanings it makes possible, I will first discuss a relatively simple term from the table, then move on to discuss the more complex phrase "mattikāḷi kaṇkoḷḷatu, nāvāṭātē!" as promised.

Let us take first, then, "nātam," the first word listed under the heading "Finances." This word is used frequently in the Drama Tongue. Artists glossed it as "paṇam," the standard Tamil word meaning "money." However, the lexical item "nātam" already exists as a standard Tamil word in its own right. The entry under "nātam" in the *Dictionary of Contemporary Tamil* reads "(musical) sound (of instruments, temple bells, etc.)" (Cre-A 1992, 617). In the Drama Tongue, then, "nātam" is money and also a familiar Tamil word meaning the sound of bells.[6] To derive a sense of these lexical borrowings, I consulted three standard dictionary sources, relying primarily on Cre-A's *Dictionary of Contemporary Tamil*. Including such information, the extended entry for this term is as follows:

Drama Tongue	*Artists' Gloss*	*English*	*Lexical Components*
nātam	paṇam	money	musical sound, as of bells

This first simple example becomes a bit more complicated (and interesting) as we move farther down the table. Continuing under the heading "Finances" to the eighth term, we find "iṇaiya nātam," a term that artists glossed for me as "iraṇṭu rūpāy," or "two rupees." Once again, however, as a lexical item in its own right, the expression "iṇaiya nātam" has a more evocative meaning in contemporary standard Tamil than this functional gloss. The term "iṇaiya nātam" couples the infinitive of the standard Tamil intransitive verb "iṇai," meaning "join together, get united; be linked; join; mingle" (Cre-A 1992, 96) with "nātam." The resulting term evokes the sound-image of a sound pair, something like "linked bells" or maybe "joined jangles." A full charting of the resonances inherent in the Drama Tongue would look like this:

Drama Tongue	*Artists' Gloss*	*English*	*Lexical Components*
iṇaiya nātam	iraṇṭu rūpāy	2 rupees	"joined jangles"

As this example from the financial domain demonstrates, Drama Tongue meanings are both referential and evocative. The "substitute" words that make up the Drama Tongue are not nonsense words but rather active standard Tamil terms whose meanings have been, rather playfully, *extended*. Language proves one of several arenas in which artists similarly extend paradigms of standard use to suit their needs, thereby creating a cover for their own rather nonstandard practices. (Two other such arenas, travel and family, are the subjects of chapters 8 and 9.)

People of the Drama Tongue

All words for persons in the Drama Tongue place people in given social roles at a drama event. So in the table's first section, "People," note that code words exist for the following categories of persons: locals, husbands and wives, sons and daughters, old men and women, children, policemen, agents, organizers, members of specific castes (high and low), and each of the repertory roles for Special Drama actors and musicians. It is the first of these categories of persons—locals—that orients the remainder of this discussion.

As noted, the code phrase "mattikkāḷi kāṇkoḷḷutu" uttered in the Drama Tongue often inaugurates use of the Drama Tongue itself. The referential gloss that artists gave of this phrase is "ūrkkārarkaḷ pārkkiṟarkaḷ" (the locals are watching). The Drama Tongue word "mattikkali" (local) was glossed as the standard Tamil word "uḷḷūrkkaran," the standard English translation of which is "a local (man)."

The concepts embedded in the standard Tamil word are themselves relevant to my argument. The adjective "uḷḷūr" (local) is a composite of two words, "uḷḷē" (inside) and "ūr" (village, town, or city; hometown). A local man, a man from inside the ūr—or an inside(ū)r, if you will—is referred to as "uḷḷūrkkārar" in standard Tamil (uḷḷūr + "kārar" [masculine person/s]). A local woman, or female inside(ū)r, is similarly an "uḷḷūrppeṇ" (uḷḷūr + "peṇ" [woman]).

These standard Tamil words for locals—inside-ūr men and women, uḷḷūrkkārar and uḷḷūrppeṇ—are tellingly replaced in the Drama Tongue by the words "mattikkāḷi" and "mattimacai." In the Drama Tongue, "matti" designates "house." In standard Tamil, "matti" means "center," used adjectivally to indicate "of the center," as in India's central government (*mattiya aracu*) (Cre-A 1992, 805). Mattikkāḷi brings center-house men and women together in a generic plural for "locals," uḷḷūrkārarkaḷ. As the landed class in these relations, mattikkāḷi have power on their side.

"Kāḷi," the word used in the Drama Tongue to refer to "man" as well as the generic plural "men," is again a standard Tamil term. "Kāḷi" names the powerful Hindu deity Kali, and by extension any female deity of dark complexion. "Mattikkāḷi" are men of the house whose power is that of centrality broadly, and of a fierce deity more specifically.[7] Locals here are solidly, even fiercely, central people in their roles as householders, a central social position in Hindu conceptions of the adult life-stage.[8]

When such centermen—the householders, the locals—step out of their houses to attend a drama, they are fascinated by the drama people, quintessential outsiders who have come to their ūr. The "insiders" stand and stare, right into the performers' very inside space. Carved out of an area of the village commons behind the stage, this temporary inside space for artists is just that: temporary. And even inside this inside space, the locals are everywhere, surrounding the artists. It is in this context that drama people say to each other, "mattikkāḷi kāṇkoḷḷutu!" as villagers pry apart with their fingers the braided palm-frond thatch walls so permeable to local eyes and ears.

In its entirety, the phrase "mattikkāḷi kāṇkoḷḷutu"—"the centermen are holding eyes"—signals artists' awareness of the locals' eyes on them. Let us turn to the latter part of the phrase. "Kāṇkoḷḷutu" is a composite idiom made of a noun and a verb from standard Tamil, though as an idiom it does not exist in standard Tamil. "Kāṇ" means eye. "Koḷ" (to take hold) is frequently used as an auxiliary verb that contributes an additional dimension of definitiveness to an action (Paramasivam and Lindholm 1980b, 313). The addition of "koḷ" to "kāṇ" here creates a noun-verb idiom for "fixing eyes"; a similar idiom that does exist in standard Tamil is "kaikoḷ" (hand + koḷ), meaning "to take charge." In "kāṇkoḷḷutu," the locals are fixing and holding their eyes on the performers, a creative way to describe what we call staring.

Generally in Hindu India eyes are regarded as both beautiful and powerful. They can be powerfully beneficent or malevolent in context-dependent ways. The concept of beneficent power located in the eyes centrally informs Hindu devotional practice, in which "darṣan"—an "exchange of vision"—is a highly sought-after relation of mutuality between the devotee and the divine through visual contact (Eck 1981). The malevolent power of the eyes—"evil eye" (kāṇ tirishti)—by contrast, is a pervasive evil that must be ritually guarded against. Anyone who stares at you may afflict you with the evil eye. Thus the sense of danger and power attending the phrase "mattikkāḷi kāṇkoḷḷutu" is far from negligible, in its characterization of locals as "center-fierce-goddess-men" and of their actions as fixing their eyes on artists.

Artists stressed that utterance of "mattikkāḷi kāṇkoḷḷutu" implies a consequent utterance, of a term that logically followed it in meaning whether voiced aloud or not (the term is listed second under "Phrases" in the table of Drama Tongue terms, on p. 290). This consequent term is "nāvāṭātē," an imperative command that artists glossed as "pēcāma(ı) iru!" in standard Tamil. Literally, it means "be without speaking," and colloquially, "shut up!" With the addition of this second phrase, the message becomes an injunction to artists to guard themselves against the centermen's eyes by taming their own tongues.

"Mattikkāḷi kāṇkoḷḷutu," then, appears to function as a kind of prompt or trigger phrase that inaugurates a series of speech acts. The first of these is the switch to the Drama Tongue itself. The need for the switch is justified in the content of the phrase "the locals are watching" itself—or, better yet, "the center-house-men-fierce-female-goddess-deities are holding eyes"—a situation to which the only appropriate response is that enacted within the utterance, a switch to the Drama Tongue.

In this sense, the utterance "mattikkāḷi kāṇkoḷḷutu, nāvāṭātē!" is simultaneously an injunction to shut up and a performative, enacting the very shift it advocates. That is, utterance of this phrase communicates a wish/need to do precisely what it simultaneously does: the need/desire to switch to the Drama Tongue is communicated by switching to the Drama Tongue. (This is a classic instantiation of a linguistic performative, wherein the utterance itself simultaneously does what it says.) Every utterance of the phrase "mattikkāḷi kāṇkoḷḷutu" in the Drama Tongue rehearses the originary, situational need and desire to inaugurate use of this very language.

The second term, "nāvāṭātē," is again etymologically evocative. "Nāvāṭātē!" breaks down into comprehensible standard Tamil roots (nā + v + āṭātē), though again the word does not exist in this particular compound configuration in standard Tamil. This is another case of hiding within the norm by extending familiar paradigms in familiar ways, though the resultant configuration is not exactly normative. "Nā" means "tongue," the more common word for which in standard Tamil is "nākku," obviously from the same root. The word "nākku" is not generally used metonymically to refer to language but rather refers literally to the organ "tongue." In the coined term "nāvāṭātē!" ("do not wag your tongue!"), the tongue is restrained by being retrained. The composite turns on the verb root "āṭu" (shake or wag), which as an emphatic negative imperative becomes "āṭātē" (āṭ[u] + ātē = don't wag), doubtlessly best glossed in English as "hold your tongue!" When centermen are holding eyes, strategic use of the Drama Tongue, with its particular holding of the tongue, is itself the best response.

The fleshed-out table for these phrases looks like this:

Drama Tongue	*Artists' Gloss*	*English*	*Lexical Components*
mattikāḷi kaṇkoḷḷatu	uḷḷūrkārarkaḷ pārkkiṟarkaḷ	locals are watching	centermen are holding eyes
nāvāṭātē!	pēcāmal iru!	don't speak/ shut up!	don't wag your tongue!

In researching etymologies and usages for "nā" and "nāvu" (tongue), I came across a term of which I had previously been unaware. Stemming from the root "nāvu," "nāvūṟu" is "harm resulting from evil tongue" (nāvu + uṟu) (University of Madras 1982, 2231). In some sense, the existence of such a term is surprising only because it seems tautological: in India the tongue is already considered an evil and harmful organ. To the same extent that eyes are beautiful and powerful, tongues are evil and dirty. Saliva, generally considered a filthy bodily substance that renders the mouth a sewer, is carried by the tongue. Kissing on the lips is censored in Tamil films not because it is too sexy but because it is too disgusting. The baring of tongues belongs to the fierce dances of evil demons and angry gods and goddesses. To stick out one's tongue at another person is a fighting gesture in Tamilnadu. Outstretched tongues often reap bloody consequences, as when those who are ritually possessed bare their tongues in prelude to drinking the blood of sacrificial animals.

There seems, then, to be a sort of sparring relationship encoded into this argot, at least on the more associative lexical levels, between the eyes of locals and the tongues of actors, like a face-off of totemic powers. Artists' internalization of stigma would explain their having adopted the nastier of the two symbols as their own in this new language. Its terms cast artists under the linguistic sign of an unappealing totem, while the phrase as a whole frames artists as unruly outsiders in need of restraint in the face of more powerful insiders.

Clearly, a relational sense of self perdures here for Special Drama artists, who remain outsiders in their own insider language. Such a case raises important questions about the assumptions made in much theoretical work on verbal expression among subordinate groups.

What Do We Expect of a Secret Language?

We continue to do anthropology precisely because all contexts are *not* the same. Not all uses of humor are the same. Not all feminisms are the same.

And not all kinds of social resistance are the same. The Drama Tongue, along with other practices of artists in the Special Drama community, keeps us aware of differences we might otherwise miss.

James Scott (1985), an important chronicler of the many diverse tactics and strategies used by subordinate groups worldwide to contest domains in which they lack social and political power, has also written specifically about the kind of speech such peoples use among themselves, which he calls "hidden transcripts" (Scott 1990). Though for the present case I find his conception of their nature insufficient in the ways I discuss hereafter, hidden transcripts clearly do exist, and Scott's concept is a valuable one.

Scott (1990) defines his notion of a "hidden transcript" among subordinate peoples as "discourse that takes place 'offstage,' beyond direct observation by powerholders" (4). Because he conceives of such private, offstage opportunities as one of the few places where subordinate peoples are free of the dictates of the power holders—by which he means, in particular, free of being "on record" in a "public transcript" that may be (and generally is) monitored by those in power—Scott expects such offstage moments to invariably express the pent-up rage of subordinate peoples (a surprisingly unmediated and "natural" emotion in his theory, as noted by Sue Gal [1995]). Scott further expects such hidden discourses to be aimed at the subversion of preexisting relations of power, again, a surprisingly non–culturally specific definition for such a context-sensitive issue.

In her thoughtfully critical review of Scott's work, Gal writes: "No doubt Scott would more easily detect the complexities of resistance and the partial or contradictory forms of hegemony if his understanding of language included more attention to linguistic form and the way that its political function is conditioned by language ideology" (1995, 420–21). Indeed, close consideration of the linguistic form and the political function of the Drama Tongue complicates the picture that Scott paints of hidden transcripts.

First, it raises questions about the finality with which he distinguishes offstage from onstage as realms of discourse. The Drama Tongue suggests instead that semipublic spaces such as the artists' permeable backstage provide an important alternative model with which to think about such realms. Second, I question Scott's notion that what subordinate peoples invariably want to express in their "offstage," or more aptly in their private, moments amounts to a pent-up rage of righteous resistance. I will consider these questions, and the insights provided by the variation between the Drama Tongue and Scott's theory, in turn.

For Special Drama artists, offstage is never in any firm sense truly "off."

Rather than dismissing the Special Drama case as anomalous, I question the model itself (isn't this what science should do?). Is there ever, in any firm sense, a truly "off" for anyone in life? Without necessarily going the full extent of Goffman's theatrical metaphor and viewing all of life as a strategic presentation of self, one must nevertheless concede that our experiences in public dialogically affect our sense of self in private. This dialogic point is simply borne out in an architecturally vivid fashion in the case of the Special Drama community. The Drama Tongue is a language designed to be used in a quite literal "offstage." Yet as we have seen, the offstage at any Special Drama event, whether backstage or at a villager's table, includes the whole village in which performers appear as outsiders. So while use of the Drama Tongue grants a degree of privacy to artists, they nevertheless remain under the watchful eyes of the insider locals even while they are offstage, remaining within Scott's "direct observation by powerholders."

This scenario complicates Scott's expectations and points out a central weakness in his conception, since both private and public communications can and often do coexist in settings that are far more nuanced than notions of either a strictly "public" or a strictly "private" transcript allow. Some of the extended etymological uses in the Drama Tongue, for instance, may well be half understood by village listeners (or at least be suggestive of meanings), in which case much of the power the argot offers its users is that of a *performance* of privacy. A performance of privacy is effective more as a metacommunication than anything. In this light, the question of whether any hidden place, hidden communication, or hidden self, for that matter, exists wholly uninformed by and out of communication with its "public" counterpart becomes moot. Rather, all such relational terms necessarily develop in and through social interaction informed by the very mutual dependency of realms distinguished as onstage or offstage.

Regarding the larger context of language ideology, Gal reminds us that in societies where language is standardized, nonstandard variants are often considered inferior and degenerate by all concerned, including the speakers themselves. This is certainly the case in the Special Drama community. The extent to which my scholarly attention to this oral argot evinced laughter from artists begins to get at the extent of its willful hiddenness and its low status as a purely oral language in a society where entextualization "classicizes" folk forms and increases their prestige (Hansen 1992, 44–45). That is, the laughter suggests that my scholarly interest prompted something like the frisson of exposure, of the tongue and of the artists who speak it, as well as a thrill at the potential realignment effected by the incongruous joining of "high" scholarship and "low" argot that threatens to lower the one and raise the other (see note 4).

The script in which Special Drama artists engage is thus quite different from either the public transcript or the hidden transcript that Scott sees as dividing our discursive worlds. Scott's public transcript is basically false behavior—behavior for show, for the record, "staged behavior" in the negative senses that so often attach to actors—for all involved. He argues against the idea that subordinate peoples internalize or incorporate dominant ideology, instead asserting that what *appears* to be consent is really only a clean act put on to escape censure. In such a scenario, public arenas are stripped of anybody's real feelings. Instead, both dominant and subordinate peoples must create hidden transcripts in which to house their true feelings and then find private arenas in which to use them. An argot, from Scott's perspective, allows people to communicate their true feelings while "covering their tracks" with new coinages.

What we find in the Drama Tongue instead is that artists' "true feelings" (if there be such things) are largely of a piece with their stigmatized role in any social situation. What is "true" is that drama artists carry with them, and constantly negotiate, a sense of self forged through ongoing social interactions. If anything, their social identity varies only in degree, not in kind, and is rendered particularly visible to us here through an analysis of the layers of intertextual and associative meanings expressed in the lexical items of their argot.

Further, since utterance of the highly laden code word for "locals" generally inaugurates a switch into artists' use of the argot, every such switch rehearses a recognition of their stigmatized status as outsiders even as it allows them an insider experience. So even if in use the Drama Tongue offers something of a reversal of the normative experience of outsiderness for its speakers—a relatively free space of insiderness in which artists can express things "off the record"—nevertheless the language formally acknowledges that such a temporary inversion of experience in no way alters the dominant terms of artists' daily experience of social exclusion. "The centermen are holding eyes, don't wag your tongue!" is an ironic injunction to speak. Its utterance ensures that offstage life is never idealized as a realm free from discursive restraint but, if anything, is transformed into a space more linguistically rich because of it.

Centered in Mobility, or, An Insider Language That Isn't

I hope this analysis of the Drama Tongue complicates theoretical assumptions about any inherent or given nature regarding private versus public speech acts. I also hope that it counters any theory of human interiority that does not recognize the extent to which self-conception is forged through linguistic interaction, in specific sociocultural arenas. Having established the extent to which Special Drama artists' insider tongue maintains their position as social outsiders in relation to a local public that surrounds them, I see the Drama Tongue as an insider language that isn't. Special Drama artists rely on persons (for employment) who rely on them (as entertainers) to continue to be outsiders *who are aware of themselves as such*. Artists cannot afford to ignore their stigmatizing social characteristics—their public, excessive hypermobility and their reputation for lacking order—but instead must keep their otherness in play if they want to remain theater artists. Theirs is a community centered in mobility. Their hidden language is a crafty linguistic mirror that winks back at the society that creates them. The Drama Tongue is a way of getting by, getting through, and getting away with some things, but it is not a way out of outsiderness.

Special Drama artists meet the evil eye with a drama tongue, retaining an understanding of their own positionality by restraining, and retraining, their linguistic practice.

8 The Roadwork of Actresses

In her preface to *Imaginary Maps*, Gayatri Spivak (1995) uses the metaphor of an intractable obstacle, a roadblock blocking women's movements worldwide, to convey what she calls a difficult truth: that "internalized gendering perceived as ethical choice is the hardest roadblock for women the world over" (xxviii). Spivak speaks of instances where the internalization of gender norms and constraints has blocked the movement of individual women down particular paths, as well as blocked the progress toward social change of collective women's movements globally.

Partha Chatterjee (1993) offers a social history of India in which women's internalization of gender norms has had a strikingly opposite effect. Chatterjee stresses the important role that Indian women's internalization of a properly gendered self-image played in building the new Indian nation, arguing that beginning in the late nineteenth century and the early twentieth, the middle-class Indian woman's ability to internalize gender constraints *eased* rather than blocked her travels out into the world. Specifically, Chatterjee suggests that it is through the internalization of a self-image of *virtuous domesticity* that middle-class Indian women have been able to maintain respectability while venturing out into the public sphere: these good women are able to carry their home identities out into the world with them.

The strategy that Chatterjee documents is an intriguing means of circumventing the censure on movement in public that confronts so many women. This ingenious strategy resolved "the women's question" for many nationalists: the middle-class Indian woman had simply to become so identified with the ideal spiritual and moral sphere of the home that these ideals remained intact wherever she went—she carried them with her, inside her.

> Once the essential femininity of women was fixed in terms of certain culturally visible spiritual qualities, they could go to schools, travel in public conveyances, watch public entertainment programs, and in time even take up employment outside the home. . . . This spirituality did not, as we have seen, impede the chances of the woman moving out of the physical confines of the home; on the contrary, it facilitated it, making it possible for her to go into the world under conditions that would not threaten her femininity. In fact, the image of

woman as goddess or mother served to erase her sexuality in the world outside the home. (Chatterjee 1993, 130–31)

Moving in public, the respectable woman is able to carry with her an inner strength forged indoors.

The case, however, is quite different for those worldly women against whom Indian nationalism's ideal middle-class and educated women were explicitly defined. These are the women whom Chatterjee identifies as "sex objects" for the "nationalist male" precisely because they are seen as "other" than his mother/sister/wife/daughter. They are neither of his kin nor of his class. Such women do not erase sexuality, as do middle-class women, they embody it: their very bodies "become the sanction for behavior not permitted" to women defined as properly feminine (Chatterjee 1993, 131).

In Tamilnadu today, whereas middle-class women are able to prise the domesticity of home from its physical confines and overlay this sensibility onto a more flexible psychic domain, Special Drama actresses who hail from the urban poor never had such a proper middle-class home in the first place. For actresses, the task of attaining the qualities of the good woman—still defined by the virtues of domesticity—requires that they constantly, vigilantly strive in their daily practice for the very physical confines that the new middle-class woman has left behind. Many actresses attempt to better their reputation as women by acting on the dominant script quite literally throughout their public journeys, seeking to re-create domesticity in its material form.

Offstage with Actresses

My focus in this chapter is on the problematic mobility of women who do *not* properly internalize gender constraints. Stage actresses are women stigmatized precisely for being too public, and for moving out into the world beyond the bounds of proper, modest feminine behavior. They have long been the paradigm of illegitimately public female bodies.[1] Not having properly internalized the gender constraints that should have blocked their road, that should have kept them indoors (or at least working in and for the maintenance of the domestic sphere), they are the very definition of the "bad" public woman. Unlike the chaste loyalty of the good wife who reveals herself to only one man, an actress's profession requires that she willingly expose herself to the gaze of many unfamiliar men, brazenly stepping out into the limelight.

Thus I write here about women and roads. More specifically, I write about my own experience of traveling certain roads and encountering certain roadblocks with certain women. I attempt to get as near as I am able to a phenomenological rendering of my travels with Special Drama actresses in the hopes that, among other things, examining my experience of being with these women will allow me some insight into their experience of being, in their own society, "other."[2]

Although the onstage styles of actresses vary widely (as do, therefore, their relations to the codified rules of the sangam), in private even actresses who are quite brazen onstage, such as Sennai Sivakami, seek to avoid unwanted attention. Likewise, those who diligently pursue the good name still live with the bad reputation of the stage actress. We have seen the spunk with which these women act onstage and the cognizance they show of their own social situations. Offstage too, actresses attempt to minimize the stigma attaching to them personally as they traverse the public sphere. The primary pragmatic challenge is how to accomplish their public artistic business with as little tainting publicness as possible.

Accordingly, roads themselves become arenas of complex negotiation. As we have seen, roads and streets are a common mise-en-scène for the highly gendered enactments represented on the Special Drama stage. The women portrayed in Special Drama comedy scenes—whether sixteen-year-old girls dancing in the streets or shrewlike wives gossiping with nosy neighbors—are invariably marked by their very publicness as having set foot *on a bad road*. Such portrayals perpetuate an already dominant association between public roads and the bad reputation of actresses as public women and shape the offstage lives of both male and female Special Drama artists.

However, while they work out of towns and cities—bringing urban ways to rural venues and thereby extending the rurban character of the interactions defining the contemporary Special Drama network—men and women have very different relations to the publicness of their profession. For example, for the most part, Special Drama actresses opt not to perform in venues that fall within a certain radius of their home—usually within ten kilometers or so—choosing to consciously separate their professional personae from their domestic lives through overtly geographic boundaries. (Sennai Sivakami's willingness to perform in the center of Madurai town on the night when Jansirani and I sat in the audience watching was a telling exception.)[3] Male artists have no such concerns and will perform anywhere. For actresses, such a restricted practice follows the overall logic of the strategy I will refer to here as their "roadwork." Actresses' choices not to perform locally, as well as their attempts to minimize a tainting publicness when they travel beyond their home locales, are means by which actresses attempt to maintain normative codes of decorum for Tamil women.

When they do go out to work in public, Special Drama actresses have ingenious means of minimizing the effects of that publicness on their local, and more personal, lives. To capture something of the quality of the simultaneously literal and metaphoric road that actresses negotiate, I offer here five fieldwork narratives. Each narrative centers on specific experiences I had on the road with actresses throughout Tamilnadu and recounts experiences that helped me understand how women who labor under the stigmatizing sign of "public women" find self-respect in their offstage lives.

In these five instances, I witnessed actresses creating private, exclusive spaces in the midst of the Tamil public sphere. Each narrative speaks of one leg in the journey to or from a Special Drama, and together they make up a voyage that begins (1) in a calendar shop in Madurai, then proceeds (2) by van or (3) by bus to (4) the backstage spaces of a performance venue, and finally (5) returns home, on foot, to Madurai. The resulting impressionistic map, drawn from my experiences traveling with specific women on specific roads, details some of the offstage spaces frequently traversed and sometimes rather ambivalently inhabited by Special Drama actresses.

My aim is to map lived, experienced spaces, not to render an objective account of things seen at a distance.[4] Each of these lived spaces is charged and remembered here with images of particular women and men of the Special Drama world and lit by the flair with which they interacted with me, as well as by their own deft pursuit of image-making practices.[5]

Interspersed with the narratives are broader analytic discussions of context and of the theoretical implications of actresses' roadwork on our understanding of the diverse range of forms feminist action takes. I present the actresses' roadwork as a set of lived, adaptive practices that operate in relation to extant gender norms defining "the good woman" (*nalla peṇ*) as categorically excluding actresses from its purview. When actresses manage to make their behavior indistinguishable from that of good women—in other words, when they appear to comply with dominant norms—they effectively stretch those norms, even alter them somewhat in the process. In expanding the category of good woman to include themselves, a note of defiant resistance joins the apparent compliance of actresses' strategies on the road, raising important questions regarding the differing benefits of such strategies for actresses and for observant analysts.

Narrative One: Regarding the Gender Dimensions of Booking a Drama

The arrangements of bookings and dates for Special Drama are negotiations that concern an artist's public appearance, a side of the business from which actresses generally distance themselves. Rather than "talking dramas" herself or making the bookings for her own public appearances directly, an actress hangs her calendar in booking shops. In 1993 there were five such shops in Madurai. Four were print shops (the same that print drama notices; see chapter 2) for whom booking artists' calendars was a side business. It was the main business in the fifth. All were very male public spaces, for although the calendars of both male and female artists hang in these shops, only men are present physically, in the flesh, that is, sitting around talking, checking on the dates of their next performances, or drumming up business for new bookings. Likewise, male representatives from a village or town interested in booking a drama come to the city to peruse these posted calendars and to check on the availability of specific drama artists, meeting at these shops to converse with those in the know about the current crop of artists. Together drama agents, drama sponsors, and drama actors regularly hang out in and around the booking shops in Madurai, all of which were located within that small two-block radius in the center of town, the little business district where actors are kings of the road but through which actresses only briskly pass on their way to and from performance venues (figs. 43, 44).

Inside the shops, the walls are lined with individual artists' calendars (fig. 45 and plate 8). Most have a separate thin page for each day of the year. The pages make a square packet of leaves which is nailed onto a cardboard backing. On this backing the name of the artist is pasted like a heading, beneath or beside which a bust photo provides further identification and allure. Often the artist's name and face share visual billing with full-color reproductions of Hindu deities (generally Ganesh or Murugan or Lakshmi), occasionally with the renowned Catholic image of the Sacred Heart, or else perhaps with a laudable regional or national cultural hero (Tiru Vallavar, Swami Vivekananda), all figures that regularly grace popular mass-produced and mass-distributed Indian calendars.[6] Then, taking an inked print of their drama notice photo block, artists collage together their own image (cut out

43 Male artists on the street in front of the Tamilnadu Drama Actors Sangam, Madurai, 1993.
44 Male artists outside a print shop in Madurai, 1993.

45 Artists' calendars hanging at Balakrishna Press in Madurai, 1998. Drama agents and artists stand by the booking table.

and pasted on with glutinous rice) and name (sometimes in fancy bold print, sometimes penned by hand) onto the backing with these more celebrated icons.

But such traditionally religious and cultural imagery is not the only fare used. Calendars that advertise consumer goods and modern fashions also figure, with results that reach almost surreal hypersymbolism, as in the pastiche pictured in figure 46 (a detail from the wall pictured in fig. 45). Here Dancer G. Lalitha has pasted her image in the center of a map of the subcontinent on a calendar for the "Viking" brand of "vests, briefs, and panties." A rather naively inked drawing of the same appears tucked into the lower right-hand corner of the board, just beside the square skirt of days: layered images above, layered days below. In a quirkily fortuitous placement, abutting Lalitha's calendar is another strikingly modern calendar, that of Dancer S. Kalaiselvi (fig. 47). Here a nattily dressed male figure with cane and bowler hat leans out over, and partially occludes, the Viking vest and brief set, while his counterpart in Western feminine garb sports a skirt that perhaps most neatly captures the visual resonances here that alternate between the cloaking and the baring of selves, all in the guise of booking time. Indeed, each artist's calendar appears as a book of days opening out under

46 Dancer G. Lalitha's calendar for the 1998 drama season.

47 Dancer S. Kaliselvi's calendar for the 1998 drama season.

her personalized headboard like a skirt, to be lifted and looked through at the buyer's whim.

Men interested in hiring an actress do not approach her directly but rather approach her calendar. An actress's calendar is in this way a material stand-in for her. It provides sponsors with a way to contract her without direct interaction, and simultaneously allows the actress to absent herself from the negotiations. Similar to the process by which good Indian girls become brides, here men engage in negotiations in which a woman's person is implicated, but not dialogically involved.[7] While he books an actress, she stays at home; an effigy of her (her personalized calendar) circulates in her stead.

Any man approaching an actress's calendar to book a drama may pick her effigy off the wall, handle it, peruse it, flip through its skirt, and read therein the unfolding story of the actress's public life: where she will be when in the coming days, where she has been in the recent past, how busy this season looks, how in demand (or not) she is this season. Penned on the backside of her calendar is the actress's performance fee, which is a private note from her, hidden from public view. If he selects her, he pens his name and his place name directly on the front of her calendar. Without her ever having to meet with him, he has arranged for her to come to his place, when he chooses, for a fee.

The shop owner, who functions as a booking agent, has a certain financial stake in these negotiations, as he earns a fee (three rupees was the going rate in 1993) every time an artist whose calendar he posts is booked for a drama. Being financially implicated in this way, the shop owner wants the calendars of popular artists in his shop. He needs to know whether a particular artist will actually attract sponsors' bookings; he needs to know each artist's value and reputation. I asked the owner of the shop whose business was exclusively booking dramas, Mr. Jeyaraman, how he ascertains this.

JEYARAMAN: I'll ask them to sing. "Show me how you sing," I'll say, and they'll sing right here in the shop. I ask many people to sing before I put their calendar up.

This surprised me, as it was the first I'd heard of such a practice.

SUSAN: Really? So, imagine that I want to hang my calendar here. Would you ask me to sing?

J: Oh no! No, I won't. I won't ask this of women.

S: Why is that?

J: We can't ask a woman to come here and sing. Can we ask a woman to come sing in a public place? If this was a house, we might ask her; here we can't.

I was intrigued. Weren't we talking about professional performers, stage actresses, the very women who *do* sing in public places? Public women par excellence? I sat there in my sari with my black box of a tape recorder, asking him endless questions, feeling like a gender freak and a bit of a boor. Actresses might be public women professionally and by night, but in their local, day-to-day lives, close to home, they tried to maintain a reputation as proper women.[8] In the daytime, in their daily local life, actresses would not come out to a public shop—the very shop where I sat and quite publicly acted the anthropologist, asking questions about these very gendered norms and practices—and perform publicly. I realized belatedly and somewhat sheepishly that Jeyaraman had been referring only to male artists when he spoke about asking them to sing, the kind of people who *should* be in shops like his (see plate 8).

Before I could even ask how it was, then, that he did ascertain the talents of an actress without asking her to sing, he volunteered the following:

JEYARAMAN: Regarding women, if we want a critical assessment, that's easy: many people will be going to see her and will be knowing about her. We can learn from so many people: they'll be saying, "This is how she talks; this is how she acts." So therefore I can guarantee her to any town.

Even her booking agent,[9] then, learns of an actress's talents only indirectly, through the eyes, ears, and words of other men who have seen and heard her onstage. Other men speak to him directly about her voice, or else they speak in and around his shop to other men hanging out in and around his shop. It is men, speaking with each other, who determine an actress's reputation, while she waits, quietly or not, at home.

Work and the Internalization of Gendered Behavior

Our internalized sense, our knowledge, of what "works" in any given social and cultural milieu is critical to our ability to act in ways that establish us as competent actors within that environment. Of course, this truism holds true only insofar as we take into account locally shared perceptions and apperceptions of who "we" are.[10] We become who we are—she or he becomes who she or he is—through the process of engaging in "the dialectic of the internalization of externality and the externalization of internality" (Bourdieu [1972] 1977, 72). That is, in learning to be cultural actors, we both internalize the external configurations and realities of our environment, and simultaneously act in relation to that external world based on our internal understandings, including our desires in relation to that world and our place within it.

In the course of such a dialectical engagement with the world around us, we invariably learn about our social standing in the terms that are locally meaningful. Thus we learn that we are male or female and concomitantly the meaning of male and female where we live; or we learn that we are rich or poor and simultaneously what that means where we live; or that we are dark skinned or light skinned, light haired or dark haired, short or tall, and so on, and simultaneously what each of these distinctions means where we live.

Because there is inequality in such hierarchical systems, shame attaches to those who fall into less-valued categories: female, poor, dark skinned, et cetera. Now, once we grasp the locally meaningful distinctions between persons, we also learn the behavioral norms associated with each distinction and category of personhood. Culturally competent action must also take account of these norms of conduct. Those already belonging to shameful categories of persons may well try harder—and may well succeed, though they are also at risk of overcompensatory hypercorrection—to maintain behaviors that might buoy them up.

Acting outside of behavioral norms threatens to shame us further, and shame is itself a notoriously potent social corrective: "it is shame, that concern for the good opinion of one's neighbors and friends, which circumscribes behavior within the moral boundaries created by shared values" (Scott 1985, 17). Shame engages when there is the possibility of a public exposure of transgression, the possibility that a state or an action will become visible to others, and is thus intimately connected to our ideas about the self and its relation to the world around us. (Guilt, on the other hand, arises when transgressions remain secret; see Geertz 1973, 401.) Shame is one of the basic human means of modulating our overall interest in the outside world, as fear of self-exposure in public potentially reduces our desire to explore the world (Sedgwick and Frank 1995, 5).

Belonging to the social category *woman* in Tamilnadu—being a South Indian woman who is linguistically and culturally competent and aware of what it means to be a member of this gender in contemporary Tamilnadu—

fundamentally entails knowing that being an actress is a shameful occupation and social identity.[11] As previously noted, many Tamil words for actress simultaneously denote whore or prostitute; "Kūtti," "kūttiyāḷ," "tāci," and "tēvaṭiyāḷ" all mean "dancing girl or prostitute," "mistress or concubine," or "dancing girl devoted to temple service, commonly a prostitute; harlot, whore." The combined effect of such derogatory terms and the discourses that fuel their existence is to keep most "good" Tamil women from daring or desiring to be actresses, to explore that world, at all.[12]

Some women do, however, take on this job. Economic realities play a dominant role in this decision and are such that a central component of the social identity of Special Drama actresses is that they are (or at least were at the time they entered the field) poor women (see introduction).

Caste and religion, the other overarching fields of socially salient distinctions that generally mark and situate people in Tamilnadu, have surprisingly far less impact on who becomes an actress than do economics. As noted, Special Drama actresses include women of every caste and religious background. Ethnicity is likewise a negligible consideration, as long as the women speak Tamil. None of these affect the ability of a woman to participate in Special Drama, though in select instances she may be able to use her ethnic or caste background to her advantage. (When the Saurashtrian community sponsored a weeklong festival in their neighborhood in Madurai in 1993, their preference was to hire artists from their own ethnic and linguistic community, among whom was Sennai Sivakami; her performance at this event was the one Jansirani and I watched together from the audience.)

The social descriptor that bears more weight in the initial picture of who an actress is in her world is education level: while actresses must be literate, the average level of conventional education attained by the actresses I interviewed was fourth standard (roughly equivalent to a fourth-grade grammar school education in the U.S. system). This is not in itself terribly unusual among poor Tamil women. While not the case in the middle class or among higher castes, a majority of Tamil girls still leave school when a marriage prospect emerges, "since her security will come from marriage rather than from her employment" (Dickey 1993, 24). The age at which a marriage prospect emerges is in itself highly variable, especially in the (preferred) case of endogamous arranged marriage where the bride and bridegroom know each other as children. In addition, for poor families, even the relatively low cost of a public school education can be prohibitive, and girl children are often removed from school before any marriage prospect for economic reasons. Actresses' training for Special Drama continues through informal arrangements with drama teachers, male elders in the field who write out the lyrics to songs and the texts of debates that the actresses must learn to occupy the repertory roles. This requires literacy, but not a high level of formal education.

Within a general context, then, where women's education is frequently sacrificed to economics (and by extension to marriage), a family's decision to allow a daughter to become an actress is still quite extreme, as it effectively kills any young woman's eventual prospect of a normal marriage. By normal here I mean a marriage arranged between the bride's and groom's families (i.e., an arranged marriage). No self-respecting groom's family will agree to have their son marry an actress (including families of male actors, as I discuss in the following chapter) because of the standard reputation of actresses as prostitutes, and the social fact that a bride's chastity is her main cultural capital. As noted, the only "marriage" route generally open to actresses (to which rare exceptions do exist) is what is euphemistically referred to as a "second marriage," or less euphemistically as being kept. The Special Drama actresses I spoke with confirmed what I observed through charting kinship relations in the acting community: 95 percent of actresses are involved in second marriages. To a remarkable extent, the continued use of derogatory Tamil terms to denote "actress" becomes a self-fulfilling prophecy, as poor young women who become actresses to earn a living effectively also eventually become mistresses.

Thus a woman's primary compensation for the loss of social standing attendant on entering this profession is economic. As previously noted, working as a Special Drama actress pays quite well in relation to other kinds of work available to this class. For example, a woman who works as a cook or a maid might earn Rs 75 per month, but working as an actress, she might earn Rs 300 *in one night*. Such relatively high wages should not, however, give the impression that Special Drama actresses are well-off once they begin on this road. In theory it is possible for an actress to accumulate a substantial income, but in practice, though actresses do alter their economic situation through this work, they remain enmeshed in relations that substantially drain that benefit.

Finally, in attempting to understand the road of the stage actress in Tamilnadu both metaphorically and quite literally, we must consider too the ineffable allure of the stage itself. There is the glamour of theatrical makeup and costumes and bright lights. There is the applause of the crowd. There is the temporary illusion of being someone else, just for a night, of a release from the strictures of day-to-day reality: the characters that Special Drama actresses play include noble queens and mythological goddesses, as well as insouciant sixteen-year-olds. Movement beyond one's normal spheres—geographic as well as postural and gestural—becomes an immediate possibility, in turn expanding the psychological and social spheres in which one normally engages with, and is engaged by, others. The bad name accorded to Tamil stage performers notwithstanding, even in a place where "the bad" does not have the "cool," sexy associations it has in many Western societies, it is nevertheless *a* social option for women who have few others, and one that allows a woman to build—as the discussion of Sennai Sivakami's strategies showed—a public persona that is the stuff of fantasy.[13]

All this can be both terrifying and exciting. When it is also a woman's way to make a living, she must be able both to tap into its extraordinariness and to find a way to normalize it to sustain her daily life and her sense of self within it. Actresses must negotiate the expansive possibilities that the life of the stage opens up in their offstage lives. In this often confusing terrain of extended mobility, I found actresses using an array of on-the-ground strategies to temper the effects of "the dialectic of the internalization of externality and the externalization of internality" characterizing their working lives.

Narrative Two: Regarding Traveling to a Drama in a Private Conveyance

Whenever they can, Special Drama artists travel to their performance venues in private rather than public vehicles. Older artists recall with nostalgia the days when they traveled in the pinnacle of secluded, enclosed, and luxurious worlds: they rode in "pleasures." "Pleasure" is the English word artists still use to refer to the private automobile, the rented Ambassador "pleasure car" that used to pick up actresses at their own door and take them directly to the performance site.[14]

Very rarely are "pleasures" used by drama parties today. Instead artists quite often pool their resources to hire a private van, the current means of avoiding public buses (figs. 48 and 49). Such drama vans are crowded. Sometimes sixteen people squeeze into a space designed for ten, where in addition the backseat is entirely taken up with artistic provisions: a large wooden foot-pedal harmonium, several drums, multiple rolls of painted canvas backdrops for scene settings, not to mention each of the actors' costume-filled suitcases. People have to sit practically on top of each other in these vans, often for many hours.

48 Dancer "Silk" Kalaiselvi at the door to the van in which she will ride to a performance venue, 1998, Madurai.

49 Male artists and a drama agent before getting in the van, 1998, Madurai.

Nevertheless, the question of why artists adamantly prefer crowded private vans to public buses is obvious: public-private distinctions as markers of prestige and social status in Tamilnadu long predate both vans and buses. The reigning logic is familiar: more-prestigious persons occupy more (and more-private) personal space, while less-prestigious persons occupy less (and less-private) space.

To me, traveling with drama artists in a van always felt risqué. Suddenly the strict women's side/men's side rules of public conveyances were lifted. The two requisite actresses in any Special Drama party would often sit side by side in the van in a two-person seat, but equally often they did not. My own presence could easily instigate multiple shifts: a woman certainly had to be seated next to me for reasons of propriety (so that I would not be forced to sit beside an unknown man), but then what about the other actress? She suddenly had increased mobility, without ever seeming to have asked for it. Inside a van, other sorts of allegiances and alliances, even intimacies, emerged easily.

Van interiors provide drama artists a means of moving through and across public roads while carrying a collective interiority, a protective group cohesiveness, with them. The world internal to the drama community creates a bubble of familiarity that stretches to the contours of every space they fill together, and in these cases it was the size of the interior of a van. I felt included in that "inside" familiarity when I rode with them. I felt freer there than almost anywhere else in Tamilnadu, engaged in a daring squeeze of closeness that was largely invisible to the outside world. I felt inside a family, of sorts, and it was a pleasure, too.

Roads and the Externalization of Gendered Behavior

Publicness is at the core of the bad reputation of the stage actress. Writing of stage actresses in North Indian popular theater, Kathryn Hansen notes that an actress is regarded as a prostitute simply by virtue of leaving seclusion to be seen in public. "Since the social construction of gender places 'good women' in seclusion, women who appear in public spaces (such as onstage) are defined as 'bad,' that is, prostitutes. Subjected to the gaze of many men, they belong not to one, like the loyal wife, but to all" (Hansen 1992, 22–23). Throughout India, a firm distinction between the public sphere of worldly activity and the domestic sphere of familial relations has long been central to the maintenance of a woman's, and thus of her family's, good reputation.

The North Indian paradigm of distinguishing between these spheres as "the home and the world" (*ghar* and *bihar*, in Hindi), and marking the distinction through the segregating practice of *pardā* (segregated living quarters), is perhaps more recognizable to Western readers than are South Indian practices of sex segregation (especially those readers familiar with the Bengali literature of Rabindranath Tagore and his 1915 novel *The Home and the World*, or Satyajit Ray's film adaptation of the same). Yet gender segregation continues to be the norm in most public venues in contemporary Tamilnadu. Restaurants, cinema halls, schools, buses, and places of worship all maintain separate sides for women and men. Such segregation is considered advantageous to all, and mutually protective; women are of course wary of the sexual advances of unknown men, but Tamil men likewise often fear the sexuality of unknown women.[15]

The indigenous Tamil terms that best articulate and name Tamil configurations of properly gendered spheres are explored in depth in A. K. Ramanujan's influential studies of classical Tamil poetry and poetics (1967, 1985) and of popular folklore genres (1986, 1991a, 1991b). Ramanujan's work introduced into scholarly discussions of South India the indigenous terms that name the continuing distinction between domestic and public spheres in all realms of Tamil life. Ramanujan first translated the terms *akam* (the inner part, or the Interior) and *puṟam* (the outer part, or the Exterior) by following the usage of classical commentators discussing the division of poems in classical Tamil anthologies dating roughly from 100 B.C. to A.D. 250. Akam poems are love poems that speak the moods of generic, unnamed lovers; puṟam poems are "usually about good and evil, action, community, kingdom; it is the 'public' poetry of the ancient Tamils" (Ramanujan 1967, 101).

In expanding his focus from the classical period to the modern, Ramanujan began to write of "an *akam-puṟam*, or domestic-public spectrum of folk genres," of which "the most *akam*, 'interior, private, familial,' in terms of teller and audience" are folktales told by women "in a kitchen while feeding the children" (1986, 46). The world of akam is finally understood as a women's space, in which its own values and attitudes come into play, as counterposed to the male-dominated puṟam world; Ramanujan writes: "Genders are genres. The world of women is not the world of men" (1991b, 53). With the most domestic scenario at one end, South Indian folk genres could be seen to range across a continuum of increasingly more public, and more male, performances, culminating in the theater: "Theater, the end-point in the continuum, is the most 'puṟam, exterior, or public' of the genres" (ibid.). Ramanujan came to see these categories of akam and puṟam as simultaneously native and analytic, as well as a common cultural base that folk and classical traditions share (Blackburn and Ramanujan 1986, 13–14). Subsequent scholars have shifted the emphasis of Ramanujan's understanding of akam and puṟam from Tamil literature to the organization of Tamil society itself: "This separation of the public and private spheres between men and women, respectively, pervades everything in Tamil society, including fiction and folk forms" (Pandian 1992, 79); "as a cardinal principle of that very culture . . . the Tamilians have divided the world into 'inner' (*akam*) and 'outer' (*puram*) categories" (Shulman 1985, 6).

Given the deep ideological roots of this gendered separation between the spheres of domestic/private/familial/interior/female, on the one hand, and the civic/public/exterior/male, on the other—a functional and symbolic ordering of the world that affects both the Tamil fictive landscape and its more mundane manifestations—the transgressions of the stage actress become all the more clear. She is engaged in performing in a most puṟam genre (the public theater) in a most public place (outdoors), and appears onstage alongside unknown men (strangers), and yet speaks publicly of *love*, the most akam of all things.

This transgression of the ideology of separate spheres stigmatizes both male and female performers of Special Drama, but the burden rests much more heavily on actresses. Many male artists indeed try to distance themselves from public women, both onstage (as we have seen in chapters 4 through 6) and off (as I detail hereafter). For public women themselves, however, disavowal is more complicated.

The genre of Special Drama itself confounds any easy division into artistic spheres of akam and puṟam by employing both male and female artists onstage together while still conveying messages of "traditional" moralism. Terukkuttu, now considered a traditional Tamil folk theater, is still performed by all-male troupes. Contemporary social dramas in Chennai have mixed-gender casts who employ realist acting conventions to represent the modern world. On this front too, then, Special Drama remains an anomaly among Tamil theatrical genres, neither abiding by traditional sex-segregated performance conventions nor fully quitting the traditional for an embrace of a coed world. In Special Drama, somewhat modernized versions of classic mythological stories are staged in fairly traditional rural venues for increasingly conventional religious purposes.[16] In all these ways, Special Drama falls through the cracks of both the modern and the traditional. Recalling

Ramanujan's dictum, we could say that this genre has no clear gender and is seen instead as indiscriminately *mixing* traditional and modern elements much as it mixes women and men. All this leaves Special Drama actresses to fend for themselves in negotiating their reputations.

Seen as too public, as moving out into the world far beyond the bounds of proper, private, modest feminine behavior, actresses must nevertheless somehow move on the ground to conduct their business. The form of this inappropriate mobility—actual travels through the public sphere on roads that lead actresses to the popular theater stage—threatens to expose the fragility of the culturally naturalized division of gendered spheres into akam and puṟam, interior/home and exterior/world. Actresses move onto public stages to enact what are meant to be the most private of relations. The actress is most unsettling precisely in her unsettledness.

Narrative Three: Regarding Traveling to a Drama in a Public Conveyance

Bakkiyalakshmi and I had finally settled on a date for me to accompany her to a drama. Bakkiya is a seasoned actress in her fifties, and we were going to a village in an area well known to her from decades of performing throughout the region.

As this village was accessible by main road, we were traveling by public bus (there is less excuse for the luxury of hiring a van when a venue can be reached by bus). All Tamil town buses, like those we took that night, have a women's side and a men's side. The words indicating which side is which are stenciled directly on the walls of the bus. When traveling in a pair, two women need have very little interaction with unknown persons on a public bus, least of all with unknown men. We had none.

We left from Madurai in the early evening and traveled into the night. To reach the sponsoring village, we had to change buses at two different stations. In the first station, our change was quick and easy. The next bus was already loading when we arrived. We simply got up from our two-person seat on the women's side of the bus from Madurai and switched to another two-person seat on the women's side of the bus from Sivaganga.

At the second station, our bus was not waiting. Bakkiya told me it would not come for another half hour. We got off the bus, and she led me to a little food stall, one among many lining the road on the side of the bus station. There a man was making a flamboyant, though common, dish, a regional specialty called "egg parota."[17] Its preparation involves terrific energy on the part of the chef. He holds two metal tools—they are shaped more like axes than knives—and bangs them down on a wide, flat metal skillet, over and over, rhythmically mixing and chopping parota and egg. It is the noisiest manner of food preparation I have ever encountered, entrancing as only an intensely loud barrage of sound can be, starting for a spell of deafening decibels at each new order and abruptly stopping again in equally deafening silence.

The chef at the stall we approached flashed a big smile at Bakkiyalakshmi. They knew each other, though I didn't catch exactly how. He was at least twenty years her junior. She introduced me, and he immediately put down his tools and led us back through his stall into a small back room. In it were a desk, a chair, and a cot. The walls were painted royal blue. He made sure I was comfortably seated in the chair and returned to his axes and skillet. Bakkiya asked me whether I would like to eat, encouraging me to do so here rather than wait for whatever food the villagers had prepared. I agreed. She left the room, and I was alone.

I sat in that little room for what felt like a long time but couldn't have been more than fifteen minutes. The wall of sound just beyond unmistakably delimited inside from outside. Where I was sitting was inside: blue walls swimming around me, a tide of deafening sound reaching me in waves. The other noises and voices and commerce beyond the walls of that room were all outside.

I realized that even on this most public of routes, taking a public bus from a public bus stand two towns away from home, Bakkiya had secured a little private space, which that night she lent to me so that I could disappear into a respite of invisibility. I sat there feeling safe and tiny, and simultaneously out of the loop and bored. How, I wondered, does Bakkiya feel when she sits there?

The Actress's Strategy of Imitating the Good Woman

An actress's battle for reputation against the stigma of unsettledness that haunts the acting profession is constant, since the very organization of Special Drama depends on performers' mobility. Recall that each artist is contracted individually for each performance, and that it is the artists' responsibility to get themselves to and from each venue. The challenge for actresses is to accrue as little tainting publicness, on the way there, as possible. For even an actress who pursues a big name in her performance style will generally want to establish as good a name for herself as possible in the negotiations of her offstage life. Why? What is the importance of a good name?

In this there are two realms of concern, the first being the impact of her good name on an actress's private life, the second being the impact of her reputation on her working life. The two are, of course, linked. Nevertheless, angling for invisibility offstage does not preclude an actress from creating the kind of hypervisible performance persona that I have discussed previously under the big-name strategy; rather, careful offstage negotiations ensure that no details of private scandal cloud the public picture in ways that are not enhancing.

As Tamil women, actresses share an awareness of the dominant values concerning women. To avoid shame, even a woman who inhabits the stigmatized identity of actress will continue to gauge her own actions in relation to those of "normal" women, that is, in terms of what is considered normal behavior for a Tamil woman. As competent members of their culture and society, actresses tend to share the same standards of social value as those who judge them. Thus an actress may be as concerned to maintain a good name in her private life as is any woman in a society that accords a good name high value.

Regarding the second realm of concern, the actress's professional and economic life, I find James Scott's discussion of the relation of class to reputation useful. Scott asks and answers the question (in relation to agrarian peasants, in his work) as follows:

> How important is a good name? Or, to put it the other way around, what is the cost of a bad name? The answer unfortunately depends a great deal on who you are, for the cost of a bad name hinges directly on the social and economic sanctions that can be brought into play to punish its bearer. In class terms, one must ask how dependent the poor are on the good opinion of the rich. . . . A good name is something like a social insurance policy for the poor against the thousand contingencies of agrarian life. (Scott 1985, 24)

An actress's reputation qua actress, as we have seen, is intricately bound up with her economic life and is inseparable from her life as a Tamil woman. For although she may be a "bad woman" by virtue of her profession, in that very professional life, rather ironically as we have seen, an actress is charged with enacting scenes of Tamil life onstage that incessantly require her to embody and voice normative moral expectations for Tamil women. Onstage, actresses must be able to speak to the overarching concerns with reputation that face all Tamil women, whether they are enacting the "good" Heroine role or the "bad" Dancer role. A thorough knowledge of this moral value system for gauging a woman's reputation precedes the ability to act either of these roles.

In their offstage attempts to garner whatever respect may be possible to them, actresses likewise use their mimetic skills. In their daily practice of public journeys, these women constantly, vigilantly strive to re-create, at least in appearance, the very physical confines of good feminine domesticity. What I am suggesting, in short, is that Special Drama actresses attempt to better their reputation as women by acting, even while offstage, on the dominant script of respectable femininity quite literally: by seeking to make their public travels offstage conform as closely as possible to the strictures, and psychic structures, of middle-class feminine domesticity.

In moving with Special Drama actresses through the streets of Tamilnadu, I saw them creating structures of enclosure (structures of the interior) even in the most public of places. These deceptively small structures of enclosure—the interiors of vans, the cardboard-backed calendars that substitute for their person in shops, or the little rooms behind street stalls in which they take respite—form what I would characterize as spaces in which actresses subtly renegotiate their status through a strategy of expansion. The creation of such varied enclosures effectively expands the category of properly domestic, feminine interior space to suddenly include actresses, the very women who otherwise, and by definition, would have no access to such a domestic identity. Through the creation of such small, secluded spaces, actresses force their inclusion as potentially "good" women into a calculus of moral virtues that otherwise categorically excludes them.[18]

Traveling with these women, I experienced viscerally how a dominant inside/outside dichotomy of good/bad morality informs their every journey, and I admired their patient, understated, and expansive response to this oppressive climate. As we traveled, actresses erected enclosures that were their own exclusive, interior spaces, spaces that slyly appropriated for themselves a dominant strategy of exclusion, everywhere we went. They strung together little islands, havens of familiarity, and hopped from one to the next as a means of remaining protected while moving through the outside.

Narrative Four:
Regarding Spatial Arrangements at a Drama Site

When artists reach their performance venue, an outdoor stage has already been erected at the site, its inside (uḷḷē) resting space and outside (veḷiyē) playing spaces already demarcated. Outside actors are visible to all, while inside is a semi-private space into which artists may disappear.

Actors change costumes, touch up their faces and hair, sleep in catnaps between scenes, chat, and snack together inside throughout the night. They prepare themselves in this collective space of inside before each stint outside. Inside, they generally maintain the decorum of women's side and men's side arrangements, though not rigidly; inside feels, in short, much like being in a privately relaxed Tamil domestic space, a home, where gender determines behavior somewhat more flexibly than in public.[19] This ability to create a familiar domestic place in the midst of the otherwise unknown and unfamiliar—an inside place where they are at least partially shielded from the public by palm thatch and a serviceable argot to feel and act in somehwat more relaxed and familiar ways—this ability is a skill actresses employ everywhere they go. Their skills traverse public and private.

Even inside the inside itself, for example, actresses maintain familiar distinctions. Backstage, they carve out a private space by tying a string across one corner and hanging a sari over it, creating a modest one-woman changing corner.

I found out just how useful a shield from the outside such an inside place could be one night when I needed to empty my bladder and my actress friends directed me to their changing corner. Squatting inside that little triangular women's space, I realized the other obvious resonance of the terms "inside" and "outside," at least in the rural context. Where there is no restroom—and the majority of people living in rural India have none[20]—"going outside" (veḷiyē pōka) means literally that. To have to go outside to relieve themselves would put actresses on par with the lower-class rural women in the audience, rather than ally them in bodily practice with middle-class women's use of an indoor toilet. Creating inside spaces such as changing corners that double as privies enables actresses to avoid all variety of unsavory outside experiences, and exposures to inclement outside environments, by fashioning inside spaces to meet their private needs.

Theoretical Grounds

Any thorough analysis of relations of stigma and stigmatized identities must necessarily engage the analyst with the critical cultural processes through which people create classificatory schemes, whether explicit or tacit. Such classificatory schemes are generated by our human "separative power" (Bourdieu 1984, 479), our power to make distinctions, to draw difference out of the undifferentiated. We also grant our distinctions—between certain persons, groups of persons, and practices—hierarchical values that frequently result in stigmatizing judgments such as normal or abnormal, moral or immoral, subject or abject. Such labeling judgments determine membership or nonmembership in social groups based on reductive and partial perceptions that focus on a particular feature, or on particular aspects (usually of behavior or of anatomy) in assigning social identity (475). Actresses, as we have seen, are stigmatized because they engage in behaviors already codified as outside Tamil norms of gendered respectability.

Analysis of the social processes concerning stigmatized identities requires first of all the recognition that such ascriptions of identity matter dearly to all involved. Bourdieu writes: "Every real inquiry into the divisions of the social world has to analyze the interests associated with membership or non-membership," for "social identity is the stake in a struggle" (476): "What is at stake in the struggles about the meaning of the social world is power over the classificatory schemes and systems which are the basis of the representations of the groups and therefore of their mobilization and demobilization" within the social world (479).

Analysis of social stigma thus runs right into the rich thicket of questions regarding the social workings of hegemony and consent, power and resistance. In struggling with their social identity, actresses seem both to collaborate with and to resist the given terms of the world in which they act; indeed, their struggles are shot through with ambivalence and ambiguity. Sherry Ortner (1995) argues that such ambivalence is a part of resistance itself.

Thinking about the variety of embodied, on-the-ground negotiations of their stigmatized identity that I have encountered among Special Drama actresses, through the kinds of experiences I write of in this chapter, has led me to recognize the wide range of possible strategies people may use to counteract stigma. These strategies are often not overtly stated but, rather, exist as "dispositions" and as the "schemes of perception and thought" that inform action: "The principle of this structuring activity is not . . . a system of universal forms and categories but a system of internalized, embodied schemes which, having been constituted in the course of collective history, are acquired in the course of individual history and function in their *practical* state, *for practice*" (Bourdieu 1984, 467). Such internalized and embodied schemes are capable of generating infinite practices "without those schemes ever being constituted as explicit principles" (Bourdieu [1972] 1977, 16).

Because the artists never discussed these as rational schemes, I analyze the embodied strategies through which artists negotiate stigma not by questioning them directly about how they *think* of their social position but by observing what they *do*, within the context and in light of the broader classificatory schemes operative in their social world, distinctions such as akam and puṟam, *uḷḷē* and *veḷiyē*. My attempts to understand actresses' roadwork are thus classically ethnographic. As Ortner (1995) notes, "Ethnography . . . has always meant the attempt to understand another life world using the self—as much of it as possible—as the instrument of knowing" (173). Habituating myself to their habitus, I treat my own experiences of actresses' roadwork as telling.

To some extent, then, my project is of a piece with the larger Foucauldian endeavor of teaching ourselves, as analysts, to recognize the variety and multiplicity of responses to power.[21] These responses include both resistance and collaboration; indeed, in the work of many theorists the distinction itself has become difficult to maintain, and rightly so (see the discussion in Ortner 1995, 175–76). Resistance and compliance shade into each other, as the ultimate meaning of an act depends so entirely on context, and contexts themselves change and evolve through these very same acts. Moreover, all too often compliance is the most effective way to resist an oppressive power. I think it behooves us, as analysts, to continue to enlarge our understanding of the myriad possible human responses to situations of unequal power, and particularly to the role that relations of stigma play in such situations.

Writing specifically about the resistance of subordinate classes, a resistance that is "close to the ground, rooted firmly in the homely but meaningful realities of daily experience" (Scott 1985, 348), Scott documents both large-scale revolts and the far more common or garden-variety evasive and defensive "weapons of the weak." These include "foot dragging, dissimulation, desertion, false compliance, feigned ignorance, slander, arson, sabotage and so on" (xvi). Christine Pelzer White has suggested that we add an inventory of "everyday forms of collaboration" to balance this list of "everyday forms of resistance," as "both exist, both are important" (White 1986, 56; cited in Ortner 1995, 176). Abandoning the form of the list for a more conceptual model, the Comaroffs suggest that resistance itself is "less a thing than a *continuum* of possibility, a range of means by which those who see themselves as dispossessed and disempowered seek, through their own agency, to regain mastery over their lives" (Comaroff and Comaroff 1993, 17).

The Comaroffs offer a useful typology of all potential forms of resistant acts ranging "across the spectrum from the most inchoate, individual, informal modes of resistance toward the more formal, public, obviously 'political' expressions of protest" (27). This continuum has a gendered aspect, as the former end—often characterized as "everyday, domestic defiance"—is, not surprisingly, home to those tactics and forms of resistance that women most frequently employ, having less access to more organized forms (38). Foucault (1980) suggests that the tendency, since the nineteenth century, to judge processes of struggle only in terms of opposition is a theoretical impoverishment that has led to dissolving all the specific problems of struggle "into the meagre logic of contradiction" (143).

Whatever the form in which we conceive of it, our understanding of the range of means that people use to seek mastery over their lives must include assimilationist collaborative strategies, which often shade into everyday forms of resistance, as well as outright refusals to collaborate that take the form of revolts, rebellions, and separatist practices. The most assiduous documentation of assimilationist collaborative strategies remains Goffman's 1963 study of stigma, in which he discusses adaptive actions such as passing; "covering" through the use of "disidentifiers"; restricting one's quotidian movement (one's "daily rounds") both geographically and socially; splitting one's discursive worlds through strategic silences (cf. Scott's "hidden transcripts," [1990]); avoiding intimacy; and in general lessening the obtrusiveness of a given stigma on a given social scene by any available means.

I understand Special Drama actresses' attempts to ease their road in the Tamil public sphere—by expanding otherwise stigmatizing gendered norms to include themselves—as an adaptive practice that is both compliant as necessary, and resistant where possible. To put it more succinctly, this roadwork is well attuned to their social world. While the schemes they employ on the road reiterate, and mimic, the forms of hegemonic power in Tamil society, the actresses' deployment of these schemes to ease their own road brings some power into their own hands. In their attempts to comply with the dominant gendered dichotomy of akam and puṟam that organizes much of the Tamil world, actresses are ambiguously faithful and subtly inexact. To use Judith Butler's terminology, their roadwork is built out of "repetitions of hegemonic forms of power which fail to repeat loyally and, in that failure, open possibilities for resignifying the terms of violation" (Butler 1993, 124). Through their embodied practices, actresses comply with the powers that stigmatize them only in such a way that their perceived compliance manages to expand their possibilities for making their home in the world. Or at least, it expands the possibilities for making what home there is for stigmatized women in the Tamil social world somewhat more comfortable. Actresses' roadwork is thus diagnostic of the complex particularities of relations of class and power in the Tamil sex/gender system.[22]

My ethnographic experiences made this set of critical approaches to consent and resistance palpable. Moving with actresses, I experienced an oscillation between havens of safety and stretches of painful overexposure. I have written here about my own experiences of vacillating between comfort and discomfort as a way of beginning to appreciate actresses' experiences on the road. As I traveled with them, I began to make my own embodied sense of their roadwork, of its system of signs and dispositions, indeed of the "imaginative universe within which their acts are signs" (Geertz 1973, 13). My feelings during our travels have become a set of signs that now signify to me, when I analyze them in terms of akam and puṟam, that I had begun, over the course of two years of moving with them, to understand viscerally what was at stake for actresses when traveling through the public sphere. I was engaging in the famous ethnographic work of "deep hanging-out" (Renato Rosaldo, quoted in Clifford 1997, 188), through which I began to understand "the character of lived experience" among actresses. Examining my own experience of being with Special Drama actresses, on their turf and in their terms, allows me additional insight into their experiences of being "other" in the context of the contemporary Tamil public sphere.

Narrative Five: Regarding Traveling Home in the Morning

The apartment building where Jansirani and I both lived in 1992 was smack in the middle of that little two-block radius of the Special Drama business district in Madurai. Most Madurai actresses try to live as near as possible to this center. Doing so minimizes the distance of their daily travels between home and a van, or home and the central bus stand, reducing their traversal of outsides by shortening the distance between insides.

The majority of male actors, on the other hand, still live in their natal villages most of the year and stay in Madurai only during the drama season, when they rent rooms in lodges in the center of town. Lodges are notorious "bad" nightlife spots, such that for a woman with an eye to her reputation, being seen in one (let alone actually staying the night in one) is not a viable option.

Jansi and I returned together from a drama one morning by bus, sleeping against each other in our seat. We arrived at the Madurai station just before 7 A.M., tried surreptitiously to unrumple ourselves, smoothed down our saris and began walking from the central bus stand to home, a distance of about five blocks.

We walked briskly through the streets. Jansi was moving very purposefully toward home. I stepped outside myself for a moment to wonder what we looked like: Does Jansi look like a woman who simply rose early this morning? Do I? (Not that I ever look simply like any woman here.) Tamil women rising early at home do things around their house, sacred ritual things, the most visible to passersby being making *kolams*, geometric patterns in rice powder that are negotiations of light lines and dark ground at the entranceway of the houses, where street touches home.[23] Kolams are one of so many respectable female daily efforts to keep the street from contaminating the home, to purify inner space and separate it from the outside. Were we, at that moment, the embodiment of the chaotic, disorderly, outside element? The very fact that we weren't at home making kolams suddenly seemed yet another proof of the mark on us. Was it obvious that we had been riding a bus, sitting up all night, our faces bearing as many pressed wrinkles as our saris? What did people think when they saw us?

This felt to me like a particularly vulnerable moment, though at the time I couldn't understand why. Rationally, the kind of danger I was familiar with from generic travels as a woman was over: night was over, we were back on familiar territory, and it was a properly respectable hour of the morning to be out and about. But I saw too how tired Jansi was, and how she had that barely containable kind of morning giddiness that comes from staying up all night. I felt scared that everything we had gone through was apparent on us; or was I perhaps picking up on her shame, as she walked, fast, not stopping to say anything to anyone? I realize now that this was a particularly vulnerable moment for her, a moment of separation from the group: we were no longer in that cocoon of sorts created by all the actors together, inside the inside spaces of their night world with their argot and their streetside networks of known people. Suddenly we were two tired women alone on the street in the broad daylight that glinted off the stray specks of green and pink glitter still stuck to Jansi's eyelids, and I felt exposed and confused, hurrying after Jansi, who was heading home so fast.

Conclusion

My own feelings when traveling with actresses reveal an unexpected sense of relief bordering on euphoria at finding havens of invisibility and familiar interiority, as well as a concomitant growing trepidation at being caught alone in public day or night. In narrating these tales from the circuit of actresses' travels between booking shops, vans, buses, backstage spaces, and roads home, I have spoken of instances where I felt uncomfortably other, as well as of times where I felt included like family; occasions when I felt invisible but somehow safe; and still others where I felt exposed and confused. While some of the sense of marginality and dislocation that pervaded my travels with actresses may have stemmed from my own psychology and cultural baggage, I have been interested here in how I began to experience their roadwork as a sensible embodied practice.

My main aim for these five narratives, however, has been to use them to illustrate the artistry of actresses' roadwork. Actresses attempt to resignify and resituate their own social position within a dominant system that persistently casts them as stigmatized other. Special Drama actresses struggle to conform to the dominant terms of gendered respectability, but in so doing, they subtly alter—by refiguring—these organizing terms themselves. Their struggle readily exposes, at least to me, the extent to which the internalization of a model of femininity based on domestic virtues affects women differently in respect to their class and social status. The internalization of a femininity based unproblematically on a securely domestic identity is a class-based privilege to which actresses by definition do not have access. Their roadwork is a hybrid of resistance and complicity, an attuned and adaptive practice that may well resignify: through their strategy of expansion, actresses include themselves in the category "good women," potentially redefining the category.

Beyond describing this adaptive practice and indicating its potential, however, questions concerning the actual effects of these practices remain. Is resignification merely a possibility, or do these practices actually effect fundamental change in the underlying circumstances of stigmatized Tamil women's lives?

Viewed in the harshest, most pessimistic light, actresses' attempts to make their conduct conform to dominant Tamil discourses of "the home and the world" have something of the pathetic, gaudy tenor of linguistic hypercorrections. Their roadwork appears as an effort to conform that actually only highlights their real inability to do so, normative status being always already out of their reach. In this light, the actresses are laughable at best; at worst, they reinscribe their own stigma.

Yet surely their roadwork strategies do help actresses in the short term: Special Drama actresses assert their right to moments of seclusion and secure them. Their practices on the road make travel less harrowing for these women. Actresses have spoken to me in many contexts about their broad hopes for the future. I have asked specifically if they envision a time when the quality of their lives might change. Even among actresses who were earning well, and whose hopes for the near future were high regarding their ability to live in greater relative financial ease within their lifetime, none thought that dominant Tamil attitudes toward their line of work would ever change. (Since then I have had many conversations with middle-class Tamilians about actresses that unfortunately convince me the actresses read this right.) Over and again, informants answered my questions about their future with an invocation of their hopes for their children. This was especially true if an actress had daughters. Jansirani has two daughters, both of whom were teenagers in 1993. She told me frequently, "I pray that this road will end with me. Let it end with me. I don't want my daughters to enter this line, or to go out onto this road." Most actresses I spoke with expressed the same wish. They had accepted that their profession would never be acceptable. In their quotidian practices, they continued to try to ease their road as best they could, but when they spoke of the future it was clear that success resided in getting off this road entirely.

Scholars, on the other hand, voice more hope regarding the question of the long-term effects of even such complicitously resistant (resistantly complicitous) practices.[24] Scott is guardedly celebratory in the concluding remarks to his study of everyday forms of peasant resistance in Malaysia. He stresses that such are our current times that we *must* highly value the short-term strategic responses to oppression that do at least provide a modicum of the small decencies that matter so much to people in the day-to-day world. Scott argues that the worldwide failure of grandiose movements for social change is all the more reason "to respect the weapons of the weak" and "to see in the tenacity of self-preservation—in ridicule, in truculence, in irony, in petty acts of noncompliance, in foot dragging, in dissimulation, in resistant mutuality, in the disbelief in elite homilies, in the steady, grinding efforts to hold one's own against overwhelming odds—a spirit and practice that prevents the worst and promises something better" (Scott 1985, 350). What that "better" might be finds an optimistic seconding voice in the Comaroffs' assertion that inchoate forms of everyday resistance inevitably "transform the consciousness of, and to one degree or another empower, those who engage in them" (Comaroff and Comaroff 1993, 20).

I vacillate between "realist" (that is, skeptical) and "populist" (celebratory) views of the effectiveness of such relatively inchoate adaptive strategies as the roadwork of Special Drama actresses. For a long time I was unable to see anything hopeful in these activities; I felt that unless the actresses could articulate the larger problems and overtly attack the rigidities of the Tamil class/gender system as a whole, nothing truly resistant was going on here. I now recognize that change occurs in many different ways, and I am less inclined to privilege the verbal as a means of effecting it. I am still skeptical of what I see as an overly optimistic assumption that inchoate forms of everyday resistance inevitably transform consciousness, but I am increasingly open to asking how gestures of defiance (even those that are ostensibly gestures of compliance) *might* transform the consciousness of those who engage in them.

In invoking actresses' consciousness, I do not mean to imply either that they do think, or that they need to think, of their own work in the same interpretive terms that I do. I am the one who constitutes their schemes as "roadwork." Actresses don't need to coin such a term, for after all they are not writing essays to be read by people unfamiliar with their social world; they are living that world. It is what their lived practices can teach us, ethnographic readers and writers, that constitutes a second level of potential long-term effects of their actions.

I certainly hope that the significance of the everyday struggles of the disempowered, and the resignifications they entail, will prove cumulative, and that the "longer-term, transnational impact" of localized populist struggles will be "to politicize and animate peripheral peoples everywhere in altogether new ways" (Comaroff and Comaroff 1993, 16). But my hope is offset by the following caution.

Mimetic repetitions—sometimes even canonically nonloyal repetitions, such as the actresses practice—can easily serve to reinscribe rather than to subvert an established order. Here I am rephrasing a question posed separately both by the Comaroffs (1993, 39) and by Judith Butler. Butler (prompted by misreadings of her own earlier work as overly celebratory) asks "whether parodying the dominant norms is enough to displace them" (Butler 1993, 125). Her answer is to recall the ambivalence of human action as reflective of "the more general situation of being implicated in the regimes of power by which one is constituted and, hence, of being implicated in the very regimes of power that one opposes." The possibility of resignification and its ultimate effects are two different matters, and as always, attempts to refigure social norms sometimes succeed and sometimes do not, and of course these outcomes resolve slowly. Must we then leave all judgments about the effectiveness of such attempts to retrospect? Perhaps I am simply too impatient. I do think it is important to free ourselves of exclusively heroic models of action. From little things, big things grow (or might). But from which small things? And will the new big things be any different from the old big things?

I will return in the epilogue to consider the longer-term effects on actresses of the various strategies in which they engage. Here I want to briefly consider who else my writing about these practices affects, a question that concerns the goals of our practice of cultural anthropology. What do we make of our fieldwork experiences and what we learn from them of different ways of being? What do we make of all the rich ethnographic information we now share, as writers and readers, about poverty and its particularities, the gory details of class struggle, and the endless inventiveness of strategies for counteracting stigma?

Scott (1985) has called the ordinary weapons of relatively powerless groups "Brechtian" forms of class struggle (xvi), and his invocation of a social critic whose medium was theater is well chosen. However, the strategies Scott documents are not Brechtian in any sense that suggests that these are themselves the political strategies Brecht advocates. Rather, Brecht's strategy was to put the struggles of the people *onstage*—and quite often his characters are women, most famously in the figure of Mother Courage, but equally in the actions of the heroines of *The Jewish Wife* and *The Good Woman of Setzuan*[25]—to show us the material specificity of the human condition. Likewise, in anthropological fieldwork we experience the world differently for a time, living in other contexts, linking ourselves up with people whose subjectivities differ from our own. People do what people must, always in particular historical circumstances. Brecht's epic theater asks the audience to look directly at these conditions and to think about them: Mother Courage makes her living off of others' dying! She is a military opportunist! She acts out of pure self-interest! The world is falling apart! Can you blame her? Would she always act this way? To change her, what must change? The world? Can we change that? Brecht stages these struggles not to suggest that they themselves are answers but to prompt *our* further questions.

The burden of changing the conditions represented onstage thus belongs to the audience. "The task of the epic theater, according to Brecht, is not so much the development of actions as the representation of conditions" (Benjamin [1939] 1969, 150). Brecht's own theatrical and theoretical act of resistance was to oppose the notions of empathy and audience identification found in the dominant theatrical conventions of his day, realism and naturalism (as is still the case in ours). His aim was to change the audience's attitude: they should sit in their seats, puffing thoughtfully on their cigars, thinking about human history ("Can we persuade them to get out their cigars?") (Brecht [1957] 1964, 39, 91–99). The play should be an "object of instruction" (42). Viewing the human condition onstage becomes the audience's rehearsal for action: when our time comes to act, may we have thought about our role first.

My own goals are similar: may the act of anthropological interpretation and representation serve to clarify our thinking regarding historical human conditions, both specifically and generally. In presenting Special Drama actresses' moves and movements on public roads, my aim has been to document these conditions and to present how actresses have dealt with them. I study actresses' roadwork as a means of understanding the complexity of inequalities of power on the ground. Special Drama actresses work on, and in, a maze of roads. I watch these women, onstage and off, sometimes moving with them, to learn about their strategies for dealing with social value systems that stigmatize and exclude them. I cannot predict where their actions will ultimately lead them, or where my representations will take me. Possibilities for further action have been opened up by prior actions, both theirs and mine. Thinking, experiencing, and writing about actresses' roadwork is my practice and my rehearsal for future action.

9 Kinship Mur̲ai

and the Stigma on Actors

An Excess Born of Lack

Special Drama artists are stigmatized for what they lack: people (and proverbs) say that actors have "no culture," "no order," "no *mur̲ai*." Yet beneath these negative locutions, in effect actors stand accused more often of *excess* than lack.

Take local standards of sociability, for example. Special Drama artists regularly create, in both their onstage work and their offstage lives, links with new and unknown persons rather than simply interacting with already known persons. In so doing, they openly operate at an extreme edge of sociability. They are more rather than less expressive of, and more rather than less engaged in, social intercourse and exchange, an abundance that is primarily met with suspicion. It is part of the business of being an actor to *pal̲aku*, to *mix* with people. Their *pal̲akkam* (custom or habit) is the practice of *familiarity*, again *pal̲akkam* (Cre-A 1992, 693–94). All these concepts are linked variations on the Tamil verbal root *pal̲aku*: people who mix with other people become *familiar* with them, and familiarity becomes their habitus.

We have already encountered other Tamil terms that similarly cast actors as people who mix with others to the point of excess. Each use speaks to particular contexts and refers to different kinds of mixing. We have heard an actress described as having an over-the-top style that "causes a sensation (*kalakkal*) by stirring things up" (*kalakalappu*); she *kalakku kalakkir̲anga* ("makes it lively, tasty, enjoyable"). We have heard the all-too-indiscriminate etymological mix of words that actors use onstage described as an impure, slangy mix that degrades the language itself, making it "koccai" or vulgar Tamil. We have seen Buffoons forestall accusations that their comedy is debased and debasing by being first to recognize that "nowadays comedy is just about mixing (sexually) with women." I will discuss here the potentially damning mix represented by intercaste or interreligious marriages, known as *kalappu kalyāṇam*, or mixed marriage; *kalappu* is the "mixing (of two that ought to be kept separate)" (Cre-A 1992, 268). Most damning of all, we will find, is marriage with actresses, who as public women should not mix with a self-respecting man's domestic life but rather be kept separate from it.

Accusations that Special Drama artists mix too freely and excessively extend to multiple social arenas. We have seen the care and concern actresses take to rein in their physical movements, moving as little as possible onstage, and restricting their offstage travels to havens of familiarity wherever possible. In these two domains, curbing physicality appears an appropriate response to the stigma of excessive mobility. There are two other domains of stigma connected to the accusation of excessive mobility, however, whose nature requires something more like psychosocial rather than physical fancy footwork. These involve accusations about the excessive mobility of artists' kinship practices. Such accusations target the onstage domain of mimesis as well as the offstage domain of marriage.

The domain of mimesis concerns the onstage embodiment of dramatic characters. In Special Drama, actors play historical heroes and mythic gods and goddesses, personages that are a far cry from artists' "real" selves. When the distinction between a true and a false self is seen as a moral matter, then anyone capable of cannily presenting a false self warrants suspicion and distrust.

The second arena in which artists are seen as suspiciously mobile and socially unrestrained is in their interpersonal relations. Actors marry and otherwise ally across caste and community lines. They create social bonds that have no ready map; who should marry the daughter of a Muslim man and a Hindu woman? Artists' alliances stretch and expand standard kinship paradigms in complicated, unruly ways that are suspect to those for whom "Tamil culture" is synonymous with a properly arranged social order that has at its base properly arranged marriage.

All such problematic mixtures read as transgressions between categories of things otherwise seen as opposed and discrete. Here I focus on the idea that artists blur boundaries between the categories of kin and stranger, and between fiction and reality. Just how such stigma affects artists lives has been the throughline of this book. Beginning with the most distanced and historical discourses, I have traced the effects of stigmatizing discourses on artists' lives, in onstage as well as offstage practices. In this chapter, I consider how accusations of excessive mixing and a concomitant lack of order affect the organization of artists' interpersonal lives onstage and off.

Kinship, Incest, and the Onstage Locus of Stigma

The stigma surrounding artists' onstage interpersonal behavior stems from a productive confusion inherent in acting itself: *acting is simulation.* What makes acting possible is mimetic imitation, the taking on of a role, of an illusory persona, or of an "other" self, at least partially and temporarily. At the root of mimesis is a slip between reality and illusion, the true and the false, even self and other. The very fact that actors "play" roles in public that are not their "real" roles in private has often, historically, made them suspect: *acting is dissimulation.* The most well-documented instances of antitheatrical prejudice to date are certainly ancient Greece (as in Plato's vision for his ideal city, *The Republic*, in which imitative actors are cast out altogether) and early modern England (where the plasticity of actors was deemed polymorphously perverse and anti-Christian, even satanic).[1] In the United States up through the first half of the twentieth century, actors were specifically banned, along with blacks and Jews, from membership in elite country clubs.[2] The fear that actors will encourage, by their example, a more general dislodging of the proper relations of social person and place clearly has a long and diverse historical pedigree (Barish 1981; Diamond 1992; Howard 1994; Agnew 1986; T. Davis 1991; Mullaney 1983).

Fieldwork discussions, with artists and nonartists alike, about Tamil stage actors' supposed lack of muṟai—usually prompted by my asking the meaning of the Tamil proverb "Actors have no muṟai, like a Ganesh-cake has no head"—exposed two levels of dissimulation in the business of acting that appeared as potential threats. Both these levels turn on interpretations of muṟai as referring to proper relations between kin. The first level, found in explanations offered by nonartists, reveals a basic distrust of mimesis as falsity. The second level, offered by artists themselves, expresses conflicts in what they see as the excess inherent in acting.

The first level of threat appears, for example, in the response I was given by a retired schoolteacher from near Madurai, now a grandfather living in Naperville, Illinois. He explained the meaning of the proverb by saying, "They are playing a husband and wife, but they are not husband and wife; there is no relation (muṟai) there." In this view, what actors present is all illusion and sheer dissimulation. The relations they portray are *not real*. The question of what real relations might in fact exist between actors is not broached; the fact that artists are *acting* is the source of their lack of muṟai.

People closer to the acting profession, however, present the matter differently. In discussing the meaning of the Ganesh-cake proverb, one young actress said, "We are actually this *mur̲ai* of father and daughter, but we are acting that *mur̲ai* of husband and wife." Such an explanation presents the problem of mur̲ai for actors as one arising from the complications of excess, rather than from a relatively simple lack. In this example, there are two mur̲ai rather than one, raising the all-too-real threat of incest by transgressing the primary distinction between marriageable and nonmarriageable kin that organizes proper relations of mur̲ai in Tamilnadu.

Endogamous, bilateral cross-kin marriage is the ideal that structures Tamil kinship terminology and classification. Mur̲ai, as the term that identifies norms of social relation, is in effect the indigenous term for designating the semantic ideals of that system as a whole. At its most prescriptive, mur̲ai speaks of proper, ideal kin relations, the most preferred being the marriage of cross-cousins. *Mur̲aikkaṭṭu*, to "wed by mur̲ai," means to marry one's *mur̲ai(p) pēṇ* ("customary bride") or *mur̲ai māppillai* ("customary groom"). Individuals are deemed customary brides or grooms based on their relationship as cross-kin (the offspring of opposite-sex siblings), as opposed to parallel-kin (who are the offspring of same-sex siblings).

To appreciate the concreteness of the centrality of mur̲ai to all discussions of kinship, let us take for example the sentence "he is to me *māmaṉ mur̲ai*" (avar eṉakku māmaṉ mur̲ai). The sentence means "his relation (mur̲ai) to me is that of māmaṉ." The word *māmaṉ* is often translated into English as "uncle," but the translation is notoriously imprecise (see Trautmann 1981 and 1987 for a full historical account of the disciplinary implications for anthropological kinship studies of this particular imprecision of translation in the work of L. H. Morgan). "Māmaṉ" is not simply uncle, but rather a term that simultaneously "comprehends the mother's brother, the father's sister's husband, and the spouse's father, genealogical relationships that are summed by a presumption that every marriage is between cross-cousins" (Trautmann 1981:23). The semantic domain of the term māmaṉ here extends to all, and only, those men who could be the fathers of cross-cousins. As an analytic paradigm, the system of preference for bilateral cross-cousin marriage is known to generations of anthropologists as the "Dravidian kinship system."[3]

And yet the set "cross-cousin marriage" too narrowly characterizes the preferential marital relations of Dravidian kinship, at least as practiced in the parts of Tamilnadu where I charted kinship relations. I say this because for a girl, her mother's brother (her māmaṉ) is not only the father of her marriageable cousin, but he is himself her potential marriage partner.

Among those with whom I spoke in the areas of central Tamilnadu in which I conducted my research, artists and nonartists alike, marriage between a girl and her maternal uncle was just as paradigmatic as marriage between cross-cousins. (Particularly in big families, the mother's younger brother may even be close to the girl in age.) Scholars generally refer to this inclusion of the parental generation within preferential marriage options from the perspective of a male ego, rather than from that of a female ego as I have done; thus the literature will refer to the set of immediate marriageable cross-kin for a man as including "his mother's brother's daughter, father's sister's daughter, and (elder?) sister's daughter" (Trautmann 1981, 217–18). I have chosen to take the perspective of a female ego regarding the marriageable relation of a girl to her māmaṉ at least in part to establish the basis on which the life story of a particular actress, whose lineage and life's work I discuss in the concluding sections of this chapter, will turn. Further, because the set of immediate cross-kin preferential marriage partners is larger than that of cross-cousins, viewing these relations from the perspective of a female ego encourages further comprehension of the term māmaṉ by recognizing that it includes "spouse." (It also, rather more disturbingly, is by extension a common, colloquial term for "pimp," yet another intimation of the ambivalent nature of the affinity provided a woman by "known" men; see ch. 5.)

Indeed Tamil women use three terms—attāṉ, maccān, and māmaṉ—interchangeably with the exclusive term for husband (purucan). That is, while "attāṉ" and "maccān" refer to the male cross-cousin (sons of a māmaṉ who is himself already married), for a female ego all three terms may also designate "husband." In the world of Tamil cinema, two of the catchiest songs ever recorded are sung by a girl flirting with either her attāṉ or her māmaṉ; such cinematic productions encode, lyrically and melodically, the tremulous, charged affective state meant to correspond to these particular marriageable kin ties.

These terms and their usages reflect an ideal, then, not exclusively of cross-cousin marriage, but of a broader class of cross-kin marriage, which is, therefore, the term I use to refer to the preferred marriage system of Dravidian kinship throughout the ensuing discussion. Its contrastive pair is the taboo on marriage with all and any parallel kin, one's mother's sister or her children and one's father's brother or his children. These parallel uncles, aunts, and cousins are, in Dravidian kinship terminology, nondistinct from one's own father, mother, and siblings. The same terms refer to male parallel cousins and brothers (annan for elder, tambi for younger) and to female parallel cousins and sisters (akka for elder, tangai for younger). Similarly the kin terms for parallel uncles and aunts derive from the terms for father and mother respectively: appā (father) becomes periyappā (big father) or cittappā (small father) depending on the birth order of these same-sex siblings, while ammā (mother) becomes periyammā (big mother) or cinnammā (small mother) accordingly.

One of the most interesting things about the system of preferential marriages encoded into Dravidian kinship terminology is how relations of affinity ensure affective states of relation. Let me clarify this assertion. In Tamil one speaks of kinship between people as a requisite relation. To determine how two people are related, for example, one asks "What need/want is he to you?" (Avar uṅkaḷukku enna vēṇṭum?). The impersonal verb form *vēṇṭum* covers the semantic domain of both "need" and "want" (impersonal here means simply that the verb does not vary according to the person, number, or gender of the noun). The construction of the question is thus "he + to you + what + need/want?". Such a locution speaks to necessity, propriety, and requirement (shoulds and musts) but equally stongly to attachments, desires, and wishes. Vēṇṭum is coupled with the dative case marker [-kku] to identify who is "the 'recipient' of the experience" of need/want, the person "to whom (or in relation to whom) this experience happens" (Paramasivam and Lindholm 1980b, 26, 38). That is, to assess muṟai one speaks in a language of the experience of need merged with desire. Or, as Margaret Trawick sensitively writes, the Dravidian system "creates longings" and "is a powerful way of conveying, igniting, or engendering certain sentiments" between and among people (Trawick 1990, 152).

Put yet another way, the affinity encoded into Dravidian kinship is as much an inherited characteristic as are blood relations themselves:"If there are prescribed or preferred mates, what does it mean, if not that affinity in a way precedes the actual marriage, . . . that affinity in a wider sense is inherited just as 'blood' relationships are?" (Dumont 1983:22). In the systemic ideal, a marital kinship bond already exists—a girl married her mother's brother's son (or her mother's brother), a boy married his father's sister's daughter—and their offspring are poised to repeat the same marriage pattern in the next generation. This makes muṟai a desired affective state as well as a matter of given consanguinial and affinal ties: one may well grow up beside one's marriageable cousin, aware of that preferential relationship and affinity from quite early in life, being told early on that this person is to be your spouse, and calling him or her by the kinship term that names such a marriageable relation. Through such experiences one feels muṟai, and muṟai feels right, bringing with it all the concomitant feelings of self-satisfaction that accompany being and behaving in the right: behaving correctly, in the right way, *muṟaippaṭiyāka*.

Such affective states make the ideal of cross-kin marriage not just a matter of pragmatics—a further link between blood relatives, with related property benefits—but one of romantic pangs as well. Dravidian kinship terminology reinscribes such affective-normative links with every use of an interchangeable term for cross-cousin, maternal uncle, and spouse.

The descriptive use of *muṟai* begins when, as with most ideals, reality is an approximation of the ideal. According to the ethnographic record, the percentage of actual cross-kin marriages among those who use Dravidian kinship terminology is not terribly high. In one scholarly estimate actual cross-kin marriages occur in only 10 to 30 percent of all marriages (Trautmann 1981:219), and in another that figure is given more loosely as "less than 50 percent of the time" (Trawick 1990: 121). Instead, the more than half of all marriages that fall short of the ideals of muṟai often conform to those ideals only after the fact; that is, they do so by continuing to use the preferential marriage kin terms to address the spouse, each such use reasserting at least the desire for the ideal affinal relation—as in our above example of the term māmaṉ being used as "a term of address for a potential marriage partner or lover" (Trawick 1990, 153), whether or not he is actually a cross-uncle. However, as with most ideals, with muṟai there are deviations and deviations, some more recuperable than others.

The ethnographic discussion I present hereafter concerns actors' valiant attempts to approximate and successfully extend the parameters of muṟai in an effort to render their deviations acceptable. One of the brilliant aspects of this terminological system is actually how easily it can assimilate difference. By addressing her new husband as attāṉ, or māmaṉ, a wife is able to normalize even a marriage to a rank outsider. While many girl children grow up calling their marriageable uncles and cross-cousins māmaṉ, maccāṉ, or attāṉ, and carry on conjugal relations familiarly from there, others bring the affective familiarity linked to such terms into a strange new conjugal relation by using the familiar terms themselves, thereby bringing their conjugal relations more in line with the ideal (to the extent that naming something makes it so).

But the situation of which the young actress earlier spoke, that of father and daughter acting as husband and wife, or of mother and son acting as wife and husband, threatens direct conflict with the incest taboo on conjugal relations with parallel kin. The horror and shame that accompany the thought of this transgression might be difficult even for artists themselves to stave off, ingrained as these sentiments are in the language of Tamil kin terms. These are the terms that they must use to speak to each other while onstage. Seen in this light, the problem for actors resides not so much in an utter lack of muṟai as in a life that necessitates certain transgressions of it: calling your father māmaṉ, or your daughter wife. The issue of whether these transgressive relations are real, or theatrical illusion, is simply rendered moot by the linguistic reality of the speech act itself. Such are the kinds of kin transgressions that society "cannot condone on pain of the destruction of the system itself" (Trautmann 1981, 227); the destruction of muṟai (*muṟaikēṭu*) is synonymous with incest (Fabricius [1779] 1972).

It is useful to pause briefly to fully recognize the difference in gravity that corresponds to the two different types of "wrong marriage" we have just encountered as possible deviations from the ideal of endogamous, bilateral cross-kin marriage. These two possible types of wrong marriage are, again, (1) a marriage "beyond the limits of kinship or of terminological recognition," that is, an exogamous marriage, and (2) a marriage between relatives that is "wrong either in respect to crossness (i.e., marriages with parallel kin), or in respect to generation, or both" (Trautmann 1981, 223–24).

These two types of wrong marriage receive entirely different receptions in the Tamil social world, which is the point that concerns us here. While the first type, marriage outside of kin relations, is a readily recuperable wrong —and indeed is easily made the stuff of comedy, as in the Buffoon-Dance duet scenario of boy meets girl, they argue, then elope—"the second case, marriage to relatives known to be related in the wrong way, is by contrast very troublesome" (Trautmann 1981, 224–25). Trautmann's explication of the differences is clear:

> Marriages that occur beyond the limits of kinship recognition pose no particular difficulties because . . . the terminology of kinship imposes itself on [these types of] wrong marriages and regularizes them. If I marry a non-relative, my spouse's father becomes classifiable with my mother's brother [māmaṉ], my spouse's mother with my father's sister, and so on. Indeed the entirety of the new relationships I acquire by marriage are integrated into those I held prior to marriage as if I had married my cross cousin. Structure, which demands cross cousin marriage, interprets history as if cross cousin marriage had occurred, and prevails. . . . On the other hand, wrong marriages between persons who recognize relationship in stipulated kinship categories pose inescapable quandaries, for prior classifications always conflict with those created by such marriages. (1981, 224–25).

Actors thus deviate from the ideal in the profoundest of ways when they act. The young actress who explained the proverb to me by saying (as did many others), "We are actually this muṟai, but we are acting that muṟai," backed up her explanation with a story about how, in fact, this very situation had come to pass. She had indeed acted as the wife to her own father onstage. Of this she said, "You can't just refuse to do the scene because he's your father. You have to do it anyway." Transgressing this foundational tenet of the Tamil social order was unfortunately a part of the job.

The story of the indignity of publicly transgressing the foundational rule of kinship is frequently retold among stage artists, to the point where it now functions as an authenticity claim for the professional stage artist, who through this difficult experience bonds with all others who share it. When invited to speak at the annual celebration of the Madurai Actors Sangam in 1992, the exceedingly popular cinema actress Manōramā used this story in just such a way to bond with her audience. She admitted to having partaken of this most defining of duplicities when, in her early life as a stage actress enacting *Valli's Wedding* on a village stage, she had played the Heroine Valli to her own son's Hero Murugan. Now a star, she used this story to establish herself as "one of us" (to borrow the chanted refrain that proved so chilling in Todd Browning's 1932 movie *Freaks*); Manōramā counted on this story to validate her in the eyes of stage artists by showing her as having felt the keenness of their plight and its deep humiliations. She used the story to establish that her own life was just like theirs in these humble, humiliated origins.

For artists, then, the proverb names an uncomfortable experience of shame and transgression, whereas for nonartists, it functions as an accusatory morality tale and moral injunction (Don't be like actors, you'll lose all muṟai!). A college professor in Madurai with whom I discussed the proverb clarified how their being without muṟai informs her view of artists: "You cannot find the proper relationship among them. They don't belong to a particular caste. So this is like the cake that is only used on one occasion; there is no continuity, and we use them only once." Here muṟai is both proper relationship and proper social home. To the professor, the lack of muṟai ensures that these actors have no social place; she does not even recognize them as a caste. Lacking muṟai, they are unregulated, and irregular; from an audience's perspective, they appear only once, not regularly for repeated turns as in ongoing, sanctioned cycles of ordered life, for here "there is no continuity."

She finds the analogy with the Ganesh-cake apt because the cake is made only for use on the day of celebration for the god Ganesh. On that day too, like the roughly formed cakes, rough-hewn clay statues of Ganesh, also made just for this day, are sold on the streets. As part of the day's ritual, the statues are taken to a watery spot—a river, a well, the ocean if possible—and submerged there to dissolve back into clay. Their dissolution is part of the celebration, as is consuming the chubby cakes. Neither icon is finely formed, nor meant to endure; both are crude and intended for fleeting enjoyment. Just like actors, the professor asserts, who come to a town or village for a single night and a single performance and then disappear.

In contrast to this nonactor's view of artists as transient and unmoored, actors' own interpretations of their proverbial lack of muṟai provide a different picture of negation. Here actors negate muṟai by having it in excess. That is, artists may not belong to a particular caste, but they are nevertheless their own, unruly, excessive caste (a caste with no culture, even). Coexistent, multiple ways of ordering relations effectively challenge any notion of a social order that relies on a unitary concept of individual persons. Instead such interpretations assume a more relational sense of identity, one that changes as contexts change.

So rather than a simple *lack* of muṟai, actors' lives open up the possibility of multiple, coexisting muṟai.[4] The Special Drama artists I know are indeed quite good at riding such fluidity, and at maintaining fluid relational identities. For example, Jansirani's family found not just one but two viable ways to incorporate me into their family. In one muṟai, I am the younger sister of the male head of their nuclear family household. As his younger sister—actually the reincarnation of his younger sister, for she died from the smallpox they contracted together as infants, while he survived—I call him *aṇṇan* (older brother) and his wife—Jansirani—*aṇṇi* (older brother's wife). Yet the closeness between her and me was and is such that Jansi also refers to me as her first child and eldest daughter, though only eight chronological years separate us. This is our second muṟai, and the one her two biological daughters choose to use in addressing me as *akka* (older sister). They choose this muṟai, that is, over that of *attai* (father's sister), or the more generic Indian-English commonplace, "Aunty." Either of these latter would equally serve as a respectful term for a visiting female household resident; akka, however, is the warmer, consanguinial choice.

What is lovely about the coexistence of these two divergent muṟai is that I have a parallel-side-kin closeness with *both* sides of the family: with him as my brother, with her as my mother, and with their two girls as my sisters. It's odd, but it works for us. We draw on each muṟai for different occasions as appropriate. When the girls attained puberty, as their attai, I provided the bracelets for their arms, as is the expected role for an attai in the puberty rites enacted by this caste. Then later, when the girls got married, they wrote to me of their confused feelings in their new households as one would to an akka, an older sister. And their mother can explain the way she misses me now as the pain of being separated from one's firstborn child, though she also occasionally asks me to speak to her husband about family matters as only a *tangai* (younger sister) could to her aṇṇaṉ.

The ease with which this family has established and maintained these two muṟai for our relationship impresses me as creative, though I have very little by way of similar instances of coexisting multiple muṟai with which to compare it, apart from Trautmann's discussion of the similarly flexible practice of making "adjustments" to conventional rules of kin terminology that some communities have been known to make in instances of wrong kin marriage.[5]

In other instances, actors' willingness to "change murai" (*muṟai māṟṟam*) might well be seen as less felicitous, and even as demonstrating a serious lack of scruples. A. S. Tangavel Vattiyar (1920–1997), a senior member of the Madurai Special Drama community, former president of the Madurai sangam, and a respected drama teacher to several generations of artists, emphasized the deceit and confusion that can result from ignoring the prescriptions of muṟai, in effect confirming the worst laypersons' assumptions about the proclivity of artists for incestuous and improper relations. (He may, of course, also have been enjoying himself by playing up this whole transgressive image at this late stage in his life; he had a certain bachelor's reputation of his own to uphold.) In the following transcript of an interview from 1992, Revathi is a young bilingual woman from Madras assisting me by asking questions I had prepared to stimulate discussions of muṟai.

REVATHI: In Tamil there is a proverb: "Actors have no muṟai, like a Ganesh-cake has no head." What does it mean? Is there any connection between this proverb and the world of music drama today, and if so, what?

A. S. TANGAVEL VATTIYAR: We say there's no muṟai, right? Well, in our country, we put everyone into a muṟai, don't we? Like he's the older one, he's the younger one, "small father" and "big father," or the "māman" or the "maccan" (nephew), right? Well, all that is not here.

R: It is not?

AST: They change it.

R: How's that? Tell us.

T: Some go wrong, no? Some do so in matters of women. Others, in anger they won't even recognize who has been their father in this field, like a guy will get work and then just forget about his father and about paying him, too. [*This is most likely a reference to his own feeling that he has been mistreated by some of his pupils, whom he refers to as his children; Tangavel was a lifelong bachelor.*] So that's it—they have no muṟai, no sense of the proper way to do things. And then, you have some people who will just change it and go on. There was a woman who was the Sinnamma [parallel kin aunt] to one guy. And he just took her away. A good woman; she was his Sinnamma.

R: His Sinnamma?

T: Yes. His mother's younger sister. She was young and good-looking. He just took her with him. What to do? That's changing muṟai (*muṟai māṟṟam*). It happens. They change muṟai, *muṟai māṟṟam*. That's how some do it. Or another way is, the son takes the income that should go to the father. The father is going year after year to dramas, and the income should be his. They do it this way too. In both cases, there is no muṟai, THERE IS NO MUṞAI! That's what they say, and they mean there is no *pāntam*, PĀNTAM ILLAI! [no respect for relationship]. Or the tangai [*younger sister*] plays Valli. Her aṇṇaṉ [*older brother*] plays Murugan. He calls her in that familiar way, "Come here, woman, go there woman" [*as a husband calls to his wife*]. Or the brother is the Hero, Sattiyavan. The sister? Savitri. So in the love scene, he embraces her. Does it all. Can you find the muṟai in that?

R: You can't find it.

T: No. In the love scene, sister and brother make love as part of the play. Then when morning dawns, they are again aṇṇaṉ-tangai. . . . For the sake of acting, I *must* make love to my sister. That's the scene!

S: So what will come of it?

T: Oh, nothing. In the morning they will be back to just aṇṇaṉ-tangai.

R: "There is no head to the cake."

T: So where is the head? On both sides it's the same; looking at it from this way or that way, it looks the same. So where is the head?

Here is the topsy-turvy confusion wreaked by not having muṟai. Not knowing the difference between up and down, top and bottom, feet and head, how can one know to interact appropriately? An actor who takes off with his sinnamma has acted as incestuously as he would if he slept with his own mother. Here we have the two senses in which muṟai is understood to refer simultaneously to proper kin relations, and to propriety in general. Muṟai stipulates the customary way of being kin and then links that to being a decent person in general. If actors play fast and loose with the former, can they be trusted in the latter?

Yet while outsiders may deem stage actors as therefore worthy of only one-time use, artists must, to continue to live, take a longer view. They appreciate that it is by dint of their ambiguous ability to appear in such confusing guises and upside-down relations—perhaps even to change muṟai itself as it suits them—that they appear, nightly, in roles as enduring and complex as those they otherwise play by day.

Two Strategies Artists Use to Counter Kin-Related Stigma

There are two primary ways in which artists confound the accusation that they do not maintain normal, muṟai-sanctioned kin relations. The first is through their actual marital patterns, and the second through their use of kin terms *as if* they were kin. In anthropological parlance, the latter is known as "fictive kinship," though the term does not do justice to the truth of the affinities forged here. If anything, I would prefer "mimetic kinship," which at least nods to the continuity that resides, in the eye of the beholder, between this offstage domain and audience perceptions of artists' transgressions onstage.

First, actual marriage patterns among artists reflect the fact that artists do frequently intermarry across the boundaries of caste and community. After marriage, like many Tamilians, artists then employ affinal kinship terms that regularize these marital bonds and normalize the appearance of their otherwise unacceptably mixed contacts. Within this general frame, however, gender casts a long shadow, as lineages of male artists shun intermarriage with actresses.

As part of my fieldwork with Special Drama artists, I charted artists' genealogies and found multiple instances of intercaste, intercommunity, and interethnic *kalappu kalyanam*. These mixed marriages effectively linked otherwise distinct artistic clans into a large acting family and, at the time of my primary fieldwork from 1991 to 1993, bound roughly half of the Special Drama community in the city of Madurai into "real" relations of kinship. Charting genealogies in the course of my interviews with Madurai artists,

I found 150 Special Drama artists of disparate caste and community background who were all linked through eleven intermarriages across five generations. Another 31 artists, all male, belonged to extended acting families not linked to artists of other castes or communities through intermarriage. Members of these male lineages voiced their determination to maintain the ideal of endogamous marriage.

I offer these numbers to give a general sense of the kind of historical terrain that exists here, which confounds the notion that artists do not maintain sanctioned kin relations. Many artists do maintain such relations, so that often when artists of disparate castes and communities call each other "brother" or "uncle," they are in fact intercaste brothers and uncles. Since I interviewed only 75 of the 353 active members of the Madurai Actors Sangam in the course of this research, there may well be other links and nonlinks among the community of which I remain unaware. By any account, however, this preliminary reckoning of the actual linking of roughly half (150 artists) of the Special Drama community through relations of marriage and intermarriage, while significant, still touches on only half the problem.

The second half of the problem concerns the ways that artists confound sanctioned kinship practices by using kin terminology even among those *not* linked by relations of intermarriage. Such use is what Goffman (1963) calls a "cover" for what might otherwise appear to be deviant—in this case, unusually free—interaction. Artists appropriate sanctioned kin terminology to establish expedient social connections where by marriage there are none. For example, an actress may call an actor "aṇṇaṉ" so that he appears as an acceptable chaperone for her in public, while in fact they are unrelated. Likewise, backstage an actress may address an unrelated younger actor as "tambi" (younger brother) to quiet any discomfort at their sharing a backstage makeup area. In many such instances, artists deploy standard Tamil kin terms liberally across caste, community, and ethnic boundaries.

Some application of kin terms to nonkin is fairly common among Tamilians. To show respect as well as family feeling to next-door neighbors or colleagues, for example, Tamil speakers often apply benign (parallel) kin terms such as aṇṇaṉ and akka, or in English (where they do not resonate with the same connotations of marriageability) the respectfully friendly terms "aunty" and "uncle."

The acting community's use of kin terms extends this common practice. Beyond such expedient uses of kin terms, Special Drama artists also maintain a network of kin address practices that extends over time to create relations of muṟai that can and do last generations. Take, for example, again the case of (my aṇṇi) Jansirani, who hails from a matriarchal acting family of five generations. Here is her daughter's explanation of muṟai among Special Drama artists, prompted by my question "Why do artists call each other by kin terms?"

> In general, one doesn't need a reason to use muṟai in address. So in offices they will call each other "Sir" and "Madam" [to show respect]. Well, if we are friendly with our next-door neighbors, we will give them respect by calling them "Aṇṇaṉ" or "Akka." In the same way, from the very beginning, this is how it was in the drama field. And that is how it has continued; that is, all the artists at that time thought of themselves as one family, an arts family, so they began to call each other by all the muṟai of family.
>
> My mother uses muṟai terms of address with everyone. Because her mother was in this field, she introduced her to how she called them, and so she too called them in this way. This practice of placing muṟai to call people [*inta muṟaivaittu kūpiṭum paḻakkam*] is used too much by artists! They all call each other by all the muṟai. Generally they call them Akka, Aṇṇaṉ, Tangai, or Tambi [using the parallel kin terms for siblings], according to their respective ages, but since some of those who came before them also had used the terms "Attai" or "Māmaṉ" [cross-kin terms] or "Sittappa" and "Periyappa" [extended generation parallel kin terms], those newly entering the field, seeing this, will follow them.
>
> So your Aṇṇi calls N. S. Varatarajan "Māmaṉ" because he called her mother Akka. Māmaṉ is the muṟai she has with him.

Jansirani's current use of the marriageable kin term "māman" to address an important male figure in the Special Drama community, about whom I have more to say shortly, thus invokes a prior kin relation between him as younger brother to Jansi's mother as older sister. Jansi's muṟai with him thus derives from a preexisting template of affinity that she inherits: it is not simply a self-motivated choice or preference. Decisions to use terms of marriageable or nonmarriageable relation may well depend on such already established relations among artists, rather than on momentary assessments of the relation between any two given people. If an actress's husband is a musician, and he calls the men with whom he plays music "brother," those musicians will already, by extension, be in a marriageable relation to his (their brother's) wife, and she will address them as "māmaṉ" when they accompany a Special Drama performance throughout the night. Such a situation may well become a joking subplot of onstage interactions, as when a Dancer looks to her māman for help when her "husband" abuses her during the Aṭipiṭi scene (see chapter 6 for all the gory details).

Perhaps unsurprisingly, it is actresses who most often use both of these kinship strategies for mitigating stigma. They hope to marry. But if not, they liberally apply kinship terminology to mask their relations with unknown men. Male artists, on the other hand, try to distance themselves from female artists as much as possible. Recall Nagaraja Bhagavattar saying to his friend Vaiyur Gopal, "We two never married drama actresses, so don't we have *culture*?" This was an offstage comment made semiprivately during a conversation-cum-interview, but male artists often make such comments quite publicly. Recall Buffoon A. R. Arumugam's onstage quip regarding the young Dancer with whom he had just performed a love duet: "Indulging in all this is wrong; there is only one woman for one man. All these others will disappear!"

In these and related strategies that artists use to mitigate stigma, gender-differentiated usages are readily apparent. Both male and female artists grapple with an overdetermined palette in trying to improve their public and private relations, often finding themselves at cross-purposes on the two fronts. That is, gender cleaves the acting community through the different experiences of male and female artists, perhaps most profoundly in their offstage domestic lives.

For both men and women, though in different ways, honoring the distinction between known versus unknown persons is hugely important. Female artists aim to convert their fellow actors into known men through actual marriage, as well as through extended use of kin terminology. Male artists aim, instead, to distance and estrange themselves from actresses as much as possible, both by keeping intact patriarchal marriage lineages and by sharply distinguishing between themselves and actresses in onstage and offstage speech. This is the gendered reality of how the notion that artists lack muṟai affects their domestic lives. Here I offer two opposing case studies of marital patterns, first in a male, then in a female, acting family.

Known and Unknown People

Known and unknown people are frequently distinguished in Tamil speech. Known people (*terintavarkaḷ*, "those who are known") are preferable to unknown people (*teriyātavarkaḷ*, "those who are unknown") in almost every type of interaction, as markedly in affairs of the heart as of the purse. Any interaction with an unknown person is suspect as potentially the first step on a path toward increased connectedness with a foreign element, leading to who-knows-what—precisely the slippery slope charted in the "love" narrative of "boy meets girl, they argue, then elope" that plays out so centrally on Special Drama stages.

In Tamilnadu generally, new and unknown alliances are guarded against and emphasis is put on strengthening the connectedness of kin networks. Known people are not necessarily people one has directly met but rather people known by one's family, and women are enjoined to regard all such known men as their protectors. The idea is that kin, even quite extended, look out for each other, and that one's physical safety as well as moral reputation is ensured by remaining within the interactive bonds of kinship and limiting outside interaction.

Actresses mitigate the stigma of interacting with unknown men by converting them into known men, both through actual intermarriage and through the extended use of kin appellations. These are understandable strategies: if the primary problem is that actresses freely interact with unknown men, then converting those men with whom they do interact from unknown to known men should help ameliorate the problem.

Accordingly, actresses see their self-respect as strengthened by the practice of treating all members of the drama community as kin, effectively converting otherwise unknown and transgressive relations into the duly known. This is how actresses often spoke of their relations within the community, giving me the impression that, as far as they were concerned, all the men in the drama community were known people to them. One of the strongest statements of this conviction came during the course of an interview I conducted with Kasturi, a young (twenty-two-year-old) Special Drama actress from Pudukkottai. When I asked her whether, if given the chance, she would act in social dramas as opposed to Special Dramas, she replied that she would not:

> In this, our dramas, all are known people [terintavarkaḷ]. In that, all are unfamiliar people [*paḻakkappaṭāta āṭkaḷ*]. They tell you to act a particular character; there are things in it we don't like. So I won't go. They want you to act all "close." We cannot go act with unknown people with whom we are not familiar [teriyāta āṭkaḷiṭam nam pōy paḻakkamillāmal naṭikka muṭiyātu].

For this young woman, the Special Drama world is the known world. Her family includes four generations of actors on her father's side (in Rangoon, Burma), as well as numerous aunts and uncles on her mother's side who act. Her own entrance into the field was unquestioned. She is the second

50 Dancer Kasturi of Pudukkottai (second from left), with her family in 1992. (Jansirani stands at far left.)

daughter in a family of five girls to whom a boy was born only as the youngest child, and the financial pressure on the eldest girls to act was strong.

Large families of girls are a severe financial burden in Tamilnadu. In this patrilocal kinship system, girls traditionally move out of their natal home and into the groom's home when they are married, taking their domestic labor contributions with them. This particular family stood to lose four hearty daughters before gaining a daughter-in-law to replace them or their labor. At the time I interviewed Kasturi, both she and her elder sister performed in Special Drama, their two younger sisters were poised to enter the field, and their brother was just six years old (fig. 50). The entire family lived on the income generated by the girls' acting. Their father frequently accompanied them to dramas as their chaperone and also "talked drama," in particular arranging dramas in which his daughters would act.

For this young actress, Special Drama artists are her "known people." Drama people (nāṭaka makkaḷ) are her family and her world. Her familiarity with this world is the condition of possibility for her acting within it, as knownness seems to profoundly shape her experience: "We cannot go act with unknown people with whom we are not familiar."

And yet, this is perhaps the ultimate paradoxical statement for a Special

Drama actress to make! It is a statement that flies directly in the face of the general appeal of Special Drama as a genre. As its name proclaims, the "specialness" of these dramas inheres precisely in the thrill of bringing together unknown people for "special" engagements. By definition, the appeal of Special Drama lies in the unknown: Unknown actors! Meeting onstage! A different partner every night! as advertisements for the genre, since its inception, have proudly proclaimed (see chapter 2). The actress's statement is, on the contrary, the voice of her experience inside the drama world, one diametrically opposed to that of outsiders.

Hers is a self-defense of perfect inversion: actors, those paradigmatic others perpetually unknown and unknowable for everyone else, are her known-people, through and with whom she establishes her own identity. It is as if her world is the roly-poly Ganesh cake, perhaps upside down but whole unto itself, and self-protective. That such a basic, definitional tenet of their art form could be experienced so differently by artists than it is by their audiences further underscores my sense that perhaps the most special aspect of Special Drama is the creativity with which artists approach their own survival in the Tamil social world.

Highly aware both of their outsider stigma and of its appeal to their audiences, actors actually manipulate to their advantage the illusion of their unknownness in performance. For example, in the debate scenes that make up the bulk of Special Drama, audiences see one actor win and the other lose, judgments that audiences make based on what they perceive as an artist's greater display of knowledge and skill. But as one actress, a relative newcomer to Special Drama, laughingly pointed out, such knowledge and skill are taught to the actors by the same two or three drama teachers working in the Madurai community. Of the two most sought-out teachers at the time, N. S. Varatarajan generally trained the Heroes, and A. S. Tangavel Vattiyar the Heroines. "So they both already know each other's style." That is, actors know of each other as performers even if they've never met, as ongoing experience in the Special Drama community continues to convert unknown into known. Kasturi put it this way: "You see someone, you hear them talk, and from experience you know: if this is how they talk, then this is how we will answer—that's our experience, isn't it?" Yet the illusion (*poy*; falsehood) of unknownness is maintained for the audience: "It's all about making an *adjustment* between ourselves and fooling the audience, that's all."

In an important sense, then, artists' unknownness is a fantasy they enact for the audience. By contrast, a safety in knownness is their fantasy of themselves. In talking again with Kasturi I realized the extent to which these contrasts structure her life when I asked her which play was her favorite. She named *Sattiyavan Savitri*, a mythic Hindu tale of the enduring love of a wife (Savitri) for her husband (Sattiyavan). In explaining to me why this is her favorite story, Kasturi spoke of her own desire for an arranged, rather than a love, marriage. It was as though that which was unavailable to her had become the stuff of her own fantasies, the very opposite of the fantasy she plays out for the audience. Audiences thrill to the unknown meetings and love marriages enacted onstage, the illicit deviation, while her own desires center on the licit norm. In her words:

> These days, only when seeing each other directly will two people choose each other. In this drama [*Sattiyavan Savitri*] it's not like that. A princess from one land and a prince from another see each other's portrait and agree to the marriage. Then until the very end they are as one, whatever the difficulty. Until the end—even when she learns that he will die—she insists on marrying only him, and she's stubborn about it. She even goes to Yemen himself [the god of death] and stubbornly argues with him, saying, "You must give back my husband's life." And she gets it back. I really like all that.

The actress stresses the enduring nature of this union as a marriage initiated through proper channels: two families of like noble status exchange an image of potential bride and groom. Their marriage is then arranged, agreed on, and enduring. Because all was done properly, even the god of death has to concede that this wife has a right to have her husband live. Her preference for this tale of acceptable marriage starkly opposes the fantasy of modern love she is hired to play onstage.

Proper unions, meetings at a distance, and loyalty and the divine recognition of rightful marriage are all things difficult to find in the real lives of actresses. Kasturi got lucky. Two years after we spoke, she did have an official, legal marriage, as the first wife to an actor with whom she had often performed. The disdainful attitudes toward actresses held by male actors usually preclude such a marriage, and indeed the father of the groom, an actor himself, blocked the idea of this marriage for several years. Finally the young couple's stubborn, perseverant belief in the rightness of their union prevailed, just as she had dared hope it would.

For the majority of artists, this is not the case. In the final sections of this chapter, I discuss two large acting families, each of whose involvement with Special Drama spans five generations. Between these two clans, a hotly contested marriage took place in 1992. This marriage provides a potent example of how differently male and female artists view their respective acting lineages, as well as how intermarriages between them establish very real relations of mu̱rai in the community.

Prestigious Patrilines and Activist Actresses

From the kinship material that I gathered in my interviews with artists, I came to recognize five progressive generations of involvement in the genre of Special Drama by the 1990s. This span of time covers the duration of the genre in Tamil drama history. The five generations can be roughly categorized as follows.

The poet-playwright generation: the 1890s through the first decade of the twentieth century
The boys company generation: 1910 through the 1930s (with blurry edges)
The generation of older artists nearing retirement: artists aged 46–75
The generation of artists playing lead roles: artists aged 16–45
The generation of children entering special drama: aged 9–15

I refer to the two family lineages I discuss here by the names of the members of the central generation, that of older artists nearing retirement, who provided me with the bulk of the information on which these charts and distinctions draw. The first is the family of drama teacher, harmonist, and Madurai Actors Sangam president N. S. Varatarajan. His is an all-male artistic lineage pridefully maintained by the family until they were "shamed" by this marriage of one of their sons to an actress. That actress belongs to the second family, that of drama company proprietor and Heroine Ambika of Karur, whose daughter, Karur Indra, a leading actress herself, married N. S. Varatarajan's nephew.

N. S. Varatarajan's Family

N. S. Varatarajan's family belongs to the Tamil caste known locally as Servar (Cērvar). The term implies a mix. Its etymological roots are in the verb *cēr*, meaning to join, combine, or unite, and so denotes association or union, mixture or compound (University of Madras 1982). Servar is a populous caste designation in the Madurai district, as well as a well-represented affiliation among the members of the Madurai Actors Sangam.[6] It is a subcaste of the Tēvar (warrior) caste. (As explained to me, the three primary subcastes of Tēvars are Maṟavār, Akampaṭiyār, and Kaḷḷar; Servar designates any union or mix of two of these three.)[7] Categorized by the Indian government as a backward caste (BC), Tēvars are the majority caste in the Madurai district and comprise roughly 65 percent of the regional population. A large bronze statue of the famous Tēvar political leader and martyr, Mutturamalinga Tevar, graces a central intersection in Madurai, and caste pride among the Tēvar population in Madurai is palpable.

My chart of the N. S. Varatarajan family kinship maps five generations (fig. 51). The poet-playwright generation contains grandfather Namasivaya Vattiyar ("Teacher from Namasivayapuram"), whose occupation his grandsons identified simply as "poet" (*pulavar*). His friend, the poet Kandasami, who was a friend and contemporary of Sankaradas Swamigal, became the guru and drama teacher to N. V.'s son Sinnatambi. Both the poet Kandasami and Swamigal were lifetime bachelors of the Maravar subcaste. Such a poet generation of elders exemplifies claims by artists that the roots of Special Drama lie in Tamil arts and letters, rather than in village theater.

By including these two men as kin in tracing his family lineage for me, N. S. Varatarajan reflects the extent to which discussions of family among Special Drama artists often include relations that are neither consanguinial nor affinal in the strict sense. These connections have, rather, a historic, even mythic, affective quality of affinity. Here in particular, a prestige claim is being asserted in the form of a lineage connection to Sankaradas Swamigal on the basis of temperament and talent rather than blood or marriage.

Sinnatambi became an actor and a drama teacher in a boys company. He had six children, three boys and three girls. Varatarajan is the eldest son. All three sons are active in Special Drama and have attained elected or appointed posts in the management of the Madurai Actors Sangam.

N. S. Varatarajan (hereafter NSV) was an important figure for me throughout my fieldwork tenure in Tamilnadu. Initially somewhat taciturn, even brusque in manner, over the years he became avuncular (perhaps as an extension of his Māmaṉ muṟai with Jansi, whom he recognized as my close friend). Early on, I sought out NSV to help me understand the old published drama scripts I had located in bookstores and through friends. He is one of the very few people I met who was able to make sense of the information on those crumbling pages, as well as make them come alive. We both, I think, enjoyed this historical work, which he interpreted as an expression of my interest in "good" drama (i.e., old, original Swamigal plays). He began to notify me when a "specially" good cast was assembled for a drama, and wel-

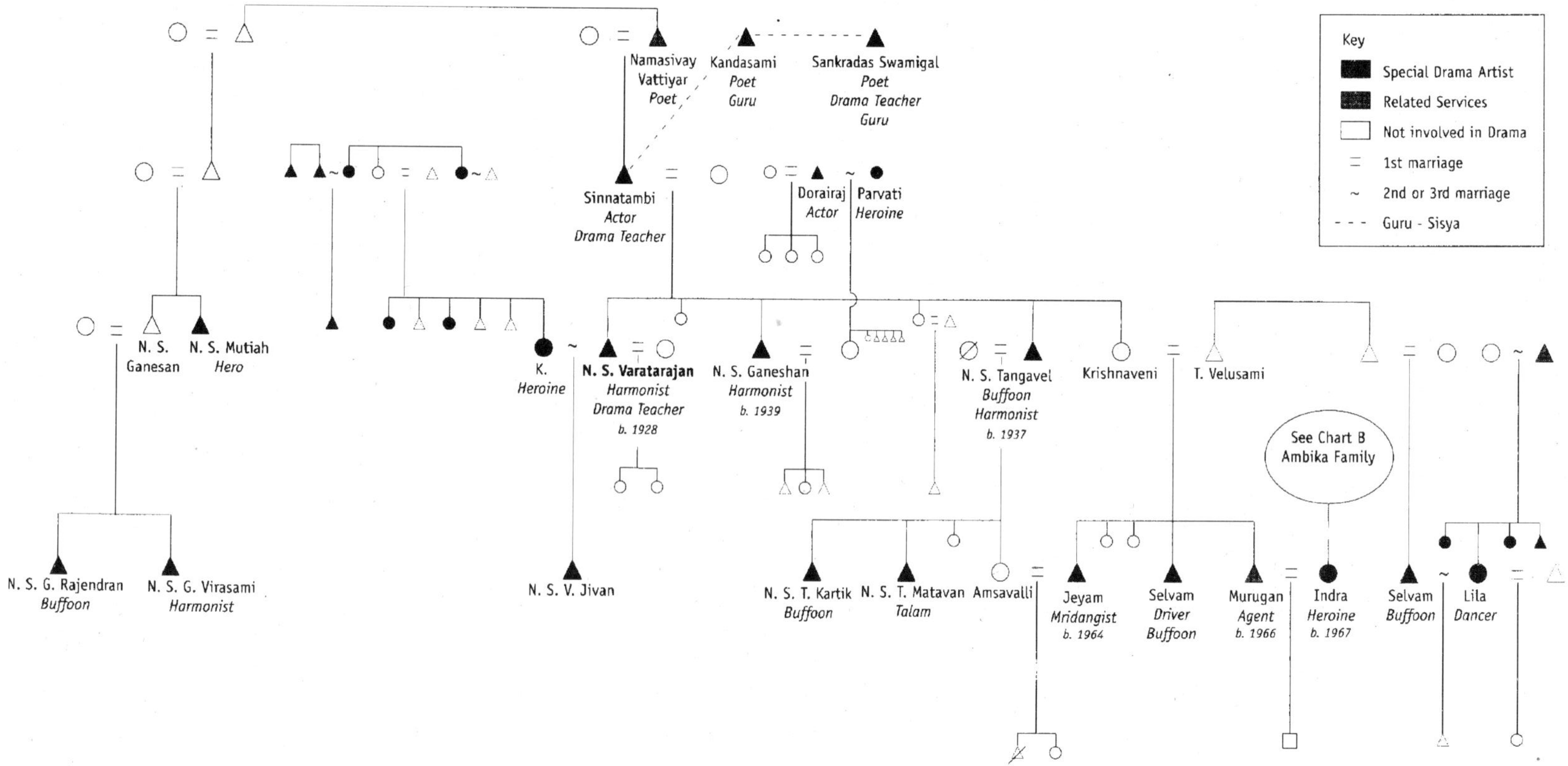

51 Kinship chart of N. S. Varatarajan lineage.

comed me to accompany the artists to the performance venue. Once there, he made sure that I was safely set up at the site before he went onstage to play harmonium all night, a courtesy I appreciated. His modulated, wait-and-see attitude toward my initial enthusiasm taught me the values of a diachronic view on the matters I sought to understand.

Born in 1927, NSV trained for ten years as an actor in the boys company in which his father taught, then in the 1940s left the company to play the harmonium in Special Drama. By the 1970s he had become a drama teacher as well, responsible for training any number of the younger generation of Special Drama actors. As a lifelong, hereditary artist possessed of what drama artists consider to be the best training available in their field, even now as a man well into his seventies NSV is one of the most steadily employed artists in the Special Drama network. He is booked to perform virtually every night in the drama season. For many dramas in which he performs he is also the drama agent, organizing performers, venue, and other requisite details of the event.

In 1994 NSV was elected president of the Madurai Actors Sangam, a post he continues to hold as of this writing. Such a prestigious status within the community is the capstone to a valued career. The features that make him so highly valued by artists include his knowledge of dramatic dialogues, music, and verse; his early training in a boys company; his ability to pass on this training as a drama teacher, especially as a teacher to other male leads; the pivotal onstage role he plays (harmonist); and the offstage figure he cuts as a patriarch in a patrilineal family of exclusively male artists. Of all these my focus here is, necessarily but nevertheless somewhat apologetically, only on the final feature in this list.

The fact that none of the women in NSV's lineage act is a significant source of family pride. All three of his sisters are married to men uninvolved in the drama community. His first two sisters married out of the family and no longer maintain any connection with the drama world at all, nor have their children entered it. His third and youngest sister, Krishnaveni, married a farmer named T. Velusami Servar, from a caste-appropriate lineage but not from within the family, who is himself uninvolved in drama. Their three sons, however, have each become involved in the drama world in some way.

The eldest son, Selvam, describes himself as having been an engineer, a driver, and a Buffoon. The middle son, Jeyam (b. 1962), is an energetic and already highly skilled mridangist who has begun to take on leadership roles in the Madurai Actors Sangam as part of the current generation of leading

Special Drama artists. Jeyam married his *muṟai peṇ*, his cross-cousin Amsavalli, daughter of his mother's brother N. S. Tangavel. She, like all the other good women in this family, remains uninvolved in Special Drama.

It is the youngest brother, Murugan, who works as a Special Drama agent, who has now seriously rocked the family boat. At the time I interviewed his mother and two older brothers, Murugan had just married Special Drama actress Karūr Indra. Before directly discussing the marriage of Murugan and Indra, however, I want to complete the portrait of NSV's family lineage traditions by discussing the complicating feature of what are euphemistically referred to as second marriages (*iraṇṭāvatu kalyāṇam*).

NSV's legal wife is a woman of his own caste who is uninvolved in Special Drama. They have two girl children, neither of whom is involved in the drama world. I have never seen, let alone met, either this wife or her children. I have, however, frequently met NSV's "second wife." K. is a tremendously gifted second-generation Special Drama actress, born in 1945. In her family, it is primarily the women who act, beginning with her mother's two sisters, then K. and her two sisters, one elder, one younger. Both of her aunts are second wives. One is the second wife of an actor whose brother also acts, and with whom she bore a child who is also an actor. Thus her familial involvement with the drama world is considerable, and a family pattern of actresses who marry as second wives is well established. Her marriage to NSV, while not legally recognized in the same way as is his other marriage, is her first and only marriage. She dates it from 1975. Together they have a son, born in 1977.

The vast majority of Special Drama actresses are second wives. Whether she seeks a husband within the drama community or outside it, an actress generally has to settle for this status, also known, rather less euphemistically than "second wife," as a *vaippaṭṭi* (kept woman) or mistress. Actresses are rarely given the respect of a legal, culturally sanctioned marriage. Such standard second-class treatment is frequently perpetuated within the acting community itself, as the NSV lineage shows. Several other patrilineal acting lineages emerged when I charted the kinship relations of other male actors of the generation of older artists, all of whom similarly took pride in not having actresses mar this picture.

Just two months after Murugan married Indra, I spoke with mridangist Jeyam, his mother Krishnaveni, his elder brother Selvam, and his sister Patma. None of them had attended their youngest brother's wedding. Through their refusal to attend, they publicly announced their vehement opposition to this move to bring an actress into the family. I asked directly why they did not want the women in their family to act. They didn't like the very idea of it, replying that they "hadn't the heart" for it. Since their grandfather's time, no woman in their family had been allowed any connection with the drama world. "The shameful time for this art began only when women came into the drama field. Our family has not had to face such a shameful situation until this time."

Somehow Varatarajan's quite public relationship with K. has been kept at a safe, second remove for this family, who could always disdainfully refer to her as his keep if they so choose. Murugan, on the other hand, actually conducted a grand wedding that showed respect for his wife. The two were engaged for over a year and prepared a proper wedding in which they officially tied a knot that now continues to rub his traditionally prestige-conscious family the wrong way.

Karūr Ambika's Family

Figure 52 provides the kinship chart of the bride's family. The Ambika clan are Reddiyars originally from the state of Andhra Pradesh, and their mother tongue is Telugu. They now live in Tamilnadu in the city of Karūr, north of Madurai.

Ambika (b. 1937) began acting at the age of five. Both her parents were actors. Her father was one of three brothers, all actors; Ambika describes their father, her grandfather Angumuttu, as a poet. Her mother, an actress, had two sisters and one brother, all of whom acted. Their mother—Ambika's grandmother Mayamai—had three sisters and one brother, none of whom acted. However, both Mayamai and her younger sister married the same man, a drama fan and bit-part actor, and many of their children and the children of another of Mayamai's sisters entered the drama field. The many intermarriages of these artists with other artists have created a dense web of muṟai that now links the members of two previously separate Muslim acting families to this Telugu-speaking Hindu family, in addition to a Malayalam-speaking Hindu family. (For visual clarity, fig. 52 does not include all these subsequent marriages.)

In 1944, when Ambika was seven years old, her parents married her to her māmaṉ, her mother's younger brother, K. T. Rattinappa. This was considered a *muṟaikkattu*, a proper marriage. He was twenty years older than his bride, and already in love with another woman, with whom he promptly ran off after the wedding ceremony. Thus though Ambika is his muṟai bride and

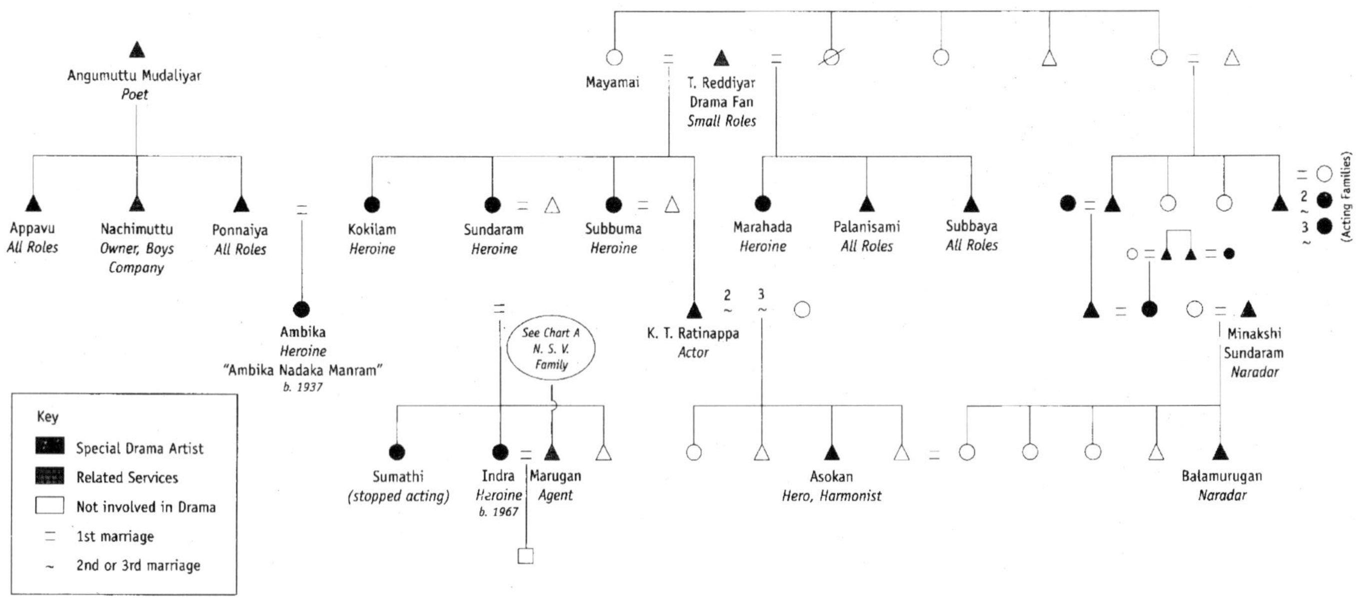

52 Kinship chart of Karūr Ambika lineage.

official first wife, she considers his lover to be his real first wife. As Ambika tells it, at age seven she was simultaneously made a child bride and a second wife, a humiliation adding insult to injury. Later, her husband took yet another wife, with whom he had four children. Subsequent intercaste, intercommunity, and interethnic intermarriages among these children have continued to link this family with numerous other families in the drama world.

Ambika speaks of her experience of child marriage as haunting her entire life. She has made her art form, Special Drama, the vehicle through which she brings an anti-child-marriage message to the world by regularly enacting onstage a story very similar to the story of her life.[8] One of the repertory dramas in the canon of plays scripted by Sankaradas Swamigal, the drama *Kōvalan Kaṇṇaki*, became the signature piece of the drama company that Ambika founded in Karūr (the Ambika Nāṭaka Maṉṟam). She has also been president of the Karūr Actors Sangam and is a drama teacher herself.

As written by Swamigal, the drama *Kovalan Kannaki* retells a famous Tamil sangam era epic from the second century A.D., *Cilappatikaram* (literally, the tale of the anklet). The story is of Kannaki, a child bride, whose husband, Kovalan, falls in love with a courtesan, spends all his time and money on her, and winds up a pauper. The righteous child bride Kannaki spends her own chaste life trying to repair the dissolute mess wrought on her husband's life by his infidelity. The famous end scene has the entire city of Madurai burning in the flames of Kannaki's righteous revenge.

The parallel between Ambika's life as an abandoned child bride and that of the epic heroine Kannaki has been the fulcrum of the actress's life and work. Ambika's revenge, and her activism, consists in performing her story through the vehicle of the *Kovalan Kannaki* drama, repeatedly, each time spreading the message to other young women at risk for the same depravities and humiliations.

The figure "of a virtuous woman rebuking society" (Weidman 2003, 199) is a common trope of many enduring Tamil stories, from the classical age of Tamil literature to the present, where its powerful rearticulation in the world of the contemporary Tamil performing arts attempts to ensure Tamil women's respectability in the era of modern culture contact. However, in the usual scenario, such stories pit the virtuous woman against the actress; the virtuous woman is never herself an actress. Amanda Weidman documents, for example, how female singers and musicians entering the world of concert stage performing in the twentieth century maintained their virtue by distinguishing themselves specifically from dancer-actresses, those women who move around and express themselves physically onstage. Respect accrued to female artists in the music world in direct proportion to their ability to distance themselves from that quintessential degraded other. For respectable middle-class women who entered the performing arts as musicians in the twentieth century, the common story is one in which the virtuous good woman defines herself precisely against those "characterless ladies," the courtesan actress, "the devadasi, a woman outside the bonds of conventional marriage," who provides "an almost unspeakable contrast against which any [self-respecting] female musician had to place herself" (Weidman 2003, 199).

Likewise the courtesan Mathavi in the *Cilappatikaram* epic, the woman on whom the dissolute Kovalan wastes all his money and time instead of using it to be a good householder and husband to Kannaki, is a Dancer. Mathavi is the bad woman, and Kannaki the home-dwelling, respectable woman. Given this common story wherein the virtuous good woman opposes the courtesan actress, Ambika's radicalism inheres in her choice to embody the subject position of the righteous woman *as an actress*. By making this play her crusade, Ambika embodies a previously unarticulated subject position. She asserts that she, an actress, can lay claim to the righteous discourse of the wronged child bride.

With this move, Ambika mobilizes the discourse of respectability for actresses. The surprising radicalism of the move lies in her embodied stance: that actresses are women also entitled to self-respecting lives. The move is made not in the overtly staged story, which follows the normal scripted lines, but rather on that powerful double level on which all performances of Special Drama operate: audiences see artists simultaneously as themselves and as the roles they play, and are constantly making judgments about this fit. It is the enduring paradox of the Special Drama actress's life that as a Heroine she must act *both onstage and off* as if she were not an actress. But here Ambika is known by all her audiences as the proprietor of the drama company that bears her name. She is that anomalous creature, a self-respecting actress, whose life's work is to argue against the humiliations that may be practiced on women in the name of "proper marriage." That is, here is a woman of the very class of women usually accused of being characterless, without culture, caste, or muṟai, asserting her right to embody the position of the child bride wronged by the injustices of social propriety in the form of muṟaikkattu, a social practice normally seen as the definition of propriety, the proper cross-kin marriage.[9]

Bringing together the two kinship sagas of the NSV clan and the Ambika clan, we see how speaking against the dominant system of traditional family lineages makes Ambika's stage acting simultaneously an act of powerful activism. Ambika speaks from experience, as a first wife, against the constraints of mu̱rai marriage. She thinks that being a first wife under such circumstances is tantamount to being second best. She is a first wife scorned, and she throws in the face of the male acting lineage their assumption that actresses cannot be righteous women by showing that it is through her enactment of her own life story of the offended child bride that she will make her mark on the drama world, and will do so from within the constraints of a classic drama, the very kind the NSV lineage also values so highly.

At age twenty-five, Ambika's daughter Indra, who works out of the much larger Special Drama network in Madurai, had already been one of the generation of leading Special Drama artists for several years. NSV's nephew Murugan, at twenty-six, had already been active as a drama agent. Indra's family had no objections to the marriage and attended in grand style, while the groom's family, as we have seen, were absent. When I left India in 1993, Indra was pregnant with their first child.

Many Mu̱rai

Both the onstage and offstage practices of the Special Drama community confound any black-and-white map that attempts to separate out the real and the fictive among its members. Artists act across this ostensible divide. Onstage, they do so through the mimetic imitation of people who they "really" are not. Offstage, they do so occasionally through the assumption of kin relations they "really" ought not to claim. Such practices taint the reputation of the acting community and stigmatize it as excessively, mimetically mobile—fluid, verging on the unstable—in social realms generally ordered by marking the right place for one and all.

However, we have seen that artists also establish and maintain kin mu̱rai in a range of ways, through appellative and affective strategies as well as by marriage. Some are creative with the former, like Jansirani, who links us with two mu̱rai. In the latter, some artists guard mu̱rai determinedly, like NSV's family. Still others make a social statement of challenging the norm, like Ambika's condemnation of society's blind adherence to mu̱raikkattu when it can actually ruin a girl's life.

We have also seen how acting itself often creates confusion in terms of mu̱rai, even for actors themselves. A brother and sister embrace each other as lovers all night, then at dawn's light are back to being brother and sister. Or mother and son, or father and daughter. Artists themselves feel these roles as discomfiting transgressions of the most deep-seated taboos. But clearly the problem here too is one of excess rather than lack, of expanded rather than singular muṟai.

Expansive, excessive, even hypermobile, actors mix elements that ought to remain discrete: styles, genres, castes, religions, and relations of all kinds. In the end, neither of the two strategies that artists use to counteract the stigmatizing reputation that they lack kinship muṟai has had much positive effect, and their alternative muṟai go unrecognized as such. Half the time, artists do actually intermarry, and the other half of the time, they act as if they are related anyway; yet neither strategy accomplishes any true conformity of artists' lives with muṟai understood as a unitary discourse of affinity that is based on cross-kin marriage as the normal course of events. Rather, given such a norm, in their offstage lives artists are essentially in a damned-if-you-do, damned-if-you-don't situation, wherein "really" intermarrying transgresses social boundaries about as much as does "faking" muṟai by using imitative naming practices to cover unsanctioned relations. At bottom, it seems, everything actors do is colored by the fact that it is they who do it: if actors are definitionally those without muṟai, all their attempts to gain muṟai are read as fakes, and blasphemies of the real.

Too many things mix in them; their stigma inheres, counter to any simple proverbial notion of lack, in their presentation of a surfeit of variables.[10] They offer orders where there should simply be order and a plurality where there should be singularity. Many people, artists and nonartists alike, glossed the Ganesh-cake piece of the proverb to me by saying, "The koḻukkaṭṭai has neither head nor tail, no clear orientation. And actors have no muṟai." True, a Ganesh-cake has neither head nor tail, neither east nor west. But both the cake and the world are round. And actors, actually, have many muṟai.

Epilogue

We have seen how actors trouble "Tamil culture" with the threat of instability, of a heightened mobility whose excesses of muṟai are decried as lack. A good metaphor for this status-which-is-not-one is flowery, so bear with me.

Every morning in villages across Tamilnadu, innumerable quantities of identical white jasmine buds are picked from jasmine bushes and brought to market. The buds are individually tied and strung together into long, fragrant white ropes, which are then purchased by, or for, women to tuck into their oiled, braided hair, the sweet smell of jasmine surrounding them all day. These flowers are appreciated when they are identical, neat and orderly, linear and of one pure scent—like the black braid itself, plaited with coconut oil. The most expensive of these jasmine strands are made from the bud variety that is straight rather than round; the straight buds line up even more precisely and neatly when tied than the round ones (plate 9).

Flower Garlands

Strands of colored blossoms are also for sale at flower stalls. These are bright orange or purple. The petals of these blossoms are unruly, not tight like the jasmine buds, and resist the best efforts at neatness and conformity. Strung bouquets of these more colorfully recalcitrant flowers go for half the price of the pure jasmine ropes. These less-expensive strands are usually worn by little girls, from whom a certain unruly exuberance is to be expected as a natural condition of childhood. A grown woman wearing the colorful strands normally worn by a girl would not be the object of derisive laughter so much as a slightly condescending compassion: she is poor but making a recognizably good effort to conform.

Finally, there is one other type of strand sold in flower stalls at market, a mixed strand of blossoms, buds, and leaves. It is not meant to be worn in the hair at all but rather is used exclusively in worship (*puja*) for gods. Any flower may be offered in puja, since gods are notoriously better suited to managing mixedness and disorder than people. These strands are called *kathambam*.

"Kathambam" means "flowers of different kinds, leaves of aromatic plants strung together," as well as the general condition of being mixed, and of mixture (Cre-A 1992). The same word is used to refer to Special Dramas made up only of comedy scenes, which are performed by Buffoons and Dancers with no dramatic roles for Heroes or Heroines at all. Kathambam performances are not considered to be *drama* at all. Though many claim to disdain such events, artists included, the sangam receipt books reveal that in the 1992 and 1993 seasons, stagings of Kathambam were the fifth most popular event for which Special Drama artists were hired (displacing a long-time repertory favorite in Madurai bookings, the mythological drama *Pavalakkodi*).

Beyond a metaphorical use of the term "kathambam" to refer to a particular, popular yet disavowed comedic event, the drama community as a whole is like a string of mixed flowers worn in the hair. Where one expects a cultivated, pure conformity there is instead a colorful multiplicity considered less than beautiful. Kathambam strands are appropriate for decorating gods, but not humans.

What to make then of people who, like mixed strands of flowers, are well placed in the service of entertaining gods but are often seen to be inappropriately mixed on a human scale? Since actors are quite clearly human rather than divine beings, their free and colorful melange is judged harshly. Only while onstage, wearing the robes of gods and representing the lives of gods, and occasionally of children, are actors indulged, revered, and respected. Such is certainly not the case when they play comedy scenes. And offstage, like everyone else, they are expected to keep their expressivity more tightly in line.

Perhaps the kind of disorder actors exhibit is too much like that of gods or children to be acceptable in the everyday world. Gods and children alike may be tricksterish, unkempt, extreme, and irrational; they are not held to, or bound by, the same social norms as adults. Gods and children can get away with social pranks that adults cannot: think of the child Krishna stealing butter, or a bit later hiding the Gopi's clothes, or of Murugan taking the guise of a tribal hunter to woo Valli, and of Naradar stirring up commotion just for the fun of it. Any number of Hindu gods gleefully don guises and call it *lila*, play, like child's play. Actors are in the business of putting on plays, a rather different matter. And yet clearly the three beings—actors, gods, and children—have some important qualities in common.

The first Indian films, silents by D. G. Phalke made in the early decades of the twentieth century, took the child Krishna as their subject, played beautifully and quite naturally by a child actor. These films provide an excellent example of a ready association of like qualities: the adorable child is a god and vice versa, and even just maybe, the adorable child is a god is an actor and vice versa. (Certainly in the merged histories of Tamil politics and Tamil cinema, the association of actors with the gods they have played onscreen has played out on-the-ground in hugely influential ways; see Pandian 1992; Baskaran 1981, 1996.) In the annual Chittirai festival in Madurai, when the goddess Meenakshi and her groom Lord Sundareshwaran are conveyed on their wedding day in a chariot through the city, they are invariably played by children. Likewise in North Indian theatrical ritual enactments of the Ram Lila, all the divine characters are played by local children (Kapur 1990). Children have long been seen in India as well suited to divine roles and to acting in general. When in exasperation Sankaradas Swamigal left his adult drama company to start a boys company, he did so on the premise that children are divinely malleable. Evidently inspired by the Tamil proverb "What won't bend at five, won't bend at fifty" (Gunasekaran 1987, 17), Swamigal clearly believed in making the child actor bend to his will in the service of a more artful staging of mythological dramas.

Given such historically linked trajectories in the representational arenas of Tamil myth, politics, and art, if gods and children are so consistently considered adorable doing disorderly things, why not actors?

The primary problem lies, as we have seen, with the illusory nature of acting itself. Actors are blasphemers of the real who *appear* as gods and children but are actually human adults. As such they should be bound by the responsibilities and social strictures of kinship, caste, and culture. The claim we have seen made repeatedly by historians and critics of Tamil drama, as well as by many artists, is above all that actors need discipline to counteract their lack of muṟai. The same discourse is reiterated by the sangam in rules and regulations that aim to rein in what are seen as the excesses of artists, regardless of the integral part that their theatrical expressivity (so often conflated with excess in these discourses) plays in making for good, captivating acting. Audiences play into both sides of this tension by paying the largest sums to Buffoons and Dancers (or to those Heroes and Heroines who behave like them) while simultaneously greeting their comedic acts with a judging, corrective laughter aligned to the status quo. Each Special Drama artist must find his or her own way to navigate these tensions, onstage and off.

Jansirani and Sivakami, 2001

Jansirani has lived her artistic life in Special Drama as a loyal worker and friend, relying heavily on interpersonal openness to support her in this community and on community itself as a kind of buffer against degradation. Sivakami, on the other hand, has always spoken of herself as an outsider even to this community, from which she expects only constraints on her art.

On my return visit to Madurai in 2001, I spent time hanging out in the sangam building and interacting with many artists I had known in the early 1990s. I wanted to see Sivakami again too, though she was never there. She would have been involved in Special Drama for over a decade by then, and I wanted to see how she had fared. I asked about her at the Sangam and learned that she still did live in Madurai, though no one knew exactly where. Her sangam membership was still current, but the clerk had no address for her.

After we had asked around for several days, one of the old men who often chaperones actresses to dramas gave us a lead. She lives over the bridge in a neighborhood on the outskirts of Madurai, the same one, in fact, where Jansi too now lives.

Jansi and I went to that place. Sivakami did not live on the street the old man thought she did. Nevertheless, fueled by her enduring determination to help me, Jansirani asked for information from strangers on the street, and we eventually found Sivakami.

She was living in a tiny one-room flat. Her widowed mother was with her at the time. She was no longer acting in dramas herself (she was of that age), but her niece was now a Dancer in Special Drama, and during the season this girl came from Madras to stay with Sivakami while she worked. This was the same girl who had stared so unflappably into my camera lens as a preadolescent. Twenty now, she had already been through too much in these nine elapsed years, including a failed marriage and the death of a child to fever. When I told Sivakami how difficult it had been to find her flat, with her old outsider sensibility still intact she replied: "Special Drama, these people are all from here, I am not, so I stay away."

Pain, and painful irony. In 2001 these two actresses, Sivakami and Jansirani, different in so many ways, both of whom had proved central to my understanding of what the life of a Special Drama actress entails and especially of the range of choices one has in that life, had come to the end of their acting careers and were now each living alone in single-room rented flats on the outskirts of Madurai, where rents were cheaper than in town.

Jansirani's two daughters have married and now live with their husband's families and have started families of their own. Her husband has moved on to a third wife. Alone after fifty, the age when it is no longer easy to find work as a Special Drama actress, this gregarious woman whose whole life had been centered around this art form and its center in Madurai now walks over the bridge into town and back again to save bus fare. And as if all the stigmas of poverty, acting, and being a second wife and now a woman alone weren't enough, a health condition has worsened over the past several years in ways that make face-to-face interactions awkward even for someone so used to mixing with all kinds of people.

Yet even in the despondency brought on by the penurious conditions of her present life, Jansirani finds ways to express her faith in the possibility of social redemption. She does not simply walk the bridge into town; she walks it barefoot, an act of humility and devotion. One must be barefoot to enter a Hindu temple, not to defile this sacred space with the animal carcass that is shoe leather. The sentiment is extended to walking on any sacred grounds, and thus one respectfully removes one's shoes to enter a Hindu home. To walk barefoot outside extends this same regard to the sanctity of the earth and one's relation to it. Saints, saddhus, gurus, bhaktiyars, devotees, and ascetics of all kinds who have stepped off the path of the Hindu householder and into a life of renunciation and devotion walk India barefoot.

The path of the religious Hindu pilgrim is open to women at two ends of their lives, when they are of either premenstrual or postmenopausal age. Their childbearing years, on the other hand, generally land women squarely within the reproductive paradigm of the wife of the householding husband, concerned with family and home, for which there are numerous wifely role models in Hindu mythology (Savitri being most often invoked as the picture of wifely loyalty). But there are also role models for Tamil women who choose a devotional path. Frequently cited among them is Auvaiyar, a female poet of the sangam era (c. 100 B.C.–250 A.D.). (The name Auvaiyar means "mother" or "respectable woman.") The poet was a professional bard in the court of a Tamil king, and she wrote both akam and puṟam poems, 59 of which are extant. While not much of her life is certain, stories, myths, and legends abound. Many of these offer solace to women who want nothing of the worldly, wifely role. As a young girl whose life revolved around her devotion to Siva, as one such legend has it, Auvaiyar did not want to switch her affections to a man. Instead she prayed to be allowed to follow the path of her devotion and received the boon of skipping entirely her child-bearing years: she was transformed over a matter of days into a "wrinkled, gray-haired, saggy-breasted woman, upon which she was overcome with joy, knowing she was safe from the world" (Gurudeva 2000, 326).

Jansirani is opting to follow an increasingly devotional path, much as I have seen other Special Drama actresses do as they age (see plate 10). Understand that these women are not involving themselves in the kind of political Hindu fundamentalism that has so violently characterized much of North Indian communal life during this same decade of which I write. The Hindu nationalist (Hindutva) ideology of the VHP (World Hindu Council) and its political wing the BJP (Bharatiya Janata Party) espouse a politics of extreme *exclusivity* that has erupted repeatedly in communal violence between Hindus and Muslims since 1992, smashing earlier Gandhian and Nehruvian founding ideals for the secular nation of India and replacing them with one designated for Hindus only. Such sentiments are the very opposite of those of the Special Drama acting community, which is, as we have seen, a community based on radical *inclusivity*: all religions welcome, all ethnicities welcome, and all castes welcome. The only codified rules concerning politics in this community are sangam rules that prohibit any mention of politics, or of any specific political parties, by artists or by drama sponsors in any connection with a Special Drama performance. Special Dramas are intended as events that overtly take themselves out of the emotionally charged political realm and instead support "the values of patriotism, cooperation, love, nonviolence, and chastity" (see appendix 1). While we may indeed recognize a politics in these categories of value themselves, nevertheless, in the decade of spiraling communal violence in which I came to know all the Special Drama artists I write of here, none sided with fundamentalist parties or espoused nationalist ideologies. When retired Special Drama actresses make devotional pilgrimages to Murugan temples or to goddess temples, these are conducted more in the spirit of Gandhian asceticism and renunciation than Hindutva.

As their careers wane, a path of increasing devotion appeals to actresses for good reason. The profession of actress has brought these women a certain disrespect all their lives, even if they were highly talented artists. Once they are done with the part of the job that gives at least short-term rewards—the pay, the applause, and that sense of righteousness that can come from even temporarily embodying high personages and expressing high ideals—

the offstage reputation of having been an actress can sting unremittingly. Alone is hard, and isolating; devotion offers succor.

> *What She Said*
>
> Shall I charge like a bull
> Against this sleepy town,
> Or try beating it with sticks,
> Or cry wolf
> Till it is filled with cries
> Of Ah's and Oh's?
>
> It knows nothing, and sleeps
> Through all my agony, my sleeplessness,
> And the swirls of this swaying south wind.
>
> O what shall I do
> To this dump of a town!
> (Auvaiyar, *Kuṟuntokai* 28, trans. A. K. Ramanujan 1967, 31)

Stigma and Its Sisters

Many of the strategies artists use to avoid stigma involve somehow hiding within the norm, or bending its parameters to include themselves. An apt (if terminologically somewhat contradictory) locution for these strategies might be "hiding out within" the norm. They are essentially minimizing strategies: they aim to minimize any stigmatizing differences between drama artists and dominant Tamil society. We see actresses using such strategies in creating private spaces in the public sphere, an attempt to garner some of the respect that insideness affords respectable women. We see such a strategy again in artists' use of kin terms to address each other. We see Buffoons use a minimizing strategy onstage to distance themselves from improperly "dirty" words (and women) through the use of stage asides and sideways glances, allying themselves instead with more proper sentiments. Finally, the sangam's strategies for elevating the reputation of the drama art and its artists, strategies that aim at increasing artists' conformity to acceptable social norms and minimizing their differences, are perhaps the fullest realization of this tack.

In all these instances, artists leave dominant distinctions between proper and improper behaviors intact while they attempt to slip themselves into the favored category. Any such strategy cuts both ways: it reinscribes the continuing salience of the dominant terms of social organization, while it also slyly subverts those same norms by *expanding* them to include artists. As such, these strategies do not involve passing or covering so much as an attitude toward dominant categories that operates on the assumption that they are, or can be made to be, more malleable than usually imagined. Therein lies their strength.

Yet however effective such strategies may be for individuals in the short term, they do not offer artists much in the way of an empowered, collective community identity. In fact, they tend to erase any base of difference from which to mobilize, offering artists no positive vantage point from which to appreciate the uniqueness of their subculture. Of the few strategies we have seen depart from this minimizing model, the first does not move toward collectivity at all. It is the strategy used by individual artists who choose to flaunt rather than flatter, and to be brazen rather than to blend. Theirs is what we might see as a strategy that maximizes difference, and what my students like to call being a "stigma diva." Here however, like Sivakami, the stigma diva—her glamour notwithstanding—seems to wind up in much the same straits as her more cautious counterparts.

Another different kind of strategy informs the Drama Tongue. While the argot clearly recognizes dominant cultural categories, it also recognizes the acting community's own differentness *as a group* in a new way, and consolidates that recognition into a new vocabulary. In so doing, the Drama Tongue prompts us to question what "insideness" means for Special Drama artists, and to pry open earlier discussions of standard structural distinctions in Tamil conceptions of inside and outside that may well be too rigid to capture the kinds of spaces, psychological and literal, inhabited by Special Drama artists. The Drama Tongue bespeaks public and private spheres that are both more connected and more permeable than they at first appear, reflecting the kinds of hybrid social spaces artists inhabit.

Building upon this, a powerful strategic use of her own hybridity appears in the activist role taken on by actress Ambika. From within a classic drama in the Special Drama repertory, she speaks up against kinship practices that keep women from living fuller lives. As both an actress and a scorned first wife and child bride, Ambika uses the Special Drama stage to challenge the inequalities of a kinship system that seems to value male prestige at the expense of women's social and self esteem.

Together, stigma-minimizing strategies, stigma-maximizing strategies, and strategies of disarming hybridity alike all aim to refigure the social world in ways that make it a more, rather than less, hospitable home for artists. In the short term these strategies are mostly effective, in their circumscribed ways. But actresses still suffer the most, and without a progressive discourse that values the long term social benefits of communities of difference and radical inclusivity, I worry that the home in this world for retired actresses will remain lonely indeed.

Appendix 1

Sangam Rules

Tamilnadu Drama Actors Sangam (Madurai)

Rules according to the Sangam founding laws of 1975 and 1978, detailing organization, the Sangam's goals, and the way it is structured

DETAILS

1. Name of this Sangam:
   Tamilnadu Drama Actors Sangam
2. This Sangam will function at the following address:
   8A/1, Sunambukara Street, Madurai-1
3. *Goals of this Sangam:*
   3a. To take the actions necessary to protect from destruction the Tamil music drama art, to reform it, and to encourage the progress of the actors and actresses who undertake it.
   3b. To make efforts to get assistance from the public, the government, and the Tamilnadu Iyal Isai Nāṭaka Manṟam [Prose-Music-Drama Society] to establish a free school and to obtain the facilities to conduct research into historical texts for the progress of drama.
   3c. To arrange to bring in appropriate teachers to teach the skills of song, dialogue, acting, and dance.
   3d. To make efforts to settle any disputes which arise between Sangam members and those with whom they interact.
   3e. To take actions against (1) those who do not give the artists their salary after the performance of a drama, (2) those artists who create unnecessary problems after receiving their money from those who contracted the drama, (3) any others who blackmail or get money from the drama actors and actresses in any other improper way, and (4) those who cancel a drama without appropriate reason, after a date has already been fixed and the advance paid.
   3f. To take up unanimous action for the progress of drama and the unity of drama artists by conducting conferences at the district, state, and national levels, to which state representatives will be sent.
   3g. To give additional assistance to members' families during both auspicious and inauspicious occasions.
   3h. To protect old dramas filled with the values of patriotism, cooperation,

love, nonviolence, and chastity, and to help conduct the new dramas of the present time [according to such values].

3i. Generally, to take up any and all actions which might aid in securing the well-being and prosperity of the actors, actresses, and musicians.

RULES

1. Name of the Sangam: Tamilnadu Drama Actors Sangam
2. Members:
   Men and women artists who either were born in Tamilnadu and have taken up work in the field of music drama, or else who were born in other parts of India but have become involved in the field of Tamil music drama, and who are above the age of eighteen but within the age of thirty-five, may join as members of this Sangam. Those under the age of eighteen who are talented in this art may join through their guardians as honorary members, but they will not have the right to vote on Sangam actions.
3. Subscription:
   One rupee will be collected as yearly dues from those who have joined as members. When new members are taken in, an entrance fee, to be decided by the Action Committee, will be collected along with the yearly dues.
4. Rights and benefits of the members of this Sangam:
   Each member of this Sangam has the right to vote on the decisions taken in the General Assembly meeting; to select the members of the Action Committee; to contest for a post in the Action Committee; and to receive the benefits which arise from the fulfillment of the Sangam's goals.
5. The Action Committee of the Sangam will decide, examining each situation, the rules to be followed by members amongst themselves, with those taking up the drama art, and with those general people organizing dramas.
6. The Action Committee will decide whether a member should be suspended from the Sangam or subject to a fine, should that member act against the rules of the Sangam, or should that member behave in such a way that might spoil the reputation of the Sangam, or should that member not pay the membership dues before the end of the month of March. If the member feels that the decision taken is against him, the member should complain within fifteen days from the date the decision was taken. This complaint will be reconsidered by the Action Committee, at which time the given decision will be final. The suspended member's membership can be canceled with an approval in the General Assembly meeting; the member on whom such action is taken must be informed of such action ten days in advance.
7. Actions to be taken against any members of the Sangam Management or Action Committee who break Sangam rules:
   If members of the Action Committee or members of the Management of this Sangam go against the rules and regulations, or if they do not present themselves in three committee meetings consecutively, the actions to be taken

against them will be decided in the monthly meeting of the Action Committee. This would then be brought to the General Assembly meeting for a final decision, where the action to be taken would be decided ultimately by the General Assembly through majority vote.

8. Management Committee:

   A. There are fifteen places: a president, a secretary, a vice president, a vice-secretary, a treasurer, and ten committee members. Each of these places will be filled through elections held in the General Assembly meeting once every three years.

   B. Those who wish to contest for a post in the Management Committee, must (1) be not less than twenty-one years of age, (2) be up to date on payment of dues, (3) have no outstanding debts to the Sangam, and (4) be someone who has not been punished for taking actions in opposition to the Sangam.

   C. Once elected, Management Committee members will hold their posts for three years. After three years, the elected member has the right to contest again, and again be elected to a post in the Management Committee.

   D. Any vacancy which arises in between elections should be filled by a majority vote at a meeting of the Management Committee. The elected member will then hold this post for the remaining period of service of this Management Committee.

9. A file containing members' addresses and full details, accounts books, and other registrations and books should be kept in the office of this Sangam. It is the responsibility of the staff persons to continue to maintain them properly. The Sangam office will be open from 9 A.M. to 1 P.M., and from 4 P.M. to 9 P.M. The registers and books should be kept in the Sangam office and should be maintained in such a way that the staff or members can look through them (they must be available for the scrutiny of any staff person or member) on any working day during the above stated timings. Any property of the Sangam should not be taken out without the permission of the Management Committee.

10. The Management Committee should meet at least once a month. Whenever the president feels that it is necessary to call for a special meeting, he can do so. The president can do so with the consent of one-third of the committee members. Through this and within ten days from the day he gets the consent, he can call for a special committee meeting. Such a committee meeting can proceed only if one-third of the total committee members are present. The matters to be discussed should be printed clearly, and notices should be distributed seven days in advance of the meeting.

11. The president should head all Sangam meetings, ensuring that they are conducted peacefully, and all actions and decisions taken must be noted down and signed by him.

12. The vice president must help the president, and take over all his responsibilities in the president's absence.

13. In the absence of both the president and the vice president, those members of

the committee who have come shall select among them one person to lead the meeting. Should a tie vote arise on any issue, he who is leading the meeting may cast the deciding vote.

14. The Sangam secretary should generally supervise and inquire after the maintenance and matters of the Sangam. Moreover he is responsible for the matters listed below.

A. Taking up letter correspondence on behalf of the Sangam. All documents should be kept with responsibility.

B. Keeping an account of the subscriptions, donations, and other funds of the Sangam by giving receipts. After expenses in accordance with the rules, the balance should be submitted to the treasurer. The secretary should help the treasurer in collections and in other works related to the accounts.

C. Recording the actions that take place within the committee meetings.

D. Ensuring, in consultation with the president, the publication of the notices and schedules of the Management Committee, and of both ordinary and special Sangam General Assembly meetings.

15. The vice-secretary should help the secretary in his work and take up the responsibilities of the secretary in his absence. But if only the secretary has the right to some decisions, he alone can make them.

16. The treasurer should maintain the accounts of this Sangam. The subscription donation and entrance fee, as well as any other gifts, should be collected by issuing receipts with the signature of the secretary. The treasurer should keep track of it in the accounts register, which should be ready for inspection by the Management Committee. The treasurer should keep with him a cash amount of 300 rupees; the balance amount should be deposited in the bank. If the president or secretary feels it necessary to spend for the Sangam, the treasurer can give the amount through proper vouchers.

17. *Yearly General Assembly Meeting*

1. The yearly General Assembly meeting will be held in the month of April. Before the meeting is held, the date of the meeting, venue, the things to be decided in the meeting and other information should be sent to all Sangam members twenty-one days in advance.

2. At least two-thirds of the total members should be present. The president can postpone the meeting if two-thirds of the members are not present for the meeting.

3. The things to be decided and fulfilled in the yearly General Assembly Meeting are given below:

a. Provide the accounts for the past year, detailing the income, expenditures, and work undertaken.

b. Elect members to the Management Committee every three years.

c. A chartered accountant should be appointed and his salary fixed for the following year.

d. The budget for the following year should be decided.

18. Any necessary corrections and changes in the Sangam's rules, and the creation of new rules, should be undertaken.
19. *Special General Assembly Meeting*
    Whenever the president feels it is necessary, he can hold a Special Meeting among the members of this Sangam. If three-fifths of the members, for any reason, apply to the president to hold a General Meeting, the president should hold a meeting within thirty days from the date of application.
20. *Funds*
    Subscription amount paid by the members of the Sangam and any drama or other programs held to collect donations are all general funds of the Sangam. The funds of the Sangam should be deposited in the name of the Sangam, in the bank selected by the Management Committee. The bank accounts should be maintained by the secretary and treasurer along with the president. The Management Committee will decide about fulfilling the aims of the Sangam from the general funds of the Sangam. In that way, it may be spent for the reasons detailed below:
    A. Apart from the amount the treasurer keeps with him for emergency expenses, the rest of the fund should be deposited in MDCC bank in the Sangam's name. The president, secretary, and treasurer of the Sangam should sign to withdraw any Sangam funds from the bank.
    B. The secretary can permit expenditures of Rs 300 between two meetings of the Management Committee. The Management Committee can permit expenditures of Rs 600 between two General Assembly meetings. For all other expenditures, the permission of the General Assembly in advance is necessary. If not, permission should be obtained in the next General Assembly meeting.
21. *Account Books*
    The fiscal year of this Sangam runs January 1 to December 31.

CORRECTING SANGAM RULES

Rules can be changed, corrected, banned, and new rules can be formulated; these special decisions can be taken with a three-quarters majority vote of the General Assembly members on the day of the General Assembly meeting.

Sangam Legal Adviser: Tiru P. S. RamaSubramaniyam, B.A., B.L.

MANAGEMENT COMMITTEE

1. Tiru M. A. Majeeth—President
2. Tiru N. S. Ganeshan—Secretary
3. Tiru N. M. Rakkappan—Vice President
4. Tiru V. S. Mukkaiyaa—Vice-Secretary
5. Tirumathi M. S. Renugadevi—Treasurer

ACTION COMMITTEE MEMBERS

1. Tiru A. S. Thangavel
2. Tiru M. M. Pichappa
3. Tiru P. M. Raamayaa
4. Tiru M. S. P. Kalaimani
5. Tiru Devi Shanmugam
6. Tiru B. Vira Chezhiyan
7. Tiru Prasat Rajendran
8. Tirumathi M. P. A. Lakshmi
9. Tirumathi A. Sitradevi
10. Tirumathi S. Kalasri

Appendix 2

Tamil Transliteration of Buffoon Selvam's Monologue, 1 April 1992

1. BUFFOON: vaṇakkam. Viṭiyum varai, nāṭakam muṭiyum varai, itē pōl
2. amaiti kāttu eṅkaḷukku nallātaravu tarumpaṭi kēṭṭukoṇṭu, kalaippaṇiyai
3. toṭaṅkukiṉṟōm.
4. muṉṉēṟa vēṇṭum.
5. ALL-ROUND: Uṅ.
6. BUFFOON: Poṟāmai paṭakkūṭātu. Ēṉ colkiṟēṉ eṉṟāl, ippaṭittāṉ vāḻkkaiyil nāṉ
7. poṟāmaippaṭṭu niṟaiya ciramappaṭṭu pōṉēṉ.
8. ALL-ROUND: Eppaṭi?
9. BUFFOON: Eṅkaḷ vīṭṭu pakkattu vīṭṭukkāraṉ veḷināṭṭukkup pōyiruntāṉ.
10. ALL-ROUND: Uṅ.
11. BUFFOON: Veḷināṭṭukkup pōṉavaṉ aṅku pōy niṟaiya cottu, paṇam ellām
12. campārittu viṭṭu vantu, iṅkē maturaiyil vantu vacatiyāka vāḻntu koṇṭiruntāṉ.
13. ALL-ROUND: Uṅ.
14. BUFFOON: Itaip pārttavuṭaṉ eṉakku poṟāmaiyaka ākiviṭṭatu.
15. ALL-ROUND: Uṅ.
16. BUFFOON: Poṟāmaiyāṉatum nāṉ nērāy eṅkaḷ appāviṭam pōyviṭṭēṉ.
17. ALL-ROUND: Uṅ.
18. BUFFOON: Eṅkaḷ appāviṭam pōy, "Appā! Appā! Nāṉ veḷināṭṭiṟku pōkiṟēṉ.
19. Eṉakku koñjam paṇam koṭuṅkaḷ, appā!" appaṭi eṉṟu kēṭṭēṉ. "Aṭa pōṭā! Iḷittavāy payalē" //
20. ALL-ROUND: Uṅ!
21. BUFFOON: "Veḷināṭṭiṟkup pōvataṟku paṇam vēṇṭām. Mutalil pāspōrṭ tāṉ vēṇṭum.
22. Pāspōrt eṭuppataṟku fōṭṭō vēṇṭum tāṉā? Pōy fōṭṭō eṭuttuviṭṭu vāṭā!" appaṭi
23. eṉṟu viṭṭār. "Cari" appaṭi eṉṟuviṭṭu nāṉum nērāy
24. 'photo-studio'vukku, pattu rūpāy vāṅkikkoṇṭu 'studio'-vukkup pōyviṭṭēṉ.
25. ALL-ROUND, HARMONIST, MRIDANGIST: (inaudible comment) *laughter*
26. BUFFOON: Mm. Āmma. 'Photo-studio'vukkup pōyākiviṭṭatu. Pōṉavuṭaṉ 'photo
27. -studio'vil uṭaṉēyākavā eṭuttut taruvārkaḷ? "Oru maṇi nēram ceṉṟu vā" eṉṟu
28. colli viṭṭār. Cari; oru maṇi nēram irukkiṟatē appaṭiyē ceṉṟu oru pāl cāppiṭṭu

29. viṭṭu varuvōm appaṭi eṉṟu nērāy pālkaṭaikku pōyākiviṭṭatu. Pāl kaṭaikkuppōy pāl cāppiṭa "Oru speshal pāl pōṭu" eṉṟu coṉṉāl, kotikka kotikka—//
30. ALL-ROUND: Uṅ.
31. BUFFOON: kaiyil cūṭu tāṅku muṭiavillai. "Cari, koñja nēram āṟaṭṭum" appaṭi eṉṟu
32. pakkattil irunta ṭēpiḷil vaittu viṭṭu pēparai pārttu koṇṭiruntēṉ. Antappakkamāy
33. vēkamāy oru peṇ—taṉ piḷḷaikku pāl illai pōlirukkiṟatu—vēkamāy vanta peṇ
34. paṭakkeṉṟu "Irantu pāl pōṭu ayyā" appaṭi eṉṟu mārāppai avacaramāy tūkkip
35. pōṭṭatu [gesture] illaiyā? Nāṉ vaittirunta pālai inta mārāppu mūṭiviṭṭatu. Nāṉ
36. pāl kuṭikka vēṇṭum. Nāṉ pāl kuṭikka vēṇṭum eṉṟāl, anta peṇ eṉṉa ceyya
37. vēṇṭum?
38. ALL-ROUND: Eṉṉa ceyya vēṇṭum?
39. BUFFOON: Eṉṉa ceyya vēṇṭum?
40. ALL-ROUND: (Teriyavillai!)
41. BUFFOON: Uṉakku teriyavillaiyā?
42. BUFFOON: Nāṉ pāl kuṭikka vēṇṭumeṉṟāl antappeṇ mārāppai tūkka vēṇṭum, //
43. ayyā!
44. MUSICIANS AND AUDIENCE: *laughter*
45. BUFFOON: Oru peṇṇiṭam pōy ippaṭic collalāmā? "Cari, namukku pāl vēṇṭām,"
46. appaṭi eṉṟu viṭṭu, nērē . . .
47. MRIDANGIST: [*plays a single hit: ding! on his drum*] //
48. BUFFOON: [*slow, exaggerated side-to-side gesture of acquiescence with the head*]
49. . . . fōṭṭō kaṭaikkup pōy fōṭṭō vāṅki viṭṭu nērē vīṭṭiṟkup pōvōm" appaṭi eṉṟu viḍḍu,
50. ALL-ROUND: Uṅ.
51. BUFFOON: "Bus-stop" kku varukiṟēṉ. Eṅkaḷ vīṭu Fatima College pōkiṟa vaḻiyil irukkiṟatu.
52. ALL-ROUND: Uṅ.
53. BUFFOON: Anta vaḻiyiltāṉ eṅkaḷ vīṭu irukkiṟatu ēḻam namparil pōka vēṇṭum illaiyeṉṟāl 73-il pōkavēṇṭum.
54. ALL-ROUND: Uṅ.
55. BUFFOON: "Cari" appaṭi eṉṟu viṭṭu "ēṟip pōyviṭuvōm" appaṭi eṉṟu viṭṭu 'bus-stop'-
56. kku varukiṟēṉ. 'Bus-stop' pūrāvum oru peṇpiḷḷai kūṭṭam! Kālaiyil. 'Office'
57. pōkiṟavarkaḷ 'office'-kkup pōkiṟārkaḷ. Vēlaiveṭṭikkup pōkiṟavarkaḷ vēlai
58. veṭṭikkup pōkiṟarkaḷ. Avaravarkal avaravar vēlaiyaip pārppataṟkāka pasil ēṟi
59. pōy koṇṭirukkiṟārkaḷ. Kūṭṭam kūṭṭam peṇkaḷ kūṭṭam kaṭṭi ēṟi kātai moykkiṟatu.
60. Nāṉum "eṉṉa ceyvatu? Passai ettaṉai passaittāṉ viṭṭuviṭṭu niṟpatu?" appaṭi
61. eṉṟu viṭṭu paṭakkuṉṟu oru pas vantatu. Atil orē peṇkaḷ kūṭṭamāy iruntālum,
62. "Paravāyillai. Aṉucarittu oru oramāy niṉṟukoḷvōm" appaṭi eṉṟu viṭṭu, oru
63. kaiyil kambiyaip piṭittukoṇṭu, oru kaiyil fōṭṭōvai piṭittukkoṇṭu, oru kālai
64. paṭikkaṭṭil mitittukkoṇṭu toṅkikkoṇṭē pōykoṇṭu irukkiṟēṉ.

65. ALL-ROUND: Uṅ.
66. BUFFOON: Oru maṉitaṉ evvaḷavu tūram toṅkikkoṇdē pōkamuṭiyum?
67. ALL-ROUND: Etil?
68. BUFFOON: Kampiyaittāṉ. Kampiyaip piṭittuttāṉ. Vēṟetai piṭittut toṅka muṭiyum?
69. “Cari” eṉṟu toṅkikoṇṭu pōykkoṇṭē irukkiṟēṉ.
70. Kai valittuviṭṭatu. Pakkattil oru 60 vayatu kiḻavi niṉṟukoṇṭu iruntatu.
71. ALL-ROUND: Uṅ.
72. BUFFOON: “Ammā! Tāyē! Nāṉum oru kaiyil niṟaiya nēramāy toṅkik koṇṭu
73. irukkiṟēṉ! Kai valikkutu.
74. Koñjam kālai tūkkikkoḷ. Nāṉ ēṟikkoḷkiṟēṉ” appaṭi eṉṟu tāṉayyā coṉṉēṉ!
75. MUSICIANS AND AUDIENCE: *laughter*
76. ALL-ROUND: Eṉṉa coṉṉāy?
77. BUFFOON: Eṉṉavā? “Koñjam kālait tūkkik koḷ. Nāṉ vaṇṭikkuḷ ēṟik koḷkiṟēṉ” eṉṟu
78. tāṉ coṉṉēṉ. Uṭaṉē antap peṇ vēṟumātiri niṉaittuk koṇṭatu.
79. “Ēṇṭā! Uṉ vayatu eṉṉa? Eṉ vayatu eṉṉa?
80. Eṉṉaip pārttu nī vantu . . . pōṭā!”
81. appaṭi eṉṟu oru aṭi aṭittu uḷḷē taḷḷi viṭṭatu.
82. ALL-ROUND: Uṅ.
83. BUFFOON: Uḷḷē taḷḷi viṭṭavuṭaṉ muṭṭi nuḻaintu uḷḷē pōy viṭṭēṉ.
84. ALL-ROUND: Uṅ.
85. BUFFOON: Muṉṉum peṇkaḷ. Piṉṉum peṇkaḷ. ‘Seats’ pūravum peṇkaḷ.
86. Orē peṇkaḷ kūṭṭam. Nāṉum oru kaiyil fōṭṭōvai vaittuk koṇṭu—caṭṭaiyil pai illai.
87. Oru kaiyil fōṭṭōvai vaittukkoṇṭu
88. oru kaiyil kampiyai piṭittu koṇṭu niṉṟu koṇṭē
89. pōykoṇṭu irukkiṟēṉ. Vaṇṭi pōy koṇṭu irukkiṟatu. Tiṭīrṉṟu ‘sudden-brake’ [*hip thrust*].
90. ALL-ROUND: Uṅ.
91. BUFFOON: Aṭṭukkuṭṭi cross, road-il.
92. ALL-ROUND: Uṅ.
93. BUFFOON: ‘Sudden-brake’ [*hip thrust*] pōṭṭāṉ. Vaṇṭi kuluṅkiyatu illaiyā?
94. Muṉṉāl peṇpiḷḷai niṟkiṟatu.
95. ALL-ROUND: Uṅ.
96. BUFFOON: 16 vayatu piḷḷai. Iṭittu viṭakkūṭātu illaiyā?
97. “Iṭippataṟku eṉṟē varukiṉṟārkaḷ” appaṭi eṉṟu viṭuvārkaḷē!
98. ALL-ROUND: Uṅ.
99. BUFFOON: Appaṭi eṉpataṟkāka niṟaiya ‘balance’ paṇṇi intak kaiyaip [*reaches*]
100. piṭittēṉ allavā? Intak kaiyil iruntu fōṭṭō kīḻē viḻuntu viṭṭatu.
101. ALL-ROUND: Uṅ.
102. BUFFOON: Kīḻē viḻunta fōṭṭō vēṟu eṅkēyāvatu viḻuntirukkak kūṭātā?
103. ALL-ROUND: Uṅ.

104. BUFFOON: Antap peṇ kālukkuk kīḻē viḻunta viṭṭatu!
105. ALL-ROUND: Appuṟam?
106. BUFFOON: Nāṉ fōṭṭō eṭukka vēṇṭum//
107. ALL-ROUND: Cari//
108. BUFFOON: Anta peṇṇiṉ kālai tūkkac colli!
109. AUDIENCE: *laughter//*
110. ALL-ROUND: Uṅ!
111. BUFFOON: Appuṟam eṉṉa ceyvatu? Oru peṇpiḷḷaiyiṭam pōy ippaṭic collalāmā?
112. "Uṉ kālait tūkkikkoḷ. Nāṉ fōṭṭō eṭukka vēṇṭum" eṉṟu?
113. MUSICIANS AND AUDIENCE: *laughter, applause.*
114. BUFFOON: Inta fōṭṭōvum vēṇṭām, veḷināṭum vēṇṭām appaṭi eṉṟu
115. viṭṭu viṭṭu, viṭṭu viṭṭu.
116. nēram kāṇātu; etāvatu oru viyāpāram paṇṇi piḻaippōm. . . .

Notes

Introduction

1 "Jāti" is the word I have translated here as caste. "Jāti" is a notoriously context-dependent term, and a usefully "fuzzy" one at that (Kaviraj 1993; Chatterjee 1993). It here refers to the actors who make up the drama world of which Mr. Bhagavattar is himself a part, within which important distinctions are possible, as the next line in our conversation makes abundantly clear. (The original Tamil line is "ē<u>n</u>e<u>nr</u>āl, kalṭshar campantamillāta oru jāti itu. Nāṭaka jāti.")

2 First narrativized in print by Rabindranath Tagore in his novel of the same name (*The Home and the World*, 1915, trans. from the Bengali by S. Tagore), this ideology has been critically discussed in a range of scholarly venues by a range of scholars of South Asian history and culture in recent years who have begun to investigate the figure of the prostitute. These include Anandhi 1997; Banerjee 1998; Chatterjee 1993; Dickey 2000; Hansen 1992; Visweswaran 1996; and Weidman 2003.

3 Mr. Bhagavattar is also an astrologer; a signpost advertising his astrological services hangs beside the front door of the house where we spoke. Astrology is a much more traditional, and acceptable, line of work than stage acting, especially for members of his Brahmin caste. The sanctioning of action in accordance with astrological alignments is closely related to the Hindu priestly function canonically served by Brahmins in Indian society.

4 The Tamil historians whose writings chart this terrain include A. N. Perumal (1981); Mu. Varadarajan (1988); M. Arunachalam (1974); S. K. Baskaran (1981); K. Sivathamby (1981); R. Rajendrasolan, "Western Influences" (Institute of Asian Studies 1990); T. K. Canmukam [Shanmugam] (1972); Vijayalakshmi Navaneethan (1985); K. A. Gunashekaran (1987); and S. Ulakanatan (1992). The works of all but the last four scholars have been published in English translation. In my citations from these works in the following chapters, I quote from published English translations where these exist, and otherwise all translations are my own.

5 Several Western scholars of Tamil theater have written on *Terukkūttu*, the indigenous street theater form that contributed thematically as well as stylistically to the development of popular modern Tamil drama (Frasca 1990; Hiltebeitel 1988; Bruin 1999). The modern form itself, however, has only recently begun to receive attention (Bruin 2001a). Frasca (1990) mentions music drama only as the "modern theater" form of *Terukkuttu*, and Hiltebeitel never mentions it at all.

6 The Karaikudi Sangam during the 1990s represented an unusual development in the history of the organizational practices of Special Drama. It bore the name "The Karaikudi Music Drama Agents and Actors Sangam" and acted as a union of agents

and artists. Agents are not generally welcomed to become members of actors sangams, since one of the primary functions of the latter is to rally in support of artists in the event of their being unfairly treated by agents. A group of devoted Karaikudi agents, however, argued—originally against the exclusionary membership policies of the mother sangam in Madurai—that theirs is a role bonded to the artists in whose interests they negotiate terms with village sponsors. Their contest of a Madurai Sangam regulation debarring agents from joining as members lost, and in the mid-1980s they opened their own association in Karaikudi. During my fieldwork this was a thriving sangam, but by 2000 it had split again into two separate unions, one for agents and another for artists.

7 These data are from Srimathi Renugadevi, the Madurai Sangam treasurer of many years. In 2001, the sangams in Erode and Coimbatore were no longer associations for Special Drama artists; instead the dramas in these regions were organized on the company model. Likewise the Perungudi Sangam was no longer included in the Special Drama network, as Perungudi actors had only one repertory play (*Kattaboman*) and consisted only of men. In their place, three new sangams located in Māyavaram, Kamuti, and Tiruchuli had entered the Special Drama network.

8 See Williams [1976] 1985.

9 The dramatic scenes in Special Drama treat the same issues but shift them to the plane of mythological characters in well-known mythic stories. For example, Valli and Murugan debate the notion of love marriage in *Valli's Wedding*. Queen Alli is a woman who reigns in a matriarchal queendom in *Pavalakkoti*. The hero Kattaboman attempts to overthrow the British invaders in *Kattaboman*. And even when he is shorn of his kingdom, Harischandra survives through the love of his wife in *Harischandra*. Thus the questions I ask here of comedy scenes would, I believe, similarly apply to dramatic scenes. No study yet addresses these questions, and I hope that my work here eventually makes doing so that much easier for anyone who attempts it.

10 For example, S. T. Baskaran (1981) writes of the company dramas that were the direct predecessors of Special Drama, and functioned as the theatrical launching pad for Special Drama artists in the early decades of the twentieth century, as follows: "the company productions barely merited the title of 'drama'; they lacked dramatic merit and were not very theatrical in performance. . . . The only qualification for an 'actor' was the ability to sing, and the most popular character of the drama was the clown who indulged in a lot of ribaldry" (41).

11 Kissing is still censored out of Tamil films, not because it is sexy but because it is considered disgusting (the mouth is a sewer, etc.).

12 Today the majority of plays in the Special Drama repertory retell Hindu mythological stories and are performed at Hindu temple festivals, but there are also Christian dramas in the Special Drama repertory that are performed for Christian church festivals. The population breakdown of the state of Tamilnadu by religious community is roughly 90 percent Hindu, 7 percent Muslim, and 3 percent Christian. Members of each of these religious communities figure among both the artists and audiences of Special Drama, though Muslim doctrine frowns on the practice of dramatic representation, and dramas treating overtly Islamic subject matter that were

popular in the early decades of Special Drama (such as *Gul-e-baqavali*, a popular Parsi drama) are now rarely if ever performed.

13 Like Special Drama, many contemporary Tamil performance genres may be hired either as purely secular entertainment or as entertainment framed within a ritual context such as the repayment of a vow to a local deity. In fact, for festivals of any length, a different entertainment is often hired each night. For example, in a three-day festival there might be a performance by a "light music orchestra" one night, a "dance drama" the next, and a Special Drama on the final night. Some of these entertainment genres are locally considered folk, others classical, and still others modern. I further situate Special Drama within such local distinctions among local genres in chapter 3.

14 Performances by music drama artists in troupes or small companies are known as "company drama" (Bruin 2001a). The designation "company drama" functions historically as the oppositional defining term to "Special Drama" within the larger field of music drama, a term that covers a wide range of types of theatrical organization.

Note here, however, that music drama artists theoretically can, historically have, and still occasionally do move back and forth between Special Drama and company drama. The same system of known repertory roles and plays that enables Special Drama to exist enables the potential exchange between Special and company dramas. Today, however, no large companies exist. Instead there are only a handful of smaller troupes performing music drama in specific regions, notably in the Tanjore district (Kodiswari 1987) and in the Kancheepuram district just South of Chennai (Bruin 2001a). Sometimes troupes exist exclusively for the performance of a particular repertory drama; for example, in the Madurai district, artists who perform exclusively the historical drama *Kattaboman* have organized into several troupes who regularly perform together, so that sponsors book the troupe as a unit rather than individual artists.

15 In that Special Drama relies on the familiarity of repertory and performance style to create a structure allowing individual artists to perform together unrehearsed, it may perhaps best be understood by American readers when compared to musical performance genres such as American jazz or Appalachian bluegrass, both of which rely on a familiar repertory (in this case, of tunes) to create a flexible performance structure in which specific artists may join together unrehearsed and "jam" onstage. (For those familiar with Indian classical music, the case is much the same: "In the performance of Hindustani music . . . the artist is judged by his ability to improvise within strictly laid-down limits" [Karnad 1989].) As in Special Drama, such a structure can accommodate and thrive on the billing of specific artists whose names are a known draw, e.g., Sonny Rollins on sax, Woody Allen on clarinet. The concept is familiar to us through other activities as well, notably games of all types. Games too employ a structure reliant on familiarity with and mastery of a set of rules that, at least theoretically, allow anyone competent and skilled in them to join the play (though of course the intricacies of personality as well as the hierarchies of class, race, and gender regularly override such theoretical democracy). Moreover,

even in theory such practices generally apply only to amateur rather than professional contexts: the sandlot baseball game and the pick-up basketball game are mere training grounds for the fiercely nationalist rhetoric of team sports. The surprises and spontaneity that enliven the amateur sport give way to the highly marketed matching of opponents in the pro game. Special Drama is a professional organizational practice that manages to sustain the enlivening characterization of an amateur sport.

American performance artists have also experimented with extending the model of play-for-fun into the world of play-for-profit in ways that aim at not losing the appeal of the spontaneous chance encounter. Contact Improvisation is a case in point. A child of 1960s counterculture ideology, this improvisational dance style was developed in the United States in the 1970s. It was begun by Steve Paxton, a Merce Cunningham company dancer who left that professional world to experiment with movement in a more ideologically egalitarian terrain. Through collective experimentation, a dance form developed that allowed artists familiar with its style and principles to come together unrehearsed and perform together live. In practice, performances were never exactly egalitarian, as the draw of "famous" names quickly grew powerful among the small group of cognoscenti who made up its practitioner and audience base (Novack 1990). Interestingly, in attempts to describe the practice of Contact Improvisation to those unfamiliar with it, its practitioners coined a new term that sought to draw on Western familiarity with the game model by referring to the dance form as an "art-sport." The promise of the unrehearsed encounter is key to the appeal of Special Drama in ways that will become clear throughout this book.

16 By 1993 international exchange rates, Rs 75 was "equivalent" to $3 in U.S. currency, Rs 300 to $12.

17 Other currently active Tamil theatrical genres that similarly follow suit are Terukkūttu (street play), an indigenous outdoor ritual epic theater; and Nāṭṭiyakkalai (country art) and Kirāmiyakkalai (village art), two categories that include local performance genres such as Karakāṭṭam (dance with a Karakam pot), Villuppāṭṭu (song with a bow), and Poykkāl Kutirai (dummy horse dance), each of which again overtly names a key element featured in performance.

18 The conundrum posed by drama people qua community resides in the fact that performers themselves, together, are a collection of excluded others: rather than an identity that originates in exclusivity and defines the boundaries of the self by marking the exclusion of an other—as in, "whatever we are, we are *not* x"—the drama community is a maximally, even radically, inclusive group. Some of the most interesting recent scholarship on the dynamics of exclusivity in community identity formation concerns whiteness. Whiteness in the United States has been the quintessential unmarked identity, the one that never needed to state what it is, only what it is *not*. This scholarship seeks to expose the "othering" on which such a stance depends (Dyer 1997; Wray and Newitz 1997; Biale et al. 1998). In this regard, one of the best features of Jenny Livingston's 1990 documentary film *Paris Is Burning* is how it manages to expose the constructedness of whiteness as an identity, rendering it open, like all others, to ridicule as well as emulation.

19 In that stigma is always a matter of the appreciation of norms and their deviations, it is intimately linked—structurally parallel, and often, I suspect, causally tied—to humor: the business of making deviations appear funny. I explore these links in my analyses of onstage comedic performances (chapters 4–6).

20 This discussion of the term *muṟai* synthesizes dictionary definitions from Cre-A1992; the Tamil Lexicon (University of Madras 1982); and Fabricius [1779] 1972.

21 Some usages allow a more open meaning, suggesting any possible "order, manner, plan, arrangement, [or] course," but unless otherwise qualified, the sense is that of "normal course," "regularity, system, routine."

22 Enumerated under the category "disgrace" is, indeed, where one finds the proverb with which we are concerned here in Rev. Herman Jensen's *Classified Collection of Tamil Proverbs* ([1897] 1989). The good reverend saw a need to organize Tamil proverbs into "proper families" but found this quite difficult, as, in his estimation, "it is hard to get such a register of sin, as proverbs almost are, into a systematic order" (ix). Such (Christian) categorical problems notwithstanding, it is clear that to be without muṟai, and moreover to be *said* to be without muṟai, is to be disgraced.

23 An appealing alternate translation would be "Between actors there is no kinship, just as this cake has no head." I am grateful to Dr. K. Paramasivam for this suggestion. I have chosen to retain the term *muṟai* untranslated to keep intact its multiple meanings.

24 The proverb is memorable for its pleasing poetic rhyme and alliteration as well as its economy of terms. Certainly one reason for employing *koḻukkaṭṭai* is for its rhyme with *kūttāṭi*, a somewhat derogatory term for actors (literally, those who play in the street: *kūttu* [street play] + āṭi [*kaḷ*] [player/s]). Rhyme in Tamil poetics is generally based on beginning sounds rather than on ending sounds as in the English tradition. This little rhyming proverb, however, has it all: the nouns *kūttāṭi* (actor[s]) and *koḻukkaṭṭai* (Ganesh-cake[s]) each take the dative case ending "ku" (to) creating a noun-plus-dative-case-ending pair (Kūttāṭikku = to actor[s], koḻukkaṭṭaikku = to Ganesh-cake[s]) of quite similar sounds, other than the additional syllable in the second term (the increased length of which is, however, somewhat offset by the two long vowel sounds in *kūttāṭi*). The predicates that follow are even more well matched in sound as well as syllabic measure: muṟai + um + illai= muṟai + any + none, or "have no muṟai"; talai + um + illai = head + any + none or "has no head" (on the use of *um* in negative contexts to signal open-ended exclusion, see Paramasivam and Lindholm 1980b, 90).

25 Due to this belief, the elephant god is often propitiated and invoked at the beginning of functions of all kinds, including artistic ones. Performances of Bharata Natyam, for example, always begin with an opening artistic offering—in this case, a dance—to Vinayakar. Many other Indian performance forms do likewise, offering as their opening piece an homage to Ganesh (Blackburn 1996; Frasca 1990; Kapur 1990). Special Drama does not generally dedicate the first song of a night of performance to Ganesh; instead, this gesture of reverence is usually devoted to his younger brother, Murugan, the god of Tamil (the language), youth, and beauty.

The state of Maharashtra is the center of grand celebrations for Vinayakar. The sweet I discuss here probably originated in Maharashtra and was adopted by Hindu Tamilians into their own celebrations.

26 Kajri Jain (2001) notes in her work on the annually renewed images of deities circulating in the popular calendars market that the figure of Ganesh is particularly plastic and perhaps the most open to modern interpretations.

27 Adapted from K. Paramasivam, "The Birth of Pillaiyar—1," in K. Paramasivam and J. Lindholm 1980a, 65–68. See also Trawick 1990, 161.

28 In *The Republic*, Plato suggests that the moral guardians of the ideal city should turn imitative actors out altogether, foreseeing a great moral danger in allowing spectators to enjoy the imitative antics of actors "lest from enjoying the imitation, they come to enjoy the reality" (1992, 395d, 398a). Here as so often, a pleasure somehow immoral lies at the root of the threat actors pose to moral order. Through Socrates' words, Plato's solution to the problem of actors is banishment: "It seems, then, that if a man, who through clever training can become anything and imitate anything, should arrive in our city, wanting to give a performance of his poems, we should bow down before him as someone holy, wonderful, and pleasing, but we should tell him that there is no one like him in our city and that it isn't lawful for there to be. We should pour myrrh on his head, crown him with wreaths, and send him away to another city" (398a). The regard here for the actor as, simultaneously, delightfully and unacceptably "other" (like divine dirt) finds an echo in the ambivalence evoked by Special Drama artists.

29 In its economical wordplay, the proverb does have a jokelike aspect. As such it fits well with Freud's hydraulic notion of a joke's "yield of pleasure" that results from "condensation" in the use of words. Joke work offers a "reduction of expenditure of psychic work" (Freud [1905] 1960, 48). For Freud, such pleasantly punny quips provide a means of circumventing inhibitory rationalism, making even what at first seemed to him "nontendentious" or innocent jokes in the end just as motivated by desire as any other joking release. In this instance, very few people have inhibitions about overtly criticizing actors, and I tend to think that the "psychic work" saved here inheres in a rhyme that is pleasingly pithy and memorable.

30 Michael Warner (1999) uses these terms in the context of a discussion of the mainstreaming desexualization of the lesbian and gay movement in the United States during the 1990s. He sees *stigmaphile* and *stigmaphobe* as different "ways of resolving the ambivalence of stigma" (75). Stigmaphiles, among whom Warner counts himself, manifest "a frank embrace of queer sex in all its apparent indignity, together with a frank challenge to the damaging hierarchies of [extant] respectability" (74). Stigmaphobes are far less disposed to challenge shame and stigma on their own terms, and put their political energy instead into vying for a place at the table. These two attitudes toward stigma represent different strategies of fighting its force. After having met several bold and brave guest artists, students in my seminar "Stigma: Culture, Deviance, Identity" coined the term "stigma diva" to describe a woman who flaunts her stigma proudly. Sivakami strikes me as a beautiful token of the type, for the contemporary Tamil context.

1. Legacies of Discourse

1 Only one freestanding biography of Sankaradas Swamigal has been published in Tamil to date (Ulakanatan 1992).

2 In a footnote to the only mention of Special Drama in his 1981 study *The Message Bearers* (24), Baskaran acknowledges that Special Drama is still staged in the southern part of Tamilnadu. This he gleaned from an interview he conducted with an actor in 1975. Nevertheless in the body of his text, as well as in a later essay where he mentions Special Drama, Baskaran continues to use the past tense.

3 I was blessed with the opportunity to meet so many artists able to speak from personal experience in drama companies, including the late A. S. Tangavel Vattiyar, the late P. S. Nagaraja Bhagavattar, the late Gnanambal, the late T. N. Sivathanu, Melur Ranjini, Ramalingasivam, Vaiyur Gopal, N. S. Varatarajan and his brother N. S. Tangavel, M. R. Kamalaveni, S. P. Rettina Pattar, T. M. Pangaja, R. Jeyalatha, Karur Ambika, M. K. Veni, N. N. Kanappa, D. P. Kuppusami, T. K. Appukutti Bhagavattar, and N. M. Sunderambal; may this account begin the work of doing justice to their years of varied experiences.

4 As an example of such elite writing for an elite class, Sundaram Pillai never intended his play *Maṉōṉmaṇīyam* to be enacted. "The play here submitted, it is needless to say, is meant for the study room and not the stage, and it is therefore written in the literary and not altogether the colloquial dialect." The manuscript was conceived as a labor of love for the Tamil language: "Among the rich and varied forms of poetic composition extant in the Tamil language, the Dramatic type so conspicuous in Sanskrit and English, does not seem to find a place. The play here submitted to the Public is a humble attempt to see whether the defect may not be easily removed. . . . No labour of love waits for demand or is hampered by considerations of its own fruitlessness, and perhaps, in this reflection will be found the best justification for the present publication." Both citations are from his 1948 English preface to *Manomaniyam* (Sundaram Pillai, Tinnevelly: South India Saiva Siddhanta Works Publishing Society), 19.

5 Parsi names the religious community of Zoroastrian immigrants in India. The Parsis migrated from Iran in the eighth century to avoid Muslim persecution, settling in the states of Maharashtra and Gujarat, and especially in Bombay. The term "Parsi theater," however, is now used to refer to "a broadly based commercial theatre whose influence extended far beyond" the Parsi community between the last decades of the nineteenth century and the first decades of the twentieth (Hansen 1998, 2292).

6 "Madras Presidency" was the colonial name for South India. In 1956 this multilingual territory was dismantled, leaving the Tamil-speaking region to continue on as "Madras state." The state name was only officially changed to Tamilnadu in 1969. For a discussion of the politics involved in the switch, see Ramaswamy 1997, 154–61.

7 This emphasis on progress through entextualization bespeaks a larger, nationwide phenomenon, consolidated after independence, of the reinvention of tradition in a new semiotics of Indian appreciation of indigenous arts. One example is the well-documented case of Bharata Natyam, now known as the "classical dance" of

Tamilnadu but previously reviled as the "nautch" dance of the Devadasis, whose transformation largely occurred in the colonial era itself (Gaston 1996; Marglin 1985; Erdman 1996; Peterson 2000; Parker 1998, Weidman 2003). Postindependence artists from a range of performance genres throughout South Asia remain intent on enhancing their status through attempts to "classicize" their art. In Sri Lanka, where the classicization of Kandyan dance became a project of the state during the 1950s, in a restructuring that seems to resonate with that of Tamil drama, "classicizing ritual dance was largely accomplished by structuring dance practices in accordance with ideas of orderliness, systematicity, and discipline" (Reed 2002, 250).

The pen is a critical tool in such revisions of the performative body. Hansen (1992) notes that the first requirement of claiming "classical" status in an Indian performance genre is that there be "a textual authority . . . that legitimates and governs the art form" (44). Entextualization as the encoding of bodily practices into written texts is a primary feature of attempts to enhance their status among artists engaged in regional performance traditions India-wide. Though these attempts now appear to be born of a vigorous national pride, the attempt to classicize through entextualization clearly began in the colonial era, when the influences of Western arts came to have such a great impact on how both practitioners and audiences reacted to what they saw.

8 While Bruin occasionally leans toward lamenting the loss of premodern Tamil rural theatrical forms in the face of the commercialization introduced by outside theatrical influences, seeing the current financial practices of music drama as a fall from the earlier grace of an "organic embedding" of kuttu in village life (2001a, 57, 61), she has nevertheless overall introduced a celebratory tone into the scholarship on music drama that is a most welcome tonic to preceding historiographic ills.

9 See Raheja 1988 on the auspiciousness of dawn for Hindu marriages.

10 Is improvisation itself the problem? Not really. For example, the pinnacle of respectable improvisation in the South Indian performing arts is undoubtedly that of highly skilled and classically trained Carnatic musicians, whose expert improvisations within a structuring *raga* (melody) and *tala* (rhythm) are unfailingly appreciated by elite, educated audiences in the big cities. Such performances involve neither words nor extraneous movements. They are pure instrumental music and as such avoid all the pitfalls into which drama seems so readily to stumble. When actors are chided for improvising, it is because it is clearly *they* who are doing so, not someone more educated, trained, or genteel.

Indeed, the difference in the respectability of drama versus comedy really arises from both who is doing the improvising and the mode in which it is done. The relative formality of dramatic scenes as opposed to comedic scenes has everything to do with the relative status of the characters portrayed. Dramatic characters are kings and queens or gods and goddesses; comedic characters are Tamil everymen and women, everyboy and girl. Every word and gesture in these ranked performances conveys distinctions of class and carriage, such that when actors improvise speech for these characters, they do so according to that character's rank.

11 I have not been able to find information on these or any subsequent issues of *The Stage Lover* in any Indian library. The first five issues were given to me by Shenbagavalli, aka Mrs. KP, shortly after the death of her beloved husband and my revered teacher, Tamil linguist Dr. K. Paramasivam. It appears that these issues originally belonged to an older male relative of KP's who was a drama buff. It was KP who first distinguished for me the two streams of Tamil drama in the twentieth century, the elite amateur drama and popular professional theater.

12 There are now Tamil music sangams, literary sangams, and actors sangams across the state. The Tamil sangam, site of prestigious linguistic activity, is located in Madurai.

13 In 1916 the Justice Party was founded and published their "Non-Brahman Manifesto." The party changed its name to the Dravidar Kazhagam (Dravidian Movement) in 1944. C. N. Annadurai, playwright and disciple of Periyar, split off from the DK in 1949 to form the DMK (Dravida Munnetra Kazhagam, or Dravidian Progress Movement). Film superstar MGR split from the DMK in 1972 to form the ADMK (Anna Dravida Munnetra Kazhagam, using Annadurai's name as its banner of distinction), which subsequently changed its name to the AIADMK (All-India Anna Dravida Munnetra Kazhagam) in 1976. The AIADMK is currently in power under the leadership of Dr. J. Jeyalalitha, who gained fame as a cinema actress and also MGR's lover and frequent leading lady. Her political party now refers to her as Mother, among other endearments; see Bate 2002 for a fascinating examination of the excesses of iconographic idolatry practiced during the reign of Jeyalalitha. See Irschick 1969 for the foundational years of separatist Tamil politics, 1916–1929.

14 The apportioning of greater prestige to the more verbal and less physical roles in popular drama carries over into other genres, particularly the music scene that is such a large part of the world of Tamil cinema. All the songs in Tamil films are dubbed. The actors in films dance, but offstage in a quiet room the playback singers stand still before microphones. ("Light music" performances of film song hits by live orchestras directly transfer this stillness of playback singers to the stage, resulting in disjunctive performances by young women whose expressive voices bear no relation to their stiff postures. Mira Nair's film *Monsoon Wedding* [2001] includes a scene that brilliantly parodies this phenomenon.) Cine playback singers gain more respect than the actors; oftentimes they are classically trained Carnatic singers, from a "good" family, et cetera. They are famous in their own right, and while their personalities and lives are discussed in film magazines and popular journals, just as are those of actors, theirs is a more respectable fame for the same reasons I have outlined here for stage artists.

15 Artists creatively sneaked freedom and anticaste messages into their dramas in songs with symbolically coded messages. For example, in a scene in *Valli's Wedding* where Valli shoos away birds from her father's millet fields, actors in the 1920s sang, "White crane, fly away home!" The elite amateur troupes who were cozy British allies, in contrast, remained apolitical during this period (Baskaran 2001, 78).

16 There is some disparity in Baskaran's account of the liberation from stigma

that their involvement in politics provided to artists who took this political ideology with them into film. Several pages later, he mentions that "the stigma attached to theatre artists was transferred to artists working in the cinema until, much later, when big money endowed the profession with a certain respectability" (Baskaran 2001, 86).

2. Prestige Hierarchies

1 This single year marks three important developments that, together, suggest 1891 as a good inaugural date for modern Tamil drama. In this year Sankaradas Swamigal began writing dramas and teaching in drama companies, Pammal Sambanda Mudaliyar founded his influential drama company Suguna Vilasa Sabha, and the play that historians regard as "the first verse drama in Tamil written under the influence of the western dramatic techniques" (IAS 1990, 495), Sundaram Pillai's *Manonmaniyam*, first appeared.

2 The drama notices in the RMRL collection are a wonderful and welcome archive. I am indebted to G. Sundar and the staff of RMRL for their invaluable services in making the collection available to scholars, as well as to James Nye, South Asia bibliographer for the library of the University of Chicago, for his perseverance of vision in making this research facility a reality. In the holdings in the RMRL collection, certain years are more heavily documented than others. In general the early years are quite well represented, while the holdings for later years are spotty. Regrettably, RMRL holds no notices from the 1950s. Hopefully, other archives will develop along these same scholarly lines and augment the critical work begun with the founding of RMRL to preserve written and visual records of Tamil popular culture.

3 I am grateful to Raja Nadikai S. P. Mina, Kalaimamani S. R. Parvati, and Kalaimamani P. S. Nagaraja Bhagavattar for generously sharing with me notices from their private papers.

4 Although this notice is undated, 1917 or 1918 is a good estimate of its imprint date, based on commonalities with other notices of the period, and the staff at RMRL have assigned it this tentative date.

5 The young Kittappa here joined his two older brothers onstage. The notice advertises S. G. Suppayaavaiyar in the Hero role of Arjuna, and S. G. Sellamaiyar in the role of Queen Alli. "S.G.S." are also initials given for the drama's "Agent and Proprietor" at the bottom, perhaps another of Kittappa's nine siblings.

6 The drama advertised in this notice is offered by a company claiming training from Sankaradas Swamigal himself (though it is three years after his death), the Madurai Sri Bala Shanmugananda Sabha. The truth of the claim lies in the participation of the TKS brothers in this company. The TKS brothers had received their initial training in Swamigal's own boys company, later temporarily joining this company (Shanmugam 1972, 270). Their names are listed prominently among those playing key roles in the drama: T. K. Shankaran as the Rajapart Rajendran, his brother T. K.

Muttusami in the Streepart role of Rukmini, and T. K. Shanmugam in another cross-dressed role as Lakshmi.

7 Note that the English side and the Tamil side do differ significantly in places; for example, the date is given in both the Western and the Hindu Tamil calendars on the right side of the notice, whereas only the Western calendar date is given on the left (a practice I discuss hereafter as part of the ritual calendar for Special Drama). Similarly, a text box in the Tamil reads "One Special Drama! An unusual meeting of Talkie stars," while on the left it announces only "Talkie Star Bramasri K. S. Devudu Iyer, Harmonist and Chorist."

8 Much of this holds true today. I know several Americans who lived in Madras during the 1990s and spoke no Tamil but who nevertheless managed quite well in English.

9 The liberal stance in the legislative debates over the language of postcolonial state rule recognized the fully assimilated place of such loan words for Tamil speakers of Jansirani's class. Liberals argued that English words had become part of the vocabulary of the Tamil speaker and were thus Tamil: "Tamil was whatever the Tamilian spoke, be it shot through with English, Sanskrit, or any other language. . . . Liberals maintained that English words like 'collector' or 'radio' were so much part of the vocabulary of the Tamil speaker that these, too, were Tamil" (Ramaswamy 1997, 166).

10 A middle-class Tamilian with no firsthand experience of the drama world with whom I recently discussed this practice offered the following comments over e-mail: "Actors and actresses are the ones who can do like this because they never care or afraid of society. But other people do highly care about society, and also worry about the comments from their society. So it is hard for an ordinary woman to do like this. Having Mom's name in initial is not at all common." The reputation of actresses as culturally defiant is clearly quite widespread and extends to gestures such as Kamalam's use of her mother's initial instead of a man's initial before her name.

11 There is a regrettable twenty-year gap, from 1944 to 1964, in the drama notice collection at the RMRL archive. I am deeply grateful to Kalaimamani S. R. Parvati for sharing with me two notices from the 1950s, which, while legible, are unfortunately not of a print quality sufficient for further reproduction here.

12 My collection consists of all the notices printed for the 1992 drama season by the Muttamil Press, the Balakrishna Press, and S. R. Printers, the three presses with the most drama notice business that year. Seventy-five percent of these notices look just like those reproduced here. Another 20 percent are double size (46 cm by 29 cm), essentially one horizontal notice atop another, and advertise two events often booked for consecutive days in the same village. In the remaining 5 percent of notices, the paper is oriented vertically, though the five artists' photos maintain the same order and placement in a rectangular relation, usually across the center of the notice. In such notices, the written text extends either above, below, or both above and below the rectangular box defined by the layout of the artists' images, which may well be why printers assert that vertically oriented notices fit more text.

13 Female artists who take on the prestigious male roles of Hero and Second Hero

are judged for their performances in these roles in the same terms as male artists are: for their heroic embodiment through speech and song. Playing these roles is, for female actresses, one way out of the stigmatizing bind into which public performance otherwise lands them, as I discuss in chapter 3.

14 *Valli* in these instances is a common shortening of the name of the play *Valli's Wedding*; this is how Special Drama artists most frequently refer to the drama in their speech.

15 Kapur's discussion of the Ramlila at Ramanagar provides a good example of the kind of powerfully devotional theater that Special Drama is *not*: a little boy who plays a god in the Ramlila "must recede in order to appear more than human, otherworldly. He must not at any cost be recognized as someone the spectators know in everyday life: he must be literally anonymous, without name" (Kapur 1990, 14).

16 I used this photograph to illustrate an essay in *Public Culture* (Seizer, 1995), accompanied by the caption "Moving in tandem." It was Carol Breckenridge, editor of the journal at that time, who was struck by how very middle-class the actresses look in this photo, and whose surprise at this alerted me to what a terrific impersonation of middle-classness surrounded me.

17 I have put the second supporting actor role (7) and the musical clarinet role (11) in brackets because both are far less regularly booked than the other artistic roles. A second supporting actor is hired only if required by the script, which is not the case, for example, in *Valli's Wedding*, the most frequently performed drama and the one I use as my template in the present discussion. Likewise the clarinet role is essentially an anomaly of the Madurai Sangam, as there is only one clarinetist in the Special Drama network, and he is a member of the Madurai Sangam.

18 The harmonium was imported from Europe in the nineteenth century. The first standard model was manufactured in Paris and patented in 1842. It had a three-octave keyboard, one set of reeds, and a single blowing pedal; more advanced models had a five-octave keyboard, four sets of reeds, and two blowing pedals, stops, and couplers. The Tamil models used today cover this whole range, including both small hand-blown models and the larger leg pedal varieties.

19 The English loan term "all-round" gets used differently by many different Indian performance genres; for example, in Parsi theater it referred to actors who played "all roles" (see Hansen 1998).

20 Should only three musicians be requested, it is the all-round drummer who is expendable; should a fancier music party be desired, a second mridangist, or sometimes a clarinetist, supplements the core group. The European clarinet has more frequently been integrated into North Indian music groups than South Indian ensembles. It figures as a central instrument in Nautanki theater orchestras, made up of harmonium, kettledrum, and clarinet or flute (Hansen 1992, 50).

21 The lower-ranking Indian-style seating in this genre provides a telling comparison with the prestige of sitting on the floor in the classical genre of Carnatic music. This difference again bespeaks the hybrid culture of Special Drama, wherein English attitudes have influenced its organization on so many subtle levels. It also speaks to how difficult it would actually be to rid Special Drama of its Western influences and still have it be itself, something the rather superficial Tamilization practiced by the state attempts to whitewash with moves such as a simple name change from "Speshal" to "Icai" Nāṭakam.

22 The role of the harmonist in Special Drama may usefully be compared with that of the *dhalang* in Javanese puppetry (Keeler 1987).

23 Exceptions to this pattern are equally telling. For example, at any venue where "traditional" arrangements are prioritized, people consciously opt for "Indian-style" seating, such as in the seating of guests at a wedding banquet where all sit cross-legged on the floor. However, in the unmarked practices of contemporary everyday life, in homes and offices throughout Tamilnadu, the person who is invited to sit down on a chair is being accorded respect, while those standing or seated on the floor occupy positions of lower rank.

24 As a Tamil drama historian writes of the comic characters in music drama, "They create the element of laughter through various means. Sometimes they even go to the extent of making fun of the audience by passing scurrilous remarks about their social behaviour. They hint at their immoral nature and make them think in shame of themselves. Sometimes they speak and act ugly features of life. Such actions are disliked by the elites and so they depreciate the general tone of the plays" (Perumal 1981, 131). Clearly the historian concurs with "the elites" in finding that comedians "depreciate" the plays as a whole.

25 Baskaran clarifies the distinction between real classical musicians and stage artists who imitate them as follows: "the difference between classical musicians and stage singers familiar with classical music must be made clear. The former were basically classical musicians and sang in concerts. The latter only acted on the stage, though some of them, after gaining fame through dramas, gave solo concerts" (Baskaran 1996, 41).

26 These figures are based on the Special Drama bookings recorded in the receipt books of the Madurai Sangam between January 1992 and July 1993. These receipt books record dramas registered through the Madurai Sangam because they employ at least one member of its members. The dramas so recorded need not, however, be performed in the Madurai district but rather include venues throughout the state. Thus one cannot conclude that *Valli's Wedding* is the most popular drama in the Madurai district, but rather only that Special Drama artists from the Madurai district are most frequently booked for this particular drama. The receipt books of other sangams likewise reflect the specialties for which their member artists are hired; the Dindigal Sangam receipt books for the 1992 drama season, for example, reveal 35 percent of bookings for *Valli Tirumanan* and an equal 35 percent for *Madurai Vīraṉ*.

27 Mythological dramas made up 27 percent of the dramas performed during these same seasons (the three other leading mythologicals, for those familiar with the repertory, were *Harischandra*, *Sattiyavan Savitri*, and *Pavalakkodi*). Another 13 percent were historical dramas, led by *Kattaboman*, a story of a South Indian king's resistance to British colonial rule (a play that includes a hysterically funny scene of Lord Colin in a red one-piece pantsuit). The final 2 percent were either "modern" dramas—primarily performances of *Iratta Kaneer* (Tears of Blood) or *Tukku Tukki* (The

Attendant), two enduring stage plays treating social issues in modern Tamil society (fidelity in the former, class in the latter) that were made into popular Tamil films in the early 1950s—or Christian devotional dramas such as *Gnana Saundiri*, *Nalla Tangal*, and *Arul Anandan*, booked by villages whose population is predominately Christian.

28 To my knowledge, no other genre of handbill for a contemporary Tamil performance genre shares these same standardized features. Fliers and posters announcing events in other contemporary Tamil performance genres appear in all shapes, sizes, and layouts. Indeed, the majority of political posters and announcements of political meetings, film posters and advertisements for film screenings, and posted public announcements for modern and social drama performances that I saw in Tamilnadu during the 1990s were laid out vertically, in the portrait printing convention.

29 I have seen remarkable exceptions to these conventions for Special Drama notices which were just that: remarkable. They involved oversize (18″ by 36″) paper of quadruple thickness (cardboard stock) printed with four different colors of ink. Only a very small number of such poster-size notices were printed in both cases that I encountered, 25 as opposed to 500. Clearly these were meant to be "special" Special Drama notices.

30 The unusual history of the worship of Lord Perumal in Valaiyangulam specifically through theatrical offerings warrants further attention. The topic evokes colorful accounts from residents of historical and mythological encounters between the villagers and Pandian kings, among others. The subject awaits further study owing to spatial constraints here.

31 For an introduction to the virtues claimed for godly vision, or *dārshan*, in Hindu India, see Eck 1981.

32 Commercial calendars sold in Tamilnadu show three sets of dates for any given day: the Tamil Hindu calendar, the Tamil Muslim calendar, and the English (Gregorian) calendar. Drama notices note only the Tamil Hindu and English Gregorian dates.

3. Discipline in Practice

1 Dumont sees "the main idea" of *Homo Hierarchachus* as "the idea of hierarchy separated from power," an idea he feels has not been sufficiently addressed by subsequent scholars (Dumont [1966] 1980, xxxv). I pursue here one small piece of his puzzle in questioning the necessity of linking status and power in thinking about the strategies of Special Drama artists. Dumont opens the door for the possibility that the two aims might be distinguished: "No doubt, in the majority of cases, hierarchy will be identified in some way with power, but there is no necessity for this, as the case of India will show" (20). It is an interesting idea, as well as a very different way of thinking about power than has generally been pursued in recent scholarship.

2 Hindu gods are often pictured as partially naked, as they are considered beyond and outside of human civilizing ties. Ascetics who follow gods may also adopt this partial nakedness, as they take themselves out of the web of human interactions and leave the householder's life to wander on religious paths semiclad. (Some of the earliest Western images of India are those of Indian ascetics, or sadhus, since early European travelers were taken with what they saw as heathen; see Cohn 1998.) I consider a number of suggestive associations between gods, children, and actors—all categories of being that bear a complicated relation to normative social practice—in the Epilogue.

3 These texts themselves have no heading but rather appear as announcements of decisions taken at a given meeting on a given date.

4 The distinction between men *parodying* and women *performing* gender in cross-dressed roles is discussed by several of the contributors to the collection *Crossing the Stage*, edited by Lesley Ferris (1993). Alisa Solomon writes: "If men dressed as women often *parody* gender, women dressed as men, on the other hand, tend to *perform* gender" (145). This distinction is largely maintained in Special Drama today, although its entailments are different from those Solomon celebrates on the American stage.

5 For a collection of essays covering a broad historical range of female-to-male cross-dressing in Western theater, see Ferris 1993.

6 "Kāyātu Kānakatē" is the key Swamigal song in *Valli's Wedding*, around which the rest of the plot of the play develops. It is a beautiful and evocative verse, likening the heroine to a deer in an evergreen grove: "Standing in the grove that never dries, / O wandering damsel, / Is a deer who is not grazing, / An unspotted deer." Artists elaborate creatively on this verse and often give their most virtuosic vocal performances at this point in the play. Some male artists also give it a sexual twist, singing of the deer's two protruding horns as its most remarkable feature, et cetera.

4. The Buffoon's Comedy

1 Special Drama artists use both the English word "joke" and the Tamil word *sirippu* to refer to jokes. Both are combined with the auxiliary verb *aṭi* (to hit), resulting in the causitive verbal usage *jōk aṭikka*, whose meaning is closest to "to crack a joke."

2 I take these useful analytic terms from the sociolinguistic work of Jakobson ([1957] 1971), Bauman (1986), and Silverstein (1996), among others. I occasionally substitute the terms "narrated text" and "narrating text" when I want to emphasize the textual features of the structures of signification under consideration. This substitution should cause no confusion, as the first terms of the pair (narrated and narrating) remain constant throughout the chapter.

3 I am grateful to P. Velraj for his assistance with the initial Tamil transcription of this performance from videotape, and for his help with a preliminary English translation. The English and Tamil texts presented here are calibrated by line number to facilitate easy cross-reference.The notational conventions used in the transcript are: // indicates point at which following line interrupts; parentheses (inaudible) indi-

cates something said but not audible; brackets and italics [*bump*] indicate gestural interjection; *ding!* indicates nonverbal interjection; capital letters (e.g., HER) indicate emphasis.

4 Seated as he is furthest downstage of all the musicians, the all-round drummer is the artist positioned physically closest to the audience. This position enables him to monitor the margins of on- and offstage and act as a potential intermediary between performers and audience, a fine instance of which we see here.

5 An iṭli is a steamed, palm-size sourdough patty made of ground rice and blackgram. Iṭli are a ubiquitous (and delicious) staple of the Tamil diet. Shops selling iṭli are quite common on the streets of Tamil towns.

6 Freud ([1905] 1960) speaks specifically of "anecdotes with a comic facade," noting that "this facade is intended to dazzle the examining eye," though indeed we may well "try to peer behind it" (126).

7 Note this first use of the verb "to lift" (tūkku), which subsequently recurs in the two remaining jokes. The simultaneity of concealing and revealing is remarkable here. The woman enters wrapped in her sari. Immediately the possibility of *lifting* the chest piece of the sari, and revealing an unmentionable object of desire, establishes that indeed her dress is appreciated by the young man as a concealment, the lifting of which would simultaneously, in Freud's terms, lift societal (both external and internalized) inhibitions and expose both her skin and his real desires, as for Freud the purpose and function of jokes is to "liberate pleasure" by "lifting inhibitions" (Freud [1905] 1960, 169).

8 Interestingly enough, renunciation plays a key role in Freud's theorizing about jokes. In keeping with his larger repression hypothesis, Freud suggests that "jokes provide a means of undoing the renunciation" demanded by "the repressive activity of civilization" (Freud [1905] 1960, 120). The argument could be strengthened and complicated by recognizing the particularity of cultural meanings of renunciation. For Freud, jokes that enable the pursuit of pleasure rather than its renunciation are attempts at "retrieving what was lost"—that is, they are alternate means of accessing infantile pleasures. Characterizing the aim of joke-work as the lifting of inhibitions on infantile pleasures also has some relevance here, as becomes clear later.

9 The success of this strategy overtly contradicts Eliot Oring's assertion that "moralizing commentary embedded within the joke is likely to prematurely reveal information that will destroy the sense of surprise" or that "any explicit didactic commentary needs to be clearly demarcated from the joke itself" (Oring 1992, 87).

10 There are many good scholarly discussions of this split between benevolent, auspicious goddesses (Sanskritic Devis) and capricious, terrifying goddesses (village *ammans*) in South India. See esp. Reynolds 1980 and Ramanujan 1986. Ramanujan discusses these two "aspects of the feminine" as "breast mothers" versus "tooth mothers." He explains that "the passive male's terror of the fierce castrating omnivorous female" stems from the fact that "the ambivalence of the Goddess is seen as the ambivalence of mothers—they are both loving and terrible" (Ramanujan 1986, 56). Of further relevance here is the observation that tooth mothers (the non-Sanskritic village goddesses) are often figured in "rough-hewn, often faceless images" (58).

11 There is always the possibility for unexpected uptakes, the possibility that some young girl in the audience will be empowered by just hearing about a crowd of women going to the office, and taking over an entire bus, no matter how the speaker or anyone else around her laughs off the suggestion. In this analysis, I focus on all that comes into play in this performance to make this the anomalous audience experience, though since I did not do a careful reception study, perhaps many more of the young girls in the audience would surprise me had I spoken with them.

12 These are familiar as three of the more advanced stages, in a total of seven named stages, of womanhood in Tamil poetry. The young woman (postpuberty) between the ages of twelve and nineteen is known as *maṅkai* (green mango); the married woman between the ages of twenty and twenty-five is called *aṛivai* (knowing); the woman age twenty-five to thirty is *terivai* (understanding); and age thirty-two and up is *per ilam pēn* (big woman). I am grateful to Daud Ali for first introducing me to such materials in discussing the *ūlā* genre of medieval Tamil poetry in the South Asia Workshop at the University of Chicago in 1994.

13 The original libidinal aim of jokes, as Freud understands it, is the sexual exposure of the other sex. The Buffoon's monologue seems tailor-made for Freud.

14 Freud's meticulous concern, throughout *Jokes and Their Relation*, with delineating the formal conditions and technical methods of jokes is based on his appreciation of jokes as providing above all a *civilized* means of pursuing libidinal pleasure. The whole project is premised on distinctions between crude versus refined society that rely, at bottom, on the establishment of separate discursive worlds for men and women, appropriate to the (in Freud's view) very different natures of their respective sexualities. See Freud [1905] 1960, 118–21.

15 For the powerful language in which the concept of layered body sheaths is evoked in Tamil, see E. Valentine Daniel 1984.

16 Several anthropologists have theorized that jokes are inherently disordering and disorganizing phenomena. Oring (1992) writes, for instance, that the task of the punch line (in his opinion, the critical distinguishing feature of the joke as literary genre) is to "disrupt the listener's traditional categories and expectations" and to "transform the perspective of the listener" through "an abrupt cognitive reorganization" (92, 85, 83). Mary Douglas (1975), in something of a twist on Victor Turner's liminal terrain, suggests that a joke is an "antirite." Whereas Turner (1977) celebrates the core of ritual as a moment of "antistructure" that ultimately facilitates the process of societal reconsolidation, Douglas (1975) sees jokes as offering "an exhilarating sense of freedom from form in general" (96). Her contention is that jokes may be distinguished from rituals as follows: "The rite imposes order and harmony, while the joke disorganizes. . . . The message of a standard rite is that the ordained patterns of social life are inescapable. The message of a joke is that they are escapable. A joke is by nature an anti-rite" (103). In stark contrast to such theories, then, in looking closely at the jokes presented in this opening act of a Special Drama, I have found that far from exerting a disorganizing or transformative impact in this particular ritual context, jokes serve to reinscribe the very conventions they blatantly taunt.

17 Here indeed A. R. Radcliffe-Brown's seminal definition of the joking relation-

ship applies in telling ways, as it highlights the centrality of participants' willingness not to take offense. Radcliffe-Brown ([1940] 1952) writes of the joking relationship: "There is a pretence of hostility and a real friendliness. To put it in another way, the relationship is one of permitted disrespect. . . . There is privileged disrespect and freedom or even license, and the only obligation is not to take offence at the disrespect so long as it is kept within certain bounds defined by custom" (91, 103).

I would suggest that such a joking relationship pertains here between the social positions of "young Tamil man" and "average Tamil woman," and that performances such as this one participate in defining "the bounds of custom." It is as though men and women here function as two separate clans (or, as is commonly remarked in Tamilnadu, two separate jātis [castes]), understood in Radcliffe-Brown's terms as "two groups, the separateness of which is emphasized" to facilitate the joking relationship may pertain ([1949] 1952, 110).

18 In that his character frequently offers up humanity in the face of institutional rigidity, the comic appeal of the pāvam man is not unlike the appeal of Charlie Chaplin's Little Tramp (I think especially of *Modern Times*), or early Woody Allen. The best theoretical plumbing of the depths of comedy as a comment on institutional rigidity is still Henri Bergson's essay "Le Rire" (Bergson [1900] 1956).

5. The Buffoon-Dance Duet

1 As noted in chapter 2, the title of the female comedic role in special Drama is "Dance," just as the male role is "Buffoon." These are both English loan words used in Tamil speech and naturalized now as Tamil words. See the list of characters on the Madurai sangam receipt in figure 28 for the whole cast array of the repertory roles in Special Drama. The title of the second act, the "Buffoon-Dance Duet," respects these role names. However, for the sake of easier and more grammatically correct reading, I have referred to the artist in the Dance role as Dancer throughout this chapter.

2 I understand the notion of synecdochic sampling here in what Howard S. Becker (1998) refers to as an "extended way, as a question of what we can say about what we didn't see on the basis of what we did see" (75). I felt more comfortable generalizing from nine closely considered performances than I did from just one, though of course my real object was to get a sense of *all* Buffoon-Dance Duet performances.

3 Among the possible relevant reasons for the lack of discussion I encountered are the following: comedy is too vulgar to talk about in general; comedy is too vulgar to talk about with a woman; comedy is too vulgar to talk about with a woman who is not a member of one's family; comedy is too vulgar to talk about with a foreigner; comedy is too vulgar to talk about with a scholar; comedy is too vulgar to talk about with a foreign scholar who is a woman and not a member of one's family; and so on.

4 Improvisation structured around a series of set relational moments was a format used productively in the context of American modern dance in the 1970s. One such method of structuring improvisation helps clarify the skeleton of the Buffoon-Dance Duet I expose here. In "Airmail Dances," Remy Charlip would send a postcard

to a dancer friend (or friends) bearing a sequence of his drawings of people engaged in particular poses—a man sliding into home base at the feet of a catcher, for example. The recipient then linked these set, sequential poses into a performance piece by improvising all the movement *in between* hitting on these particular images. The five structuring story moments in the Buffoon-Dance Duet likewise allow for individual artists to fill in the transitions between them with their own creativity and style.

5 While stages are generally temporary structures, villages that sponsor many dramas every year, such as Valaiyangulam, have raised common funds to put a concrete floor permanently in place.

6 Mudras are stylized, symbolic gestures used in Indian dance and ritual. I adopt my use of "lite" here from the American food industry, to refer to something that offers a suggestion of substance without the presence of real substance. Here the Dancer manages to suggest Bharata Natyam style and form without actually performing Bharata Natyam. For example, the hand mudras she uses are simple gestures from colloquial Tamil life, rather than the more abstract symbols codified into a gestural system in Bharata Natyam. Similarly, when she closes a movement phrase with the traditional tripartite flourish from Bharata Natyam, she never adopts the low, bent-kneed posture of the classical Bharata Natyam Dancer but rather skims the surface of the movement, maintaining an upright posture throughout.

Note a similar use of "light" in current usage in the Tamil live music performance industry, where "light music orchestras" increasingly perform cinema songs on stages where classical South Indian Carnatic music was previously performed. Within such groups, their more classically oriented numbers are also referred to as "light classical."

7 Middle-class women's styles and fashions in Tamilnadu, both international and Indian (jeans, T-shirts, salwar kameez, etc.), no longer adhere strictly to either the tāvaṇi or the sari norm. This shift in middle-class fashions has begun a considerable trickle down to the lower classes, which is why I have qualified my description of this dress practice with the term "traditionally." Nevertheless, for the majority of Tamil women and postpubescent girls, especially in rurban areas, their clothing choices remain either saris or tāvaṇi sets, and the tāvaṇi set remains a signifier of unmarried status.

8 The duet lends itself to Lacanian psychological interpretations in interesting ways. It seems to enact the range of dynamics suggested in Lacan's writings on the mirror stage: in a state of longing for the lost world of the imaginary, these two seem to hold on to some primary dreams, like cranky children stuck in an adult world of *logos*. Indeed, a bit later in the duet, when Buffoon and Dancer exchange love vows, they use baby-talk voices.

9 This is the only singular usage of the second person in this exchange. After use of the exclusive "we" is established, all other uses of "you" also switch to the matching plural; e.g., line 10: "only if we give it can you [plural] drive it."

10 A similar lesson was pointedly addressed to the kids sitting in the audience up front when Shridhar, a Buffoon from Madurai, prepared to embark on the contest

segment of a duet with Dancer Silk by first establishing that this young audience knew all that was at stake: "Who are we? We are men! We are heroes! Yes! And in what does the heroism of men consist? This [*physically erecting the head of the microphone*] is the heroism of men!" The duet is a crash course in sexual symbolism as well as sex education.

11 According to the A&E television network's 1999 documentary *Love Chronicles: Arranged Marriages*, 50 percent of love marriages worldwide end in divorce, whereas 85 percent of arranged marriages endure.

12 I first encountered this essay as an unpublished paper (Ramanujan 1991b). It has subsequently been posthumously published (Ramanujan 1997) with the unfortunate omission by the editors of the story itself, Ramanujan's translation of which is to be found instead in another book (Beck et al. 1987).

6. The Aṭipiṭi Scene

1 Marshall Sahlins's study of color perception is relevant here: biologic structures of the mind—whether of the arcing possibilities of the full color palette, or of the wide range of human affects and emotions—"constitute a set of organizational means and possibilities at the disposition of the human cultural enterprise" (1976, 2). They remain only possibilities until we make them meaningful in situ.

2 A panchayat is the meeting of all in a village for a public airing of grievances and problems, at which the nattamai presides as arbiter and judge who metes out a course of reparation.

3 Kovalan is the husband of Kannaki in the famous sangam-era Tamil epic *Cilappatikaram*. He is seduced by a Dancer, and keeping her as his mistress reduces him to ruin.

4 The paradigmatic distinction between benevolent versus dangerous types of Hindu female deities has been widely discussed in the literature on South India. See especially Ramanujan 1986; Hawley and Wuff 1982; Hart 1973; Wadley 1980.

5 Holly Baker Reynolds notes that in what at first seems paradoxical but in the end proves to be in keeping with central Tamil cultural values, women aspire to the wifely-goddess role that keeps them subordinate out of a general preference for an ordered social world. "Women themselves are the staunchest supporters of a system that normatively renders them subservient and subordinate to men. . . . Why do women opt for goddesses such as Laksmi who are paragons of wifeliness, purity, and benevolence, instead of *ammans* who are independent, passionate, and capricious? . . . The benevolent goddesses express an ordered, regulated, and properly classified world. To opt for the married goddess, then, is to opt for a world of order on cosmic, social, and existential levels" (Reynolds 1980, 43–44). In her assumption that opting for the "world of order" would be the obvious Tamil choice, Reynolds thinks like most Tamilians I met, for whom the disorder represented by the acting community was anathema.

6 Senthil Gowndamani is an act of two male comedians who figure as comic relief

in innumerable Tamil films of the late twentieth century. In all these popular entertainment genres, whether play or film, the comic action is entirely separate from the dramatic action, and skits or sketches such as the Aṭipiṭi scene stand (or fall, repeatedly) on their own merits.

7 What is surprising is that, under the rubric of the "classical," so many theater theorists have conflated the two very different traditions of Greek and Sanskrit theater (see Sue-Ellen Case 1991). I argue here that these different traditions entail very different spectatorial relations as well, several of which are relevant to the syncretic, hybrid theater of Special Drama.

8 Most literature on humor recognizes that not all laughter is humorous laughter. There is indeed a larger methodological question here: Should one assume that laughter is even a set whose various members are at all related? Is malicious laughter in any way related to joyous laughter, hysterical laughter to conspiratorial laughter? Perhaps the best approach to theorizing about laughter is to regard each type of laughter as requiring its own theory. Certainly in reading the literature on humor theory, one has the strong sense that each theory derives from and primarily addresses only the specific instances from which it builds. Though this may be a truism for all theory, it is particularly glaring in this field. As John Morreall (1987) writes: "The major difficulty in constructing a comprehensive theory [of laughter] is that we laugh in situations which are so diverse that they seem to have nothing in common but our laughter. . . . In the face of this diversity, many have suggested that there could not be a single formula which covered all laughter situations. The correct approach, they say, is not to look for an essence of laughter, but to treat laughter situations in the way Wittgenstein treated games, as a set whose members show only family resemblances" (128). Morreall himself nevertheless attempts a universal theory, summed up in the adage "Laughter results from a pleasant psychological shift." I hesitate at any such move, as laughter in use is what interests me, not a generalization that would mitigate the particularity of each instance.

Another problem that exercises me here but is never directly addressed in humor literature is that of assessing another's laughter. How can we tell, from the outside, precisely what kind of laughter we witness in another? I aim here to understand a responsive laughter that is not my own, making this a particularly ethnographic quest.

9 In discussing the audience's enjoyment, Neelam invokes a collective sensibility —what she refers to as "the tastes of all Tamil people"—that seems to function differently from the psychological processes of individual identification, introjection, incorporation, and transformation historically active in the bourgeois spectatorship of Western dramatic realism (Diamond 1992). The model is based on psychoanalytic theory, in which identification is understood as the "psychological process whereby the subject assimilates an aspect, property or attribute of the other and is transformed, wholly or partially, after the model the other provides" (Laplanche and Pontalis 1973, 205).

10 The word 'mā is short for ammā (woman; lady; mother).

11 Silvan Tompkins's psychological affect theories would be a good place to begin thinking further about shame and contempt in this performative context. Compar-

ing Tompkins's ideas on shame to the kinds of affective continuities held to pertain between audience and performer in classical rasa theory could prove particularly productive; "Shame is the most reflexive of affects in that the phenomenological distinction between the subject and object of shame is lost" (Sedgwick and Frank 1995, 136).

On the power of public opinion to shame, Bowen suggests that among the Tiv, "public complaining" works to cement familial relationships, as the fear of public shaming keeps the family together in anticipatory avoidance of outsiders' comments (Bowen 1954, 73–74). Shame as a public catalyst for domestic transformation is clearly at the crux of the Aṭipiṭi scene as well.

7. The Drama Tongue and the Local Eye

1 On the fetishization of criminal cant by the bourgeoisie of early modern England, see Reynolds 1999. More recent U.S. parallels to this desire to find radical political answers among the artistically creative underclass readily spring to mind, such as the slumming of rich white New Yorkers heading to Harlem to hear jazz singers scat in the 1920s, or even the overwhelming success of gangsta rap among white college kids today.

2 "Bāshai" is a Tamilization of the Sanskrit word "bhāṣā," meaning language or speech, especially vernacular speech. The Tamil use of "bāshai" is somewhat differently defined in different sources. The comprehensive *Tamil Lexicon* offers the following second meaning, which makes the artists' choice apparent: "Secret language, expressive signs or signals, serving as a mode of communicating ideas; kuḻuukkuṟi" (University of Madras 1982, 2644). Johann Philip Fabricius's missionary dictionary offers "language, speech, tongue" (Fabricius [1779] 1972, 684), and the modern Cre-A dictionary defines "bāshai" only as "language," and "kuḻuukkuṟi" as "jargon, argot" (Cre-A 1992, 717).

3 While the subcultural deployment of encryption is clearly not unique to the Special Drama community in India, whether any other Indian argot shares the specific qualities of the Drama Tongue that interest me here, I cannot say. Do other Indian argots similarly capture an outsider identity in an insider tongue? A comparative study focusing on speakers' terms of self-reference and self-identity in a range of argots from different social contexts is a project that would be well worth undertaking. As a comparison of argots within India, it could point to important regional differences among professions and classes. If undertaken as a comparison of argots cross-culturally, such a focus would undoubtedly raise questions about the relationship between subcultural languages, their speakers' self-conception, and the ideology of their larger cultural homes.

4 When faced with my scholarly attention to their oral inventiveness, Drama Tongue speakers invariably laughed at the incongruity of such serious attention to their strategically oral play. My attention turned what had previously existed only in the realm of the word-of-mouth into an objectified text-artifact, in a sense aligning

their argot with the more highly valued language of standard written Tamil. This surprising realignment was itself then enfolded in a joking relationship with me about the language that seemed to turn on a new hierarchy of outsiderness, as "secret" insider words in the mouth of such an extreme outsider as myself seemed to provide an experience of incongruity that was an infallible trigger to laughter. Usually this took the form of pleasurable, if somewhat embarrassed, surprise. I think I was aided in this relatively friendly response to my anthropological scrutiny by the history of affection for, even devotion to, the Tamil language that has historically played such a large part in twentieth-century Tamil politics. The cultural penchant for taking pride and pleasure in the Tamil language has been documented by historical accounts of Tamil revivalism (Irschick 1969) and specifically of acts of devotion to the Tamil language itself (Ramaswamy 1997). In the twentieth century, Tamilians deified the Tamil language as a symbol of Tamil culture, and this love of Tamil contributed to the general goodwill with which my own linguistic attempts, both in standard Tamil and in the Drama Tongue, were consistently met by my informants.

5 I hesitate to assert that this table represents a complete compilation of Drama Tongue terms, first because of the idiosyncrasies of its generation (having begun with a comparative list, it may also have been partially defined by that list), and second because the Drama Tongue is a living language in a constant state of creative flux and growth.

6 Are Special Drama artists necessarily aware of the prior and/or etymological definitions of the words redeployed in the Drama Tongue? This is a question not so much of competence in speaking the Drama Tongue as it is of the kind of knowledge that competence in standard Tamil entails. Or in any language, for that matter; what does it mean to know a language? Does one need to know all the meanings of a given word? Need one know every word in the language well enough to use it, or well enough to comprehend it?

It might be possible to approach a contained version of such questions, as they relate to the particular terms redeployed in the Drama Tongue, by attempting empirically to gauge informants' knowledge of standard Tamil vocabulary through methods such as questionnaires or overt discussions. I did not attempt any such research. Perhaps it would prove fruitful, though empirical approaches seem plagued by profound philosophical questions concerning the nature of linguistic knowledge itself: might we not "know" the meanings of words in our native tongue even when we can't actually define them? An empirical method here might test informants on their abilities for metapragmatic reflection rather more than on the kinds of knowledge that underlie their ability to understand the sense of the meanings at play in the redeployment of any standard Tamil lexeme in the hidden language of the Drama Tongue. Rather than attempt any definitive answer to a question that may not have one, I offer two further points of information that pertain in this particular situation.

First, the *Dictionary of Contemporary Tamil* (Tamil-Tamil-English) first published by the Madras publishing house Cre-A in 1992 is just that: it attempts to include definitions of only those Tamil words and meanings in current use in the late twentieth century. Given the esteemed group of Tamil scholars who made up its board of compilers, I trust that this dictionary represents a repository of the language as used and understood by contemporary native Tamil speakers. The definitions present in the Cre-A dictionary are those I have used to unpack the lexical building blocks of the Drama Tongue and are those I assume contemporary speakers of standard Tamil to know as they use the language.

I have supplemented my own understanding of the lexical items in question by consulting two other, older dictionaries of the Tamil language in the course of this work. The most comprehensive source of Tamil-Tamil-English definitions remains the six-volume *Tamil Lexicon* published by the University of Madras in 1982. The *Tamil Lexicon* includes an exhaustive compilation of words from all the previously existing Tamil lexicographical sources and provides etymologies for the majority of its entries. The other source I have consulted is Fabricius's *Tamil and English Dictionary*, a missionary text first published in 1779, whose fourth edition was revised and enlarged for publication in 1972; it is the latter revised edition that I have consulted. However, for the readings of lexical items deployed in the Drama Tongue that I present here, I have limited my analysis to the contemporary definitions given in Cre-A 1992.

Second, the community of Special Drama artists varies widely in education level. Some of the artists I interviewed had been officially "educated" only to the fourth standard (roughly equivalent to a grammar school education up to the fourth grade), while at least one had completed a master's degree (M. Phil.). In addition, as noted earlier, the Special Drama community includes many artists whose mother tongue is not Tamil, but who have mastered Tamil as an acquired language to the point where they speak flawlessly. Given this diversity in education and socialization, some speakers of the Drama Tongue would certainly know the standard meanings of the lexical items redeployed in the Drama Tongue, while others might not.

A similar range of variance would of course also hold true for the village audience that overhears artists speaking the Drama Tongue, though in general the transparency of its component terms does not seem to pose any threat to the ability of the Drama Tongue to function effectively as a secret language. The primary reason that transparency of its component terms does not pose a functional problem to the ability of the Drama Tongue to serve as a secret means of communication is that audience members *expect to be unable* to understand these artists. This expectation is one of the sequelae of the stigmatized status generally granted stage artists. Their otherness is expected, and talk among artists is consequently expected to be unintelligible to outsiders. This means that a minimum effort applied to concealing communication will prove effective, as is indeed what we find in the largely transparent construction of the Drama Tongue.

The expectation that artists are in some profound way unintelligible to outsiders stems from the larger belief that artists lack order. The extent to which this expectation of unintelligibility affects audience comprehension of the onstage performances of Special Drama is itself a question. I have often wondered how much of the speech onstage audiences understand; they clearly appreciate much of what occurs onstage, though whether that appreciation is based on full verbal comprehension remains questionable. Educated native Tamil speakers whom I hired to transcribe passage of dramas from videotapes showed extreme variation in their ability to do so. Thus an empirical study regarding lexical knowledge would, at the very least, draw a widely varied response, the primary usefulness of which might inhere in reopening the very philosophical questions it would aim to stave off.

7 The common standard Tamil word "vīṭṭukkāraṉ" combines the Tamil terms for house and man to mean both landlord and husband. The latter is not a gloss for "mattikkāḷi" in the drama tongue; nevertheless the commonality between husbands and landlords as persons of power does lend weight, it seems, to the conjunction of house and man in the drama tongue and imbues "local man" with a further sense that the designated person is a man in a position of power.

8 The householder and the ascetic are seen as opposite life choices. The spiritual path of the latter is defined as a renunciation of the duties of the former. The potential similarity between actors' itinerant lives and the hagiographies of Hindu saints and ascetics suggests a potential proximity of actors with gods. The inability of Special Drama actors to benefit from such a notion and its attendant respect again points to the effects of stigma in artists' lives.

8. The Roadwork of Actresses

1 Chatterjee's 1993 discussion of the specifically Indian paradigm of the actress as highly stigmatized public woman (135–57) is well supplemented by Hansen (1992, 1999), Dickey (1993, 61–64), and Pandian (1992, 79–90). Of course, actresses were also paradigmatically stigmatized public women in Victorian England (T. Davis 1991; Walkowitz 1998), as well as in the earlier Elizabethan period (Howard 1994), a history that is by no means easily separable from its colonial sequelae under the Raj.

2 I aspire here to what Michael Jackson (1989) terms "radical empiricism," a style and methodology that seeks "to encourage us to recover a lost sense of the immediate, active, ambiguous 'plenum of existence' in which all ideas and intellectual constructions are grounded" (3).

3 This is a telling exception for two reasons. Sennai Sivakami's choice was simultaneously an act of disidentification with Madurai (as is her stage name itself, with its reference to Chennai) and an overt assertion of the bonds of her ethnic identity as a Saurashtrian. The drama in which she performed was part of a weeklong festival sponsored by the Saurashtrian community in Madurai, and the stage was erected in the neighborhood where many Saurashtrians live.

4 Keith Basso's ethnographic project of making Apache maps rather than "Whiteman's" maps is one good, relatively recent example of this important distinction in research orientations to mapping in particular (1996). Likewise, in a broader frame, rather than privileging the visual as the sole mode of perception valuable to social scientific method, I join a host of others (Jackson 1989; Fabian 1983; Bourdieu [1972] 1977; Turner 1985; Myerhoff 1978) in understanding participant observation as an endeavor that engages the researcher's whole person in perception. I particularly like

Jackson's proposal of a radically empirical method that entails "working through all five senses, and reflecting inwardly as well as observing outwardly" (1989, 8).

Thus in this chapter I treat my own experiences as primary data, since like Jackson I define the experimental field "as one of interactions and intersubjectivity" (4). Such methods necessarily spark all manner of complex psychological relations between researchers and subjects, including transference, countertransference, identification, and disidentification. Rather than shy away from these complexities, I see promise in recognizing that it is because of such human relations that anthropology is such a rich science. In Myerhoff's deceptively simple words, "You study what is happening to others by understanding what is going on in yourself" (cited in Frank 1995, 213).

5 In the tradition of memory training developed by the sixteenth-century Jesuit priest Matteo Ricci, human memory is significantly aided by images that are "lively and not too static, they must arouse strong emotions" (Spence 1984, 25–26).

6 Marketed throughout India, the most popular images on such mass-marketed calendars vary by region and by era; see Jain 2001.

7 In marital negotiations, mothers actively participate. In drama negotiations, as this narrative seeks to illustrate, only men participate. Nevertheless, in both cases the woman whose life is at the center of the negotiation is curiously silent.

8 As the remainder of this chapter should make clear, even these women who are the epitome of public women care intensely that they not be seen as such, especially locally *where they live*, as is the case for this shop in Madurai (for actresses who live in Madurai). As the not-within-ten-kilometers practice suggests, many actresses will not perform unless they are far enough away from their domestic lives (from where they are known, local women) that the consequences to their reputations decrease.

Why should women who perform publicly, whose reputations for modesty have already largely been shattered, nevertheless attempt to conform to normative codes of gendered virtue? It seems these are the only codes that matter and that a woman must deal with these in some way. For many actresses, the public sphere seems to be divided into a differentiated continuum of publicness, either relatively more or relatively less proximate to her domestic sphere. Thus there is a proximate public sphere, relatively close to home, wherein a woman's reputation is reflected directly in her domestic life, as well as affected by it. In that more proximate sphere, a woman attempts to be seen as not an actress at all. In the less proximate public sphere where the woman is known primarily as an actress, she attempts instead to stave off the bad reputation through other roadwork techniques and strategies. Thus the same principles of womanly virtue affect her wherever she goes, though distancing herself from her own home allows her to more easily create a fictive self on the road whose modesty is signaled by her roadwork practices.

9 Mr. Jeyaraman calls himself a "power agent" (using the English terms). He reasoned that this is an appropriate epithet for his work, since he does not directly book dramas, as does a drama agent, but rather is empowered by the artists to book dramas on their behalf with many drama agents.

10 Dell Hymes's preliminary definition of the concept of communicative compe-

tence is still relevant for the basic foundation I am laying here. Hymes saw linguistic competence as intimately engaged with cultural knowledge, since in addition to grammar, "a child acquires also a system of its use, regarding persons, places, purposes, other modes of communication, etc.—all the components of communicative events, together with attitudes and beliefs regarding them" (cited in Briggs 1988, 6).

11 Despite the stigma on the acting profession as a whole for women, many more Tamil women are willing and eager to act onscreen than onstage. Chennai is filled with young women who are aspiring film starlets. The screen has a cachet that the stage does not have, as cinema *stars* manage to elevate otherwise stigmatizing behaviors into the realm of cultic fascination and allure. The alchemy that converts a Tamil actress into a cinematic superstar deserves a separate study and is yet unwritten; one key question for such a study would be the extent to which fame mitigates stigma, for whom and to what effect. For not even a Tamil female cinema star can escape the popular logic by which her chosen profession *proves* that she is, at core, a "bad" woman. In a passage on the reputation of female Tamil cinema stars, Sara Dickey (1993) writes: "The basis for the stigma attached to actresses seems to be related primarily to the sentiment that no 'good woman' would display herself in public. . . . Nice women would not show themselves to the public, so these women must have been bad before they became actresses" (63).

In Tamil cinema, as recent scholarship makes clear, actresses remain purveyors either of the bad road or of a fantasy wherein bad women still get the goods. Indeed, it seems more likely that it is the women in the cinema audience who experience relief from the realities of Tamil women's roles. M. S. S. Pandian (1992) suggests that Tamil films offer female audiences a "liminal experience" wherein "the rigidly imposed rules of society are relaxed for brief periods" (81). Dickey similarly notes the escapist appeal of Tamil films for their audiences, as well as the extent to which "the pleasure of that escape derives from its roots in real-life and psychological stresses" (175).

12 The stigma of prostitution seems to vary far less cross-culturally than do the legal regulations concerning its practice. See Pheterson 1993 for a valuable discussion of how "actual whore life" differs from "the whore stigma" in the West. The stigma of prostitution, and the shame and dishonor it entails, is everywhere meant to deter women from work that could potentially empower them, at least financially if not also sexually and psychologically (Pheterson 1993); equally, sex workers' rights activists argue that "empowering sex workers empowers all women, for the whore stigma is used to discipline women in general" (McClintock 1993, 3). The extent to which the whore stigma structures dominant notions of middle-class women's morality cannot be overemphasized; nonprostitute women are socialized into a morality that is specifically middle-class in ways they don't necessarily realize when, for example, they expect working women to refuse any and all work that might be construed as socially irresponsible, to which one sex worker commented, "Morals like that require a budget" (McClintock 1993, 8).

13 In the United States this whole realm of associations has had enormous popular culture appeal, from James Dean's *Rebel without a Cause* in the 1950s to the girl group TLC, whose album *Crazy, Sexy, Cool* propelled them to fame in the 1990s. Regardless of the deluge of Western popular-culture influences in India that has continued from the colonial through to the postcolonial era, such an allure of the bad seems not to have fundamentally affected a system of social values wherein goodness is the desired cooling balm in an overly hot and overly crowded cultural and geographic climate. But such metaphor mixing is dizzying, and the dangers of misinterpretation in attempting such a large discussion in a footnote are overwhelming; instead I refer the reader to two studies of South Indian cinema that discuss the ubiquitous Tamil cinematic plot of a good Tamil man curing a young woman of her bad Western ways and thereby converting her to an acceptable loving wife (Pandian 1992; Dickey 1993), as well as to an entirely different angle on the meanings of "cool" and "hot" in Hindu India in relation to sexuality in the ethnosociological work of McKim Marriott (1989, 1998). On how "bad" social roles have nevertheless ironically offered a refuge of sorts for some Indian women historically, see Veena Oldenburg's 1990 essay on Lucknow courtesans, whose lives and practices Oldenburg celebrates as giving "a completely ironic slant to the notion of respectability" (266).

14 Ambassador is the brand name of the first model of automobile manufactured in India.

15 Two recent scholarly reckonings of the Tamil state of affairs regarding the purported effects of transgressive female sexuality in public reveal just how fundamental to contemporary Tamil gender relations is a notion of the inherent benefits of sex segregation: "Women possess a great amount of inherent power (*cakti*)—greater than men—but if this power is not limited and directed by a father, husband or brother it will lead to harmful events (such as illicit sexual liaisons) destructive to the woman's kin group and even to the fruitfulness of the land they live on" (Wadley 1980; Reynolds 1980, cited in Dickey 1993, 27).

The manner in which female sexuality is socially constructed in Tamil society, as elsewhere, is that an independent woman (i.e., a woman who is not under male domination) is seen as sexually threatening and subversive. Even in popular Hinduism, goddesses who are not under male domination are more feared as potentially destructive than goddesses with male consorts (Shulman 1980, 144–57). This male anxiety over female sexuality is only heightened when the woman in question presents herself as a transgressor of socially prescribed norms, be they related to dress, space, or anything else (Pandian 1992, 85).

Even though pardā does not take the same form in South India that it does in the North, then, a notion of the proper gendering of domestic and public spheres clearly informs Tamil sensibilities in fundamental ways.

16 The designation "modern" in the world of Tamil theater has generally meant the use of three specific elements of theatrical presentation: the proscenium arch, with its raised stage and side wings; the division of a play into acts and scenes; and the creation of sets for these scenes, generally in the form of painted backdrops (see chapter 1 in this volume, and also Kapur 1991; Karnad 1989).

17 Parota is a thin, layered flat bread made of wheat flour.

18 Note how the Special Drama actresses' tactic here for dealing with their difference from the norm—that of acting *as if* they were already included in a preexisting category intended to exclude them—differs significantly from a tactic that has recently been so central to U.S. identity politics: the creation of discrete new categories of identity to help stigmatized persons locate themselves as other. Instead, the actresses' tactic of expanding the category "good woman" (rather than accepting a definition of its contours that has them always already outside it) seems to employ the kind of tactical misrecognition that José Muñoz discusses as "disidentification," defined as "a survival strategy that is employed by a minority spectator to resist and confound socially prescriptive patterns of identification" (Muñoz 1999, 106, 28). Of course, any identification includes misrecognitions (Sedgwick 1990, 61; cited in Muñoz 1999, 8). Muñoz's contribution to this arena is his vision for how to use dominant culture "as raw material to make a new world" (Muñoz 1999, 196). Seeing oneself as capable of belonging where one is not meant to be and acting critically on that perception—acting on a "disidentificatory desire," in Muñoz's terms—treats the world as a place where relations of identification are as highly fluid, mobile, and destabilizing as Plato feared they were, where imitation inspires life to truly resemble art, and where dominant, exclusive cultural categories become terms whose relational nature is suddenly malleable in human hands.

19 Some gender separations are also maintained in most Tamil homes; for example, women eat separately, after men. Likewise, backstage at a Special Drama event, women and men arrange their suitcases of costumes on separate sides of the available space and sit behind their open suitcases, each with a hand mirror propped in its lid, to apply their makeup.

20 According to John Burns, writing of rural India in the *New York Times* in 1996, "700 million of the country's 930 million people, having no toilets, either defecate into buckets or on open land."

21 Numerous studies of society, culture, and history have significantly contributed to this endeavor in recent decades; primary influences on my own work have been Comaroff and Comaroff 1993; Halperin 1995; Scott 1985, 1990; and Sedgwick 1990.

22 On using resistance, broadly conceived, as a diagnostic of power, see Abu-Lughod 1990.

23 David Shulman (1985) writes of the kolam as a negotiation of the threshold between akam and puṟam as follows: "The mistress of the house, or a daughter, or perhaps a trusted servant, has laid out this pattern upon arising in the morning: she may have selected a traditional design of geometric shapes intertwined, or, if her intentions are more elaborate, two peacocks, perhaps, emerging from a maze. One cannot enter the house without passing through this man-made [*sic*] focus of auspicious forces, which sets up a protective screen before the home. Of course, one cannot see the screen itself, but only its focal point at the threshold, the point at which it emerges into form—a complex form at that, carefully planned and executed, a reflection of some inner labyrinth externalized here at the boundary, the line dividing the inner and the outer, the pure from the chaotic" (3).

24 The Comaroffs discuss the split between celebratory and realist positions that scholars have taken on questions of the long-term effects of resistance, noting the vigor of the ongoing argument between the two (1993, 16).

25 There are particularly strong continuities between the dilemmas of Tamil actresses and that of Brecht's good woman of Setzuan. Brecht's heroine experiences an ongoing conflict between a moral injunction to be "good," and her need to be "bad" in order to survive economically. Nor do the similarities stop there: to negotiate this conflict, Brecht's good woman also resorts to acting; she plays two versions of herself—good and bad—off against each other throughout the drama (Brecht 1947).

9. Kinship Muṟai and the Stigma on Actors

1 See Barrish 1981 for the antitheatrical prejudice historically, and Jean L. Howard's *The Stage and Social Struggle in Early Modern England* (1994) for the satanic accusations against actors there.

2 My grandmother, Florence Victor, remembers well the membership policies of the Beverly Hills Country Club in the 1940s and 1950s, when she and her husband were new Jewish arrivals to the Los Angeles entertainment industry. Private communication, 2002.

3 The paradigm was first discussed anthropologically by Lewis Henry Morgan in 1870, within an unfortunate evolutionary comparative rubric of "classificatory" (theirs, aka primitive) versus "descriptive" (ours, aka evolved) kinship systems.

4 In general, muṟai is a singular ideal. The question of multiple muṟai that properly exist might well arise here: aren't relations of multiple muṟai established when a cousin becomes a wife?

The answer is no: this singularity of the role is precisely what the Dravidian kinship terminological system accomplishes and why it is good to think with—it provides anyone who holds the assumptions of a different kinship system a chance to recognize the encoding of normative cultural ideals in all kin terminologies that naturalize social relations. When a Tamil girl marries her male cross-cousin, his mother/her aunt becomes her mother-in-law. So, one might ask, doesn't the young woman now have two kinds of muṟai with the older woman? No; there is no shift in muṟai here, no doubling effect, as the terminological position of these two roles, aunt and mother-in-law, had never been distinguished in the first place: her aunt was, in the terminology of address, already her potential mother-in-law, a woman she *already* called "Attai." The same cross-cousin marriage ideal encoded into Dravidian kinship terminology had already made the Attai's son the bride's *Attan*, cousin and husband, since childhood.

5 Here Trautmann's attention to the few instances in the ethnographic record of peoples who use the Dravidian kinship terminology that shed light on the kinds of adjustments or "conventional alterations" that some communities make to accommodate wrong-kin marriages is welcome as a means to begin to theorize broader accommodations of new kinship practices. None of the instances Trautmann summarizes touch specifically on that primary incestuous transgression that actors face, but rather are confined to parallel-cousin, instead of cross-cousin, marriage transgressions (Trautmann 1981, 225–28). Nevertheless the possibility of people making adjustments to terminology, and creating newly recognized conventions, is part of what makes actors' attempts to ameliorate their social standing through incorporative and creative uses of kin terminology not entirely without precedent.

6 I cannot claim to offer an accurate statistical breakdown of sangam members by caste, though perhaps half of the Madurai Special Drama community affiliate in some sense with the Servar caste community. One reason for this is the centrality to the Madurai community of the family I describe here.

7 Dr. K. Paramasivam, personal communication, 4 January 1992.

8 Several actresses told me they felt similarly about acting the role of Valli in *Valli's Wedding*. Valli is asked by Murugan, who is himself already married to Devaiyanai, to become his second wife. A great portion of the dramatic action of this play is taken up with Valli's argument against the practice of second marriage as disrespectful to women. By playing Valli onstage, these actresses felt they had a chance to speak about a role they play in real life.

9 Social reform crusades concerned with Indian women's domestic lives were big in Britain and the United States as well as India in the nineteenth century. More than fifty years after the 1891 colonial age-of-consent law was enacted in India regarding Hindu marriages, it still had not really affected the lives led by lower-class women like Ambika. In postcolonial times, though in some ways already overdetermined, these issues are no longer (at least overtly) defined from outside but rather are now identified as problems by those who live them: women like Ambika, who themselves experienced child marriage, testify to those like her who are still at risk.

Several middle-class Indian theater activists are doing related work in rural areas and regularly encounter villages where women suffer from social troubles supposedly eradicated under colonial law. Actress Mangai and her troupe in Tamilnadu and actress Susuma and her one-woman shows in Maharashtra have both recounted such experiences to me in personal communications. The Tamil writer C. S. Lakshmi has produced a documentary film on Ambika's life and work, entitled simply *Ambika*, through the auspices of Sparrow (Sound and Picture Archives for Research on Women, Mumbai India, 2003).

10 In the terms that McKim Marriott and Ronald Inden (1974) use to describe interactive styles of personhood in the Indian context, artists are "maximally transactive" in their social relations. In subsequent work, Marriott theorizes interactive styles in the Hindu world in the even more precise terms of mixing, marking, and unmatching.

Synthesizing a wealth of ethnographic information from various parts of India, Marriott (1998) has developed what he terms "an ethnosociology that can deal systematically with the distinctive culture of the region" (279). Marriott's model is of the multidimensional logics that undergird social action in South Asia. Speaking of any large world area as a singular cultural entity, even when that entity is a system of relative social positions, risks turning the culture concept into a static whole. It is therefore a view many anthropologists reject, recognizing how historical contingency and the vicissitudes of interpretive practice contribute to what we see where.

In my own focus on artists' strategies for dealing with social stigma, I view their work and lives as engagements in a historical, and fundamentally contingent, problem. These differences notwithstanding, there are many continuities between my observations of the negotiations that Special Drama artists make to deal with stigma and Marriott's charting of the social logics revealed by ethnographic findings across India, and supported by his own readings of Hindu philosophical texts.

Marriott's ethnosociological model is based on three axes, each of which represents a continuum from more to less pure, respectively. The three axes are unmixing versus mixing, unmarking versus marking, and matching versus unmatching. Each of these three continua corresponds in important ways to the multiple dimensions I discuss as stigmatizing Special Drama artists.

First and foremost is the common perception that actors engage in too much mixing of all kinds. In Marriott's terms, mixing generates a kind of interactive "heat" through the activity of varied social exchanges, interchanges, and intersections; it is opposed to unmixing, which is a way people can attain "coolness" by "internalising their resources," that is, by keeping to themselves, and "potentialising their energies" rather than squandering them in mixing with others (Marriott 1998, 282). The practice of intercaste love marriage that actors (and, even more so, actresses) engage in stigmatizes them in the domain of too much mixing. Second, actors are marked by engaging in behaviors that are themselves ranked as low, such as physically providing services for money. A third stigmatizing dimension of actors' interactions is that which Marriott discusses as unmatching. He defines unmatching processes as "actions considered to be alien or inappropriate to entities' own properties, whether actual, past, imagined, or desired" (282). This describes well the stigma that confronts actors simply for *acting*, for playing false roles, and for representing themselves, even in imaginary and mythic contexts, as personages other than who they otherwise are.

Marriott's terms thus help to identify the intersecting dimensions of the stigma that artists negotiate. To summarize, unmatching corresponds to the stigma of engaging in mimetic processes and the proffering of false selves. Engaging in too much mixing corresponds to the stigma placed on artists for their practices of intermarriage and fictive kin strategies, as well as the diversity and inclusivity of the community in general. The stigma that is marking speaks to how artists are marked by their excessive mobility, and their participation in a service economy. Marriott's systematization of these concepts allows him to envision people's social lives according to their positions in the intersecting planes of these socially defining concepts. In such a charting, Special Drama artists would appear as inhabitants of the highly impure intersection of these three interactive fields of social relations, the bottommost corner of a metaphorical "cube" of Hindu ethnosociology, explicitly labeled in some of Marriott's diagrams as the figurative location of prostitutes, whores, and sluts, in others as the locus of impure coupling, insult, disgust, and wild and loathsome things of all forms (Marriott 1989, 1993, 1998). The ways in which Special Drama artists are stigmatized by a combination of mixing, unmatching, and marking take shape in the terms and tropes of the local Tamil discourses on excessive mobility that I have introduced throughout this book.

Works Cited

Abu-Lughod, Lila. 1990. "The Romance of Resistance: Tracing Transformations of Power through Bedouin Women." *American Ethnologist* 17, no. 1 (February): 41–55.

Agnew, Jean-Cristophe. 1986. *Worlds Apart: The Market and the Theater in Anglo-American Thought, 1550–1750*. New York: Cambridge University Press.

Ali, Daud. 1994. "The Arrows of Kama: Engendering the Court through the Gaze." South Asia Workshop, University of Chicago, 8 February 1994.

Anandhi, S. 1997. "Sexuality and the Nation: 'Ideal' and 'Other' Women in Nationalist Politics, Tamilnadu, c. 1930–47." *South Indian Studies* 4:195–217.

Anderson, Benedict. 1992. *Imagined Communities*. Rev. ed. New York: Verso.

Apffel Marglin, Frederique. 1985. *Wives of the God-King: The Rituals of the Devadasis of Puri*. Delhi: Oxford University Press.

Appadurai, Arjun, Korom, Frank J., and Margaret A. Mills, eds. 1991. *Gender, Genre, and Power in South Asian Expressive Traditions*. Philadelphia: University of Pennsylvania Press.

Apte, Mahadev L. 1985. *Humor and Laughter: An Anthropological Approach*. Ithaca, N.Y.: Cornell University Press.

———. 1992. *Humor and Communication in Contemporary Marathi Theater: A Sociolinguistic Perspective*. Pune: Linguistic Society of India.

Ardener, Shirley, ed. [1981] 1993. *Women and Space: Ground Rules and Social Maps*. Oxford: Berg.

Aristotle. 1982. *Poetics*. Trans. James Hutton. New York: Norton.

Arunachalam, M. 1974. *An Introduction to the History of Tamil Literature*. Tiruchitrambalam, India: Gandhi Vidyalayam.

Bakhtin, Mikhail M. [1935] 1981. "Discourse in the Novel." In *The Dialogic Imagination*, trans. Caryl Emerson and Michael Holquist. Austin: University of Texas Press.

———. [1965] 1984. *Rabelais and His World*. Trans. Helene Iswolsky. Bloomington: Indiana University Press.

Banerjee, Sumanta. 1990. "Marginalization of Women's Popular Culture in Nineteenth Century Bengal." In *Recasting Women: Essays in Indian Colonial History*, ed. Kumkum Sangari and Sudesh Vaid. New Brunswick, N.J.: Rutgers University Press.

———. 1998. *Under the Raj: Prostitution in Colonial Bengal*. New York: Monthly Review Press. (First published as *Dangerous Outcast: The Prostitute in Nineteenth Century Bengal* in 1998 by Seagull Books, Calcutta, India.)

Barish, Jonas. 1981. *The Antitheatrical Prejudice*. Berkeley: University of California Press.

Barnett, Marguerite Ross. 1976. *The Politics of Cultural Nationalism*. Princeton, N.J.: Princeton University Press.

Baskaran, S. Theodore. 1981. *The Message Bearers: The Nationalist Politics and the Entertainment Media in South India, 1880–1945*. Madras: Cre-A.

———. 1996. *Eye of the Serpent: An Introduction to Tamil Cinema*. Madras: EastWest Books.

———. 2001. "Persistence of Conventions: 'Company Drama' and the Tamil Cinema." *Seagull Theatre Quarterly*, no. 31:75–88.

Basso, Keith H. 1979. *Portraits of "the Whiteman": Linguistic Play and Cultural Symbols among the Western Apache*. Cambridge: Cambridge University Press.

———. 1996. *Wisdom Sits in Places*. Albuquerque: University of New Mexico Press.

Bate, J. Bernard. 2000. "Meedaittamil: Oratory and Democratic Practice in Tamilnadu." Ph.D. diss., Department of Anthropology, University of Chicago.

———. 2002. "Political Praise in Tamil Newspapers: The Poetry and Iconography of Democratic Power." In *Everyday Life in South Asia*, ed. Diane P. Mines and Sarah Lamb, 308–25. Bloomington: Indiana University Press.

Baugh, John, and Joel Sherzer, eds. 1984. *Language in Use: Readings in Sociolinguistics*. Englewood Cliffs, N.J.: Prentice-Hall.

Bauman, Richard. 1977. *Verbal Art as Performance*. Long Grove, Ill.: Waveland Press.

———. 1986. *Story, Performance, and Event: Contextual Studies of Oral Narrative*. Cambridge: Cambridge University Press.

———. 1993. "Disclaimers of Performance." In *Responsibility and Evidence in Oral Discourse*, ed. Jane H. Hill and Judith T. Irvine. Cambridge University Press.

Bauman, Richard, and Joel Sherzer, eds. 1974. *Explorations in the Ethnography of Speaking*. London: Cambridge University Press.

Beck, Brenda E. F. 1982. "The Courtship of Valli and Murugan: Some Parallels with the Radha-Krishna Story." In *The Divine Consort: Radha and the Goddesses of India*, ed. J. S. Hawley and D. M. Wulff. Boston: Beacon Press.

Beck, Brenda E. F., et al., eds. 1987. *Folktales of India*. Chicago: University of Chicago Press.

Becker, Howard S. 1998. *Tricks of the Trade: How to Think about Your Research While You're Doing It*. Chicago: University of Chicago Press.

Ben-Amos, Dan. 1982. *Folklore in Context*. New Delhi: South Asian Publishers.

Ben-Amos, Dan, and Kenneth S. Goldstein, eds. 1975. *Folklore: Performance and Communication*. The Hague: Mouton.

Benjamin, Walter. [1939] 1969. "What Is Epic Theater?" In *Illuminations*, trans. Harry Zohn. New York: Schocken.

Bergson, Henri. [1900] 1956. "Laughter." In *Comedy*, introduced by Wylie Sypher. New York: Doubleday Anchor.

Bharatiyar, Subramanian. [1909] 1981. "Cankita visayam" [The Issue of Music]. In *Bharatiyar Katturaikal* [Essays of Bharatiyar], ed. A. Tirunavukkarasu. Madras: Vanathi Pathipakkam.

Biale, David, Michael Galchinsky, and Susannah Heschel. 1997. *Insider/Outsider*. Berkeley: University of California Press.

Blackburn, Stuart. 1996. *Inside the Drama-House: Rama Stories and Shadow Puppets in South India*. Berkeley: University of California Press.

Blackburn, Stuart, and A. K. Ramanujan. 1986. Introduction to *Another Harmony: New Essays on the Folklore of India*, ed. Stuart Blackburn and A. K. Ramanujan. Berkeley: University of California Press.

Bogden, Robert. 1988. *Freak Show: Presenting Human Oddities for Amusement and Profit*. Chicago: University of Chicago Press.

Boon, James A. 1983. "Folly, Bali, and Anthropology, or Satire across Cultures." In *Text, Play, and Story*, ed. Edward M. Bruner. Long Grove, Ill.: Waveland Press.

Booth, Wayne C. 1982. "Freedom of Interpretation: Bakhtin and the Challenge of Feminist Criticism." *Critical Inquiry* 9:45–76.

Bougainville, Louis-Antoine de. [1772] 1967. *A Voyage around the World*. Ridgewood, N.J.: Gregg Press.

Bourdieu, Pierre. [1972] 1977. *Outline of a Theory of Practice*. Trans. Richard Nice. Cambridge: Cambridge University Press.

———. 1984. *Distinction: A Social Critique of the Judgement of Taste*. Trans. Richard Nice. Cambridge: Harvard University Press.

Bowen, Elenore Smith. 1954. *Return to Laughter: An Anthropological Novel*. New York: Anchor.

Brecht, Bertolt. 1947. *The Good Woman of Setzuan*. Trans. Eric Bentley. New York: Grove.

———. 1955. *Mother Courage*. Trans. Eric Bentley. New York: Grove.

———. [1957] 1964. *Brecht on Theatre*. Ed. and trans. John Willett. New York: Hill and Wang.

———. 1965. *The Jewish Wife*. Trans. Eric Bentley. New York: Grove.

Briggs, Charles. 1988. *Competence in Performance: The Creativity of Tradition in Mexicano Verbal Art*. Philadelphia: University of Pennsylvania Press.

British Association for the Advancement of Science. 1874. *Notes and Queries on Anthropology for the Use of Travellers and Residents in Uncivilized Lands*. London: Edward Stanford, Charing Cross.

———. n.d. [c. 1895]. "Forms of a Schedule Prepared by a Committee of the British Association for the Advancement of Science Appointed to Organize an Ethnographical Survey of the United Kingdom." Unpublished circular.

Bruin, Hanne de. 1999. *Kattaikkuttu: The Flexibility of a South Indian Theatre Tradition*. Gonda Indological Series 7. Groningen: Egbert Forsten.

———. 2000. "Naming a Theatre in Tamil Nadu." *Asian Theatre Journal* 17, no. 1 (Spring): 98–122.

———. 2001a. "The History of the Rural *Natakam* or 'Drama' in North Tamilnadu." *Seagull Theatre Quarterly*, no. 31:56–74.

———. 2001b. "Introduction." *Seagull Theatre Quarterly*, no. 31:2–6.

Bullock, Barbara E. 1996. "Popular Derivation and Linguistic Inquiry: Les Javanais." *French Review* 70 (2): 180–91.

Burns, Elizabeth. 1972. *Theatricality: A Study of Convention in the Theatre and in Social Life*. London: Longman Group.

Burns, John F. 1996. "Accident or Mass Murder? India's Food-Poisoning Mystery." *New York Times*, 19 August.

Butler, Judith. 1990. *Gender Trouble: Feminism and the Subversion of Identity*. New York: Routledge.

———. 1993. *Bodies That Matter: On the Discursive Limits of "Sex."* New York: Routledge.

Cage, Ken. 2003. http://www.mambaonline.com/feature/feature_kencage.htm (accessed 9 July).

Case, Carole. 1984. "Argot Roles in Horseracing." *Urban Life* 13, nos. 2–3 (October): 271–88.

Case, Sue-Ellen. 1991. "The Eurocolonial Reception of Sanskrit Poetics." In *The Performance of Power*, ed. Sue-Ellen Case and Janelle Reinelt, 111–27. Iowa City: University of Iowa Press.

Chatterjee, Partha. 1993. *The Nation and Its Fragments: Colonial and Postcolonial Histories*. Princeton, N.J.: Princeton University Press.

Chatterjee, Sudipto. 2001. "From Colonial *Jatra* to Native Theatre: Hybrid Aesthetics of Nineteenth Century Bengali Theatre." *Seagull Theatre Quarterly*, no. 31:24–32.

Clark, Michael. 1970. "Humor and Incongruity." *Philosophy* 45: 20–32.

Clifford, James. 1997. "Spatial Practices: Fieldwork, Travel, and the Disciplining of Anthropology." In *Anthropological Locations*, ed. Akhil Gupta and James Ferguson, 185–222. Berkeley: University of California Press.

Cohn, Bernard S. 1987. *An Anthropologist among the Historians and Other Essays*. Delhi: Oxford University Press.

———. 1988. "The Command of Language and the Language of Command." In *Subaltern Studies IV*, ed. Ranajit Guha. Delhi: Oxford University Press.

———. 1998. "The Past in the Present: India as a Museum of Mankind." *History and Anthropology* 11 (1): 1–38.

Comaroff, John L., and Jean Comaroff. 1993. "Resistance and Rebellion in Black South Africa, 1830–1920: Awful Acts, Lawful Facts, and Illegal Imaginings on a Colonial Frontier." Unpublished proposal to the American Bar Foundation and the University of Chicago.

———. 1995. "New Persons, Old Subjects: Rights, Identities, Alternative Modernities." In *From Revelation to Revolution: Christianity, Colonialism, and Consciousness in South Africa*, vol. 2. Chicago: University of Chicago Press.

Cre-A. 1992. *Kriyāviṉ Taṟkālat Tamiḻ Akarāti* [Dictionary of Contemporary Tamil]. Madras: Cre-A.

Daniel, E. Valentine. 1984. *Fluid Signs: Being a Person the Tamil Way*. Berkeley: University of California Press.

Davis, Nathalie Zemon. 1975. "The Reasons of Misrule" and "Women on Top." In *Society and Culture in Early Modern France*. Palo Alto: Stanford University Press.

Davis, Tracy C. 1991. *Actresses as Working Women: Their Social Identity in Victorian Culture*. New York: Routledge.

Diamond, Elin. 1992. "The Violence of 'We': Politicizing Identification." In *Critical Theory and Performance*, ed. Janelle G. Reinelt and Joseph R. Roach. Ann Arbor: University of Michigan Press.

Dickey, Sara. 1993. *Cinema and the Urban Poor in South India*. Cambridge: Cambridge University Press.

———. 2000. "Permeable Homes: Domestic Service, Household Space, and the Vulnerability of Class Boundaries in Urban India." *American Ethnologist* 29, no. 2 (May): 462–89.

Douglas, Mary. 1966. *Purity and Danger*. New York: Routledge.

———. 1975. "Jokes." In *Implicit Meanings: Essays in Anthropology*. London: Routledge.

Dumont, Louis. [1957] 1986. *A South Indian Subcaste: Social Organization and Religion of the Pramalai Kallar*. Trans. M. Moffatt, L. Morton, and A. Morton. Delhi: Oxford University Press.

———. [1966] 1980. *Homo Hierarchicus: The Caste System and Its Implications*. Trans. Mark Sainsbury, Louis Dumont, and Basia Gulati. Chicago: University of Chicago Press.

———. 1983. *Affinity as Value: Marriage Alliance in South India, with Comparative Essays on Australia*. Chicago: University of Chicago Press.

Durkheim, Emile. [1893] 1964. *The Division of Labour in Society*. London: Routledge.

———. [1895] 1950. *The Rules of Sociological Method*. Glencoe, Ill.: Free Press of Glencoe.

———. [1912] 1965. *The Elementary Forms of the Religious Life*. New York: Free Press.

———. [1950] 1957. *Professional Ethics and Civic Morals*. London: Routledge and Kegan Paul.

Dyer, Richard. 1997. *White*. New York: Routledge.

Eck, Diana L. 1981. *Darsan: Seeing the Divine Image in India*. Chambersburg, Pa.: Anima Books.

Elias, Norbert. 1974. "Towards a Theory of Communities." Foreword to *The Sociology of Communities*, ed. Colin Bell and Howard Newby. Portland, Oreg.: Frank Cass.

English, James F. 1994. "Introduction: Humor, Politics, Community." In *Comic Transactions: Literature, Humor, and the Politics of Community in Twentieth-Century Britain*. Ithaca, N.Y.: Cornell University Press.

Erdman, Joan. 1996. "Dance Discourses: Rethinking the History of the 'Oriental Dance.'" In *Moving Words: Rethinking Dance*, ed. Gay Morris. New York: Routledge.

Fabian, Johannes. 1983. *Time and the Other: How Anthropology Makes Its Object*. New York: Columbia University Press.

Fabricius, Johann Philip. [1779] 1972. *Tamil and English Dictionary*. 4th ed. Tranquebar: Evangelical Lutheran Mission.

Farrell, Ronald A. 1972. "The Argot of the Homosexual Subculture." *Anthropological Linguistics* 14:97–109.

Feld, Steven. [1982] 1990. *Sound and Sentiment*. 2nd ed. Philadelphia: University of Pennsylvania Press.

Ferris, Lesley, ed. 1993. *Crossing the Stage: Controversies on Cross-Dressing*. London: Routledge.
Firth, Raymond. [1936] 1983. *We, the Tikopia*. Stanford, Calif.: Stanford University Press.
Foucault, Michel. 1978. *The History of Sexuality*. Vol. 1. Trans. Robert Hurley. New York: Vintage.
———. 1980. *Power/Knowledge*. Ed. Colin Gordon, trans. Colin Gordon et al. New York: Pantheon.
Frank, Gelya. 1995. "The Ethnographic Films of Barbara G. Myerhoff: Anthropology, Feminism, and the Politics of Jewish Identity." In *Women Writing Culture*, ed. Ruth Behar and Deborah A. Gordon. Berkeley: University of California Press.
Franklin, Karl J. 1975. "A Kewa Religious Argot (New Guinea)." *Anthropos* 70:713–25.
Frasca, Richard Armando. 1990. *The Theater of the Mahabharata: Terukkuttu Performances in South India*. Honolulu: University of Hawaii Press.
Freud, Sigmund. [1905] 1960. *Jokes and Their Relation to the Unconscious*. Trans. and ed. James Strachey. New York: W. W. Norton.
Gal, Susan. 1995. "Language and the 'Arts of Resistance.'" *Cultural Anthropology* 10, no. 3:407–24.
Gandhi, Gopalkrishna, ed. 1983. *Tamilnadu District Gazetteers: Pudukkottai*. Madras: Government of Tamilnadu.
Gaston, Anne-Marie. 1996. *Bharata Natyam: From Temple to Theatre*. New Delhi: Manohar Publishers.
Geertz, Clifford. 1973. *The Interpretation of Cultures*. New York: Basic Books.
Gennap, Arnold van. [1909] 1960. *The Rites of Passage*. London: Routledge.
Giddens, Anthony. 1971. *Capitalism and Modern Social Theory: An Analysis of the Writings of Marx, Durkheim, and Max Weber*. Cambridge: Cambridge University Press.
Girard, Rene. 1978. "Perilous Balance: A Comic Hypothesis." In *"To Double Business Bound": Essays on Literature, Mimesis, and Anthropology*. Baltimore: Johns Hopkins University Press.
Goffman, Erving. 1963. *Stigma: Notes on the Management of Spoiled Identity*. Englewood Cliffs, N.J.: Prentice-Hall.
———. 1974. *Frame Analysis*. New York: Harper and Row.
———. 1979. "Footing." *Semiotica* 25 (1–2): 1–29.
Gopalratnam, V. C. 1981. "Tamil Drama." In *Indian Drama*, 2d rev. ed., 119–26. New Delhi: Publications Division, Ministry of Information and Broadcasting, Government of India.
Gunasekaran, K. A. 1987. *Tamiḻ Nāṭakamum Cankaratās Cuvāmikalum* [Tamil Drama and Sankaradas Swamigal]. Sivagangae: Annam.
Gurudeva. 2000. "Saint Auvaiyar Ma." In *Loving Ganesha*. 2nd ed. Kapaa, Hawaii: Himalayan Academy.
Gutman, Judith Mara. 1982. *Through Indian Eyes*. New York: Oxford University Press.
Halperin, David. 1995. "The Queer Politics of Michel Foucault." In *Saint Foucault: Towards a Gay Hagiography*. New York: Oxford University Press.

Handke, Peter. [1972] 1977. *Three by Peter Handke*. New York: Bard (Avon Books).
Hansen, Kathryn. 1992. *Grounds for Play: The Nautanki Theatre of North India*. Berkeley: University of California Press.
———. 1998. "Stri Bhumika: Female Impersonators and Actresses on the Parsi Stage." *Economic and Political Weekly* (Mumbai), 29 August 1998, 2291–2300.
———. 1999. "Making Women Visible: Gender and Race Cross-Dressing in the Parsi Theatre." *Theatre Journal* 51 (2): 127–48.
Haraway, Donna J. 1988. "Situated Knowledges: The Science Question in Feminism and the Privilege of Partial Perspective." *Feminist Studies* 14, no. 3.
———. 1991. "A Cyborg Manifesto: Science, Technology, and Socialist-Feminism in the Late Twentieth Century." In *Simians, Cyborgs, and Women: The Reinvention of Nature*. New York: Routledge.
Hart, George L., III. 1973. "Women and the Sacred in Ancient Tamilnad." *Journal of Asian Studies* 32, no. 2 (February): 233–50.
Hawley, John Stratton, and Donna Marie Wulff, eds. 1982. *The Divine Consort: Radha and the Goddesses of India*. Boston: Beacon Press.
Hebdige, Dick. 1979. *Subculture: The Meaning of Style*. London: Methuen.
Heckel, Angelika. 1986. *Natyasastra*. Bangalore: IBH Prakashana.
———. 1989. "Rasa: The Audience and the Stage." *Journal of Arts and Ideas* (New Delhi), nos. 17–18:33–42.
Hillery, George A., Jr. 1955. "Definitions of Community: Areas of Agreement." *Rural Sociology* 20 (June).
Hiltebeitel, Alf. 1988. *The Cult of Draupadī: Mythologies from Gingee to Kuruksetra*. Vol. 1. Chicago: University of Chicago Press.
Howard, Jean E. 1994. *The Stage and Social Struggle in Early Modern England*. London: Routledge.
Hughes, Stephen P. Forthcoming. "Music in the Age of Mechanical Reproduction: Drama, Gramophone, and the Beginnings of Tamil Cinema." *Journal of Asian Studies*.
Hutton, J. H. 1946. *Caste in India: Its Nature, Function, and Origins*. Cambridge: Cambridge University Press.
Hutton, James. 1982. Introduction to *Aristotle's Poetics*, trans. James Hutton. New York: Norton.
Hymes, Dell. 1971. "Sociolinguistics and the Ethnography of Speaking." In *Social Anthropology and Language*, ed. Edwin Ardener. London: Tavistock.
———. 1990. *Foundations in Sociolinguistics: An Ethnographic Approach*. Philadelphia: University of Pennsylvania Press.
IAS. *See* Institute of Asian Studies.
Inden, Ronald. 1990. *Imagining India*. Oxford: Blackwell.
Institute of Asian Studies. 1990. "Western Influences on Tamil Drama." In *Encyclopaedia of Tamil Literature*, vol. 1. Madras: Institute of Asian Studies.
Irschick, Eugene F. 1969. *Politics and Social Conflict in South India: The Non-Brahman Movement and Tamil Separatism, 1916–1929*. Berkeley: University of California Press.
———. 1986. *Tamil Revivalism in the 1930s*. Madras: Cre-A.

Ishwar, M. V. 1911. "Some Aspects of the Profession of an Actor: A Plea for Professional Theatres of Educated People." *The Stage Lover* (Madras) 1, no. 3 (October).
———, ed. 1911a. *The Stage Lover* 1, no. 1 (August).
———. 1911b. *The Stage Lover* 1, no. 2 (September).
———. 1911c. *The Stage Lover* 1, no. 3 (October).
———. 1911d. *The Stage Lover* 1, nos. 4–5 (November–December).
Iyal Icai Nāḍaka Manram. 1992. *Kalaimāmaṇi Virutu Vaḻaṅkum Viḻā, 1992 Cirappumalar* (Catalog Celebrating the 1992 Great Artist Awards Ceremony). Chennai: Tamiḻnāṭu Iyal Icai Nāṭaka Manram (Madras: The Tamilnadu Prose-Music-Drama Association).
Jackson, Michael. 1989. *Paths toward a Clearing: Radical Empiricism and Ethnographic Inquiry*. Bloomington: Indiana University Press.
Jacobson, Doranne. 1978. "The Chaste Wife: Cultural Norm and Individual Experience." In *American Studies in the Anthropology of India*, ed. Sylvia Vatuk. New Delhi: Manohar.
Jain, Kajri. 2001. "Vernacularising Capitalism: Sivakasi and Its Circuits." (Manuscript.)
Jakobson, Roman [1957] 1971. "Shifters, Verbal Categories, and the Russian Verb." In *Roman Jakobson: Selected Writings*, vol. 2. The Hague: Mouton.
Jameson, Fredric. 1972. *The Prison-House of Language: A Critical Account of Structuralism and Russian Formalism*. Princeton, N.J.: Princeton University Press.
Jenkins, Ron. 1994. *Subversive Laughter: The Liberating Power of Comedy*. New York: Free Press.
Jensen, Herman. [1897] 1989. *A Classified Collection of Tamil Proverbs*. New Delhi and Madras: Asian Educational Services.
Jowitt, Deborah. 1985. "Balancing Heaven and Hell." *Village Voice*, 30 April, 97.
Kannabiran, Kalpana. 1995. "Judiciary, Social Reform, and Debate on 'Religious Prostitution' in Colonial India." *Economic and Political Weekly* 30 (43): 59–69.
Kaplan, Charles D., Helmut Kampe, and Jose Antonio Flores Farfan. 1990. "Argots as a Code-Switching Process: A Case Study of the Sociolinguistic Aspects of Drug Subcultures." In *Codeswitching as a Worldwide Phenomenon*, ed. R. Jacobson. New York: Peter Lang.
Kapur, Anuradha. 1990. *Actors, Pilgrims, Kings, and Gods: The Ramlila at Ramnagar*. Calcutta, India: Seagull Books.
———. 1991. "Notions of the Authentic." *Journal of Arts and Ideas* (New Delhi), nos. 20–21 (March).
———. 1993. "The Representation of Gods and Heroes: Parsi Mythological Drama of the Early Twentieth Century." *Journal of Arts and Ideas* (New Delhi), nos. 23–24 (January): 85–107.
Karnad, Girish. 1989. "Theatre in India." In "Another India," special edition, *Daedalus: Journal of the American Academy of Arts and Sciences* 118 (4): 331–52.
Kaviraj, Sudipta. 1993. "The Imaginary Institution of India." In *Subaltern Studies VII: Writings on South Asian History and Society*, ed. Partha Chatterjee and Gyanendra Pandey. Delhi: Oxford University Press.

Keeler, Ward. 1987. *Javanese Shadow Plays, Javanese Selves*. Princeton, N.J. Princeton University Press.

Kersenboom-Story, Saskia C. 1987. *Nityasumangali: Devadasi Tradition in South India*. Delhi: Motilal Banarsidass.

———. 1995. *Word, Sound, Image: The Life of the Tamil Text*. Oxford: Berg Publishers.

Kirshenblatt-Gimblett, Barbara. 1975. "A Parable in Context: A Social Interactional Analysis of Storytelling Performance." In *Folklore: Performance and Communication*, ed. Dan Ben-Amos and Kenneth S. Goldstein. The Hague: Mouton.

Kishwar, Madhu, and Ruth Vanita. 1987. "The Burning of Roop Kanwar." *Manushi* (New Delhi), nos. 42–43:15–25.

Kodiswari, M. S. 1987. *Nāṭṭuppura Icai Nāṭakaṅkaḷ: Taṉjai Māvaṭṭam* [Folk Music Drama: Tanjore District]. Madras: Madras University, Pachaiyappan College.

Laclau, Ernesto. 1991. "Community and Its Paradoxes." In *Community at Loose Ends: The Miami Theory Collective*, ed. Miami Theory Collective. Minneapolis: University of Minnesota Press.

Laplanche, J., and J-B. Pontalis. 1973. *The Language of Psycho-Analysis*. Trans. Donald Nicholson-Smith. New York: Norton.

Leach, Edmund. 1964. "Anthropological Aspects of Language: Animal Categories and Verbal Abuse." In *New Directions in the Study of Language*, ed. Eric H. Lenneberg. Cambridge: MIT Press.

Lewis, Oscar. [1955] 1986. "Peasant Culture in India and Mexico: A Comparative Analysis." In *Village India: Studies in the Little Community*. Chicago: Midway Reprint Edition.

Lorde, Audre. 1982. *Zami: A New Spelling of My Name*. Freedom, Calif.: Crossing Press.

Malinowski, Bronislaw. 1922. *Argonauts of the Western Pacific*. London: George Routledge and Sons.

Maloney, Clarence. 1974. *Peoples of South Asia*. New York: Holt, Rinehart, and Winston.

Mandel, Oscar. 1970. "What's So Funny: The Nature of the Comic." *Antioch Review* 30, no. 1:73–89.

Mannheim, Bruce. 1995. "On the Margins of *The Couple in the Cage*." *Visual Anthropology Review* 11, no. 1 (Spring): 121–27.

Maraimalai Adigal. [1925] 1980. Preface to the Second Edition. In *Cintanaik Kaṭṭuraıkaḷ* (Philosophical Essays), 9–40. Madras: SISSW.

Marglin, Frederique Apffel. 1985. *Wives of the God-King: The Rituals of the Devadasis of Puri*. Delhi: Oxford University Press.

Marriott, McKim. 1976. "Hindu Transactions: Diversity without Dualism." In *Transaction and Meaning: ASA Essays in Social Anthropology*, vol. 1. Philadelphia: Institute for the Study of Human Issues.

———. 1989. "Constructing an Indian Ethnosociology." *Contributions to Indian Sociology* 23:1–39.

———. 1993. Various unpublished diagrams of the Hindu Constituent Cube, shared with the author in personal communication.

———. 1998. "The Female Family Core Explored Ethnosociologically." *Contributions to Indian Sociology* 32, no. 2:279–304.

Marriott, McKim, and Ronald B. Inden. 1974. "Caste Systems." In *Encyclopaedia Britannica*, 15th ed.

Maurer, David. 1931. "Carnival Cant." *American Speech* 6:327–37.

McClintock, Anne. 1993. "Sex Workers and Sex Work: Introduction." *Social Text* 37:1–10.

McLean, Adrienne L. 1997. "The Thousand Ways There Are to Move: Camp and Oriental Dance in the Hollywood Musicals of Jack Cole." In *Visions of the East: Orientalism in Film*, ed. Matthew Bernstein and Gaylyn Studlar. New Brunswick, N.J.: Rutgers University Press.

Mehrotra, R. R. 1977. *Sociology of Secret Languages*. Simla: Indian Institute of Advanced Study.

Mehta, Kumudini. 1960. "English Drama on the Bombay Stage in the Late Eighteenth and in the Nineteenth Century." Thesis, University of Bombay.

Microsoft. 2000. "Indian Languages." Microsoft Encarta online encyclopedia. http://encarta.msn.com.

Miner, Horace M. 1968. "Community-Society Continua." In *International Encyclopedia of the Social Sciences*, vol. 4. London: Crowell, Collier, and Macmillan.

Mitchell, William E. 1992. "Introduction: Mother Folly in the Islands." In *Clowning as Critical Practice*. Pittsburgh, Pa.: University of Pittsburgh Press.

Mitter, Partha. 1977. *Much Maligned Monsters: History of European Reactions to Indian Art*. Oxford: Clarendon Press.

———. 1994. *Art and Nationalism in Colonial India, 1850–1922*. Cambridge: Cambridge University Press.

Modleski, Tania. 1988. *The Women Who Knew Too Much: Hitchcock and Feminist Theory*. New York: Methuen.

Morreall, John, ed. 1987. *The Philosophy of Laughter and Humor*. New York: State University of New York Press.

Mouffe, Chantal. 1991. "Democratic Citizenship and the Political Community." In *Community at Loose Ends*, ed. Miami Theory Collective. Minneapolis: University of Minnesota Press.

Mudaliyar, Pammal Sambanda. 1998. *Pammal Campanta Mutaliyarin Urainatai Nulkal*. Vol. 1. Chennai: International Institute of Tamil Studies. [A compilation of earlier 1962, 1969, and 1938 publications.]

Mukerji, Chandra, and Michael Schudson. 1991. "Introduction: Rethinking Popular Culture." In *Rethinking Popular Culture: Contemporary Perspectives in Cultural Studies*, ed. Chandra Mukerji and Michael Schudson. Berkeley: University of California Press.

Mukherjee, Bharati. 1989. *Jasmine*. New York: Ballantine.

Mullaney, Steven. 1983. "Strange Things, Gross Terms, Curious Customs: The Rehearsal of Cultures in the Late Renaissance." *Representations* 3 (Summer): 40–67.

Muñoz, José Esteban. 1999. *Disidentifications: Queers of Color and the Performance of Politics*. Minneapolis: University of Minnesota Press.
Murray, Thomas E. 1993. "The Folk Argot of Midwestern Gangs." *Midwestern Folklore* 19, no. 2:113–48.
Myerhoff, Barbara. 1978. *Number Our Days*. New York: E. P. Dutton.
Nancy, Jean-Luc. 1991a. *The Inoperative Community* [Communauté désūvrée]. Ed. Peter Connor, trans. Peter Connor, Lisa Garbus, Michael Holland, and Simona Sawhney. Minneapolis: University of Minnesota Press.
———. 1991b. "Of Being in Common."
Nārāyaṉ, Aṟantai. 1981. *Tamiḻ Ciṉimāviṉ Katai* [The Story of Tamil Cinema]. Madras: New Century Book House.
Narayan, R. K. [1982] 1996. *Malgudi Days*. Madras: Indian Thought Publications.
———. 1987. *The Mahabharata*. New Delhi: Vision Books.
Naregal, Veena. 2001. "Provincial Elites, Urban Intellectuals and a New Marathi Theatre." *Seagull Theatre Quarterly*, no. 31:7–33.
Navaneethan, Vijayalakshmi. 1985. *Nāṭaka Viḻikaḷ* [Drama Eyes]. Madurai: Kuṟiñci Malar Veḷiyīṭu.
Newton, Esther. 1972. *Mother Camp: Female Impersonators in America*. Englewood Cliffs, N.J.: Prentice Hall.
———. 2000. *Margaret Mead Made Me Gay*. Durham: Duke University Press.
Novack, Cynthia J. 1990. *Sharing the Dance: Contact Improvisation and American Culture*. Madison: University of Wisconsin Press.
Oldenburg, Veena Talwar. 1990. "Lifestyle as Resistance: The Case of the Courtesans of Lucknow, India." *Feminist Studies* 16, no. 2:259–88.
Oring, Elliott. 1992. *Jokes and Their Relations*. Lexington: University Press of Kentucky.
Ortner, Sherry. 1995. "Resistance and the Problem of Ethnographic Refusal." *Comparative Studies in History and Society* 37, no. 1 (January): 173–93.
Pandian, M. S. S. 1992. *The Image Trap: M. G. Ramachandran in Film and Politics*. New Delhi: Sage.
Paramasivam, K., and James Lindholm. 1980a. *A Basic Tamil Reader and Grammar*. Vol. 1, *Readings*. Evanston, Ill.: Tamil Language Study Association.
———. 1980b. *A Basic Tamil Reader and Grammar*. Vol. 2, *Annotations*. Evanston, Ill.: Tamil Language Study Association.
Parker, Kunal. 1998. "'A Corporation of Superior Prostitutes': Anglo-Indian Legal Conceptions of Temple Dancing Girls, 1800–1914." *Modern Asian Studies* 32 (3): 559–633.
Paxson, Heather. 2002. "Rationalizing Sex: Family Planning and the Making of Modern Lovers in Urban Greece." *American Ethnologist* 29, no. 2:307–34.
Peacock, James. [1968] 1987. *Rites of Modernization*. Chicago: University of Chicago Press.
Perumal, A. N. 1981. *Tamil Drama: Origin and Development*. Madras: International Institute of Tamil Studies.
Peterson, Indira Viswanathan. 2000. "Reading the Temple-Dancer as Sati: From

South Indian Legend to Goethe's Poem *Der Gott und die Bajadere*." Paper presented at the meetings of the Association for Asian Studies, San Diego, Calif., 11 March 2000. (Manuscript, a longer version of the presented paper.)

Pheterson, Gail. 1993. "The Whore Stigma: Female Dishonor and Male Unworthiness." *Social Text* 37:39–64.

Pinney, Christopher. 1997. *Camera Indica: The Social Life of Indian Photographs*. Chicago: University of Chicago Press.

Plato. 1992. *Republic*. Trans. G. M. A. Grube, revised by C. D. C. Reeve. Indianapolis: Hackett.

———. 1993. *Philebus*. Trans. Dorothea Frede. Indianapolis: Hackett.

Poplin, Dennis E. 1979. *Communities: A Survey of Theories and Methods of Research*. 2nd ed. New York: Macmillan.

Pratt, Mary Louise. 1986. "Fieldwork in Common Places." In *Writing Culture*, ed. J. Clifford and G. E. Marcus. Berkeley: University of California Press.

Radcliffe-Brown, A. R. [1940] 1952. "On Joking Relationships." In *Structure and Function in Primitive Society*. Glencoe, Ill.: Free Press.

———. [1949] 1952. "A Further Note on Joking Relationships." In *Structure and Function in Primitive Society*. Glencoe, Ill.: Free Press.

Rajam, V. S. 1986. "Anaṅku: A Notion Semantically Reduced to Signify Female Sacred Power." *Journal of the American Oriental Society* 106:257–72.

Ramanujan, A. K. 1967. *The Interior Landscape: Love Poems from a Classical Tamil Anthology*. Trans. A. K. Ramanujan. Bloomington: Indiana University Press.

———. 1970. "Towards an Anthology of City Images." In *Urban India: Society, Space, and Image*, ed. Richard G. Fox. Monograph and Occasional Papers Series, Monograph no. 10. Durham, N.C.: Duke University Program in Comparative Studies on Southern Asia.

———. 1973. Introduction to *Speaking of Siva*, trans. A. K. Ramanujan. New York: Penguin.

———. 1985. *Poems of Love and War from the Eight Anthologies and the Ten Long Poems of Classical Tamil*. New York: Columbia University Press.

———. 1986. "Two Realms of Kannada Folklore." In *Another Harmony: New Essays on the Folklore of India*, ed. Stuart H. Blackburn and A. K. Ramanujan. Berkeley: University of California Press.

———. 1989. "Telling Tales." *Daedalus: Journal of the American Academy of Arts and Sciences* 118, no. 4:239–62.

———. 1991a. "Toward a Counter-System: Women's Tales." In *Gender, Genre, and Power in South Asian Expressive Traditions*, ed. Arjun Appadurai, Frank J. Korom, and Margaret A. Mills. Philadelphia: University of Pennsylvania Press.

———. 1991b. "A Flowering Tree: A Woman's Tale." Manuscript in A. K. Ramanujan Papers, University of Chicago Special Collections.

———. 1997. *A Flowering Tree and Other Oral Tales from India*. Ed. Stuart Blackburn and Alan Dundes. New Delhi: Penguin.

Ramaswami Sastri, K. S. 1956. Preface to *Nāṭyasāstra of Bharatamuni*, vol. 1, 2nd ed. Baroda: Oriental Institute.

Ramaswamy, Sumathi. 1992. "Daughters of Tamil: Language and the Poetics of Womanhood in the Tamilnad." *South Asia Research* 12, no. 1:38–59.
———. 1993. "En/gendering Language: The Poetics of Tamil Identity." *Society for Comparative Study of Society and History*, 683–725.
———. 1997. *Passions of the Tongue: Language Devotion in Tamil India, 1891–1970*. Berkeley: University of California Press.
Rangacharya, Adya. 1980. *The Indian Theatre*. New Delhi: National Book Trust.
———. 1986. *Natyasastra*. Bangalore: IBH Prakashana.
Ray, Satyajit. 1984. *The Home and the World*. Produced by the National Film Development Corporation of India, written and directed by Satyajit Ray.
Reed, Susan. 2002. "Performing Respectability: The Berava, Middle-Class Nationalism, and the Classicization of Kandyan Dance in Sri Lanka." *Cultural Anthropology* 17, no. 2:246–77.
Reynolds, Bryan. 1999. "Criminal Cant: Linguistic Innovation and Cultural Dissidence in Early Modern England." *LIT: Literature, Interpretation, Theory* 9, no. 4:369–95.
Reynolds, Holly Baker. 1980. "The Auspicious Married Woman." In *The Powers of Tamil Women*, ed. Susan S. Wadley. Syracuse, N.Y.: Maxwell School of Citizenship and Public Affairs.
Richmond, Farley P., Darius L. Swann, and Phillip B. Zarrilli, eds. 1990. *Indian Theatre: Traditions of Performance*. Honolulu: University of Hawaii Press.
Royal Anthropological Institute of Great Britain and Ireland. 1951. *Notes and Queries on Anthropology*. 6th ed. London: Routledge and Kegan Paul.
Rubin, Gayle S. 1975. "The Traffic in Women." In *Toward an Anthropology of Women*, ed. Rayna R. Reiter. New York: Monthly Review Press.
Russo, Mary. 1986. "Female Grotesques: Carnival and Theory." In *Feminist Studies/Critical Studies*. Bloomington: Indiana University Press.
Sacks, Harvey. 1974. "An Analysis of the Course of a Joke's Telling in Conversation." In *Explorations in the Ethnography of Speaking*, ed. R. Bauman and J. Sherzer. London: Cambridge University Press.
Sahlins, Marshall. 1976. "Colors and Cultures." *Semiotica* 16:1–22.
———. 1993. "Goodbye to Tristes Tropes: Ethnography in the Context of Modern World History." *Journal of Modern History* 65 (March): 1–25.
———. 1996. "The Sadness of Sweetness: The Native Anthropology of Western Cosmology." *Current Anthropology* 37, no. 3:395–428.
Sandoval, Chela. 1991. "U.S. Third World Feminism: The Theory and Method of Oppositional Consciousness in the Postmodern World." *Genders*, no. 10:1–24.
Scott, James C. 1985. *Weapons of the Weak: Everyday Forms of Peasant Resistance*. New Haven, Conn.: Yale University Press.
———. 1990. *Domination and the Arts of Resistance: Hidden Transcripts*. New Haven, Conn.: Yale University Press.
Sedgwick, Eve Kosofsky. 1985. *Between Men: English Literature and Male Homosocial Desire*. New York: Columbia University Press.
———. 1990. *Epistemology of the Closet*. Berkeley: University of California Press.

Sedgwick, Eve Kosofsky, and Adam Frank. 1995. "Shame in the Cybernetic Fold: Reading Silvan Tomkins." In *Shame and Its Sisters: A Silvan Tomkins Reader*, ed. Eve Kosofsky Sedgwick and Adam Frank. Durham, N.C.: Duke University Press.

Seizer, Susan. 1995. "Paradoxes of Visibility in the Field: Rites of Queer Passage in Anthropology." *Public Culture* 8, no. 1:73–100.

Shanmugam, T. K. 1972. *Eṉatu Nāṭaka Vāḻkkai* [My Life in Theater]. Madras: Vāṇati Patippakam.

Shulman, David Dean. 1980. *Tamil Temple Myths: Sacrifice and Divine Marriage in the South Indian Saiva Tradition*. Princeton, N.J.: Princeton University Press.

———. 1985. *The King and the Clown in South Indian Myth and Poetry*. Princeton, N.J.: Princeton University Press.

Siegel, Lee. 1987. *Laughing Matters*. Chicago: University of Chicago Press.

Silverstein, Michael. [1987] 1995. "Shifters, Linguistic Categories, and Cultural Description." In *Language, Culture, and Society*, 2nd ed., ed. Ben Blount. Long Grove, Ill.: Waveland Press.

———. 1996. "The Secret Life of Texts." In *Natural Histories of Discourse*, ed. Michael Silverstein and Greg Urban. Chicago: University of Chicago Press.

Singer, Milton. 1972. *When a Great Tradition Modernizes*. New York: Praeger.

Sivathamby, Karthigesu. 1981. *Drama in Ancient Tamil Society*. Madras: New Century Book House.

Spence, Jonathan D. 1984. *The Memory Palace of Matteo Ricci*. New York: Viking Penguin.

Sperber, Dan, and Dierdre Wilson. 1981. "Irony and the Use-Mention Distinction." In *Radical Pragmatics*, ed. Peter Cole. New York: Academic Press.

Spivak, Gayatri Chakravorty. 1995. Translator's preface to *Imaginary Maps: Three Stories by Mahasweta Devi*. New York: Routledge.

Stallybrass, Peter, and Allon White. 1986. *The Politics and Poetics of Transgression*. Ithaca, N.Y.: Cornell University Press.

Stocking, George W., Jr. 1994. "Reading the Palimpsest of Inquiry: Notes and Queries and the History of British Social Anthropology." Huxley Memorial Lecture, Oxford University, manuscript on file in the Museum of Mankind Library.

Sykes, Gershom. 1958. *The Society of Captives*. Princeton, N.J.: Princeton University Press.

Tagore, Rabindranath. [1915] 1985. *The Home and the World*. Trans. Surendranath Tagore. London: Penguin.

Thapar, Romila. 1987. "Traditions versus Misconceptions: Romila Thapar Talks to Madhu Kishwar and Ruth Vanita." *Manushi* (New Delhi), nos. 42–43:2–14.

Tonnies, Ferdinand. [1887] 1957. *Community and Society*. Ed. and trans. Charles P. Loomis. New York: Harper Torchbook.

Trautmann, Thomas R. 1981. *Dravidian Kinship*. Cambridge: Cambridge University Press.

———. 1987. *Lewis Henry Morgan and the Invention of Kinship*. Berkeley: University of California Press.

Trawick, Margaret. 1990. *Notes on Love in a Tamil Family*. Berkeley: University of California Press.

Turner, Victor. [1969] 1977. *The Ritual Process: Structure and Anti-Structure*. Ithaca, N.Y.: Cornell University Press.

———. 1985. *On the Edge of the Bush: Anthropology as Experience*. Ed. E. L. B. Turner. Tucson: University of Arizona Press.

Ulakanatan, S. 1992. *Cuvāmi Caṅkaratācar* [Sankaradas Swamigal]. Madras: Pāri Nilaiyam.

University of Madras. 1982. *Tamil Lexicon*. 6 vols. Madras: University of Madras.

Varadarajan, Mu. 1988. *A History of Tamil Literature*. Trans. E. Sa. Visswanathan. Delhi: Sahitya Akademi.

Viswanathan, Gauri. 1989. *Masks of Conquest: Literary Study and British Rule in India*. New York: Columbia University Press.

———. 2000. "Literacy and Conversion in the Discourse of Hindu Nationalism." *Race and Class* 42, no. 1: 1–20.

Visweswaran, Kamala. 1996. "Small Speeches, Subaltern Gender: Nationalist Ideology and Its Historiography." In *Subaltern Studies IX*, ed. Shahid Amin and Dipesh Chakrabarty. New York: Oxford University Press.

Wadley, Susan S., ed. 1980. *The Powers of Tamil Women*. Syracuse, N.Y.: Maxwell School of Citizenship and Public Affairs.

Walkowitz, Judith R. 1998. "Going Public: Shopping, Streetwalking, and Sexual Harassment in Victorian London's West End." *Representations* 62 (Spring): 1–30.

Warner, Michael. 1999. *The Trouble with Normal: Sex, Politics, and the Ethics of Queer Life*. New York: Free Press.

Washbrook, D. A. 1989. "Caste, Class and Dominance in Modern Tamil Nadu: Non-Brahmanism, Dravidianism, and Tamil Nationalism." In *Dominance and State Power in Modern India: Decline of a Social Order*, ed. Francine R. Frankel and M. S. A. Rao, 204–64. Delhi: Oxford University Press.

Weidman, Amanda. 2003. "Gender and the Politics of Voice: Colonial Modernity and Classical Music in South India." *Cultural Anthropology* 18, no. 2:194–232.

White, Christine Pelzer. 1986. "Everyday Resistance, Socialist Revolution, and Rural Development: The Vietnamese Case." *Journal of Peasant Studies* 13, no. 2:49–63.

Willeford, William. 1969. "The Fool and the Woman." In *The Fool and His Scepter*. Chicago: Northwestern University Press.

Williams, Raymond. [1976] 1985. *Keywords: A Vocabulary of Culture and Society*. Rev. ed. New York: Oxford University Press.

Wilson, Peter J. 1969. "Reputation and Respectability: A Suggestion for Caribbean Ethnology." *Man* 4, no. 1:70–80.

Wray, Matt, and Annalee Newitz. 1997. *White Trash: Race and Class in America*. London: Routledge.

Young, Iris Marion. 1990. "The Ideal of Community and the Politics of Difference." In *Feminism/Postmodernism*, ed. Linda J. Nicholson. New York: Routledge.

Index

PERMISSIONS

I have presented earlier versions of several of the following chapters in other venues. The material in chapter 4 first appeared as "Jokes, Gender, and Discursive Distance" at the International Society for Humor Studies conference in Ithaca, New York, in June 1994, and then again at the Association for Asian Studies Meeting in Washington, D.C., in April 1995. It appeared in print in *American Ethnologist* 24, no. 1 (February 1997).

The material in chapter 5 first appeared as "Sociospatial Paradigms on the Tamil Popular Stage" in October 1994 at the South Asia Workshop at the University of Chicago, and subsequently at the South Asia Conference in Madison, Wisconsin, later that fall.

The material in chapter 6 was first presented as "Laugh Till It Hurts: Domestic Violence on the Tamil Popular Stage" at the Conference on Visual Media, Mass Communication, and Violence in South Asia, at the University of Texas, Austin, in April 2001, and as part of the Feminist Anthropology Speakers Series, Occidental College, Los Angeles, later that same month. It was again presented under the auspices of the United States Educational Foundation in India, Chennai, in November 2001.

The material in chapter 8 first appeared as "Road Work: Offstage Scripts for Acting the Ideal Tamil Woman," at the South Asia Conference in Madison, Wisconsin, in October 1996; the Association for Asian Studies Meeting in Chicago, Illinois, in March 1997; the graduate student conference on Space in South Asia at the University of Chicago in May 1997; and at the second annual South Asian Women's Conference in Los Angeles, September 1997. At the Scripps College Faculty Seminar in March 2000, it benefited from a reading by James C. Scott and faculty from the Claremont Colleges. It appeared in print in *Cultural Anthropology* 15, no. 2 (May 2000).

The useful comments of discussants, audience members, organizers, anonymous readers, and journal editors at each of the aforementioned venues have significantly influenced the form in which you encounter the ideas in this book. I am grateful to all these interlocutors for helping me hone my scholarship and for keeping things interesting.

SUSAN SEIZER is an associate professor

of anthropology and of gender & women's studies

at Scripps College in Claremont, California.

Library of Congress Cataloging-in-Publication Data

Seizer, Susan.
Stigmas of the Tamil stage : an ethnography of Special Drama artists in South India / Susan Seizer.
p. cm.
Includes bibliographical references and index.
ISBN 0-8223-3432-1 (cloth : alk. paper)
ISBN 0-8223-3443-7 (pbk. : alk. paper)
1. Ethnology—India—Tamil Nadu. 2. Theater—Anthropological aspects—India—Tamil Nadu. 3. Theater and society—India—Tamil Nadu. 4. Folklore—Performance—India—Tamil Nadu. 5. Tamil Nadu (India)—Social life and customs. I. Title.
GN635.I4S37 2005
306.4'848'0954'82—dc22 2004019405